THE LEGEND OF ZELDA™

Ocarina of Time

OCARINA OF TIME—THE GAME

The Legend of Zelda™: *Ocarina of Time* was developed for the Nintendo 64 game platform and originally released in 1996 as part of *The Legend of Zelda*™ series of games. *Ocarina of Time* became a huge success, selling over 7 million units worldwide and winning several industry awards.

AKIRA HIMEKAWA

Because of *Ocarina*, I wanted to have control of Link, so I bought *Smash Bros*. If you make all four characters Link and have a battle, it may just be my imagination, but Blue Link appears to be the most cruel, ruthless and brutal. The next strongest one is the calm Purple Link. Next is the passionate Red Link. Hang in there, Green Link!

Akira Himekawa is the collaboration of two women, A. Honda and S. Nagano. Together they have created nine manga adventures featuring Link and the popular video game world of *The Legend of Zelda*™, including *Ocarina of Time*, *Oracle of Seasons* and *Four Swords*. Their most recent work, *Legend of Zelda*™: *Phantom Hourglass*, is serialized in *Shogaku Rokunensei*.

THE LEGEND OF ZELDA™
– OCARINA OF TIME –
PART 2
VIZ Kids Edition

STORY & ART BY
AKIRA HIMEKAWA

Original Japanese edition
"ZELDA NO DENSETSU - TOKI NO OCARINA - GE"
published by SHOGAKUKAN Inc.

Translation/John Werry, Honyaku Center Inc.
English Adaptation/Steven "Stan!" Brown
Touch-up Art & Lettering/John Hunt
Cover & Interior Design/Izumi Hirayama & Sean Lee
Editor/Mike Montesa

Printed in the U.S.A.

Published by VIZ Media, LLC
P.O. Box 77010
San Francisco, CA 94107

10 9 8 7 6 5
First printing, December 2008
Fifth printing, July 2010

www.viz.com

RATED A FOR ALL AGES
PARENTAL ADVISORY
LEGEND OF ZELDA is rated A and is suitable for readers of all ages.
ratings.viz.com

www.vizkids.com

THE LEGEND OF ZELDA™
OCARINA OF TIME

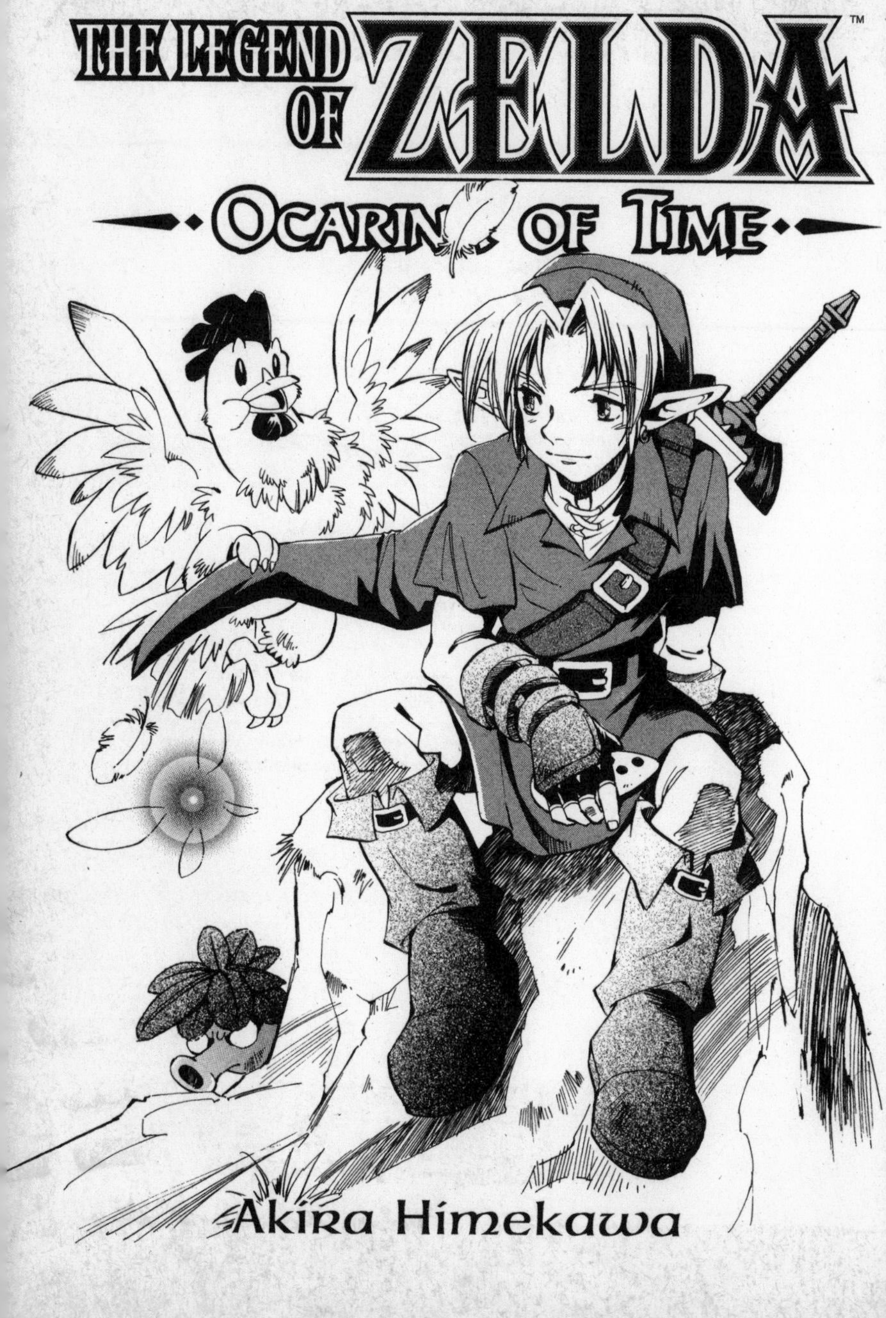

Akira Himekawa

THE LEGEND OF ZELDA
OCARINA OF TIME

PART 2

CONTENTS

HERO OF TIME

OCARINA OF TIME – BONUS STORY

HERO OF TIME – BONUS STORY

CHAPTER 5
SHADOW GUIDE: SHEIK

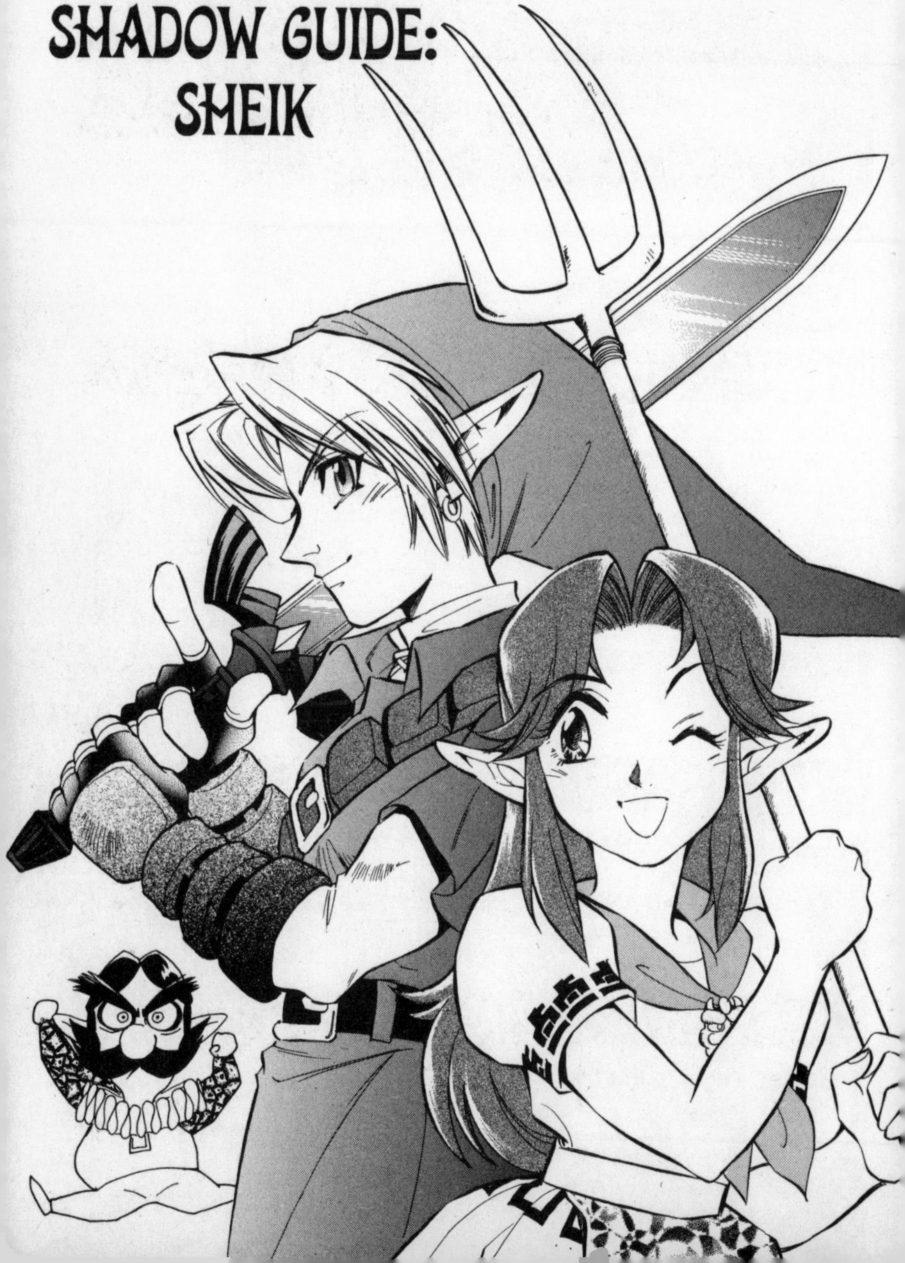

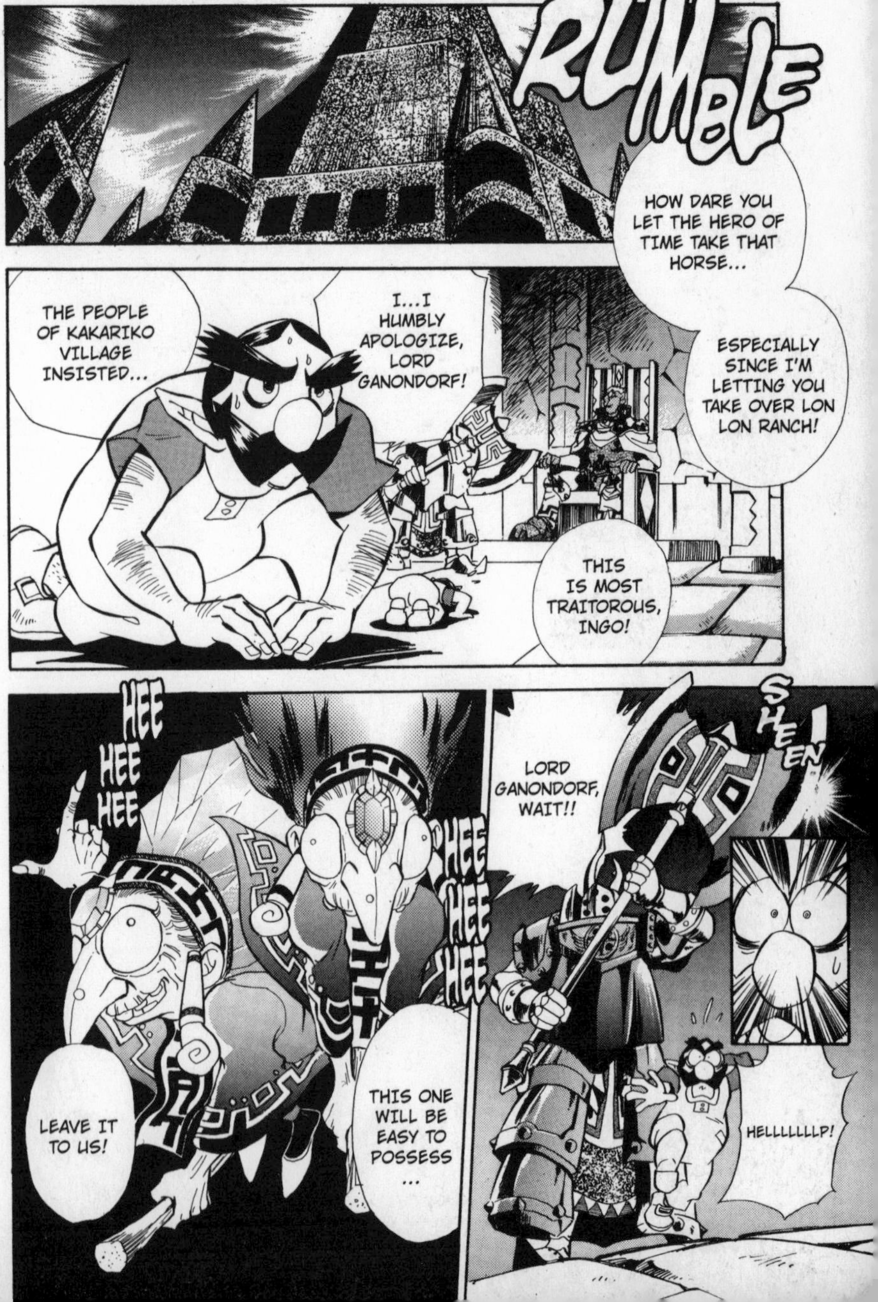
RUMBLE
HOW DARE YOU LET THE HERO OF TIME TAKE THAT HORSE...
ESPECIALLY SINCE I'M LETTING YOU TAKE OVER LON LON RANCH!
THIS IS MOST TRAITOROUS, INGO!
I...I HUMBLY APOLOGIZE, LORD GANONDORF!
THE PEOPLE OF KAKARIKO VILLAGE INSISTED...
SHEEN
LORD GANONDORF, WAIT!!
HELLLLLLLP!
HEE HEE HEE
THIS ONE WILL BE EASY TO POSSESS...
HEE HEE HEE
LEAVE IT TO US!

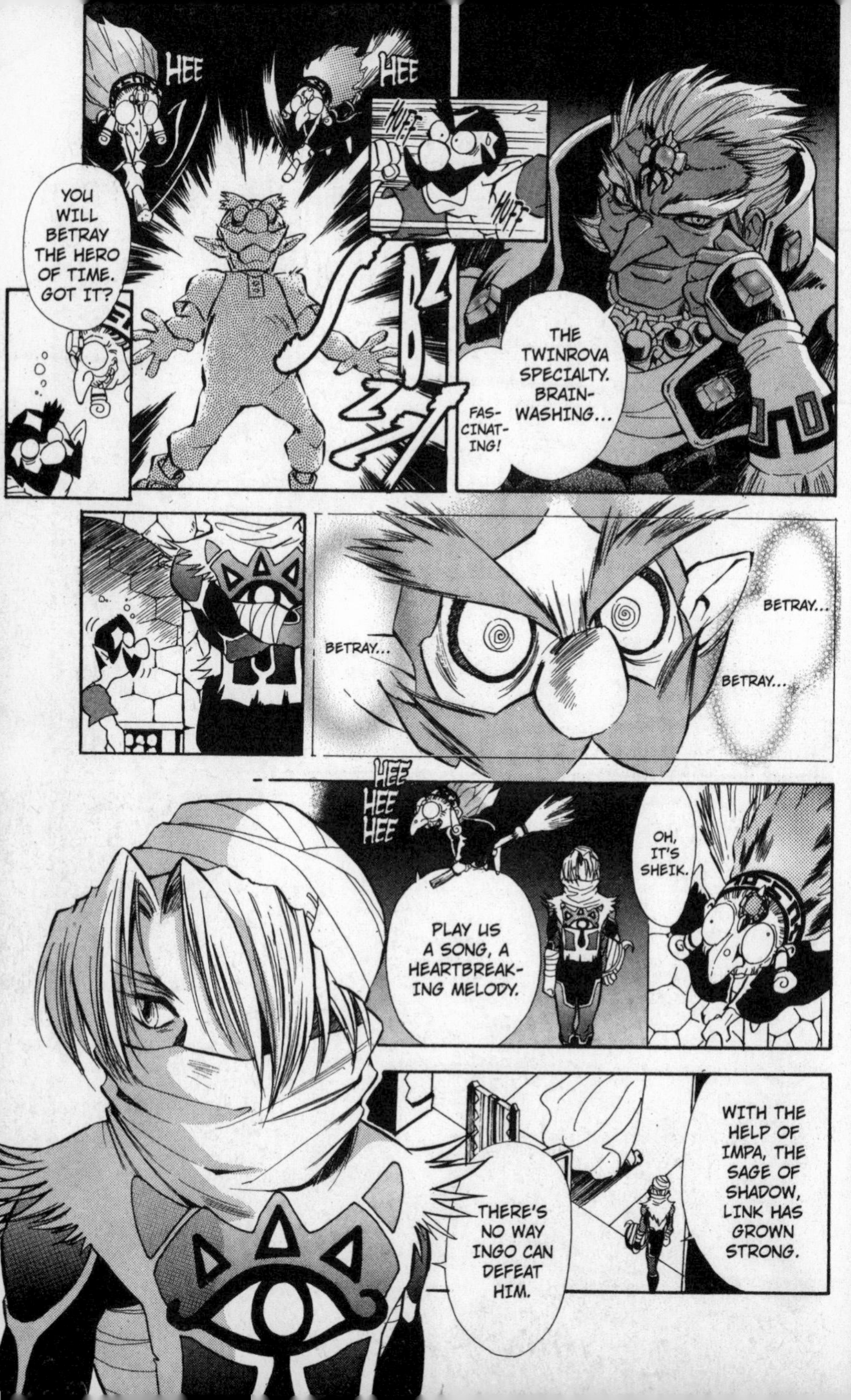

THE TWINROVA SPECIALTY. BRAIN-WASHING...
FAS-CINAT-ING!
HUFF
HUFF
HEE
HEE
YOU WILL BETRAY THE HERO OF TIME. GOT IT?
BZZZ
BETRAY...
BETRAY...
BETRAY...
OH, IT'S SHEIK.
HEE HEE HEE
PLAY US A SONG, A HEARTBREAK-ING MELODY.
WITH THE HELP OF IMPA, THE SAGE OF SHADOW, LINK HAS GROWN STRONG.
THERE'S NO WAY INGO CAN DEFEAT HIM.

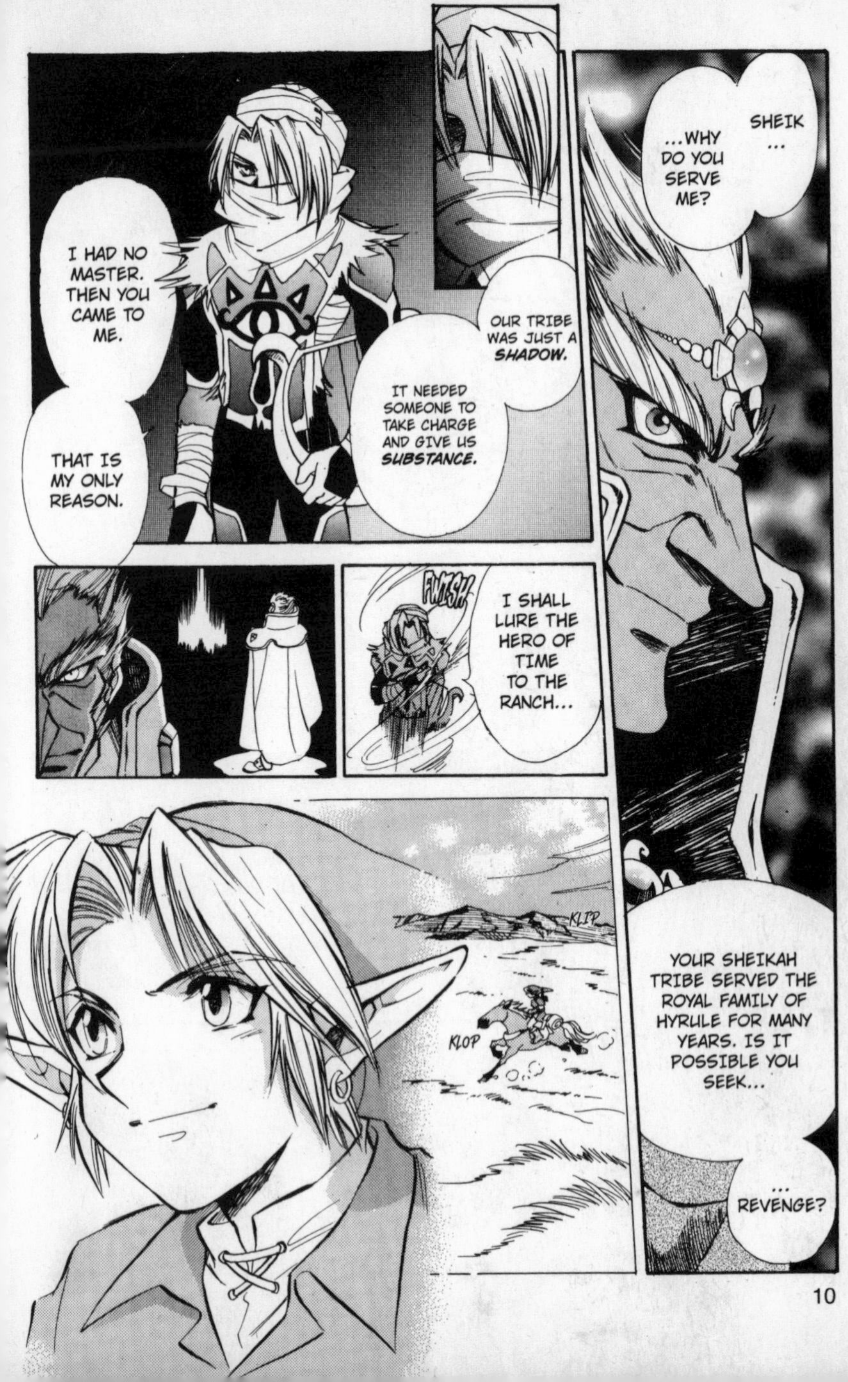
SHEIK ...
...WHY DO YOU SERVE ME?
YOUR SHEIKAH TRIBE SERVED THE ROYAL FAMILY OF HYRULE FOR MANY YEARS. IS IT POSSIBLE YOU SEEK...
... REVENGE?
OUR TRIBE WAS JUST A **SHADOW.**
IT NEEDED SOMEONE TO TAKE CHARGE AND GIVE US **SUBSTANCE.**
I HAD NO MASTER. THEN YOU CAME TO ME.
THAT IS MY ONLY REASON.
FWISH!
I SHALL LURE THE HERO OF TIME TO THE RANCH...
KLIP
KLOP

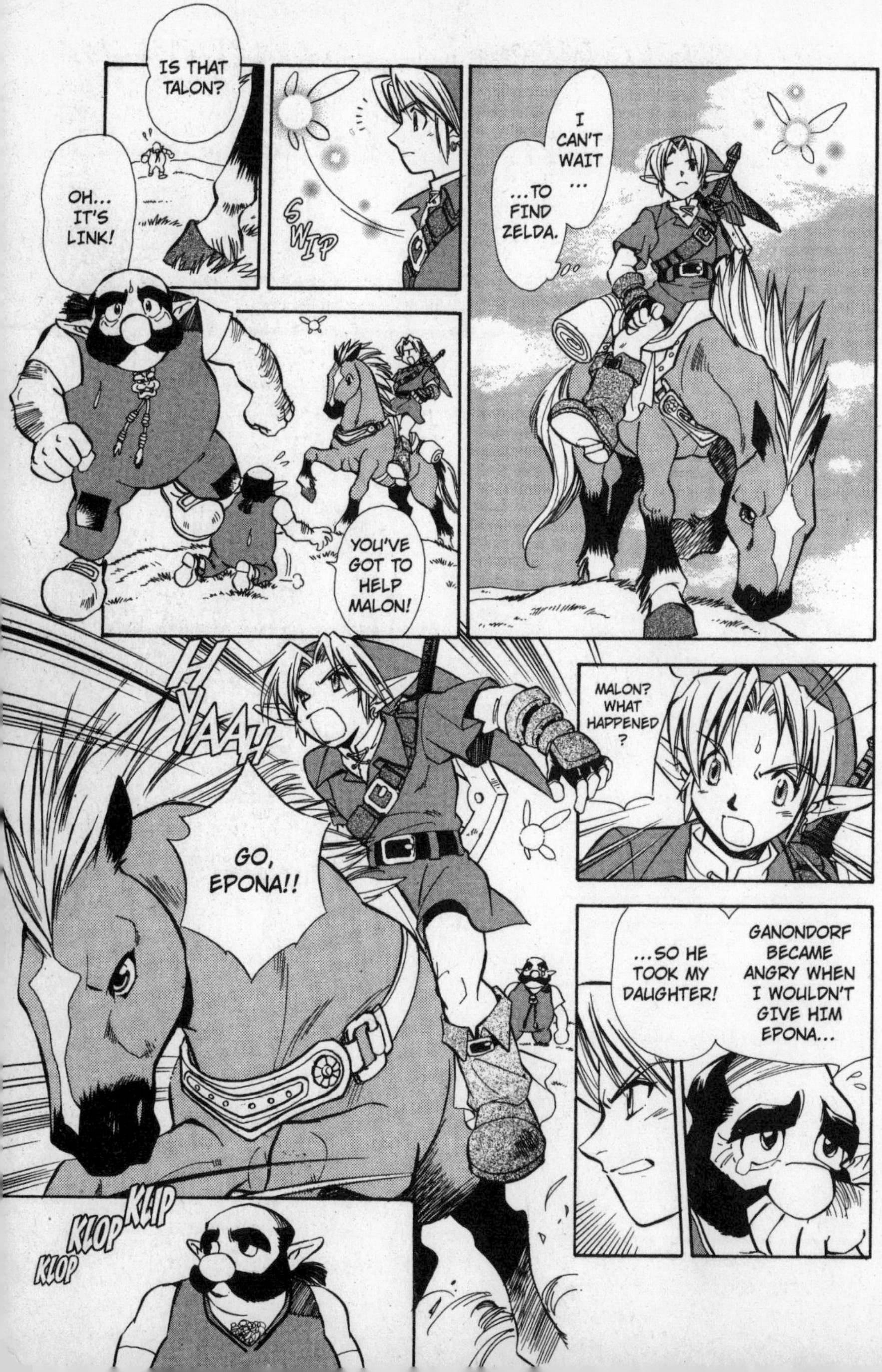

I CAN'T WAIT ...
...TO FIND ZELDA.
SWIP
IS THAT TALON?
OH... IT'S LINK!
YOU'VE GOT TO HELP MALON!
MALON? WHAT HAPPENED?
GANONDORF BECAME ANGRY WHEN I WOULDN'T GIVE HIM EPONA...
...SO HE TOOK MY DAUGHTER!
HYAAH
GO, EPONA!!
KLIP
KLOP
KLOP

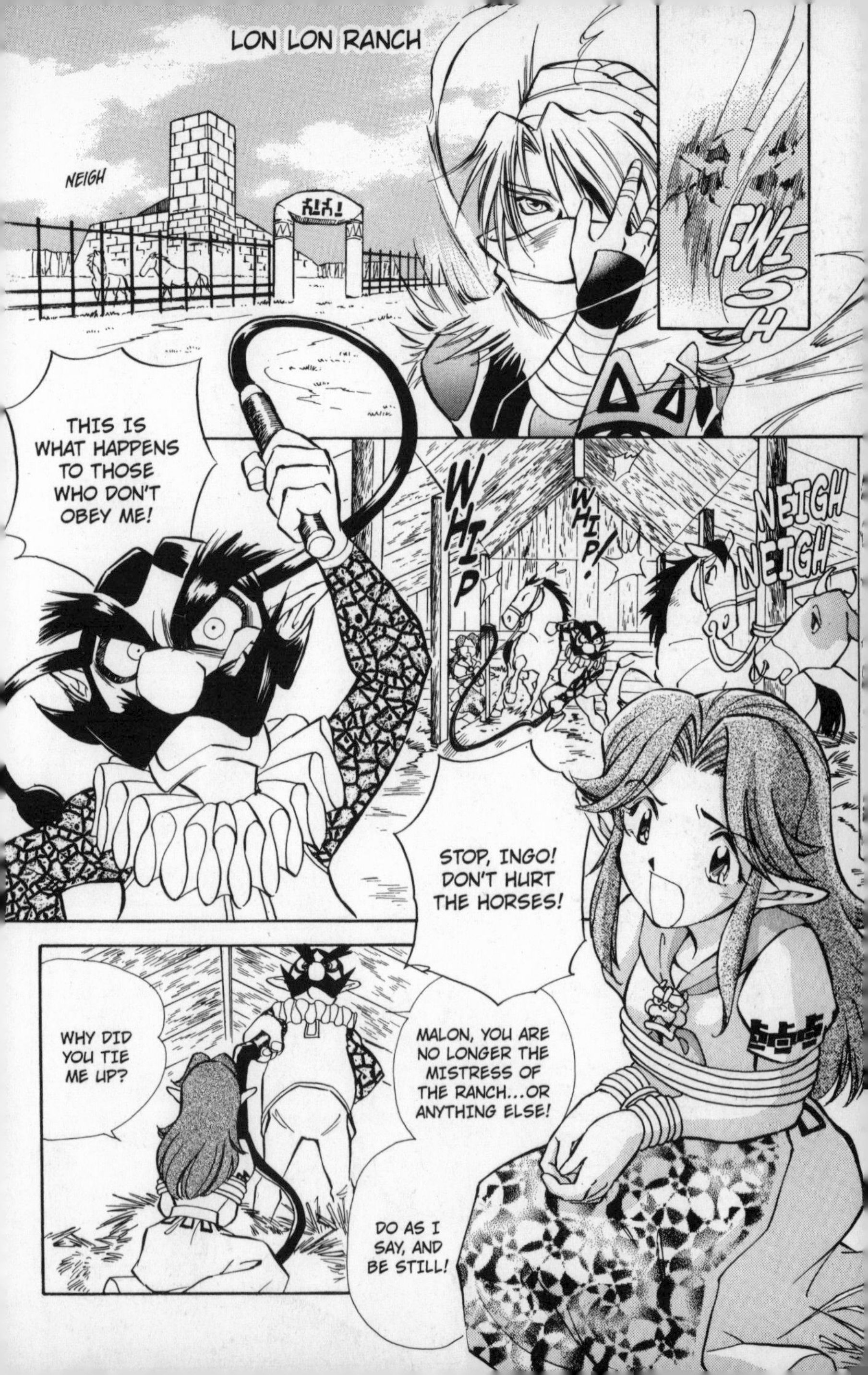
FWISH
LON LON RANCH
NEIGH
WHIP
WHIP!
NEIGH NEIGH
THIS IS WHAT HAPPENS TO THOSE WHO DON'T OBEY ME!
STOP, INGO! DON'T HURT THE HORSES!
WHY DID YOU TIE ME UP?
MALON, YOU ARE NO LONGER THE MISTRESS OF THE RANCH...OR ANYTHING ELSE!
DO AS I SAY, AND BE STILL!

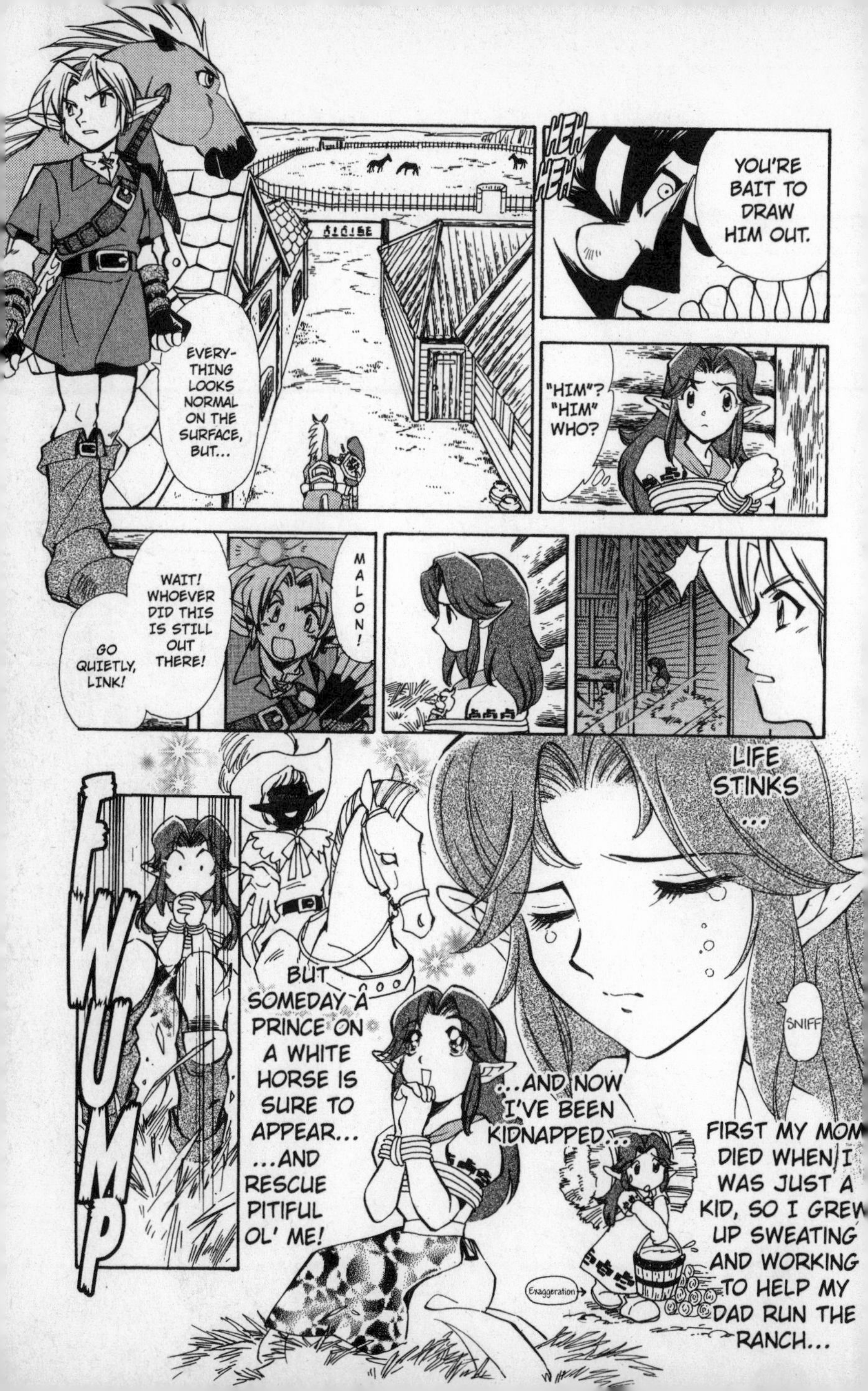
HEH HEH
YOU'RE BAIT TO DRAW HIM OUT.
"HIM"? "HIM" WHO?
EVERY-THING LOOKS NORMAL ON THE SURFACE, BUT...
MALON!
WAIT! WHOEVER DID THIS IS STILL OUT THERE!
GO QUIETLY, LINK!
LIFE STINKS...
SNIFF
FIRST MY MOM DIED WHEN I WAS JUST A KID, SO I GREW UP SWEATING AND WORKING TO HELP MY DAD RUN THE RANCH...
Exaggeration
...AND NOW I'VE BEEN KIDNAPPED...
BUT SOMEDAY A PRINCE ON A WHITE HORSE IS SURE TO APPEAR...
...AND RESCUE PITIFUL OL' ME!
FWUMP

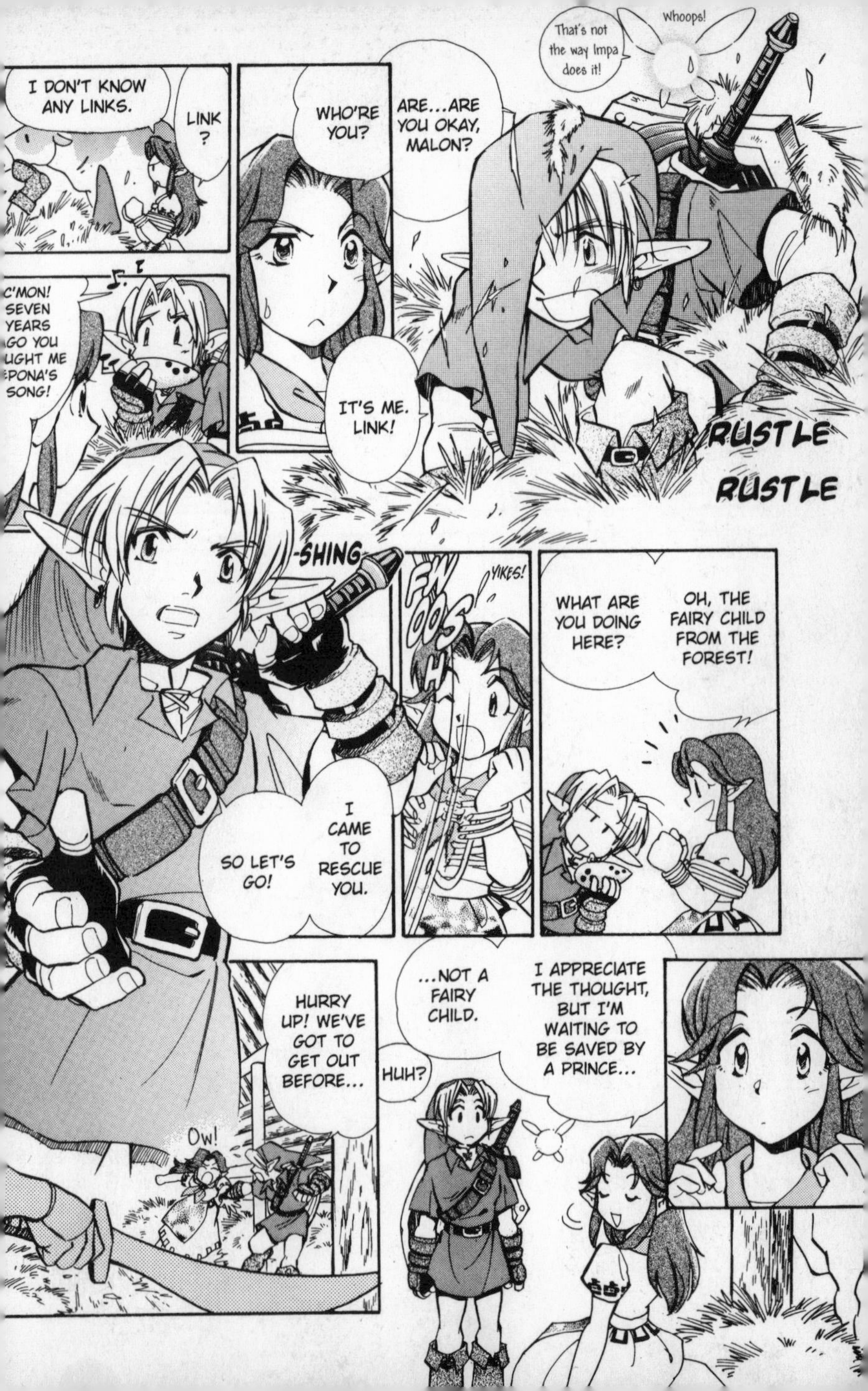
Whoops!
That's not the way Impa does it!
ARE...ARE YOU OKAY, MALON?
RUSTLE
RUSTLE
WHO'RE YOU?
IT'S ME. LINK!
LINK?
I DON'T KNOW ANY LINKS.
C'MON! SEVEN YEARS GO YOU UGHT ME PONA'S SONG!
OH, THE FAIRY CHILD FROM THE FOREST!
WHAT ARE YOU DOING HERE?
YIKES!
FWOOSH
SHING
I CAME TO RESCUE YOU.
SO LET'S GO!
I APPRECIATE THE THOUGHT, BUT I'M WAITING TO BE SAVED BY A PRINCE...
...NOT A FAIRY CHILD.
HUH?
HURRY UP! WE'VE GOT TO GET OUT BEFORE...
OW!

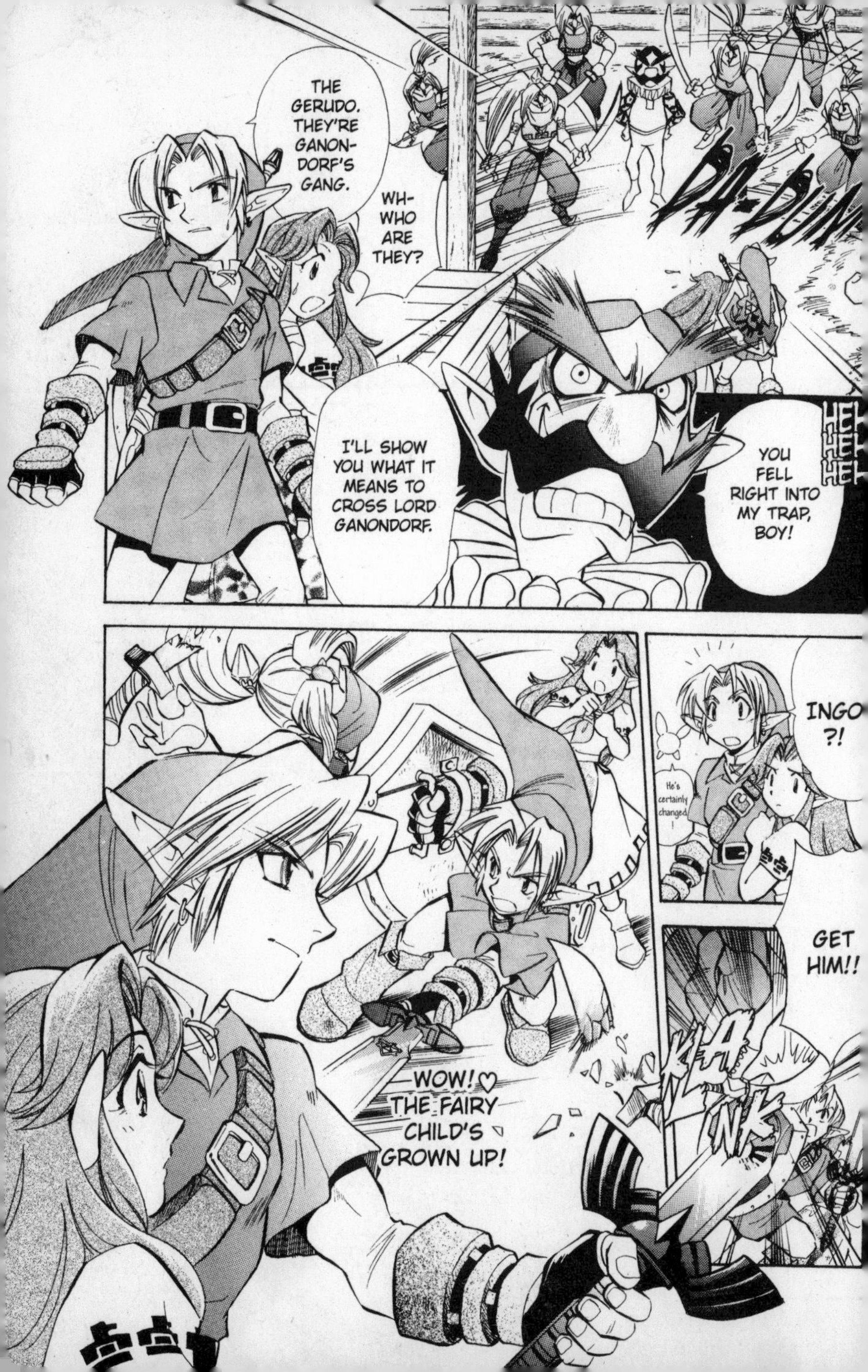
DA-DUM
HEH HEH HEH
YOU FELL RIGHT INTO MY TRAP, BOY!
I'LL SHOW YOU WHAT IT MEANS TO CROSS LORD GANONDORF.
WH-WHO ARE THEY?
THE GERUDO. THEY'RE GANON-DORF'S GANG.
INGO ?!
He's certainly changed!
GET HIM!!
KLANK
WOW! ♡ THE FAIRY CHILD'S GROWN UP!

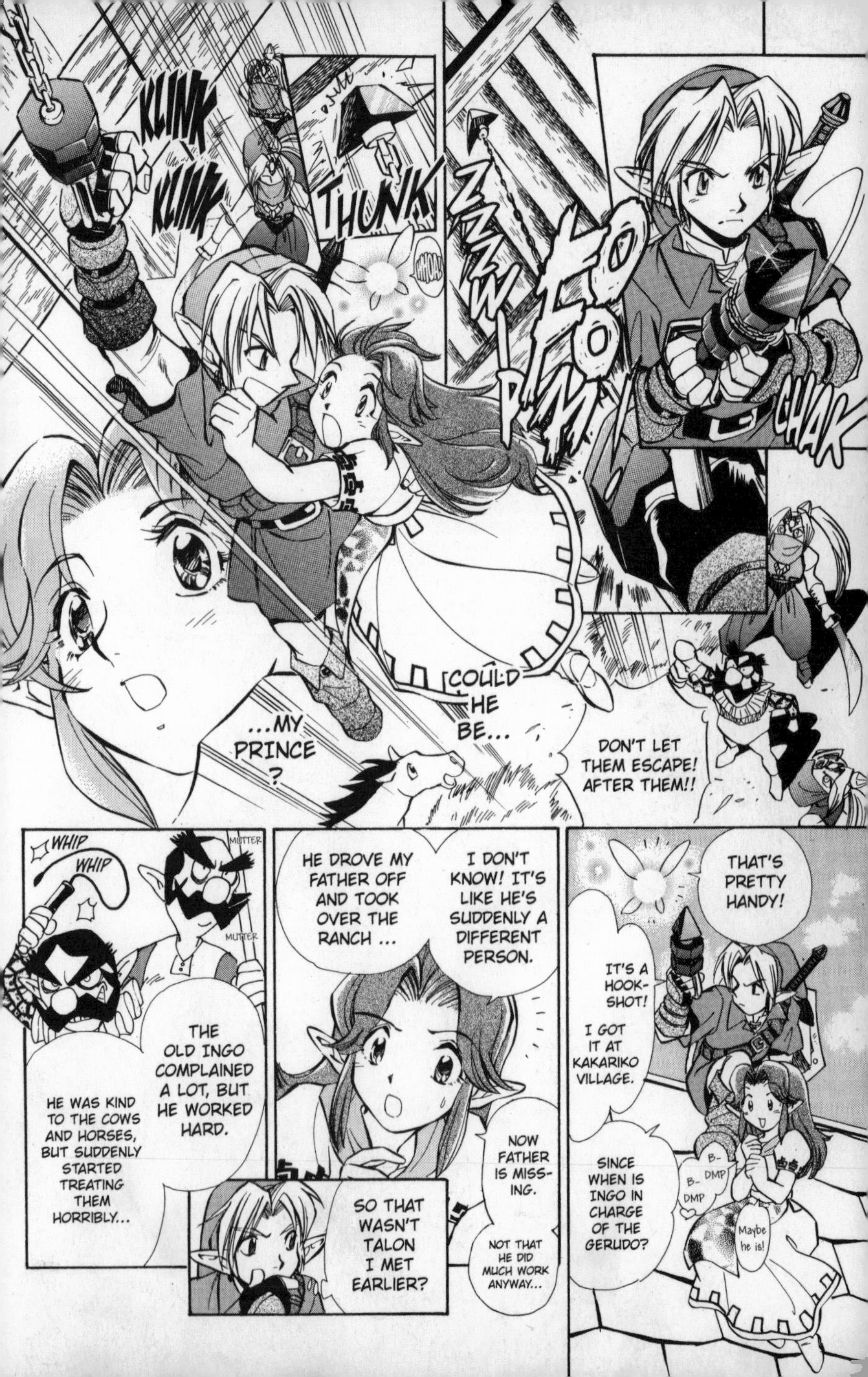
CHAK
THUNK
KLINK
KLINK
WHOA!
DON'T LET THEM ESCAPE! AFTER THEM!!
COULD HE BE...
...MY PRINCE?
THAT'S PRETTY HANDY!
IT'S A HOOK-SHOT!
I GOT IT AT KAKARIKO VILLAGE.
SINCE WHEN IS INGO IN CHARGE OF THE GERUDO?
B-DMP
B-DMP
Maybe he is!
I DON'T KNOW! IT'S LIKE HE'S SUDDENLY A DIFFERENT PERSON.
HE DROVE MY FATHER OFF AND TOOK OVER THE RANCH ...
NOW FATHER IS MISSING.
NOT THAT HE DID MUCH WORK ANYWAY...
SO THAT WASN'T TALON I MET EARLIER?
MUTTER
MUTTER
WHIP
WHIP
THE OLD INGO COMPLAINED A LOT, BUT HE WORKED HARD.
HE WAS KIND TO THE COWS AND HORSES, BUT SUDDENLY STARTED TREATING THEM HORRIBLY...

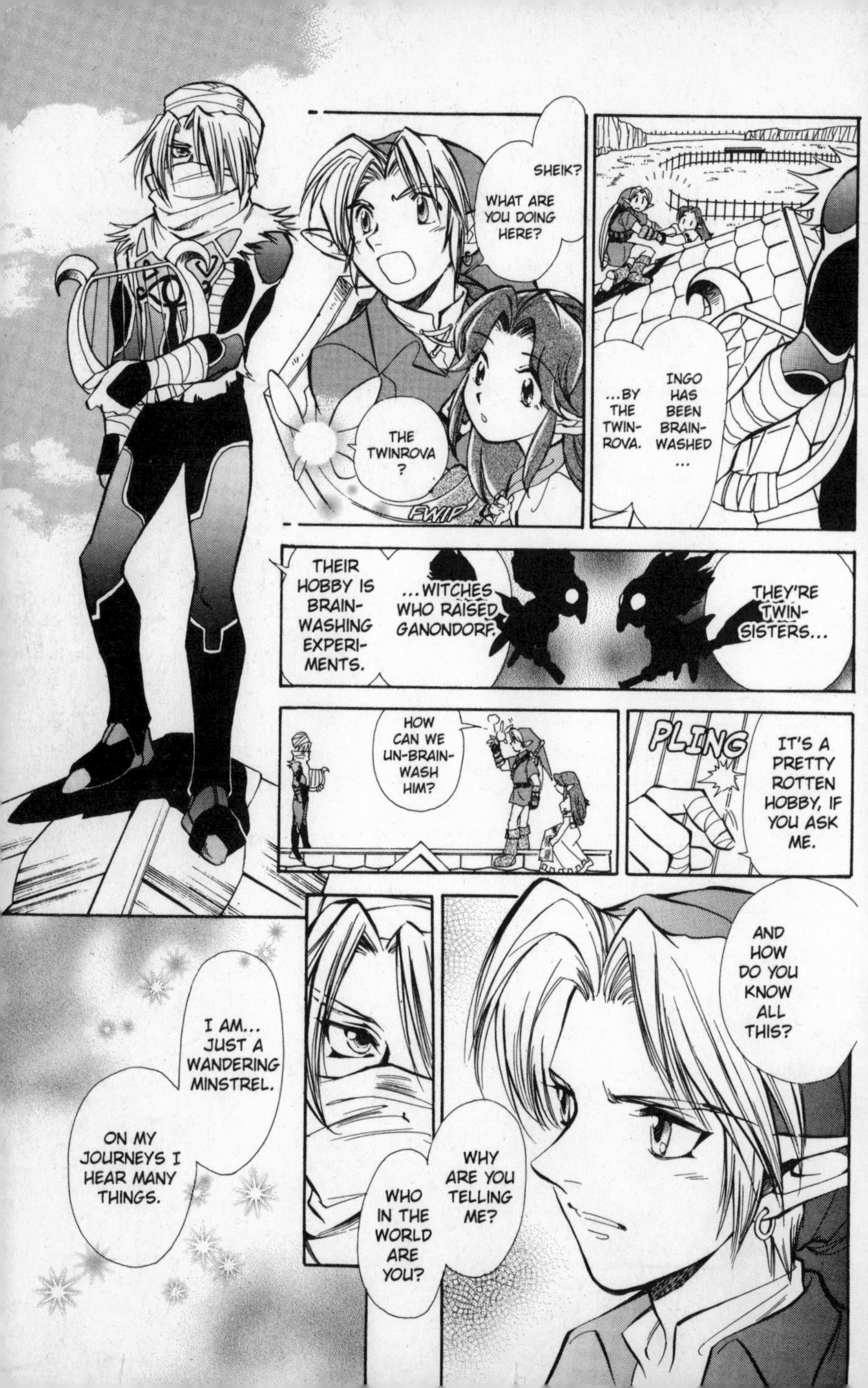
INGO HAS BEEN BRAIN-WASHED...
...BY THE TWIN-ROVA.
SHEIK? WHAT ARE YOU DOING HERE?
THE TWINROVA?
FWIP
THEY'RE TWIN-SISTERS...
...WITCHES WHO RAISED GANONDORF.
THEIR HOBBY IS BRAIN-WASHING EXPERI-MENTS.
PLING
IT'S A PRETTY ROTTEN HOBBY, IF YOU ASK ME.
HOW CAN WE UN-BRAIN-WASH HIM?
AND HOW DO YOU KNOW ALL THIS?
WHY ARE YOU TELLING ME?
WHO IN THE WORLD ARE YOU?
I AM... JUST A WANDERING MINSTREL.
ON MY JOURNEYS I HEAR MANY THINGS.

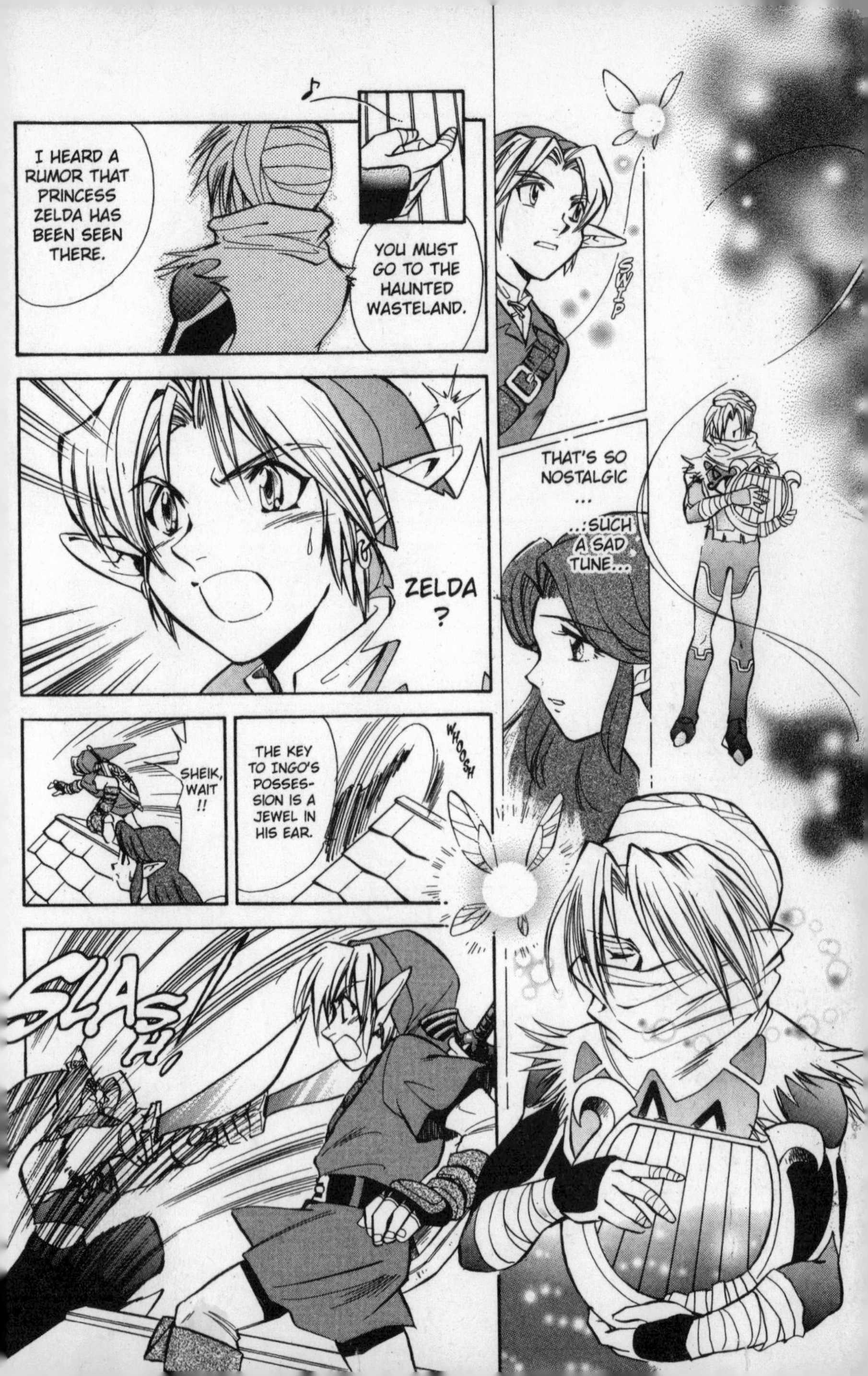

SWIP
THAT'S SO NOSTALGIC ...
...SUCH A SAD TUNE...
YOU MUST GO TO THE HAUNTED WASTELAND.
I HEARD A RUMOR THAT PRINCESS ZELDA HAS BEEN SEEN THERE.
ZELDA ?
WHOOSH
THE KEY TO INGO'S POSSES-SION IS A JEWEL IN HIS EAR.
SHEIK, WAIT !!
SLASH!

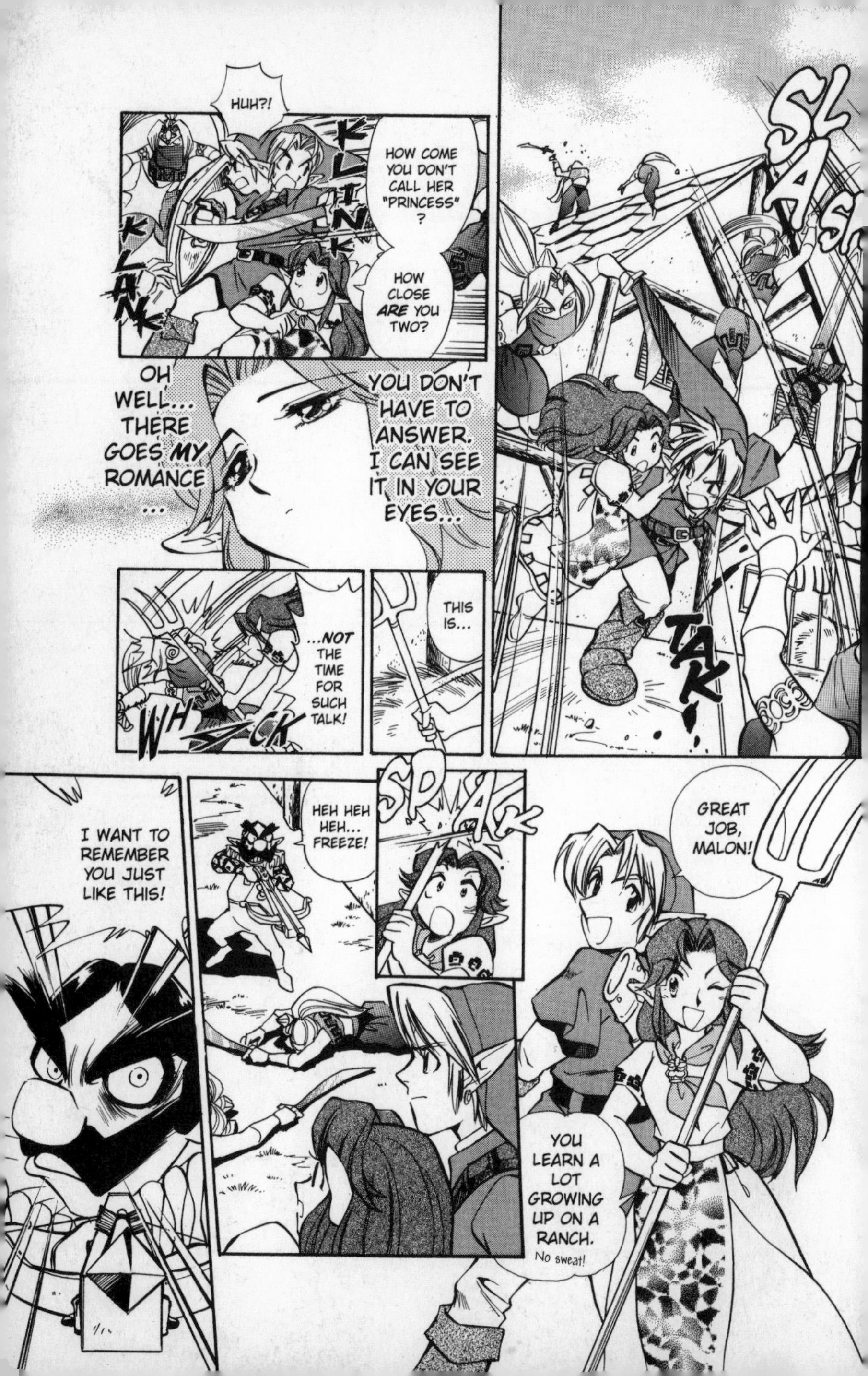
SLASH
TAK
HUH?!
KLINK
KLANK
HOW COME YOU DON'T CALL HER "PRINCESS"?
HOW CLOSE ARE YOU TWO?
YOU DON'T HAVE TO ANSWER. I CAN SEE IT IN YOUR EYES...
OH WELL... THERE GOES MY ROMANCE...
THIS IS...
...NOT THE TIME FOR SUCH TALK!
WHACK
GREAT JOB, MALON!
YOU LEARN A LOT GROWING UP ON A RANCH.
No sweat!
SPAK
HEH HEH HEH... FREEZE!
I WANT TO REMEMBER YOU JUST LIKE THIS!

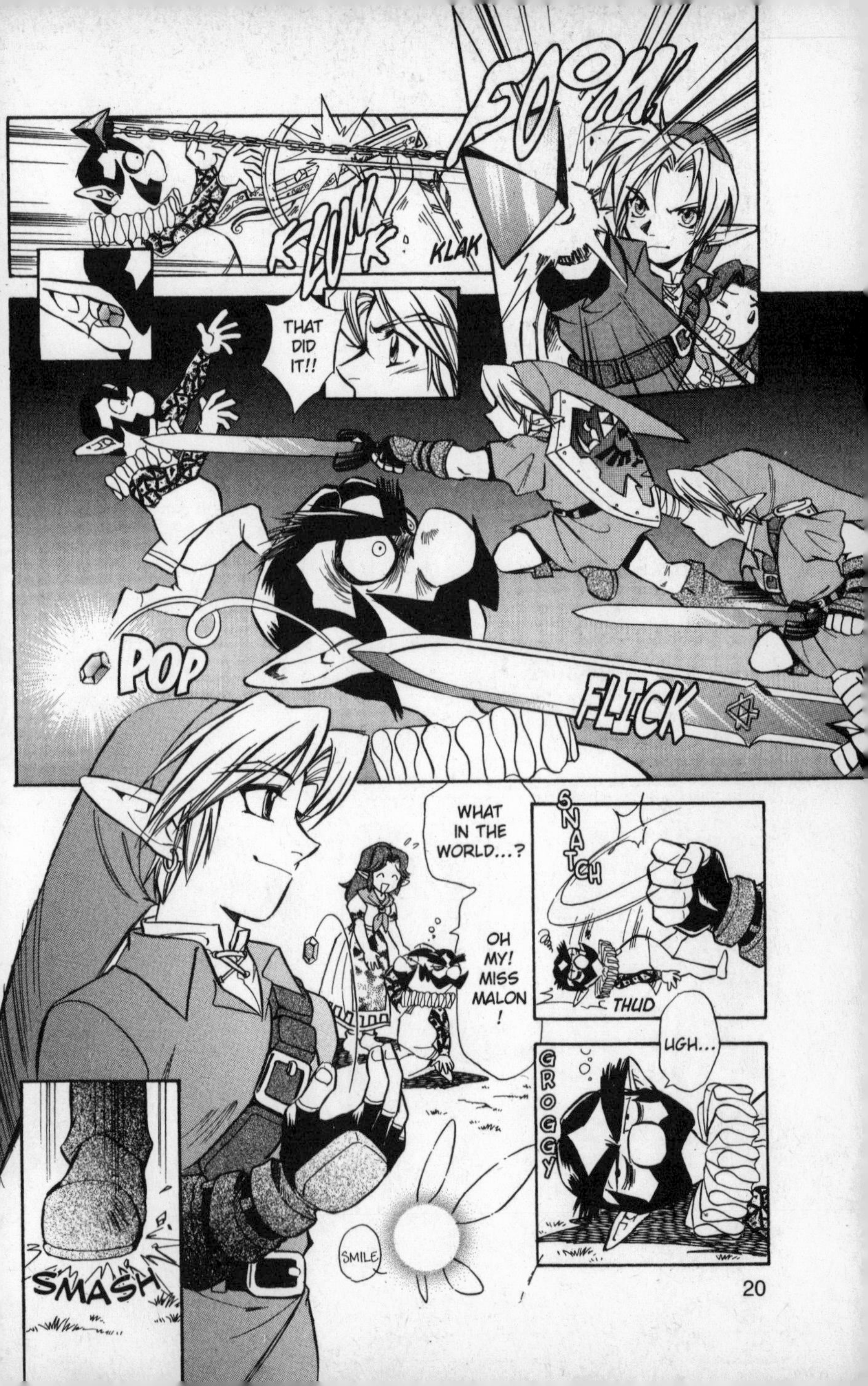
FOOM
KLINK
KLAK
THAT DID IT!!
POP
FLICK
SNATCH
THUD
UGH...
GROGGY
WHAT IN THE WORLD...?
OH MY! MISS MALON!
SMILE
SMASH

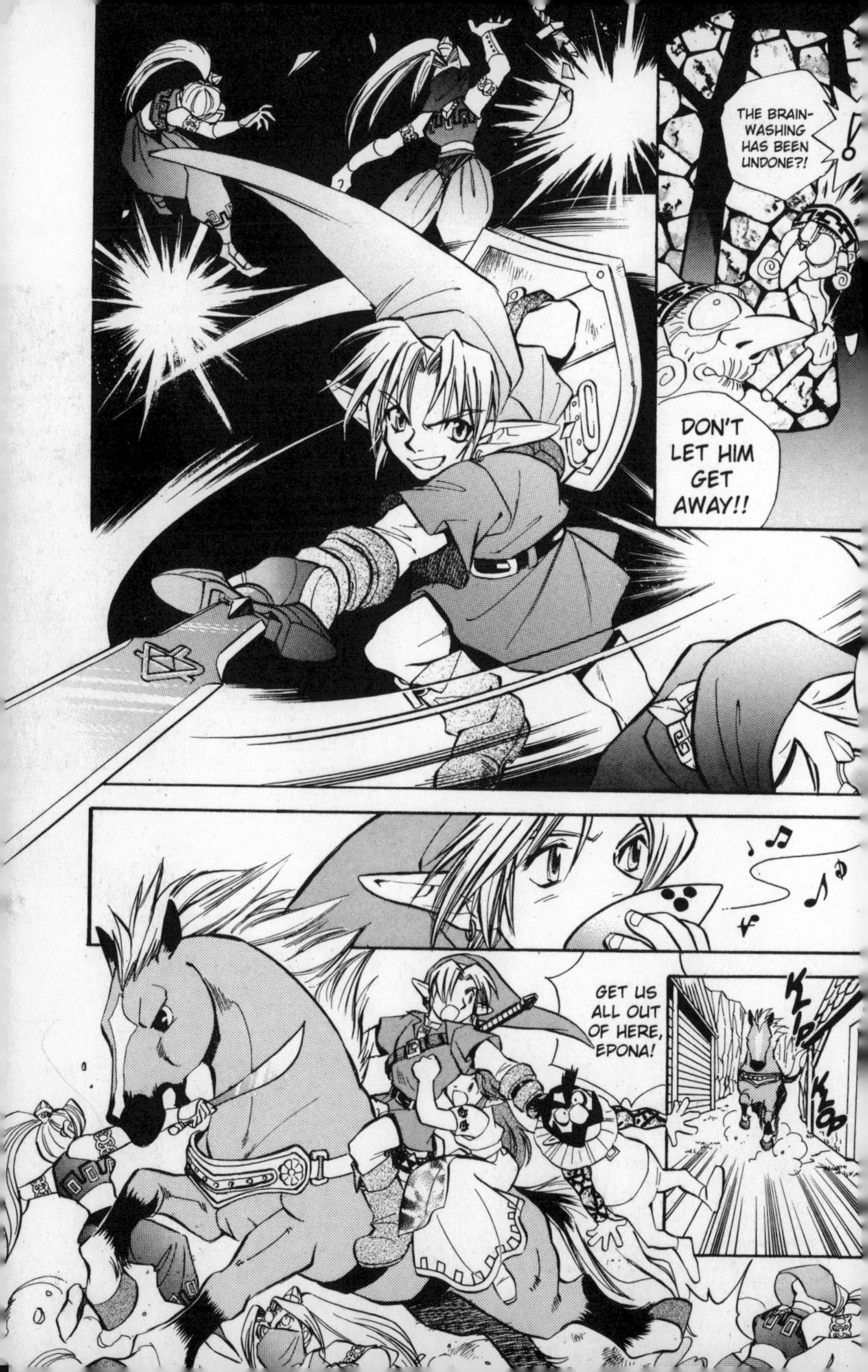
THE BRAIN-WASHING HAS BEEN UNDONE?!
!
DON'T LET HIM GET AWAY!!
KLIP
KLOP
GET US ALL OUT OF HERE, EPONA!

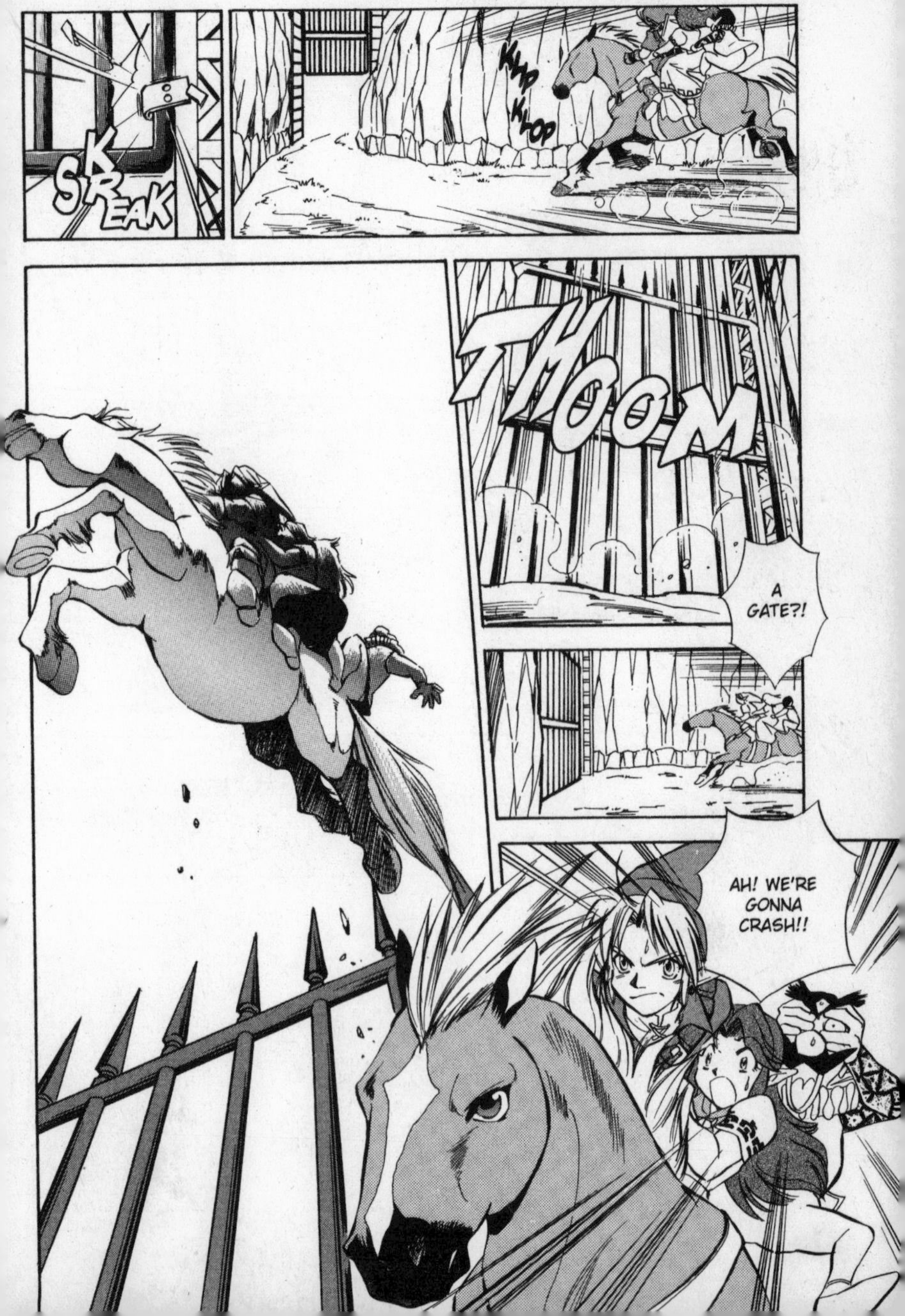
KLIP KLOP
SKREAK
THOOM
A GATE?!
AH! WE'RE GONNA CRASH!!

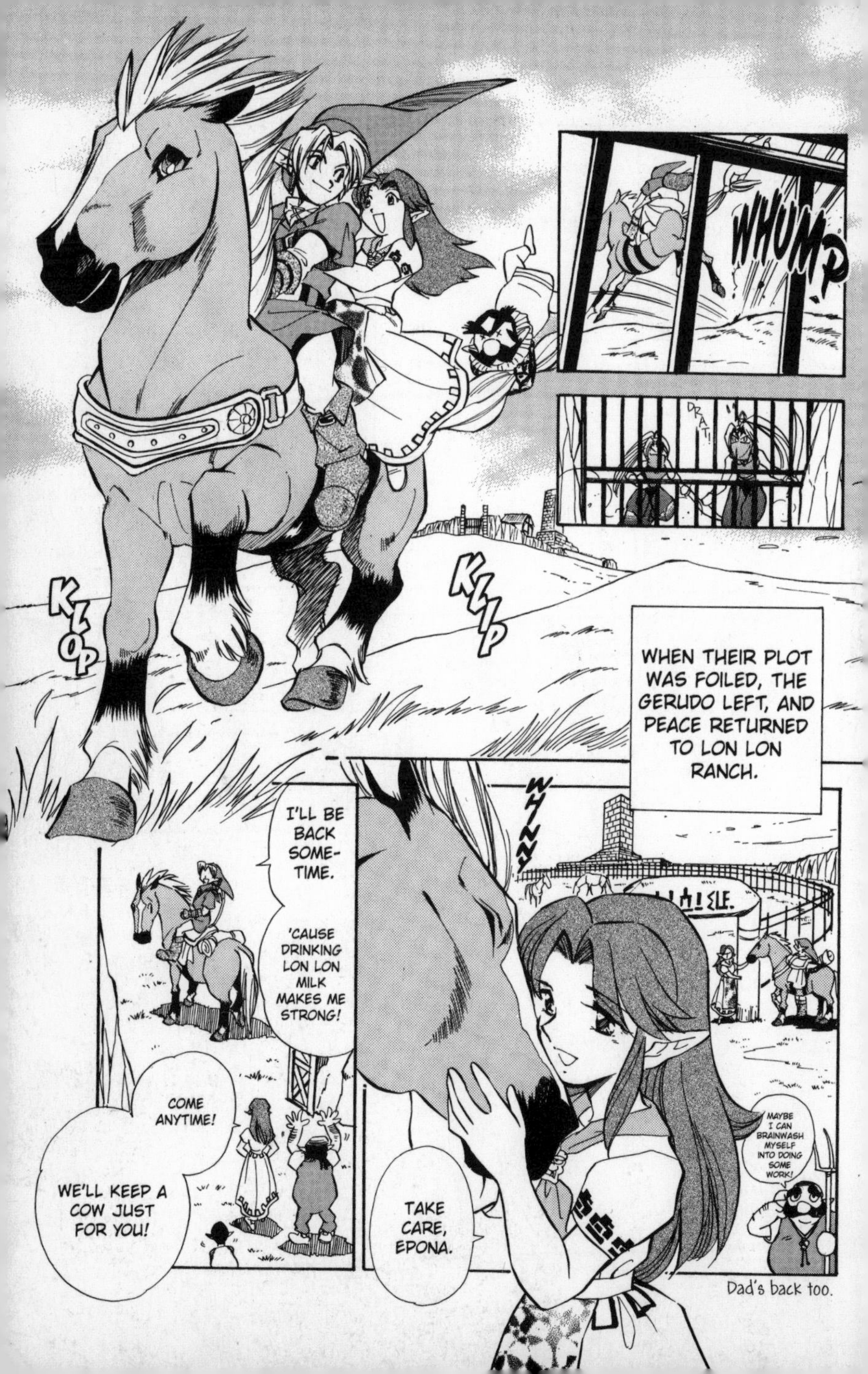
WHUMP
DRAT!
KLIP
KLOP
WHEN THEIR PLOT WAS FOILED, THE GERUDO LEFT, AND PEACE RETURNED TO LON LON RANCH.
WHINNY
MAYBE I CAN BRAINWASH MYSELF INTO DOING SOME WORK!
TAKE CARE, EPONA.
Dad's back too.
I'LL BE BACK SOME-TIME.
'CAUSE DRINKING LON LON MILK MAKES ME STRONG!
COME ANYTIME!
WE'LL KEEP A COW JUST FOR YOU!

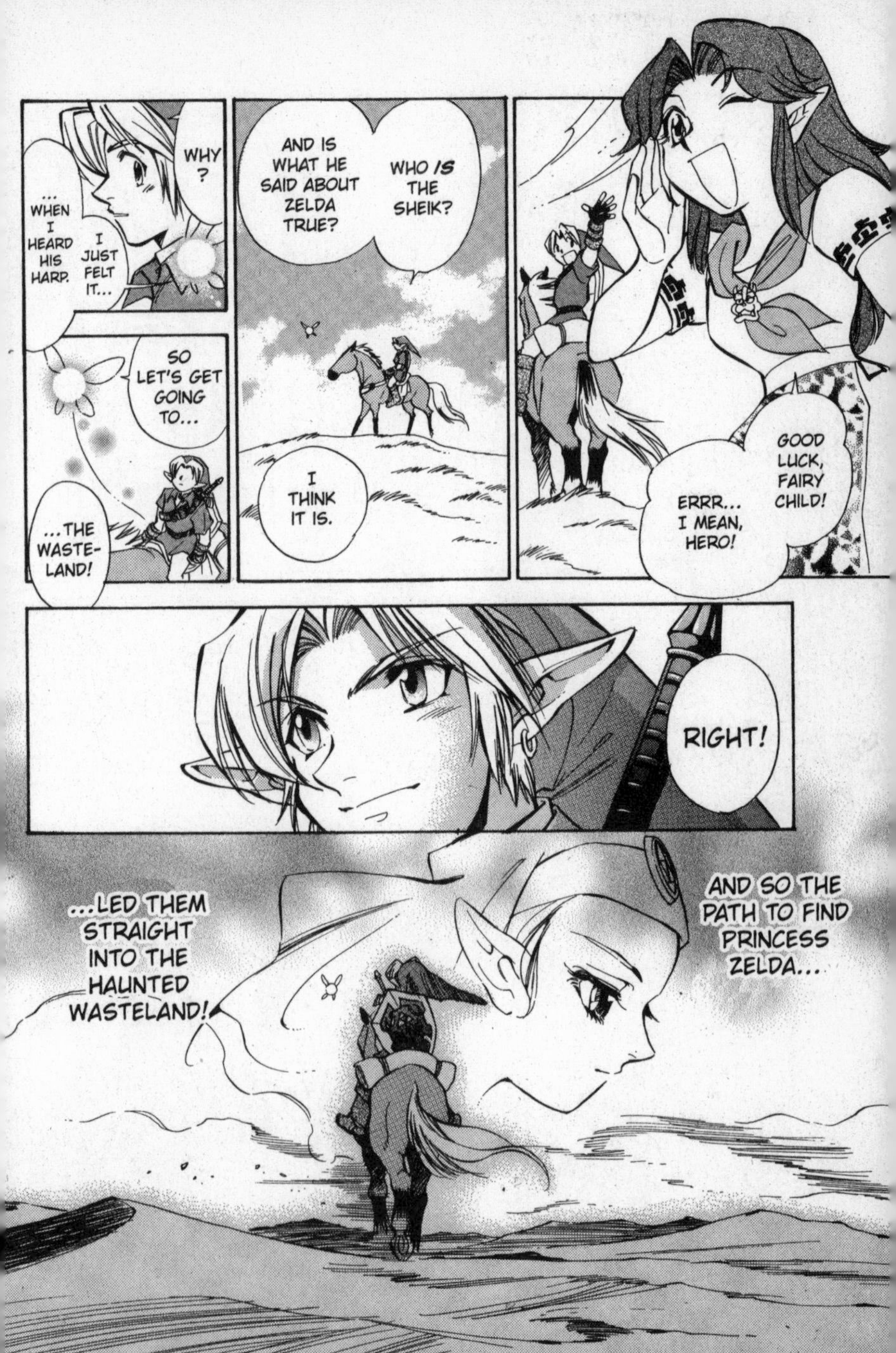
GOOD LUCK, FAIRY CHILD!
ERRR... I MEAN, HERO!
WHO *IS* THE SHEIK?
AND IS WHAT HE SAID ABOUT ZELDA TRUE?
I THINK IT IS.
WHY?
I JUST FELT IT...
...WHEN I HEARD HIS HARP.
SO LET'S GET GOING TO...
...THE WASTE-LAND!
RIGHT!
AND SO THE PATH TO FIND PRINCESS ZELDA...
...LED THEM STRAIGHT INTO THE HAUNTED WASTELAND!

CHAPTER 6
THE HAUNTED WASTELAND

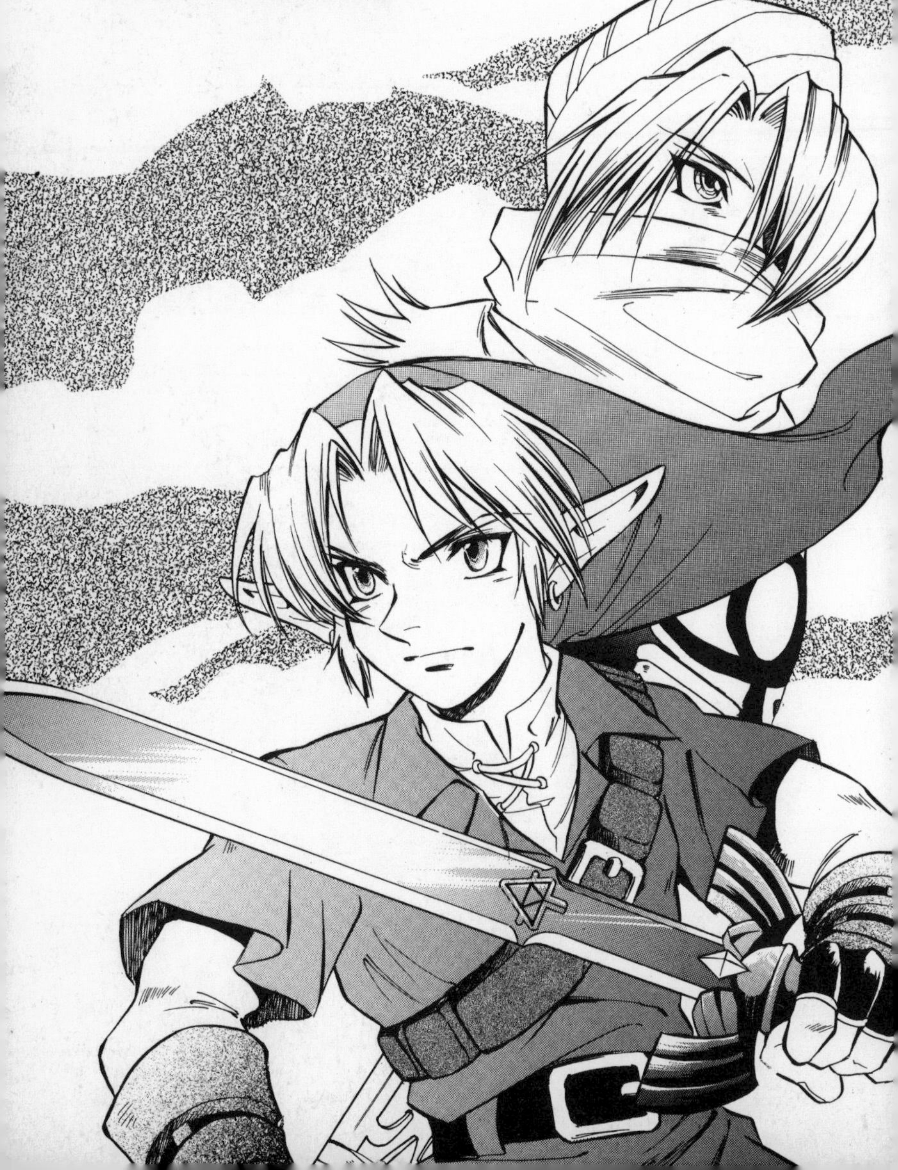

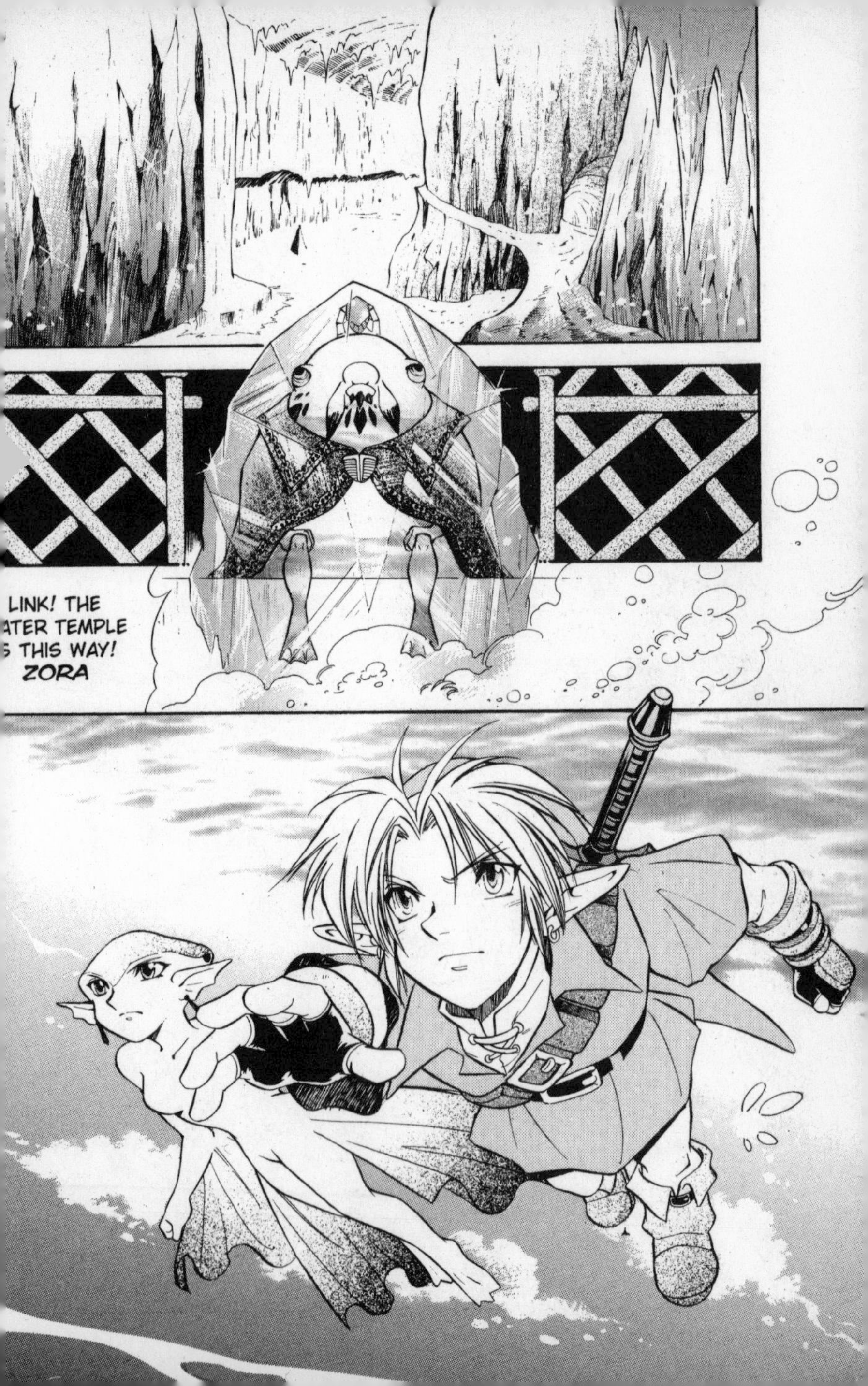
LINK! THE
ATER TEMPLE
S THIS WAY!
ZORA

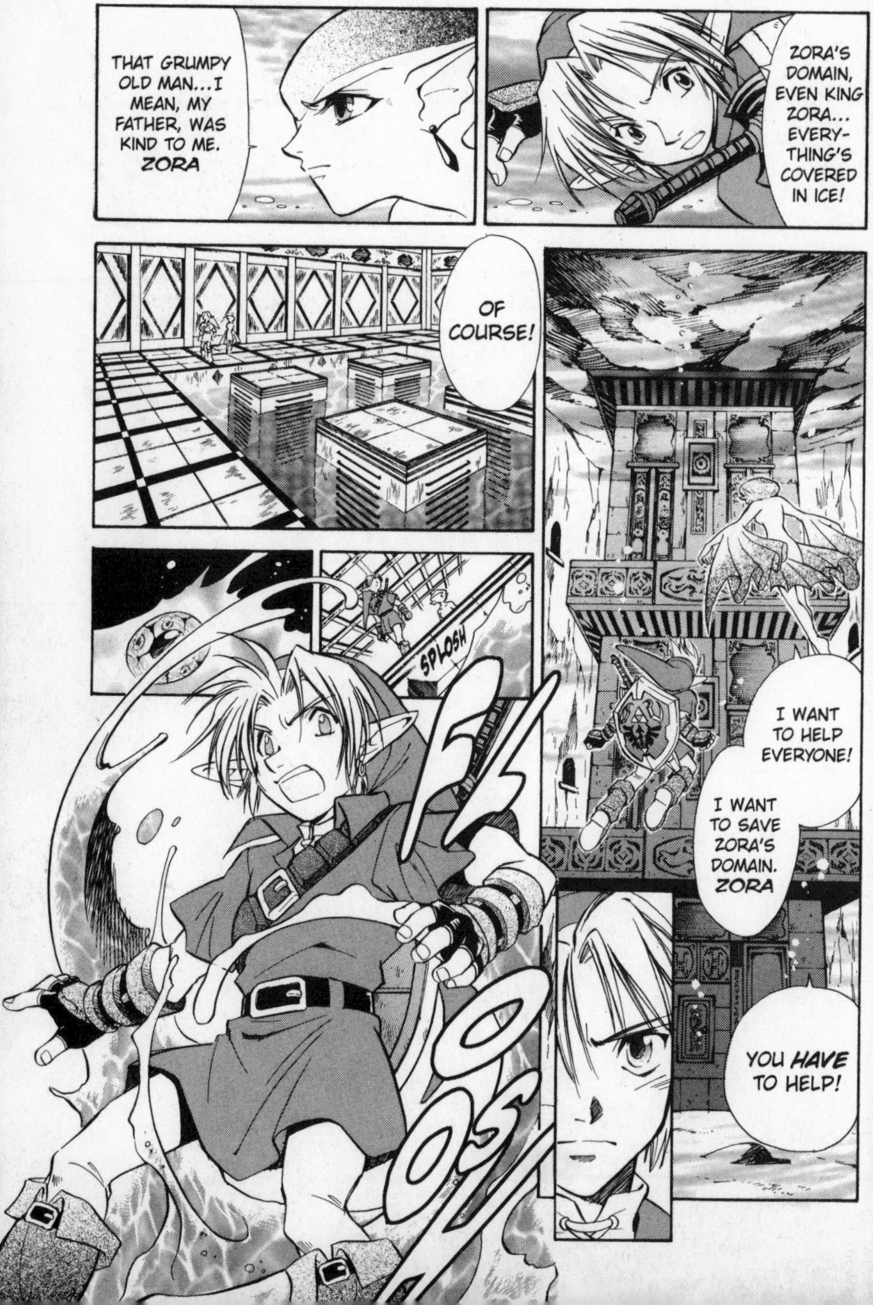
ZORA'S DOMAIN, EVEN KING ZORA... EVERY-THING'S COVERED IN ICE!
THAT GRUMPY OLD MAN...I MEAN, MY FATHER, WAS KIND TO ME. ZORA
I WANT TO HELP EVERYONE!
I WANT TO SAVE ZORA'S DOMAIN. ZORA
YOU HAVE TO HELP!
OF COURSE!
SPLOSH

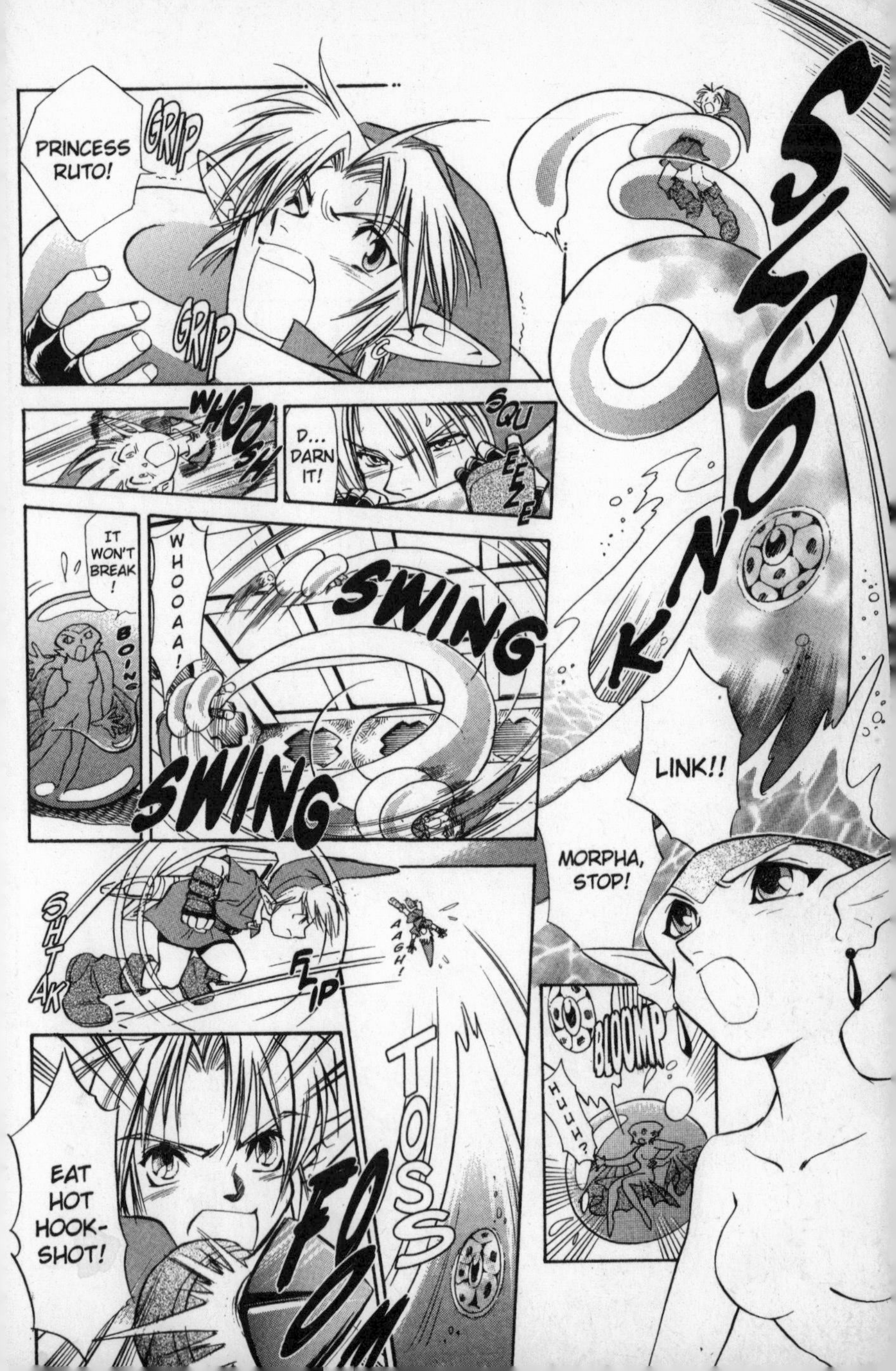
SHOOONK
LINK!!
MORPHA, STOP!
BLOOMP
HUUH?
PRINCESS RUTO!
GRIP
GRIP
SQUEEZE
D... DARN IT!
WHOOSH
SWING
SWING
WHOOOAA!
IT WON'T BREAK!
BOING
FLIP
AAGH!
SHTAK
TOSS
FOOM
EAT HOT HOOK-SHOT!

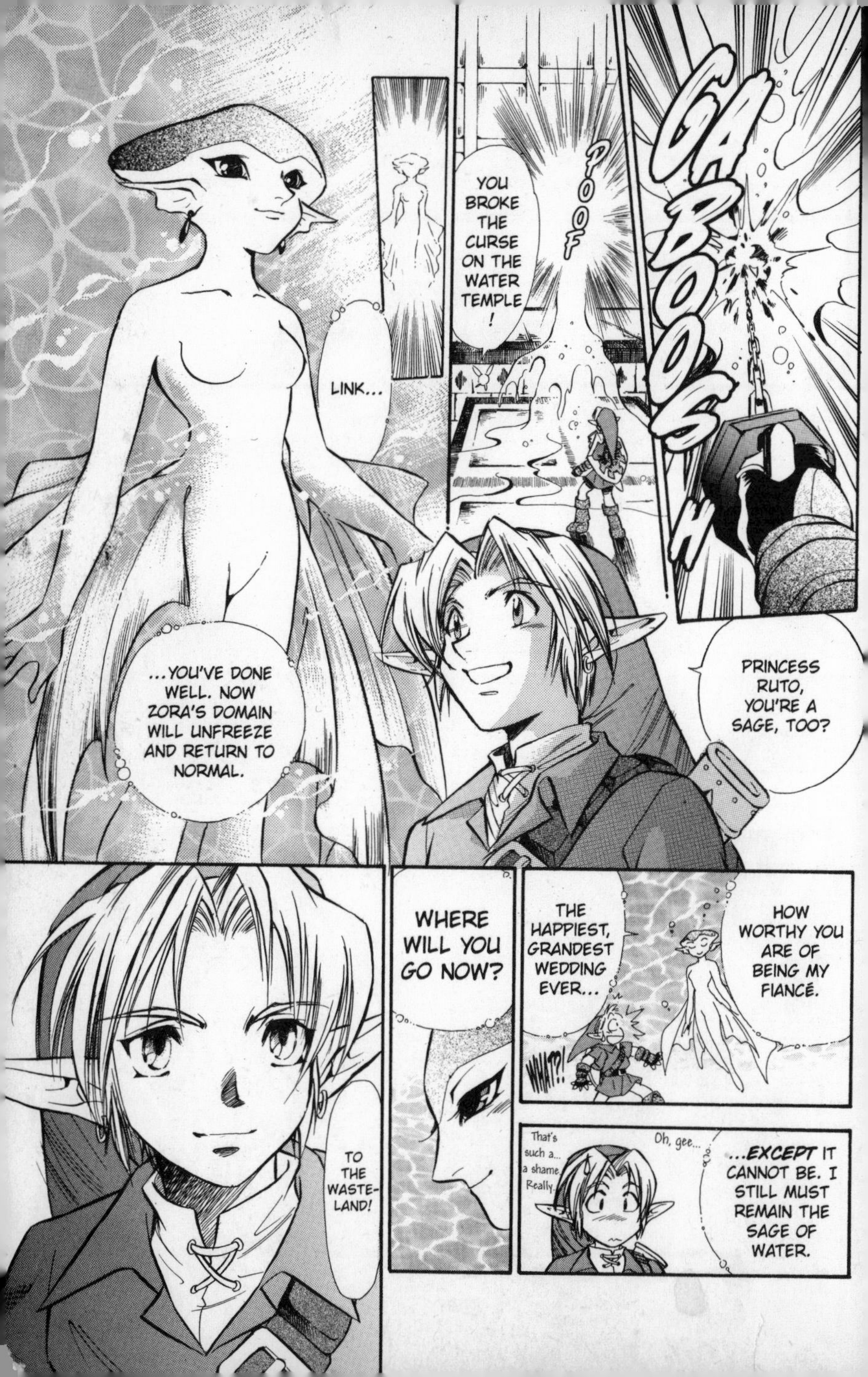
GABOOOSH
POOF
YOU BROKE THE CURSE ON THE WATER TEMPLE!
LINK...
PRINCESS RUTO, YOU'RE A SAGE, TOO?
...YOU'VE DONE WELL. NOW ZORA'S DOMAIN WILL UNFREEZE AND RETURN TO NORMAL.
HOW WORTHY YOU ARE OF BEING MY FIANCÉ.
THE HAPPIEST, GRANDEST WEDDING EVER...
WHAT?!
...*EXCEPT* IT CANNOT BE. I STILL MUST REMAIN THE SAGE OF WATER.
Oh, gee...
That's such a... a shame. Really.
WHERE WILL YOU GO NOW?
TO THE WASTE-LAND!

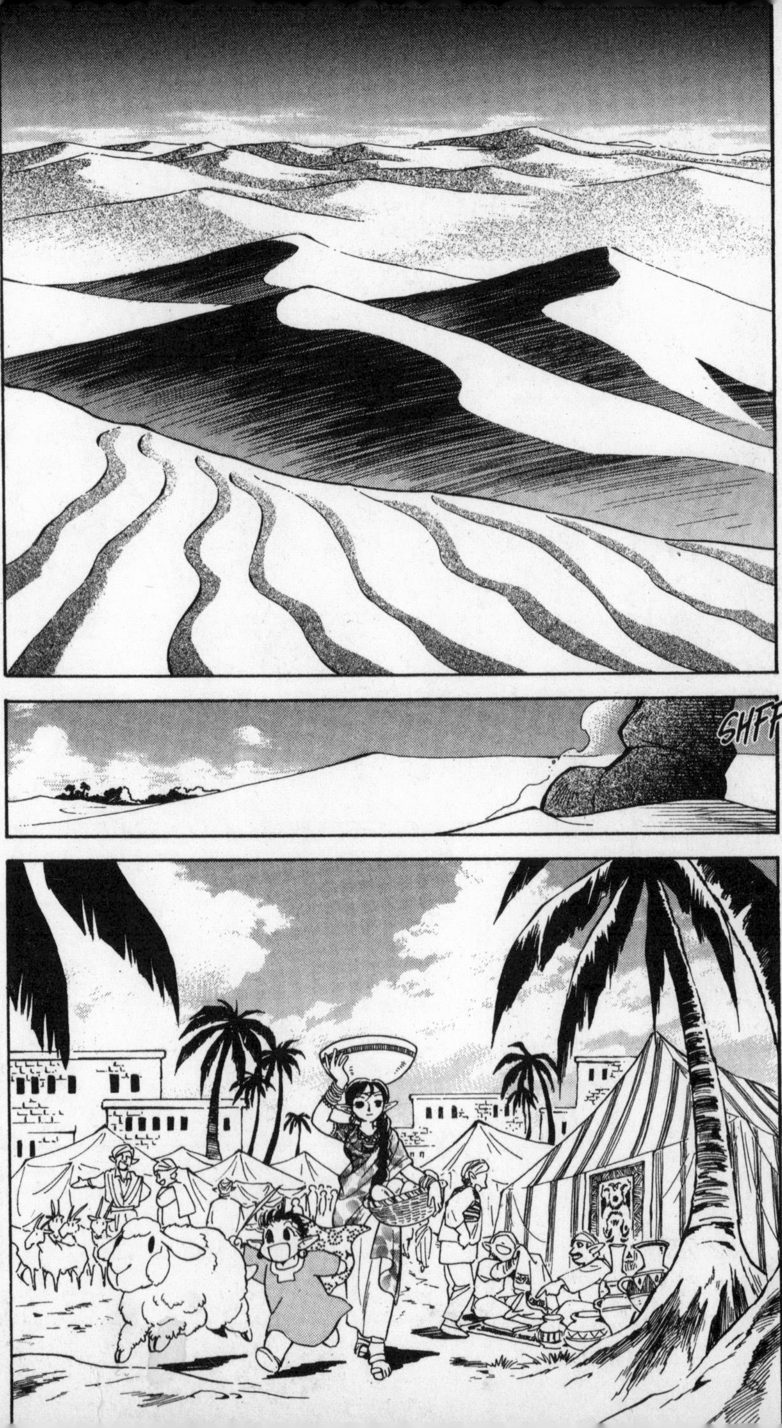
SHFF

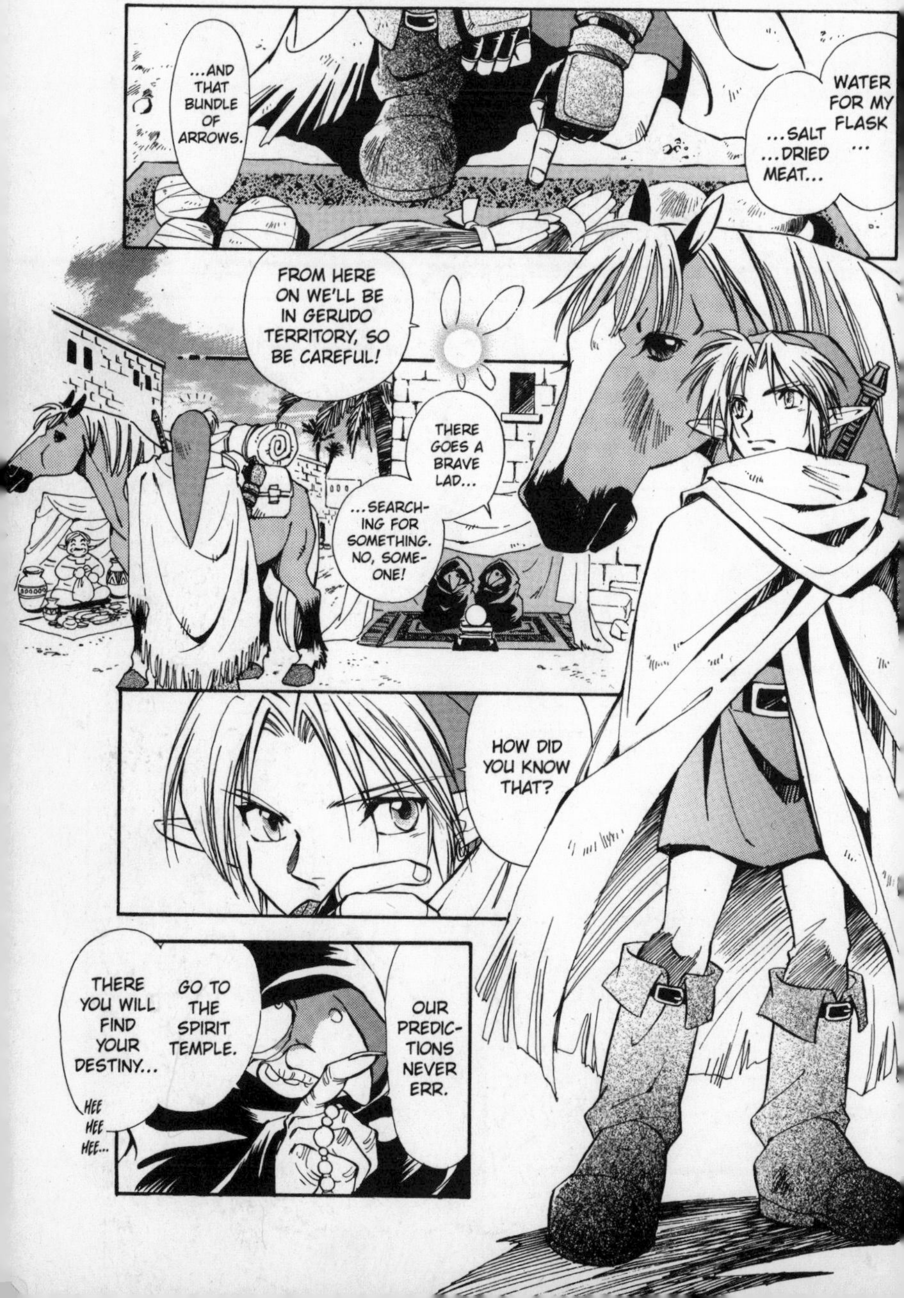
WATER FOR MY FLASK ... ...SALT ...DRIED MEAT...
...AND THAT BUNDLE OF ARROWS.
FROM HERE ON WE'LL BE IN GERUDO TERRITORY, SO BE CAREFUL!
THERE GOES A BRAVE LAD...
...SEARCHING FOR SOMETHING. NO, SOMEONE!
HOW DID YOU KNOW THAT?
OUR PREDICTIONS NEVER ERR.
GO TO THE SPIRIT TEMPLE.
THERE YOU WILL FIND YOUR DESTINY...
HEE HEE HEE...

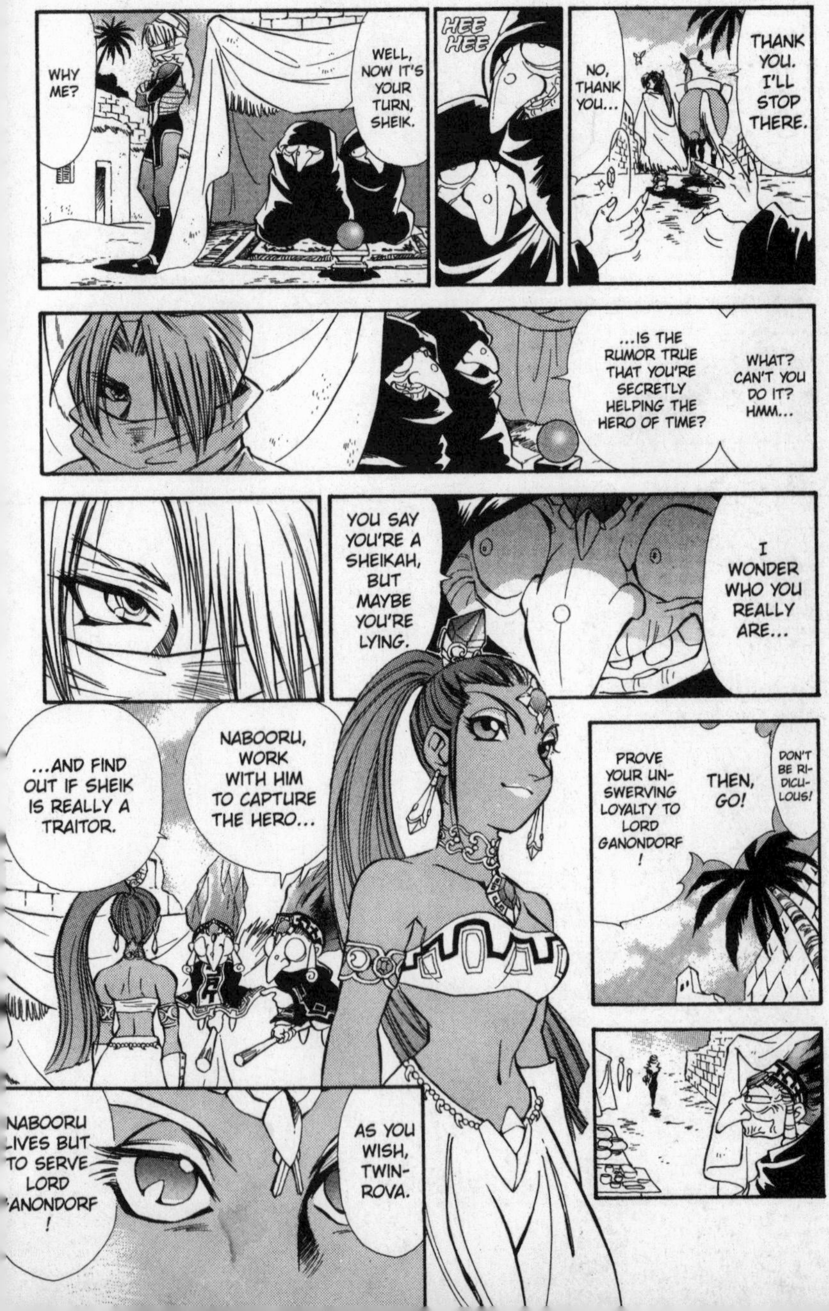
THANK YOU. I'LL STOP THERE.
NO, THANK YOU...
HEE HEE
WELL, NOW IT'S YOUR TURN, SHEIK.
WHY ME?
WHAT? CAN'T YOU DO IT? HMM...
...IS THE RUMOR TRUE THAT YOU'RE SECRETLY HELPING THE HERO OF TIME?
I WONDER WHO YOU REALLY ARE...
YOU SAY YOU'RE A SHEIKAH, BUT MAYBE YOU'RE LYING.
DON'T BE RIDICULOUS!
THEN, GO!
PROVE YOUR UNSWERVING LOYALTY TO LORD GANONDORF!
NABOORU, WORK WITH HIM TO CAPTURE THE HERO...
...AND FIND OUT IF SHEIK IS REALLY A TRAITOR.
AS YOU WISH, TWINROVA.
NABOORU LIVES BUT TO SERVE LORD GANONDORF!

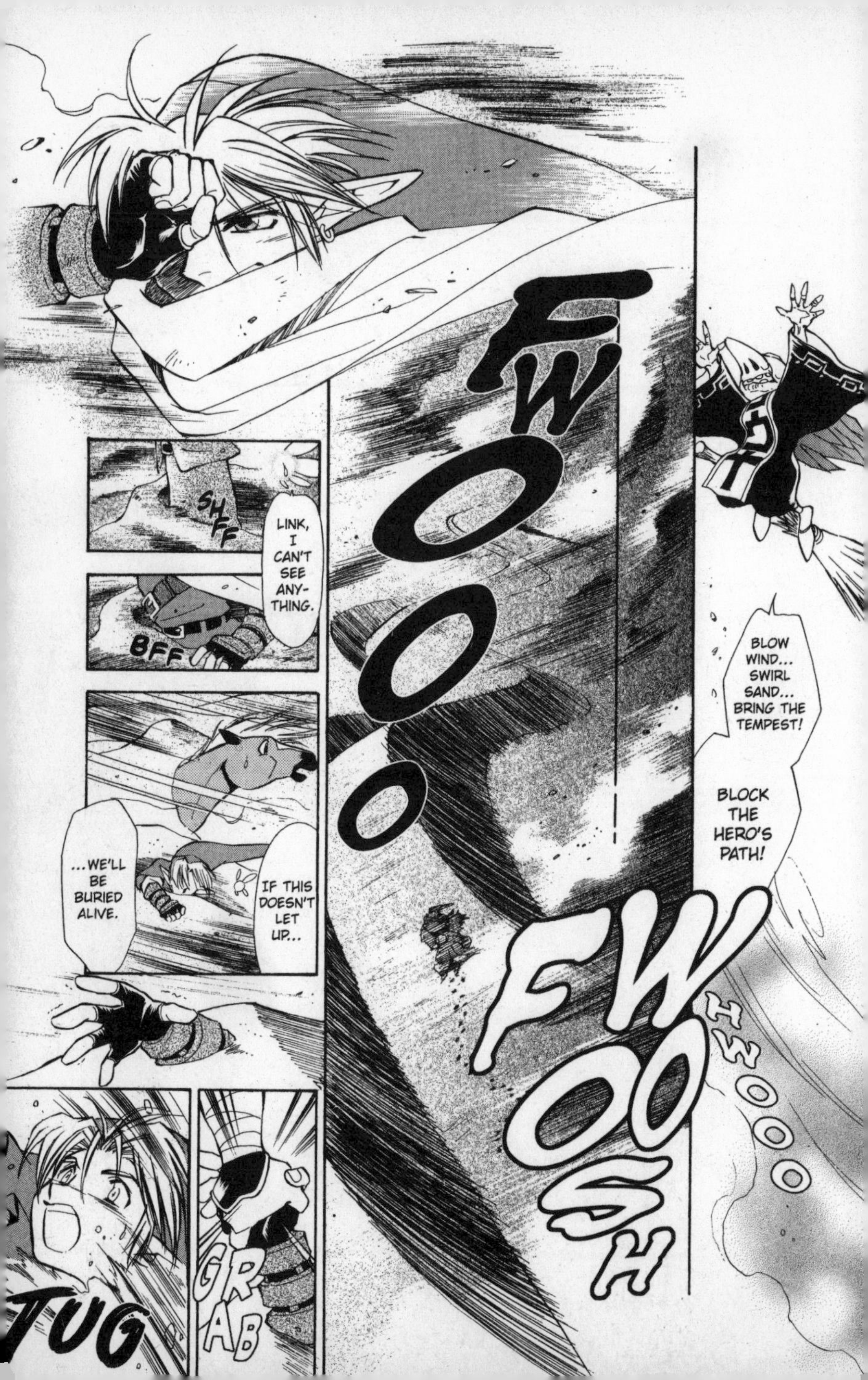
FWOOOOO
BLOW WIND... SWIRL SAND... BRING THE TEMPEST!
BLOCK THE HERO'S PATH!
FWOOSH
WHOOOO
SHFF
LINK, I CAN'T SEE ANYTHING.
BFF
IF THIS DOESN'T LET UP...
...WE'LL BE BURIED ALIVE.
GRAB
TUG

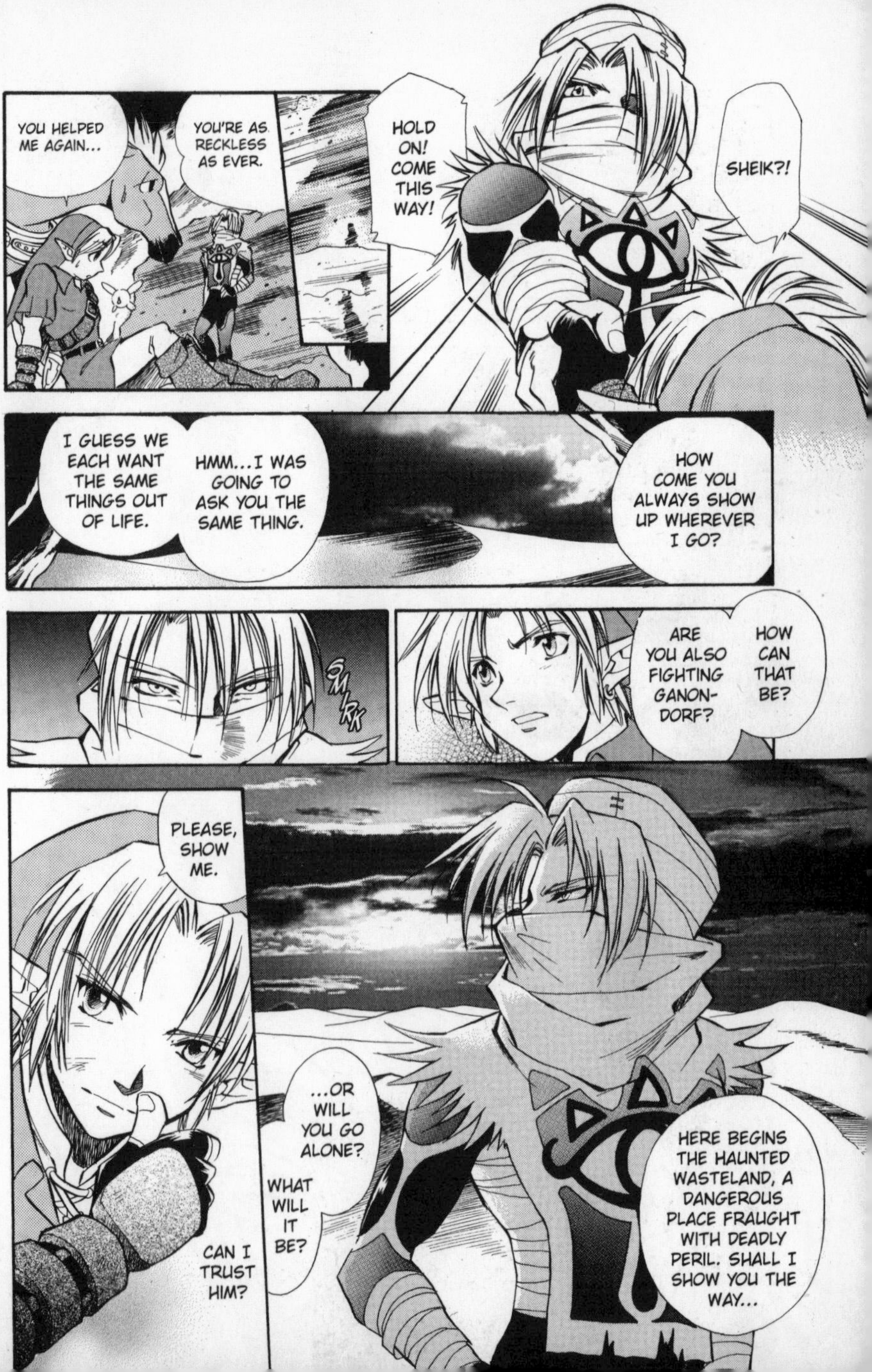
SHEIK?!
HOLD ON! COME THIS WAY!
YOU'RE AS RECKLESS AS EVER.
YOU HELPED ME AGAIN...
HOW COME YOU ALWAYS SHOW UP WHEREVER I GO?
HMM...I WAS GOING TO ASK YOU THE SAME THING.
I GUESS WE EACH WANT THE SAME THINGS OUT OF LIFE.
HOW CAN THAT BE?
ARE YOU ALSO FIGHTING GANON-DORF?
SMIRK
HERE BEGINS THE HAUNTED WASTELAND, A DANGEROUS PLACE FRAUGHT WITH DEADLY PERIL. SHALL I SHOW YOU THE WAY...
...OR WILL YOU GO ALONE?
WHAT WILL IT BE?
CAN I TRUST HIM?
PLEASE, SHOW ME.

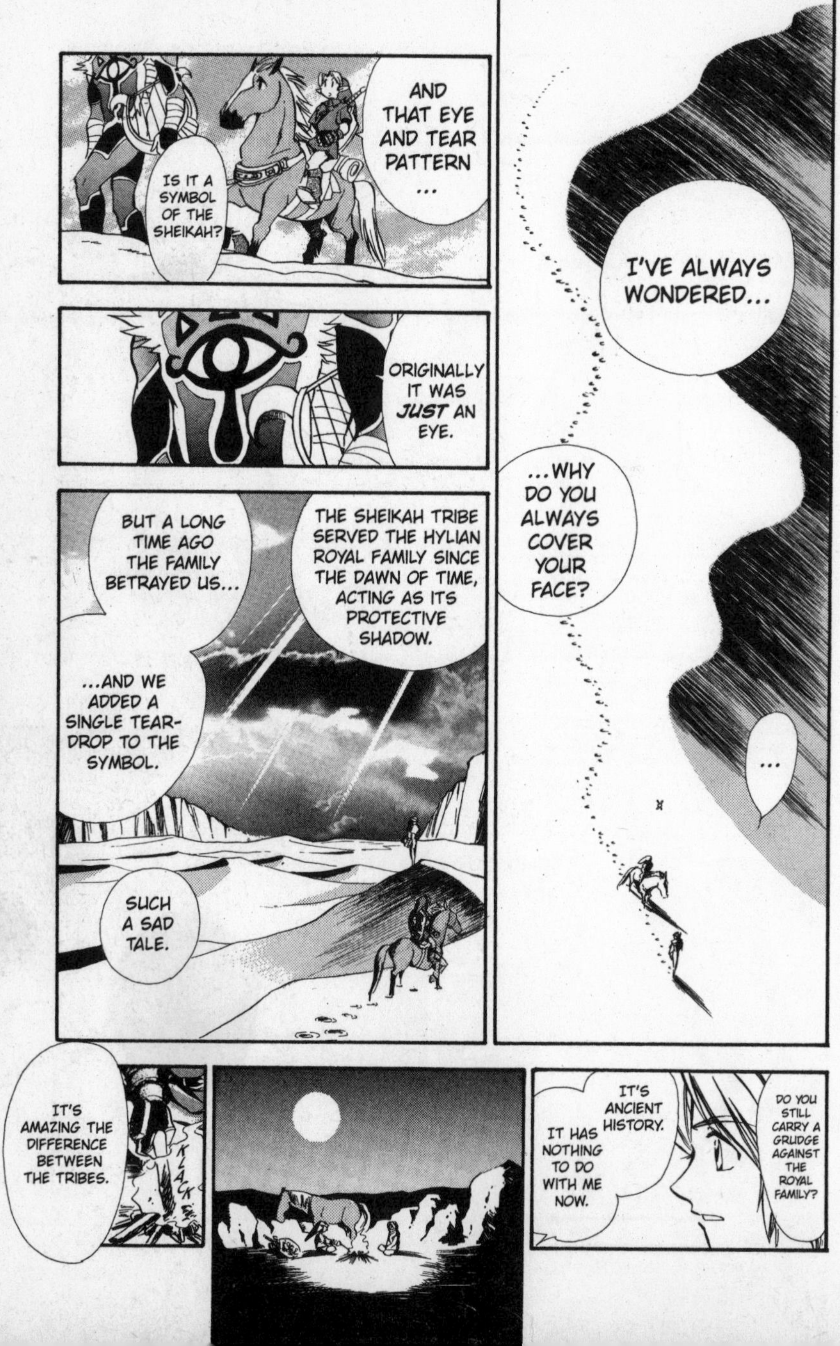
I'VE ALWAYS WONDERED...
...WHY DO YOU ALWAYS COVER YOUR FACE?
...
AND THAT EYE AND TEAR PATTERN ...
IS IT A SYMBOL OF THE SHEIKAH?
ORIGINALLY IT WAS *JUST* AN EYE.
THE SHEIKAH TRIBE SERVED THE HYLIAN ROYAL FAMILY SINCE THE DAWN OF TIME, ACTING AS ITS PROTECTIVE SHADOW.
BUT A LONG TIME AGO THE FAMILY BETRAYED US...
...AND WE ADDED A SINGLE TEAR-DROP TO THE SYMBOL.
SUCH A SAD TALE.
DO YOU STILL CARRY A GRUDGE AGAINST THE ROYAL FAMILY?
IT'S ANCIENT HISTORY.
IT HAS NOTHING TO DO WITH ME NOW.
IT'S AMAZING THE DIFFERENCE BETWEEN THE TRIBES.
KLACK

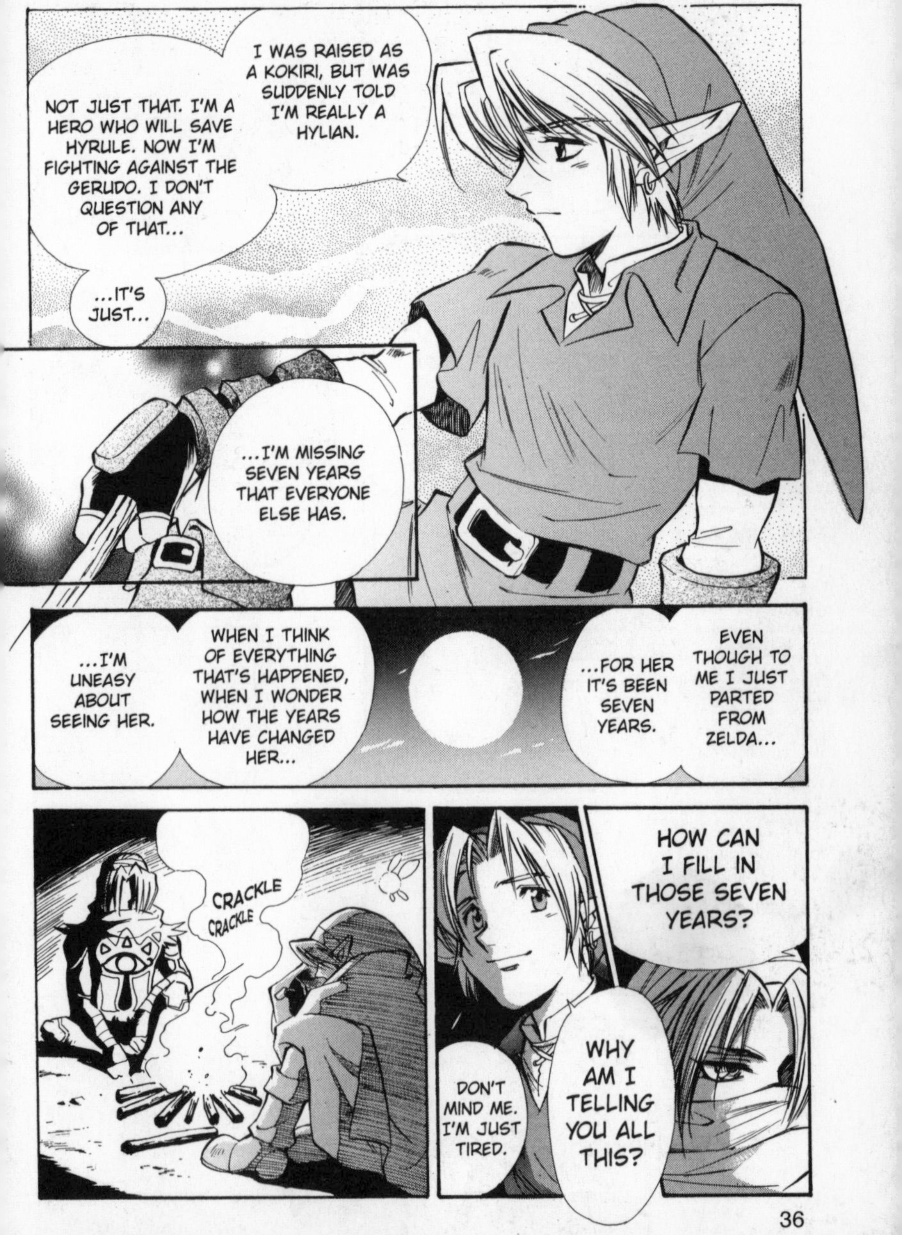
I WAS RAISED AS A KOKIRI, BUT WAS SUDDENLY TOLD I'M REALLY A HYLIAN.
NOT JUST THAT. I'M A HERO WHO WILL SAVE HYRULE. NOW I'M FIGHTING AGAINST THE GERUDO. I DON'T QUESTION ANY OF THAT...
...IT'S JUST...
...I'M MISSING SEVEN YEARS THAT EVERYONE ELSE HAS.
EVEN THOUGH TO ME I JUST PARTED FROM ZELDA...
...FOR HER IT'S BEEN SEVEN YEARS.
WHEN I THINK OF EVERYTHING THAT'S HAPPENED, WHEN I WONDER HOW THE YEARS HAVE CHANGED HER...
...I'M UNEASY ABOUT SEEING HER.
HOW CAN I FILL IN THOSE SEVEN YEARS?
WHY AM I TELLING YOU ALL THIS?
DON'T MIND ME. I'M JUST TIRED.
CRACKLE
CRACKLE

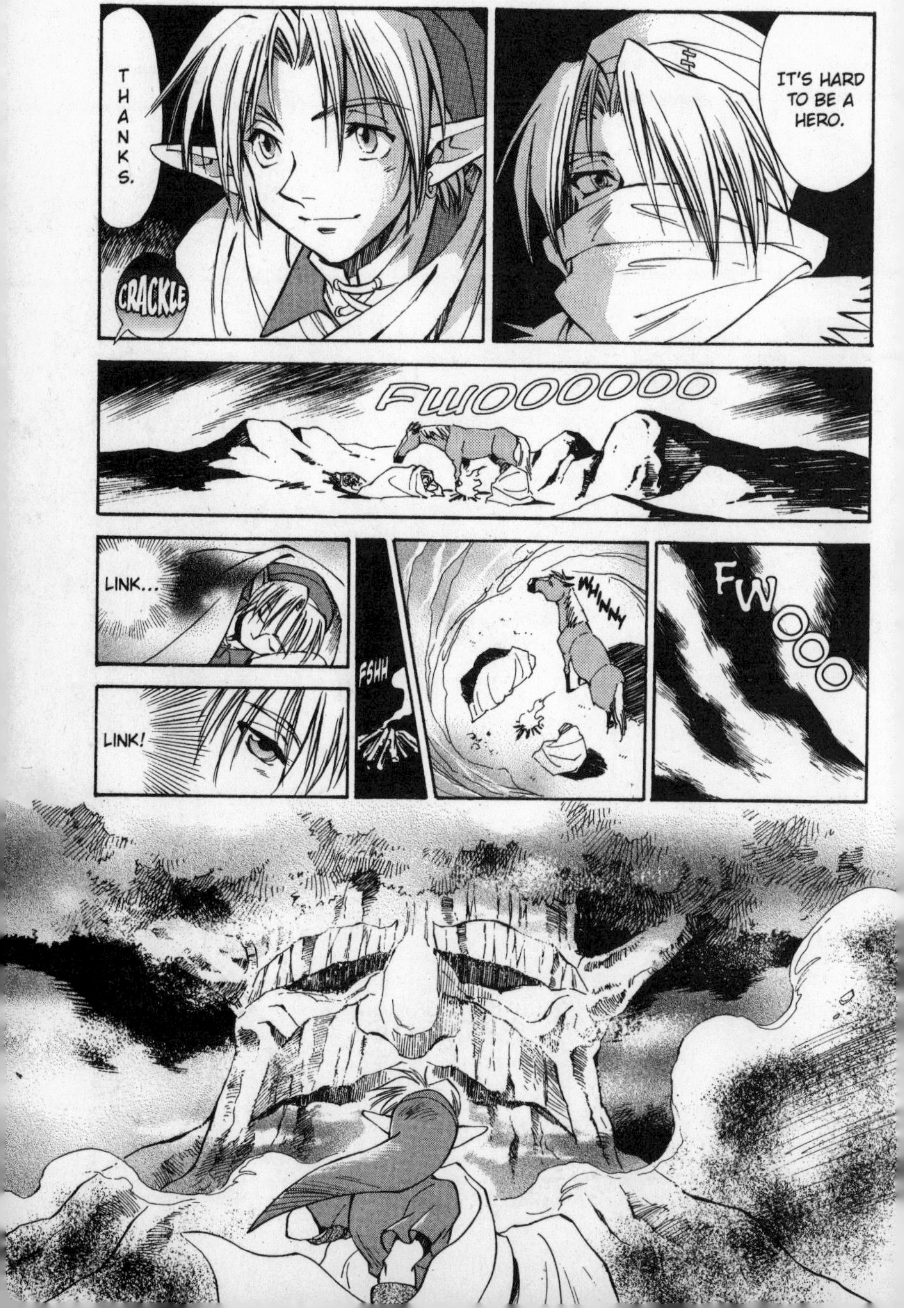
IT'S HARD TO BE A HERO.
THANKS.
CRACKLE
FWOOOOOO
FWOOO
WHINNY
FSHH
LINK...
LINK!

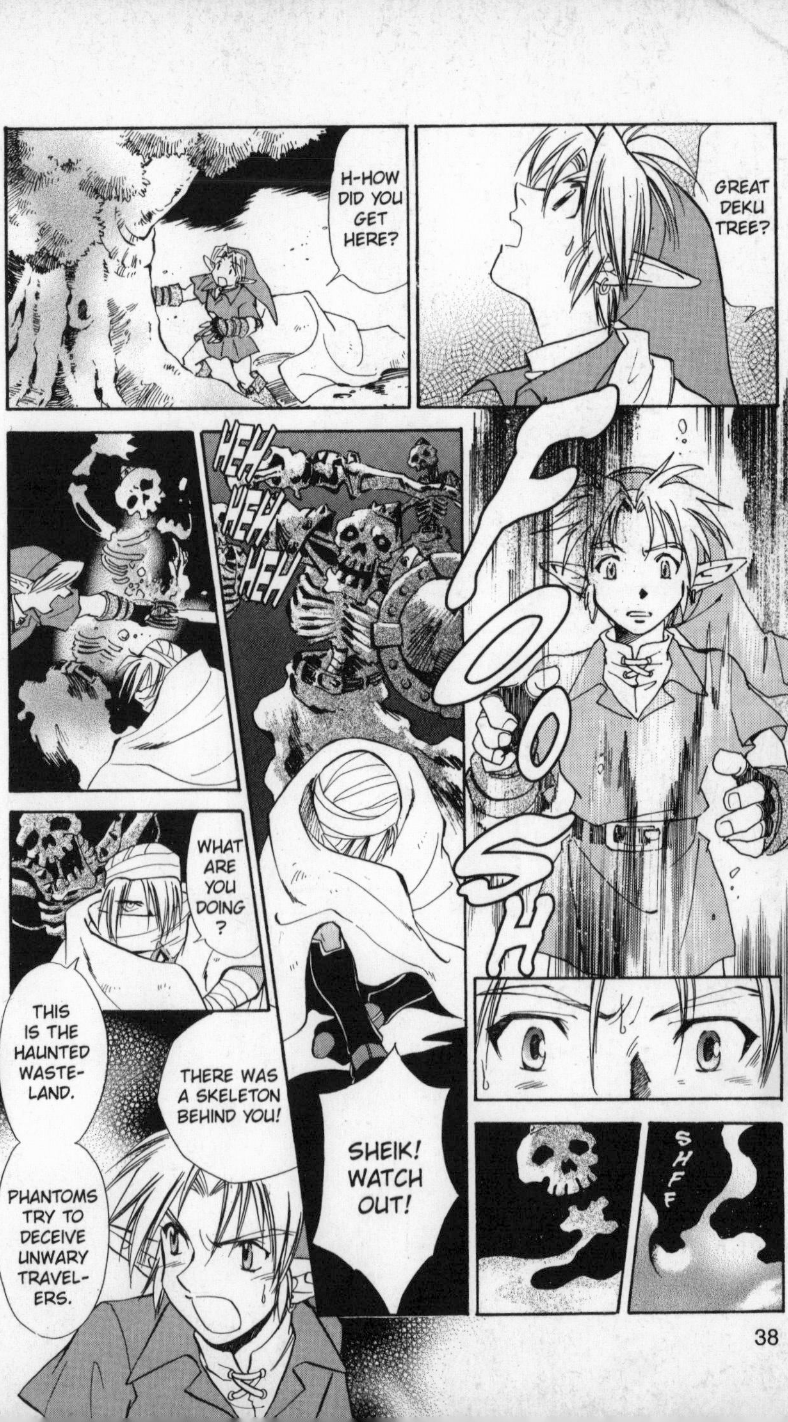
GREAT DEKU TREE?
H-HOW DID YOU GET HERE?
SOOSH
HEH HEH HEH
WHAT ARE YOU DOING?
SHFF
SHEIK! WATCH OUT!
THERE WAS A SKELETON BEHIND YOU!
THIS IS THE HAUNTED WASTE-LAND.
PHANTOMS TRY TO DECEIVE UNWARY TRAVEL-ERS.

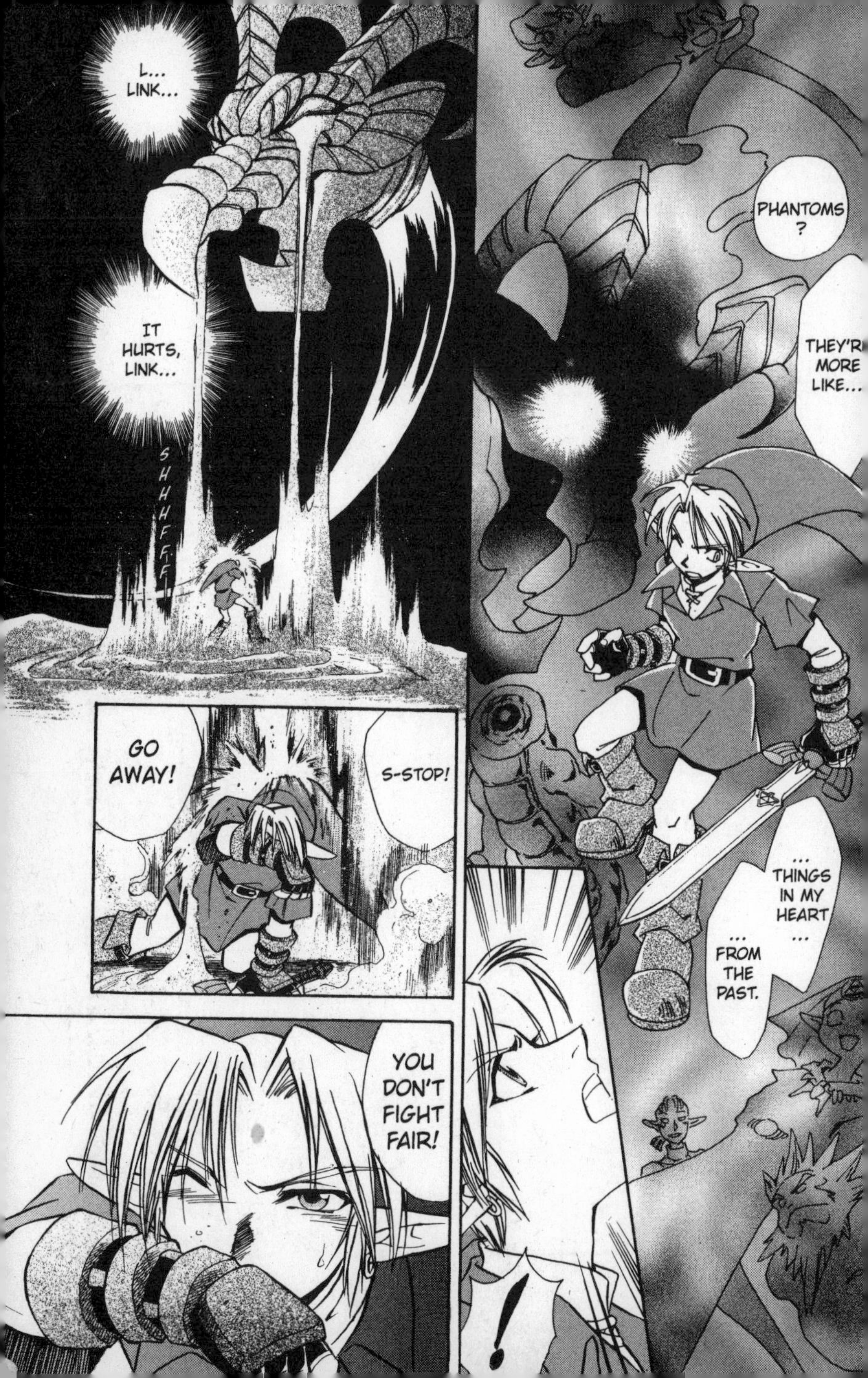
PHANTOMS ?
THEY'R MORE LIKE...
...THINGS IN MY HEART...
...FROM THE PAST.
L... LINK...
IT HURTS, LINK...
SHHHFFF
S-STOP!
GO AWAY!
YOU DON'T FIGHT FAIR!

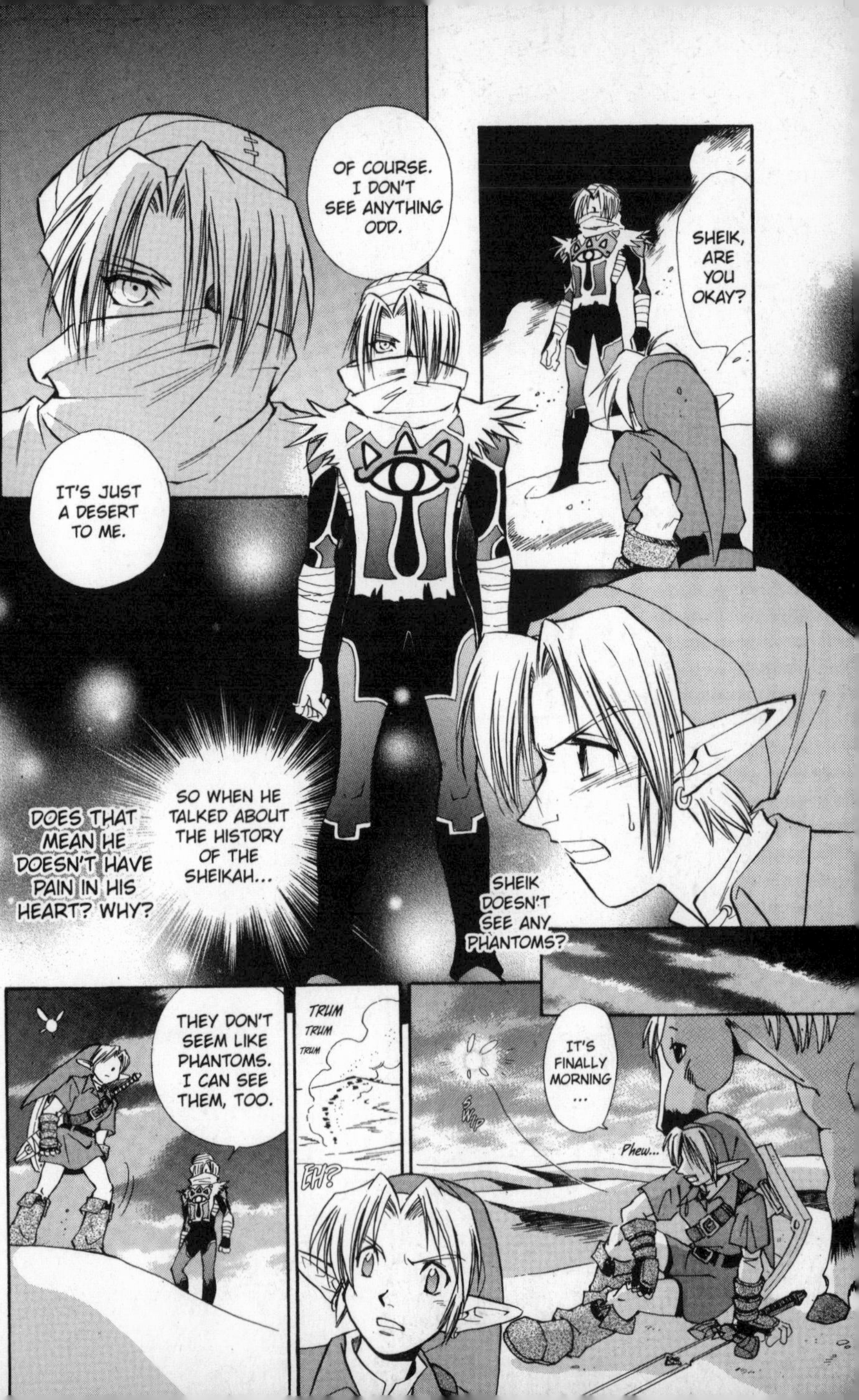
SHEIK, ARE YOU OKAY?
OF COURSE. I DON'T SEE ANYTHING ODD.
IT'S JUST A DESERT TO ME.
SHEIK DOESN'T SEE ANY PHANTOMS?
SO WHEN HE TALKED ABOUT THE HISTORY OF THE SHEIKAH...
DOES THAT MEAN HE DOESN'T HAVE PAIN IN HIS HEART? WHY?
IT'S FINALLY MORNING ...
Phew...
TRUM
TRUM
TRUM
SWIP
EH?
THEY DON'T SEEM LIKE PHANTOMS. I CAN SEE THEM, TOO.

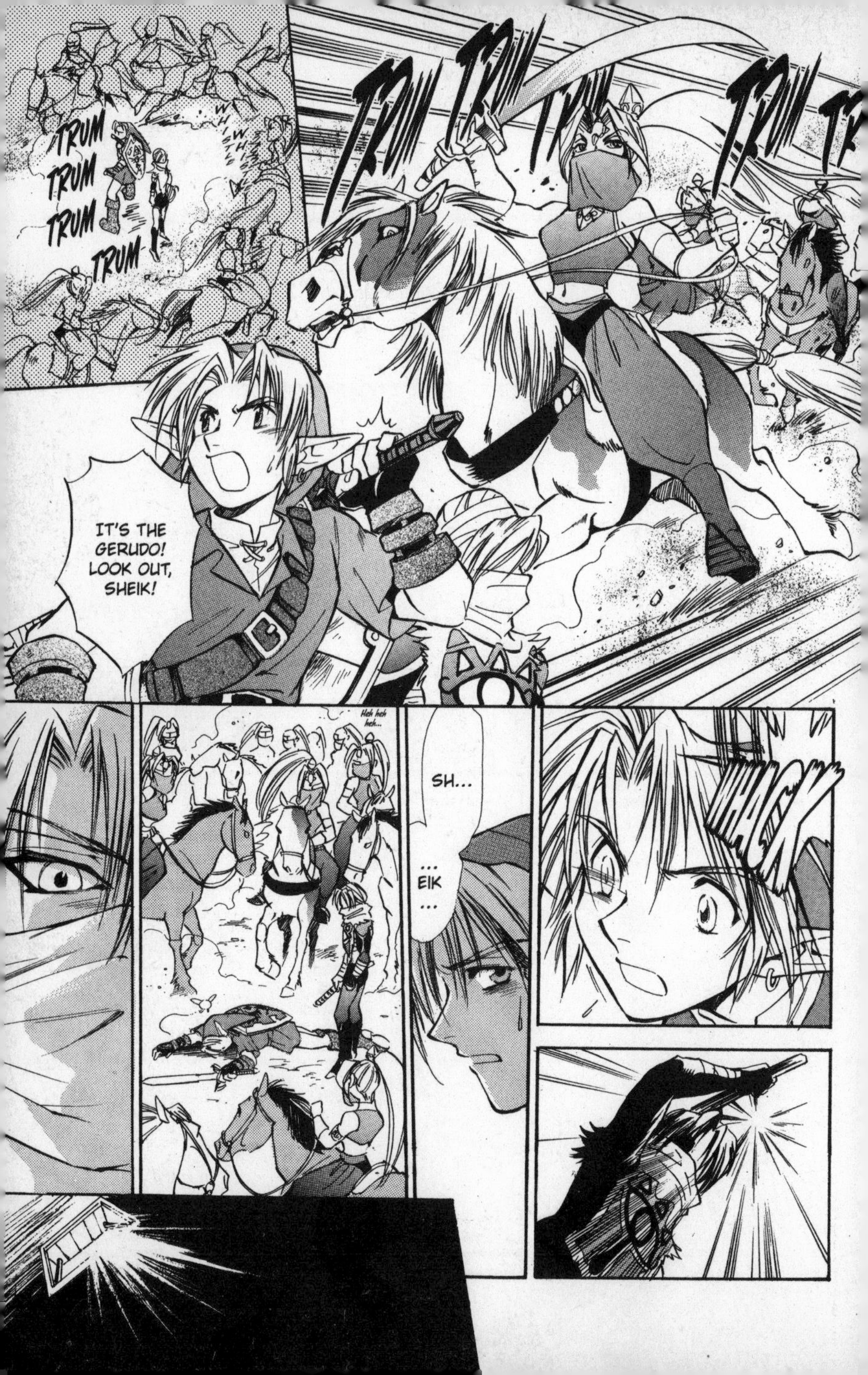
TRUM
TRUM
TRUM
TRUM
IT'S THE GERUDO! LOOK OUT, SHEIK!
WHACK
SH...
... EIK ...
Heh heh heh...

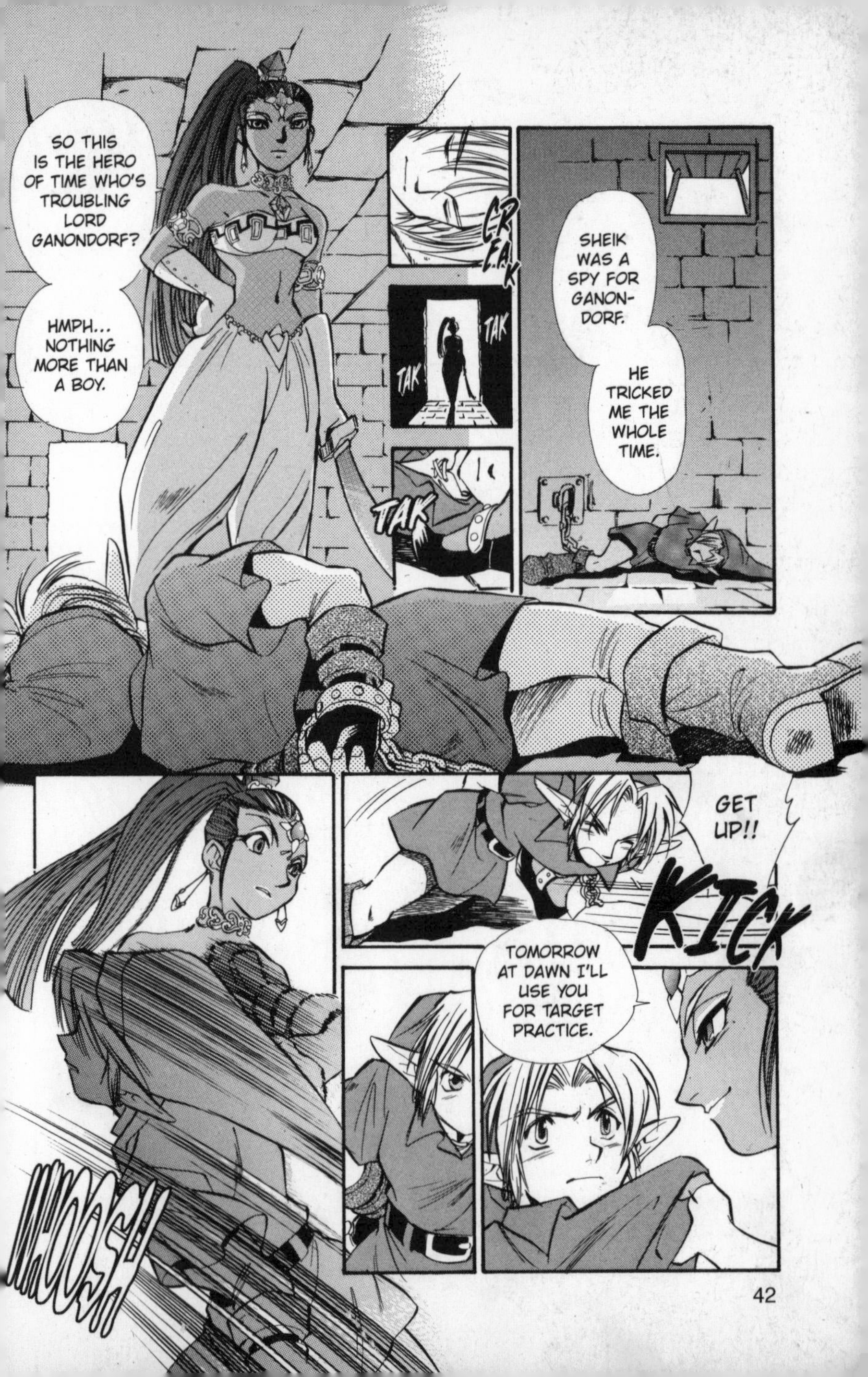
SHEIK WAS A SPY FOR GANON-DORF.
HE TRICKED ME THE WHOLE TIME.
CREAK
TAK
TAK
TAK
SO THIS IS THE HERO OF TIME WHO'S TROUBLING LORD GANONDORF?
HMPH... NOTHING MORE THAN A BOY.
GET UP!!
KICK
TOMORROW AT DAWN I'LL USE YOU FOR TARGET PRACTICE.
WHOOSH!

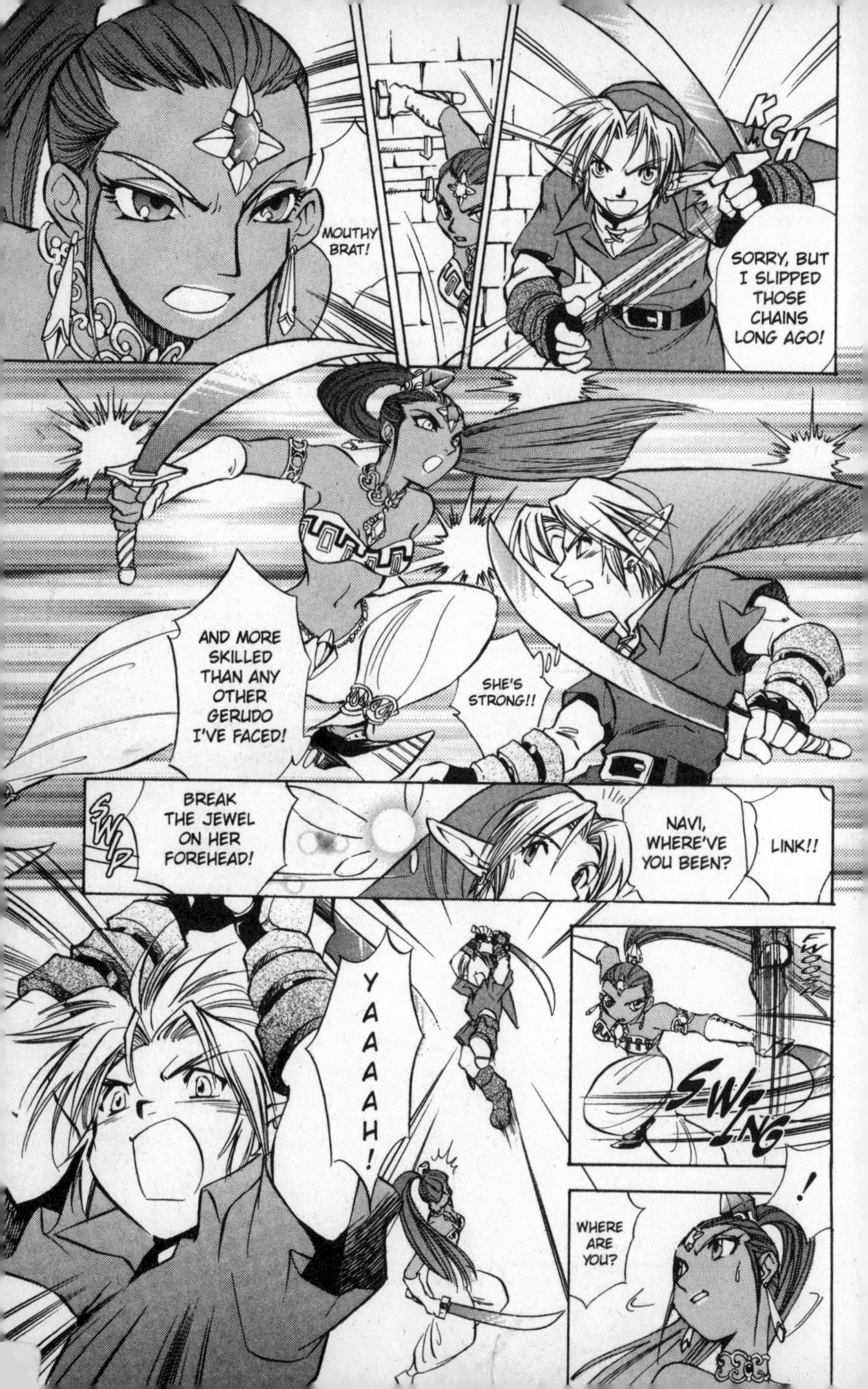
KCH
SORRY, BUT I SLIPPED THOSE CHAINS LONG AGO!
MOUTHY BRAT!
SHE'S STRONG!!
AND MORE SKILLED THAN ANY OTHER GERUDO I'VE FACED!
LINK!!
NAVI, WHERE'VE YOU BEEN?
BREAK THE JEWEL ON HER FOREHEAD!
SWIP
FWOOM
SWING
!
WHERE ARE YOU?
YAAAAAH!

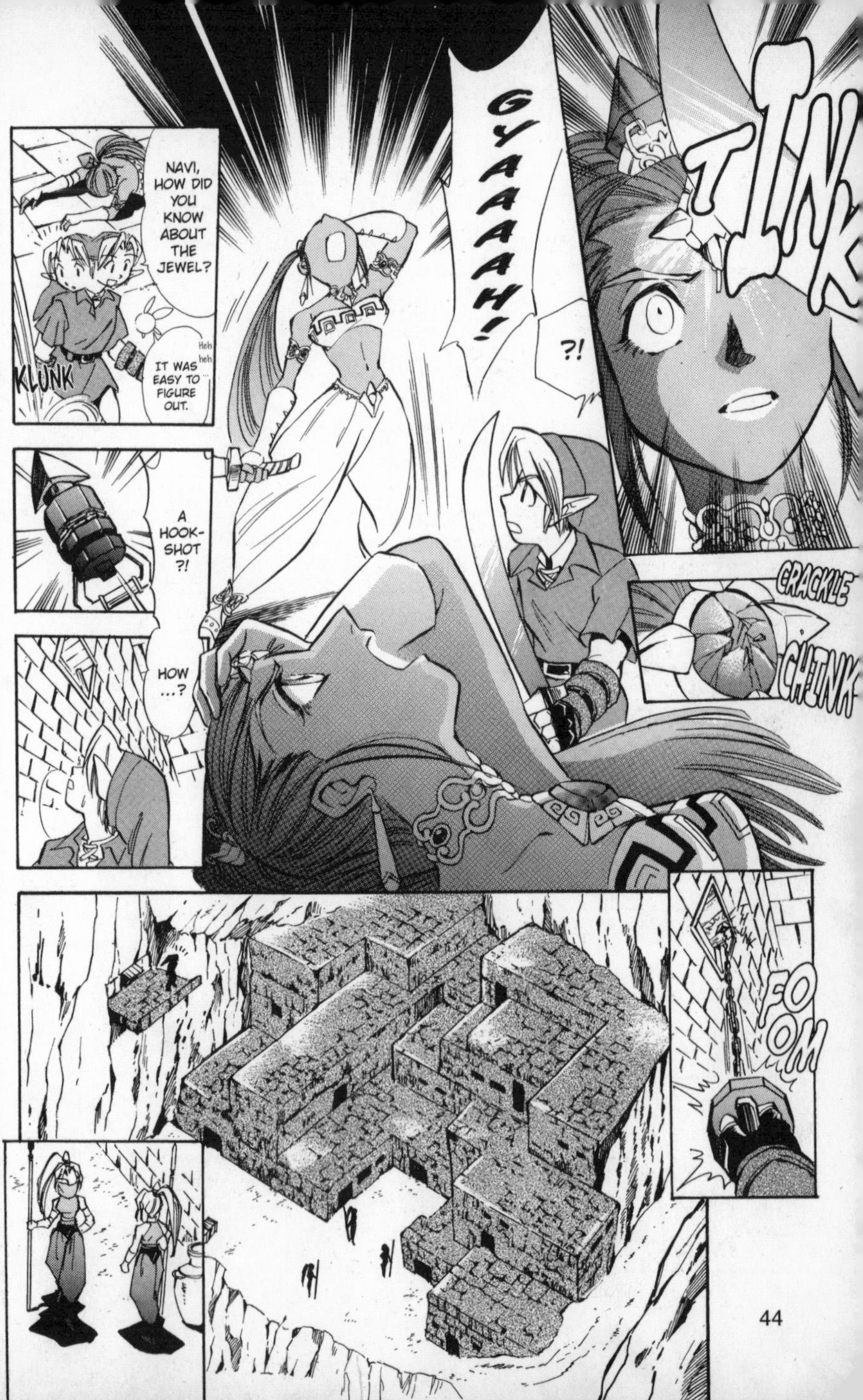
TINK
?!
CRACKLE
CHINK
GYAAAAAH!
NAVI, HOW DID YOU KNOW ABOUT THE JEWEL?
KLUNK
Heh heh...
IT WAS EASY TO FIGURE OUT.
A HOOK-SHOT ?!
HOW ...?
FOOM

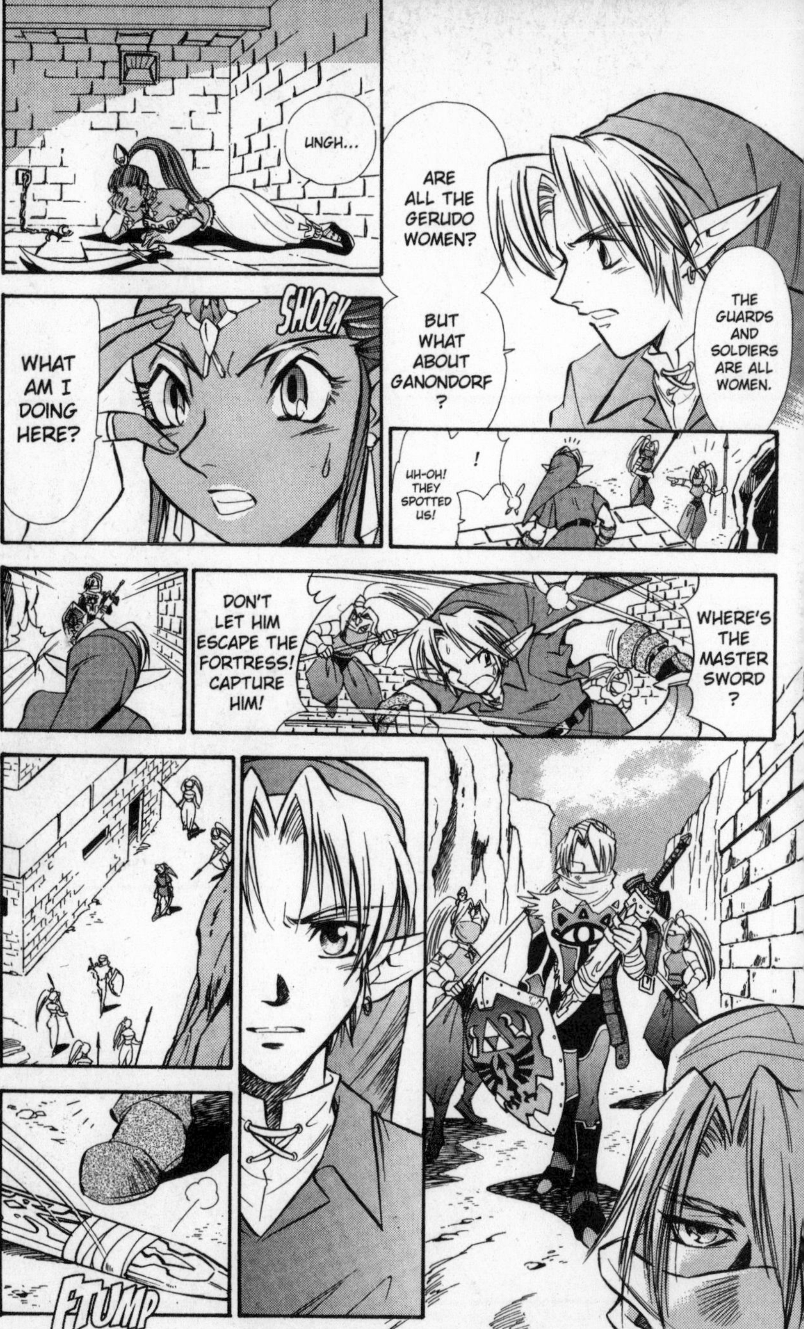
THE GUARDS AND SOLDIERS ARE ALL WOMEN.
ARE ALL THE GERUDO WOMEN?
BUT WHAT ABOUT GANONDORF?
UNGH...
SHOCK
WHAT AM I DOING HERE?
!
UH-OH! THEY SPOTTED US!
WHERE'S THE MASTER SWORD?
DON'T LET HIM ESCAPE THE FORTRESS! CAPTURE HIM!
FTUMP

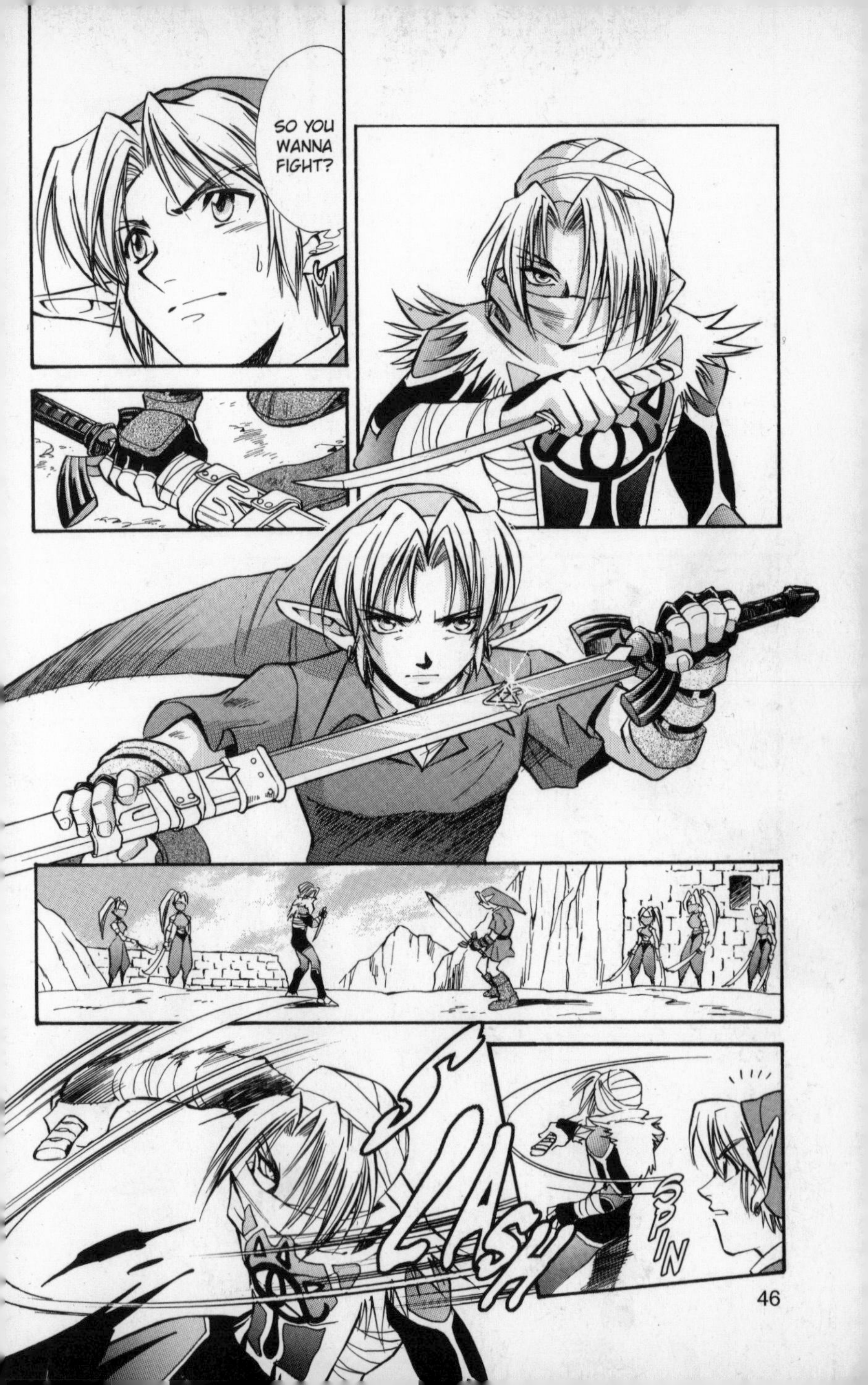
SO YOU WANNA FIGHT?
CLASH
SPIN

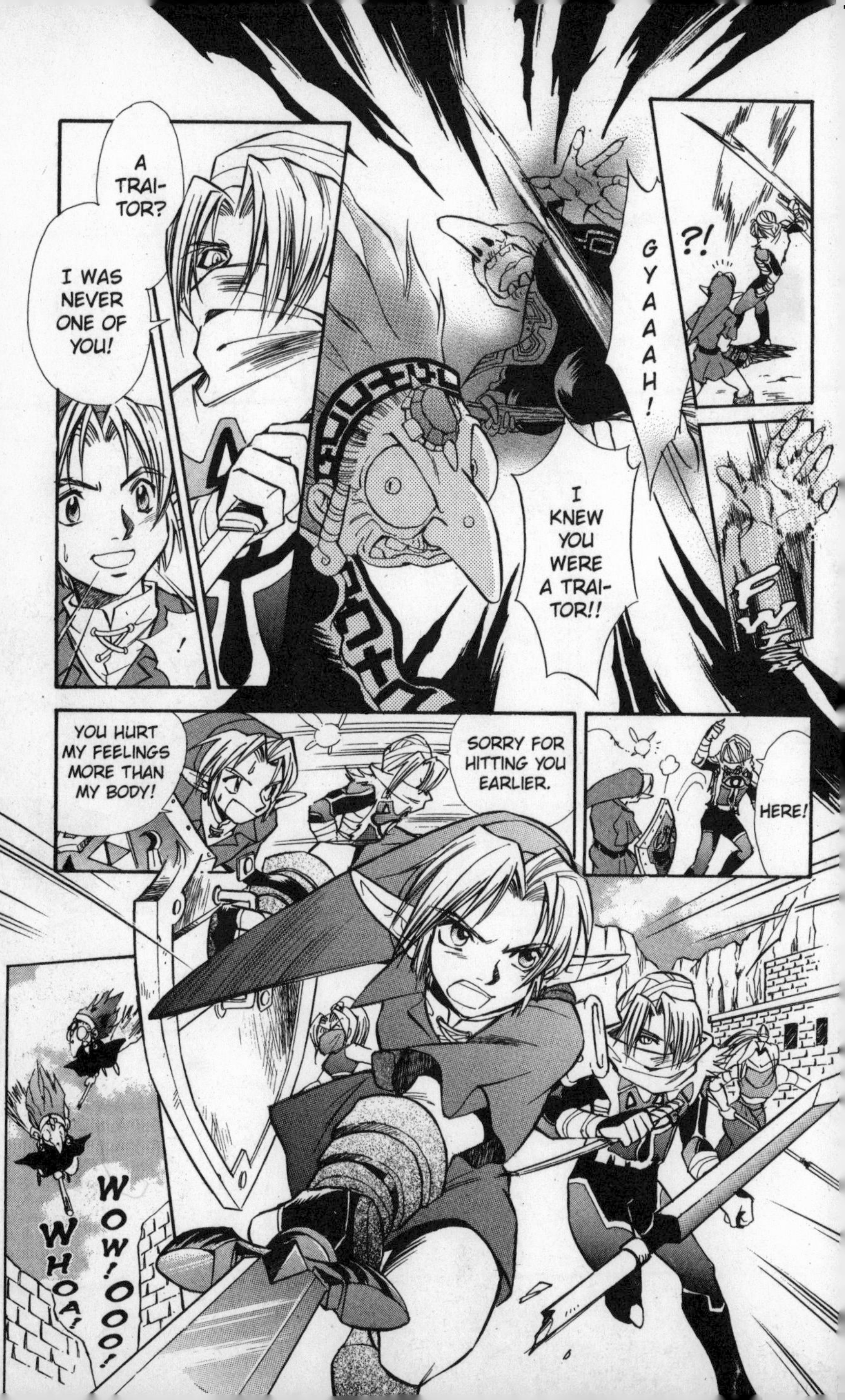
?!
GYAAAAH!
I KNEW YOU WERE A TRAI-TOR!!
A TRAI-TOR?
I WAS NEVER ONE OF YOU!
HERE!
SORRY FOR HITTING YOU EARLIER.
YOU HURT MY FEELINGS MORE THAN MY BODY!
WOW!OOO!
WHOA!

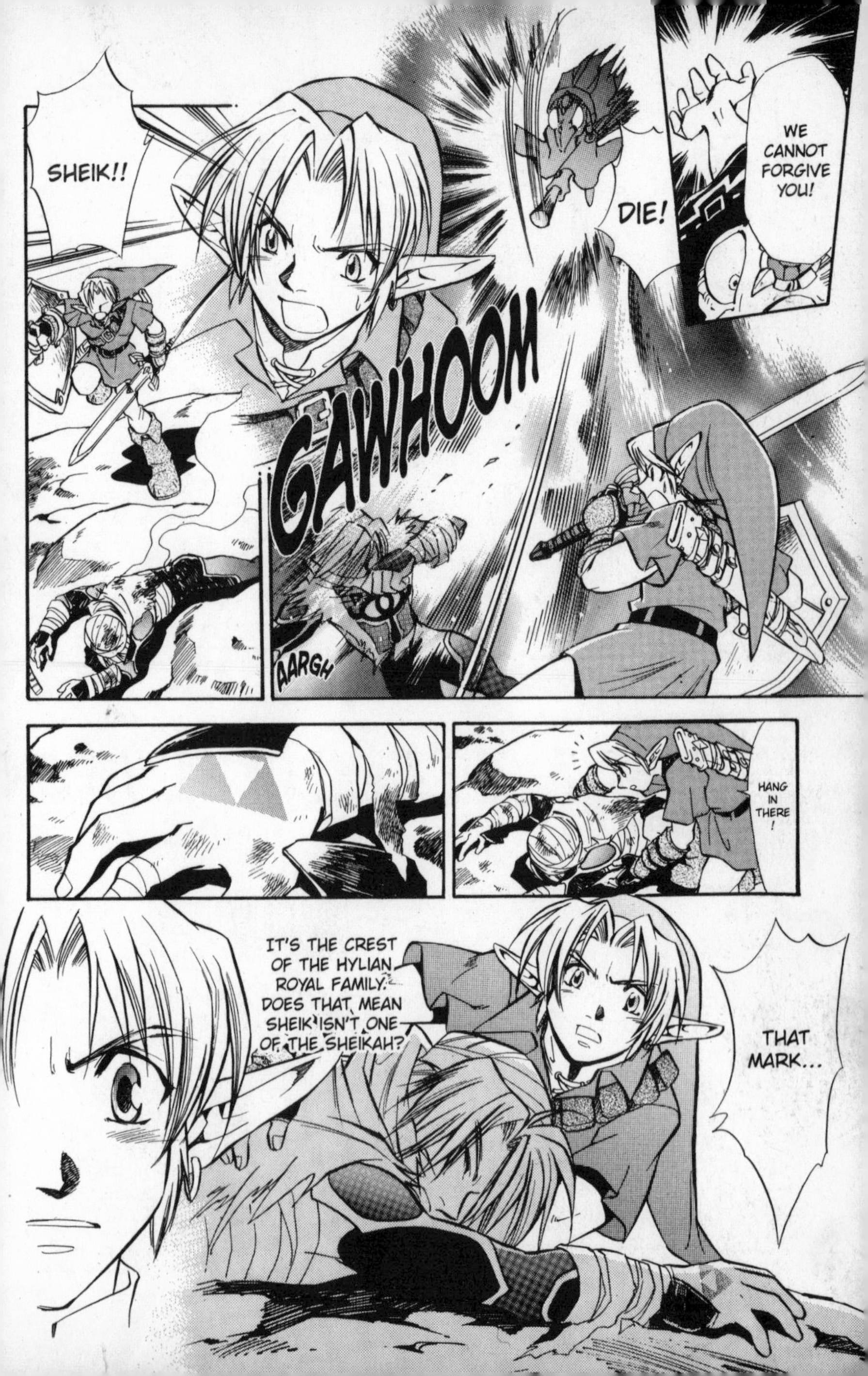
WE CANNOT FORGIVE YOU!
DIE!
GAWHOOM
AARGH
SHEIK!!
HANG IN THERE!
THAT MARK...
IT'S THE CREST OF THE HYLIAN ROYAL FAMILY. DOES THAT MEAN SHEIK ISN'T ONE OF THE SHEIKAH?

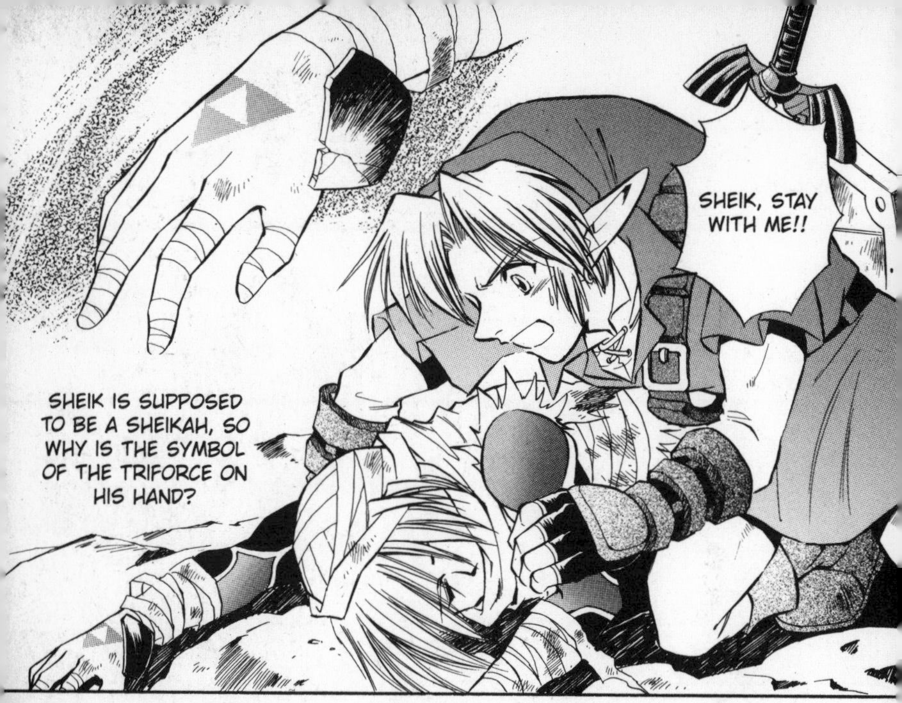
SHEIK, STAY WITH ME!!
SHEIK IS SUPPOSED TO BE A SHEIKAH, SO WHY IS THE SYMBOL OF THE TRIFORCE ON HIS HAND?

CHAPTER 7 A FATEFUL REUNION

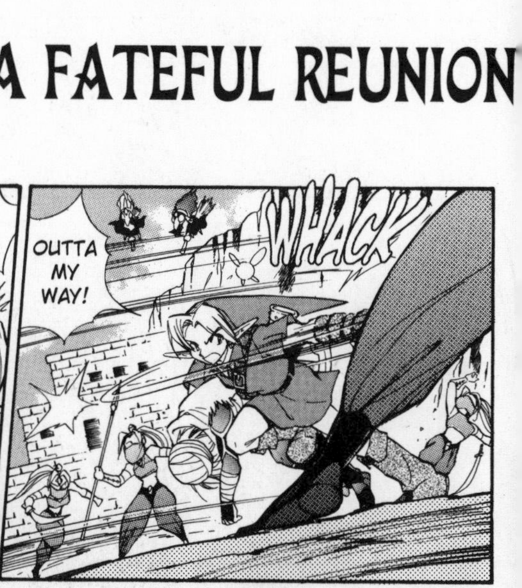
OUTTA MY WAY!
WHACK

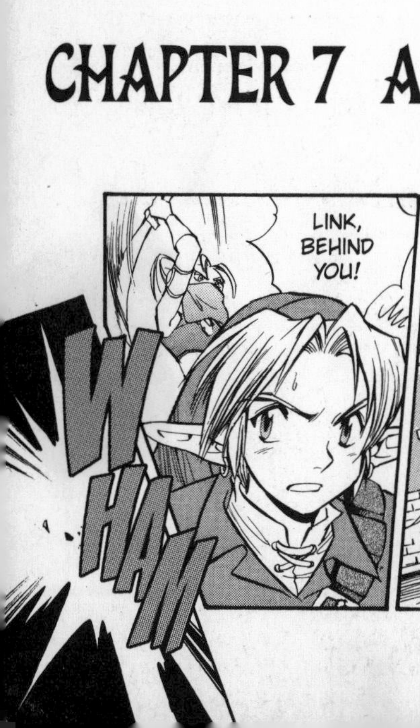
LINK, BEHIND YOU!
WHAM

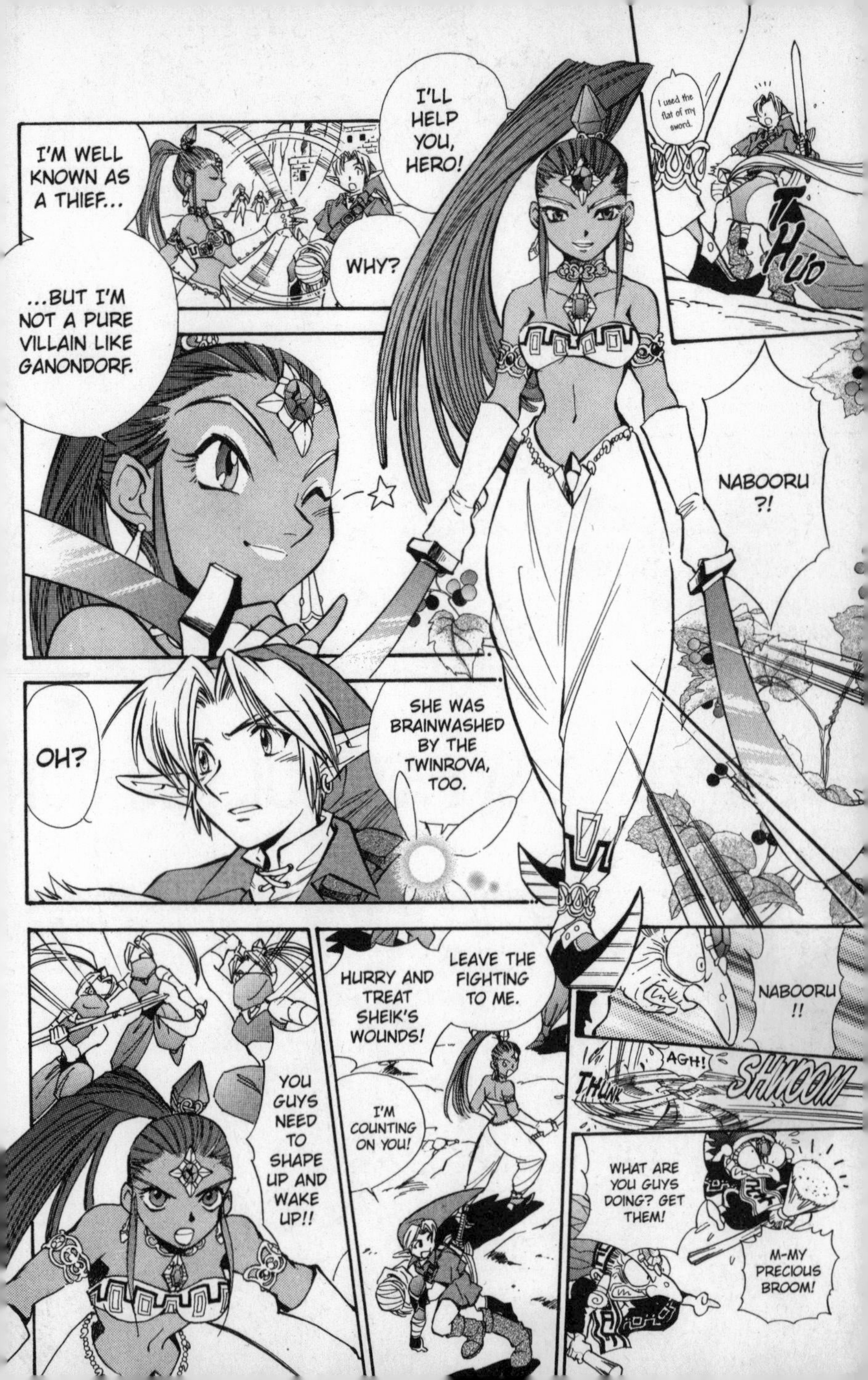
I used the flat of my sword.
THUD
NABOORU ?!
I'LL HELP YOU, HERO!
WHY?
I'M WELL KNOWN AS A THIEF...
...BUT I'M NOT A PURE VILLAIN LIKE GANONDORF.
SHE WAS BRAINWASHED BY THE TWINROVA, TOO.
OH?
NABOORU !!
SHWOOM
AGH!
THUNK
WHAT ARE YOU GUYS DOING? GET THEM!
M-MY PRECIOUS BROOM!
LEAVE THE FIGHTING TO ME.
HURRY AND TREAT SHEIK'S WOUNDS!
I'M COUNTING ON YOU!
YOU GUYS NEED TO SHAPE UP AND WAKE UP!!

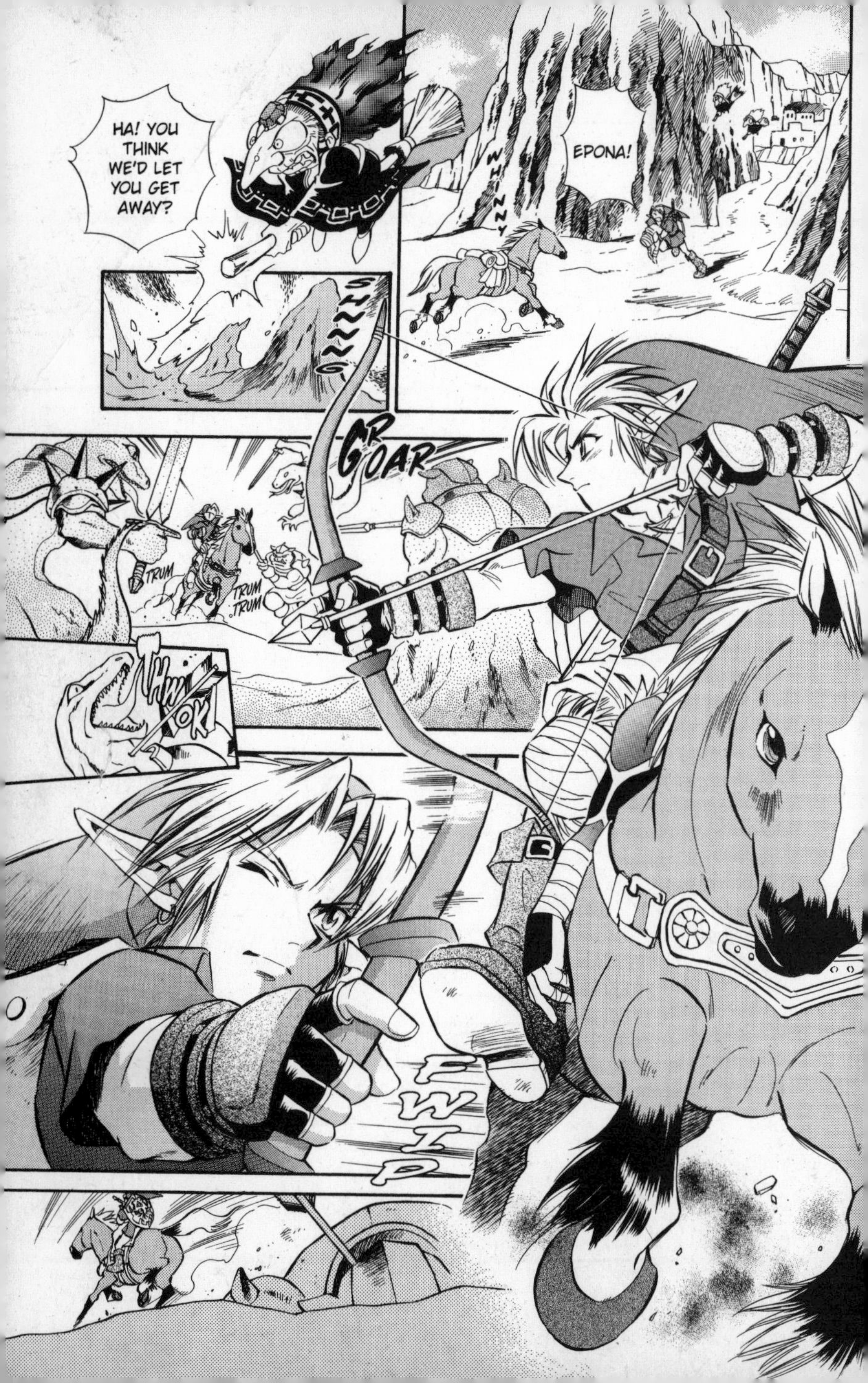
EPONA!
WHINNY
HA! YOU THINK WE'D LET YOU GET AWAY?
SHNNNG
GROAR
TRUM
TRUM TRUM
THWOK
FWIP

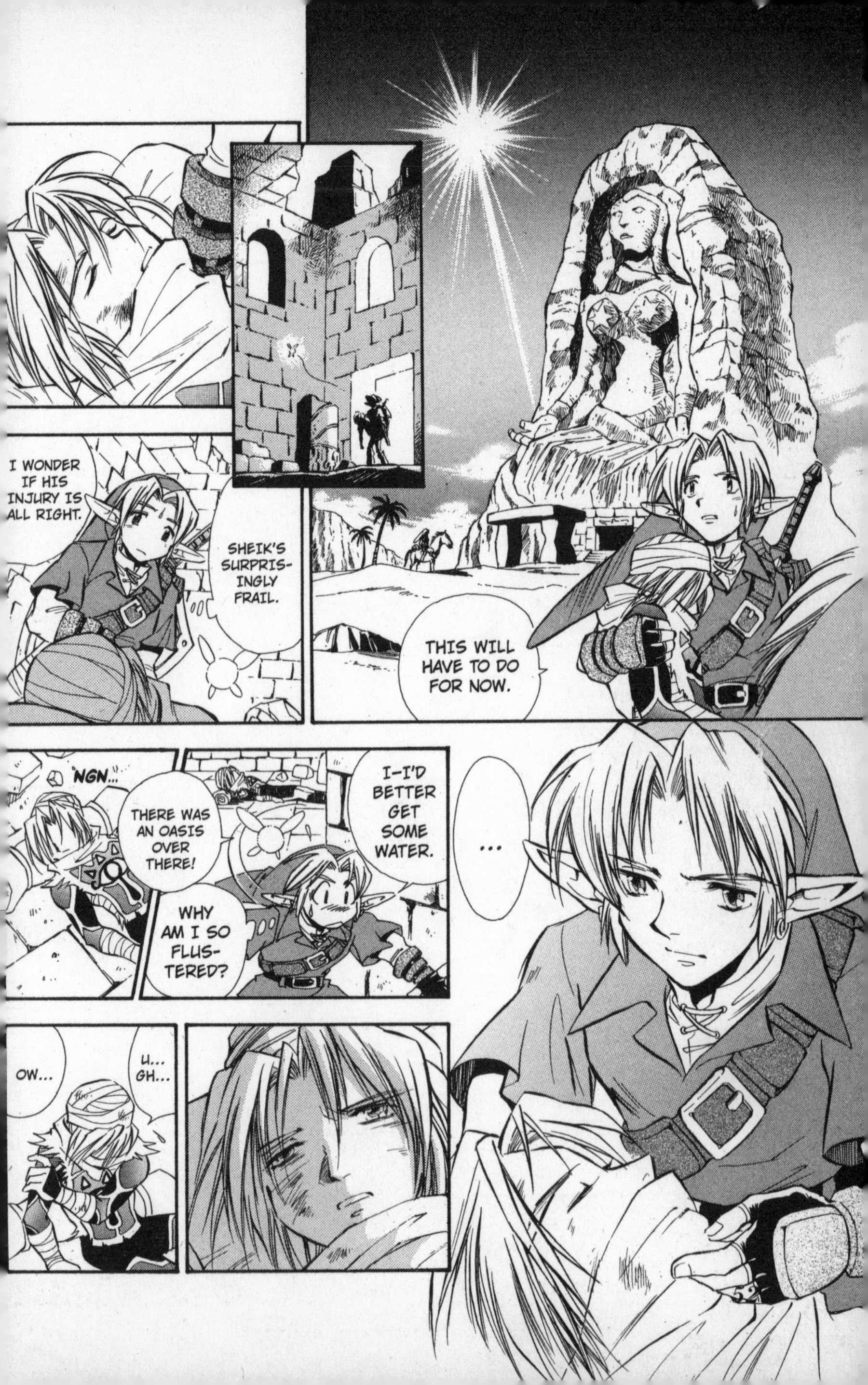
THIS WILL HAVE TO DO FOR NOW.
SHEIK'S SURPRISINGLY FRAIL.
I WONDER IF HIS INJURY IS ALL RIGHT.
...
I-I'D BETTER GET SOME WATER.
THERE WAS AN OASIS OVER THERE!
WHY AM I SO FLUSTERED?
NGN...
U... GH...
OW...

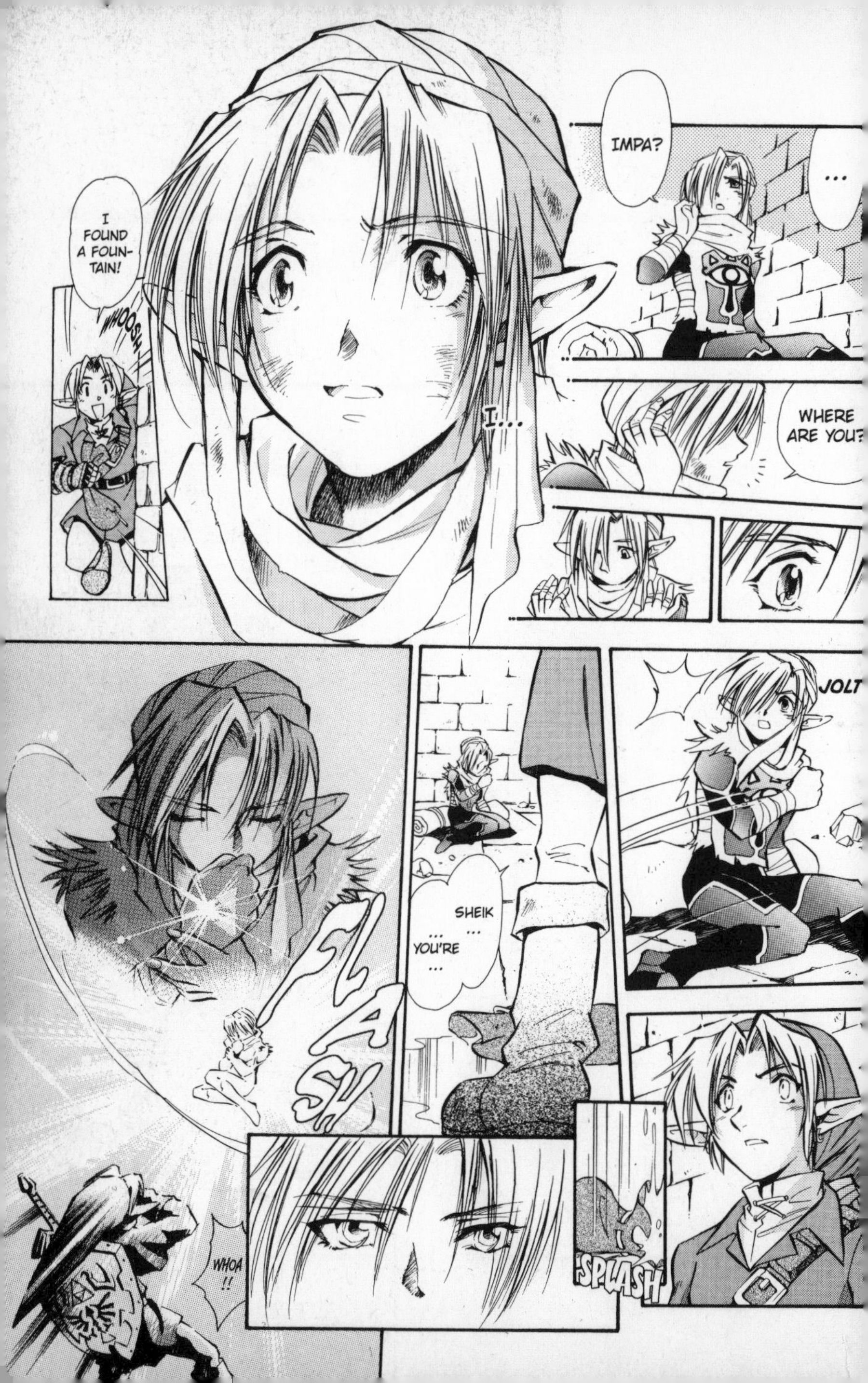
IMPA?
...
WHERE ARE YOU?
I...
I FOUND A FOUN-TAIN!
WHOOSH
JOLT
SHEIK ... ... YOU'RE ...
SPLASH
FLASH
WHOA !!

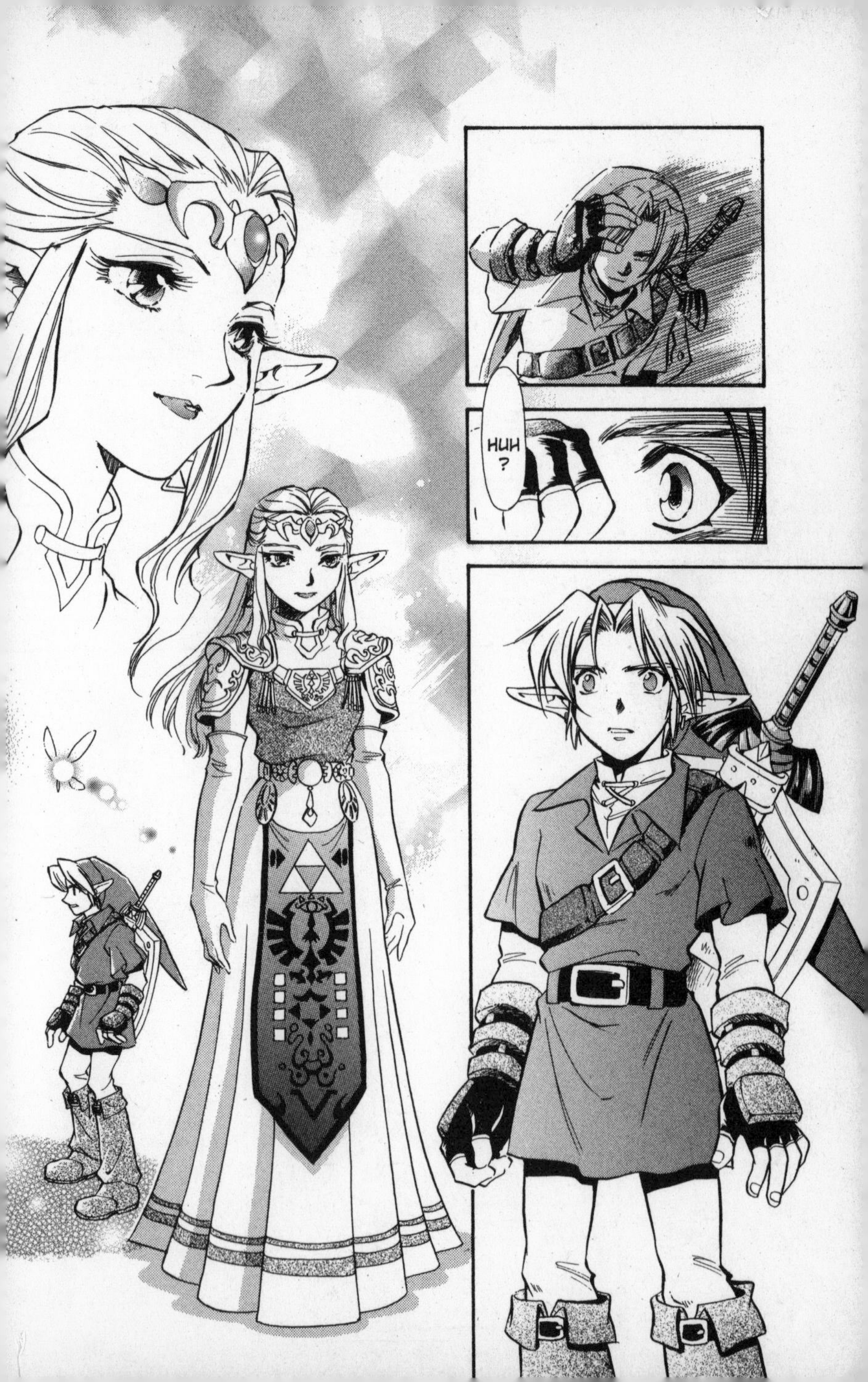
HUH?

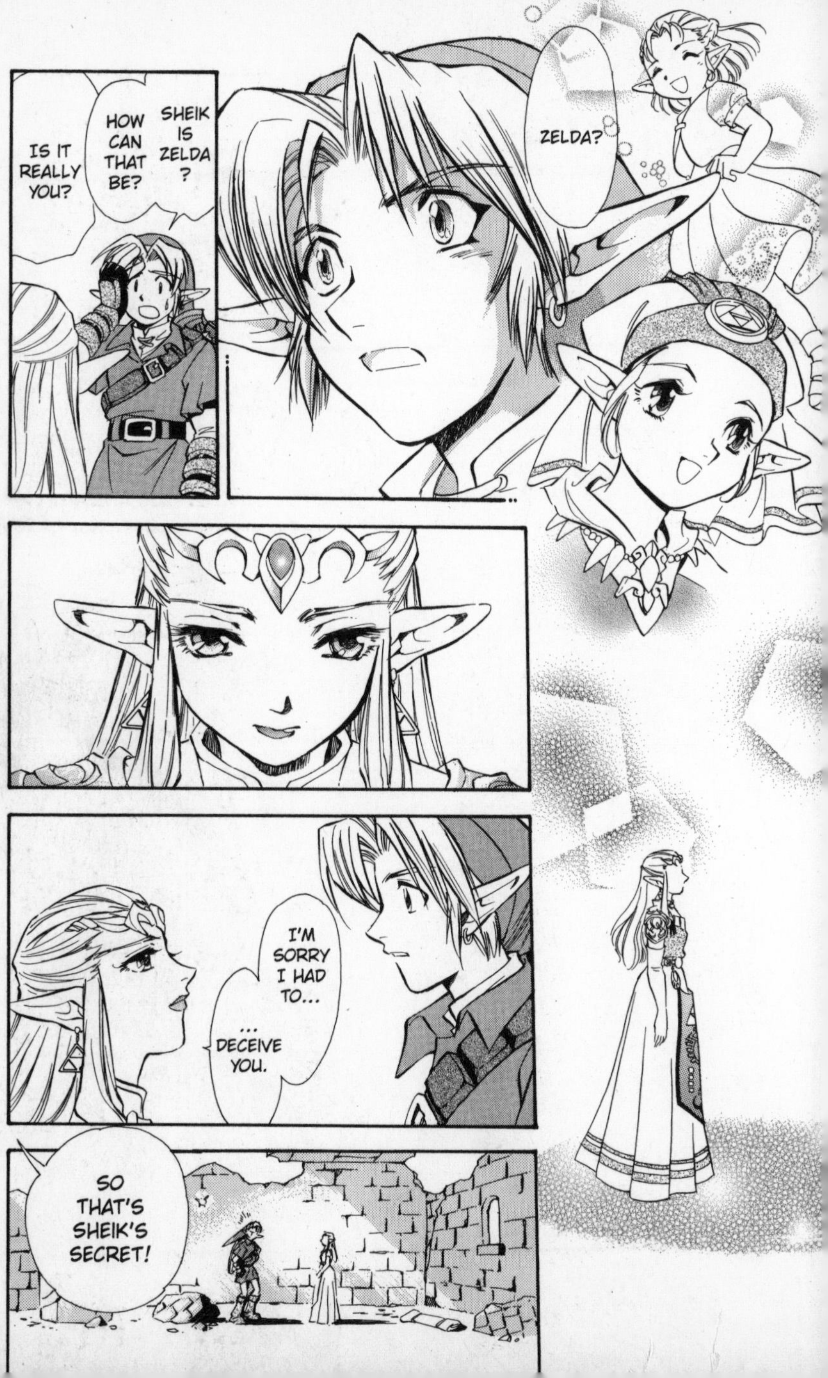
ZELDA?
SHEIK IS ZELDA?
HOW CAN THAT BE?
IS IT REALLY YOU?
I'M SORRY I HAD TO...
... DECEIVE YOU.
SO THAT'S SHEIK'S SECRET!

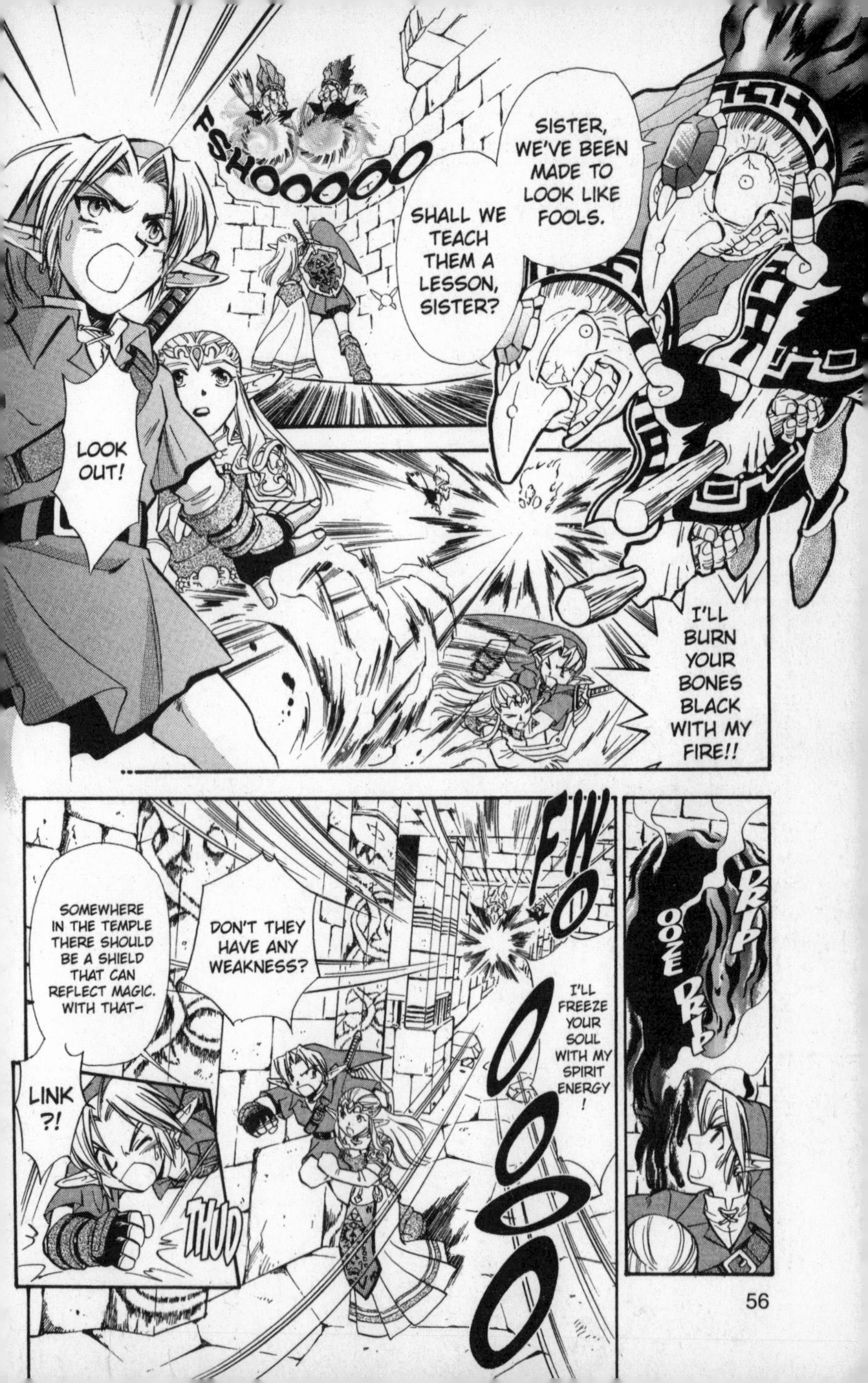
SISTER, WE'VE BEEN MADE TO LOOK LIKE FOOLS.
SHALL WE TEACH THEM A LESSON, SISTER?
FSHOOOOOO
LOOK OUT!
I'LL BURN YOUR BONES BLACK WITH MY FIRE!!
OOZE
DRIP
DRIP
FWOOOOOO
I'LL FREEZE YOUR SOUL WITH MY SPIRIT ENERGY!
DON'T THEY HAVE ANY WEAKNESS?
SOMEWHERE IN THE TEMPLE THERE SHOULD BE A SHIELD THAT CAN REFLECT MAGIC. WITH THAT-
LINK?!
THUD

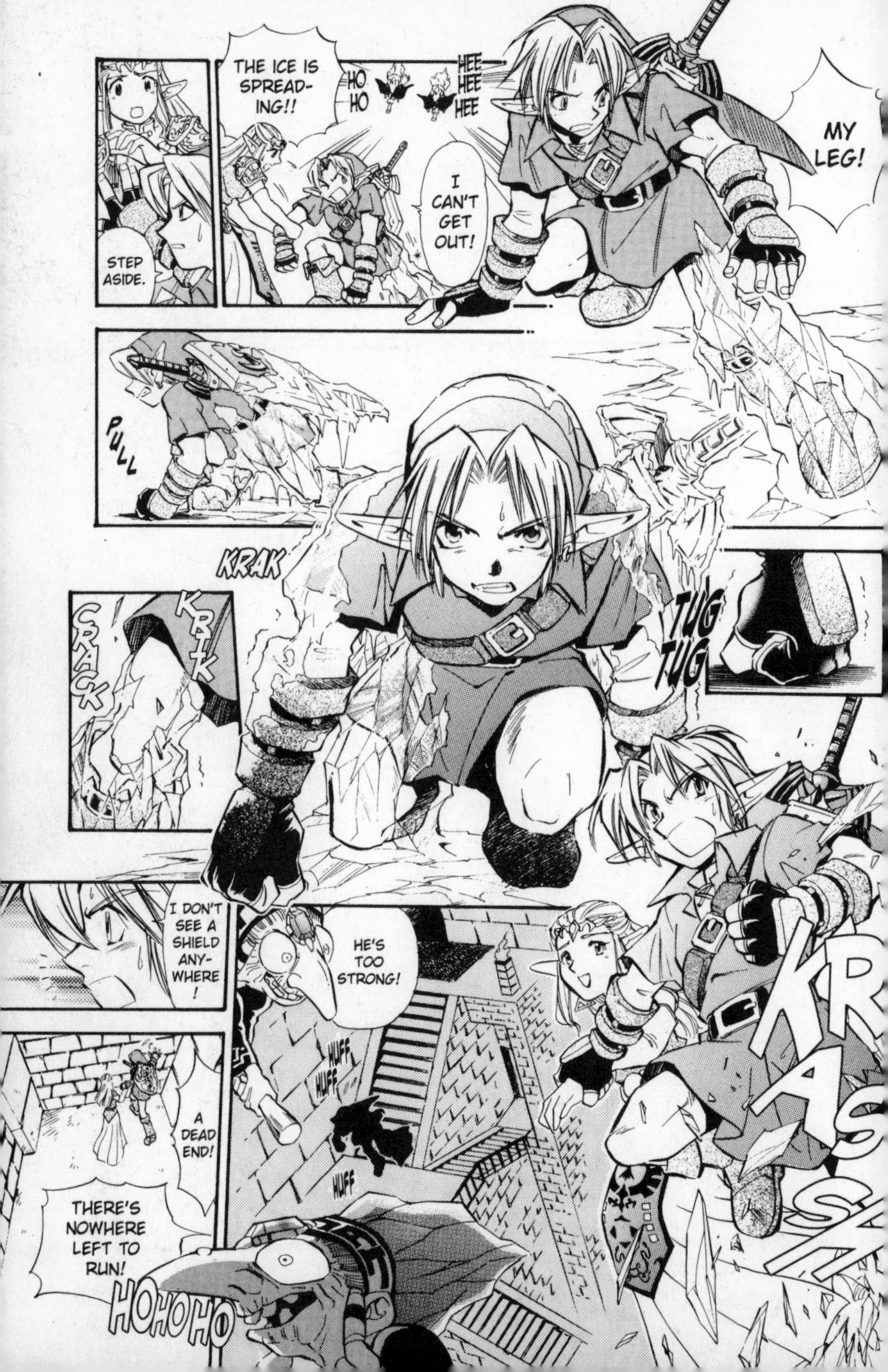

MY LEG!
HEE HEE HEE
HO HO
THE ICE IS SPREADING!!
I CAN'T GET OUT!
STEP ASIDE.
TUG TUG
KRAK
PULL
KRIK
CRACK
KRASH
HE'S TOO STRONG!
HUFF HUFF
HUFF
I DON'T SEE A SHIELD ANYWHERE!
A DEAD END!
THERE'S NOWHERE LEFT TO RUN!
HOHOHO

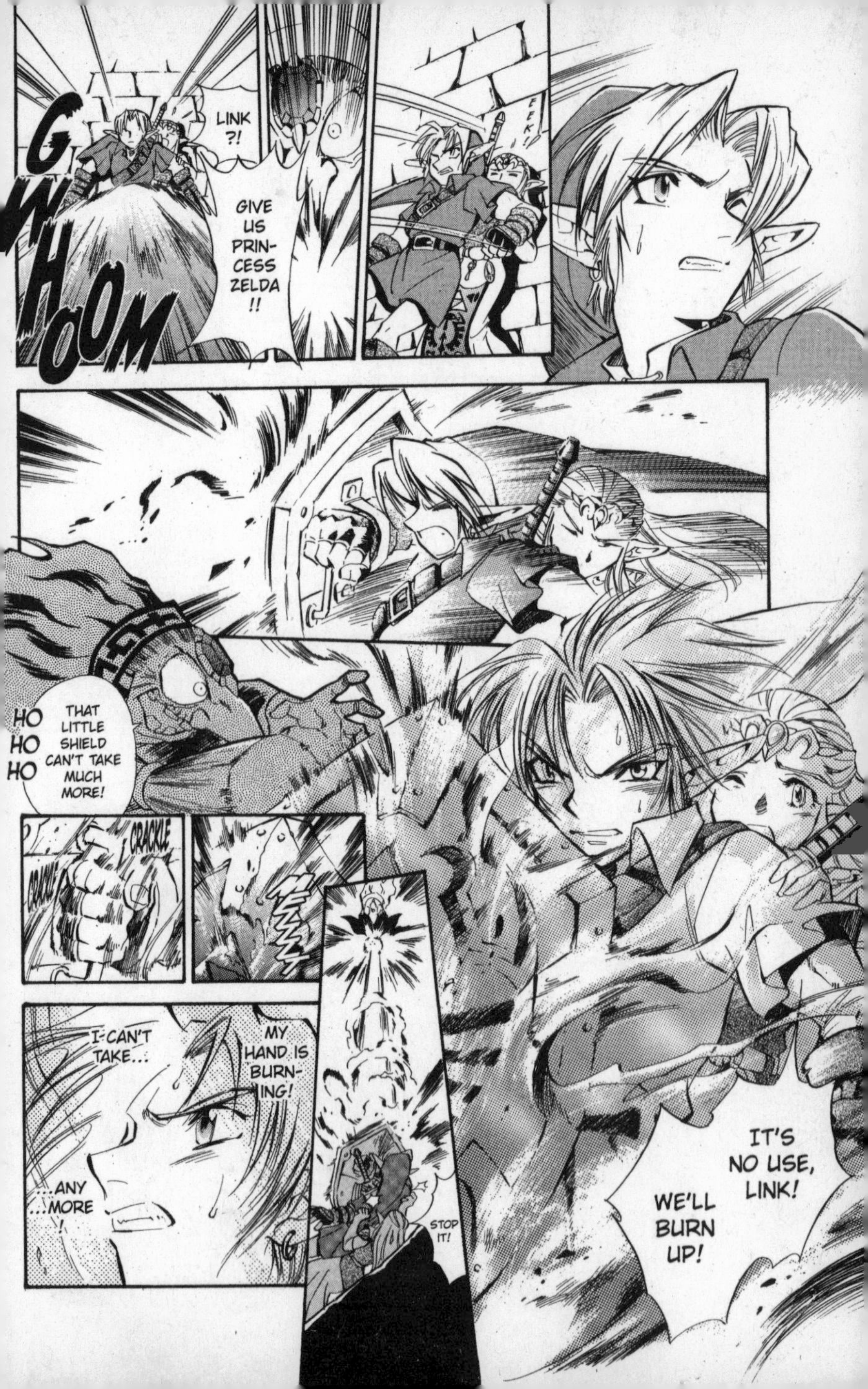
EEK!
LINK ?!
GIVE US PRINCESS ZELDA !!
GWHOOM
HO HO HO
THAT LITTLE SHIELD CAN'T TAKE MUCH MORE!
IT'S NO USE, LINK!
WE'LL BURN UP!
CRACKLE
CRACKLE
STOP IT!
MY HAND IS BURNING!
I-CAN'T TAKE...
...ANY ...MORE !

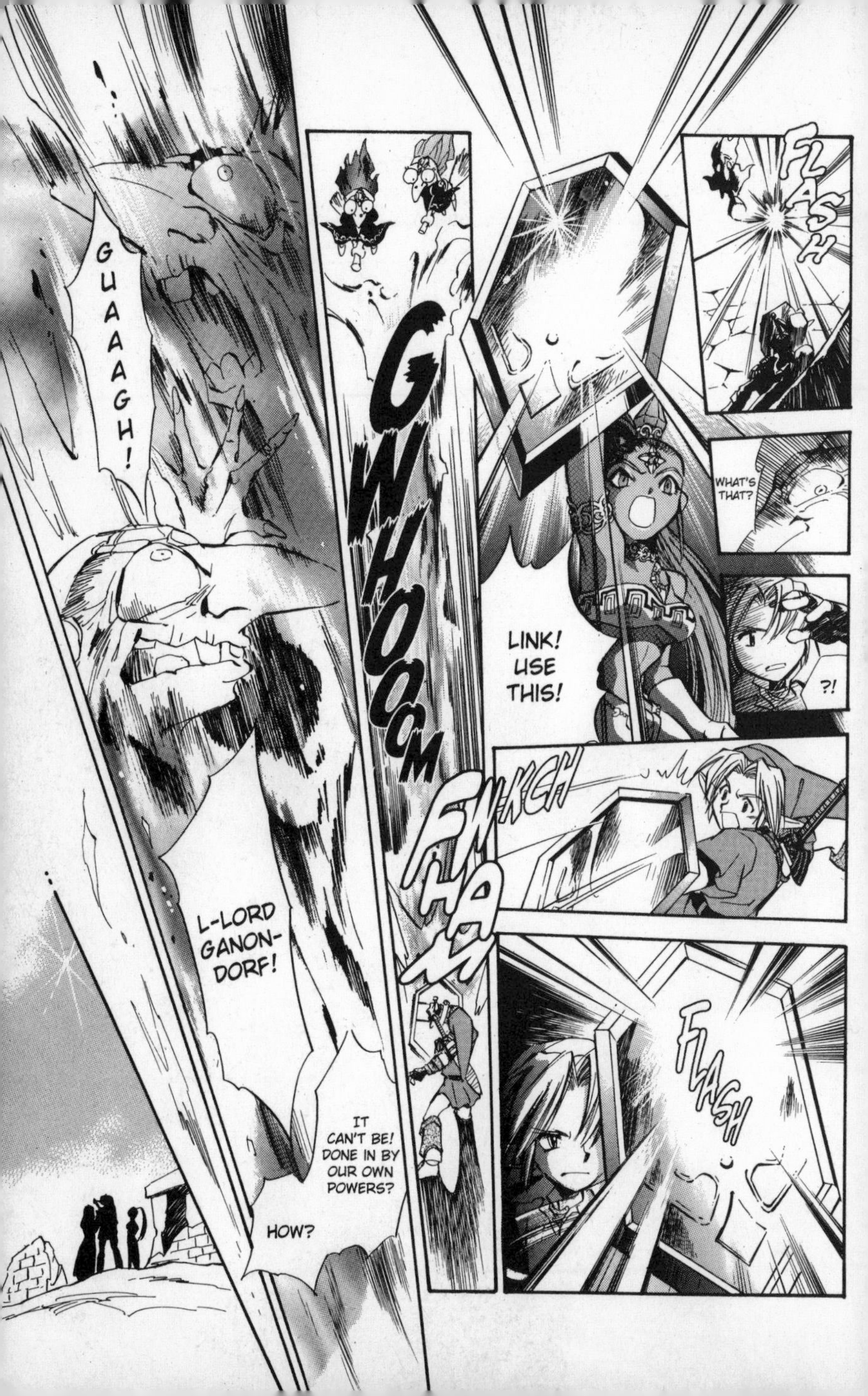
FLASH
WHAT'S THAT?
LINK! USE THIS!
?!
FWKCH
FWHAM
FLASH
GWHOOOM
GUAAAAGH!
...
L-LORD GANONDORF!
...
IT CAN'T BE! DONE IN BY OUR OWN POWERS?
HOW?

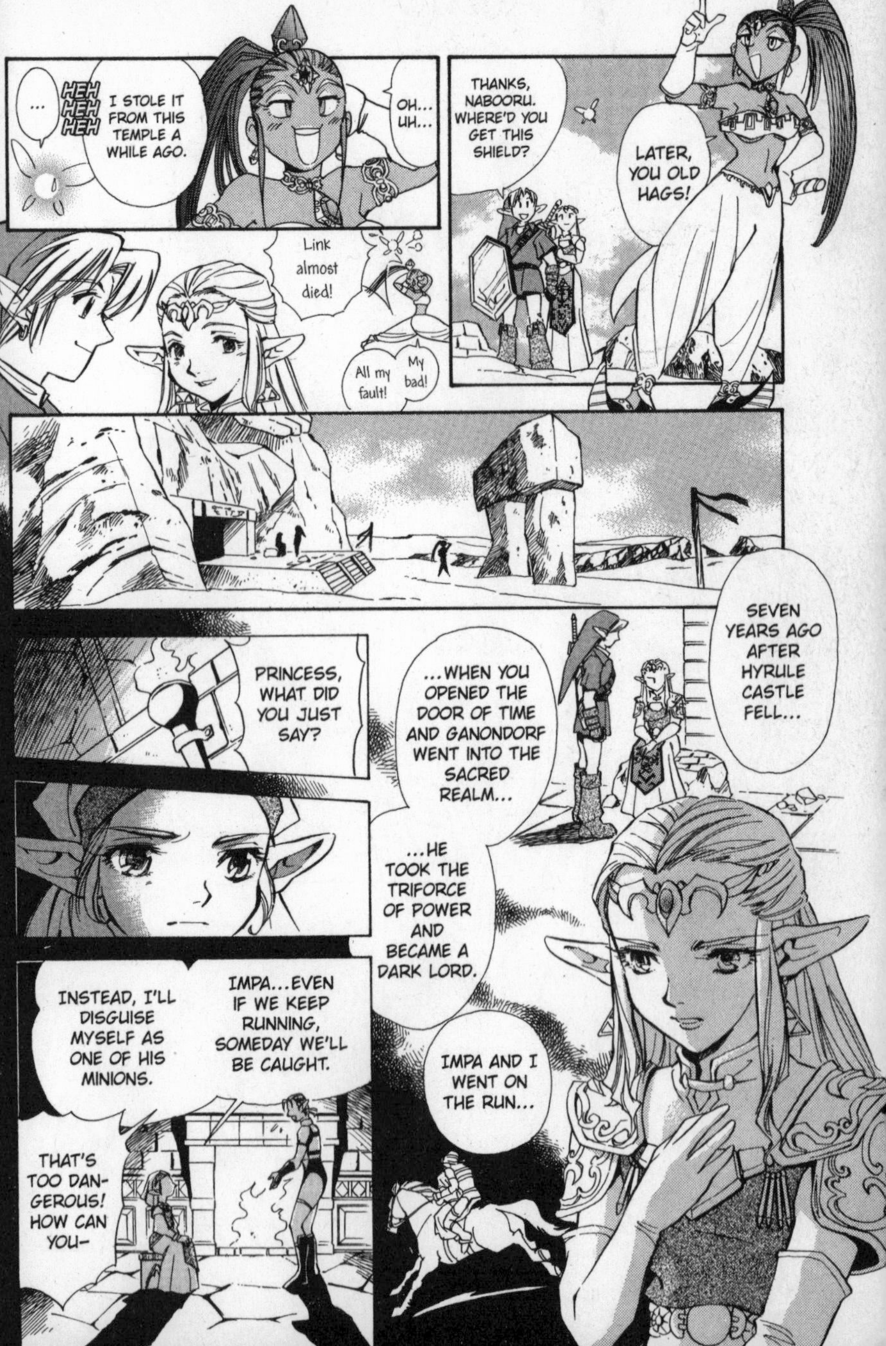
THANKS, NABOORU. WHERE'D YOU GET THIS SHIELD?
LATER, YOU OLD HAGS!
OH... UH...
I STOLE IT FROM THIS TEMPLE A WHILE AGO.
HEH HEH HEH
...
Link almost died!
My bad!
All my fault!
SEVEN YEARS AGO AFTER HYRULE CASTLE FELL...
...WHEN YOU OPENED THE DOOR OF TIME AND GANONDORF WENT INTO THE SACRED REALM...
...HE TOOK THE TRIFORCE OF POWER AND BECAME A DARK LORD.
IMPA AND I WENT ON THE RUN...
PRINCESS, WHAT DID YOU JUST SAY?
IMPA...EVEN IF WE KEEP RUNNING, SOMEDAY WE'LL BE CAUGHT.
INSTEAD, I'LL DISGUISE MYSELF AS ONE OF HIS MINIONS.
THAT'S TOO DANGEROUS! HOW CAN YOU-

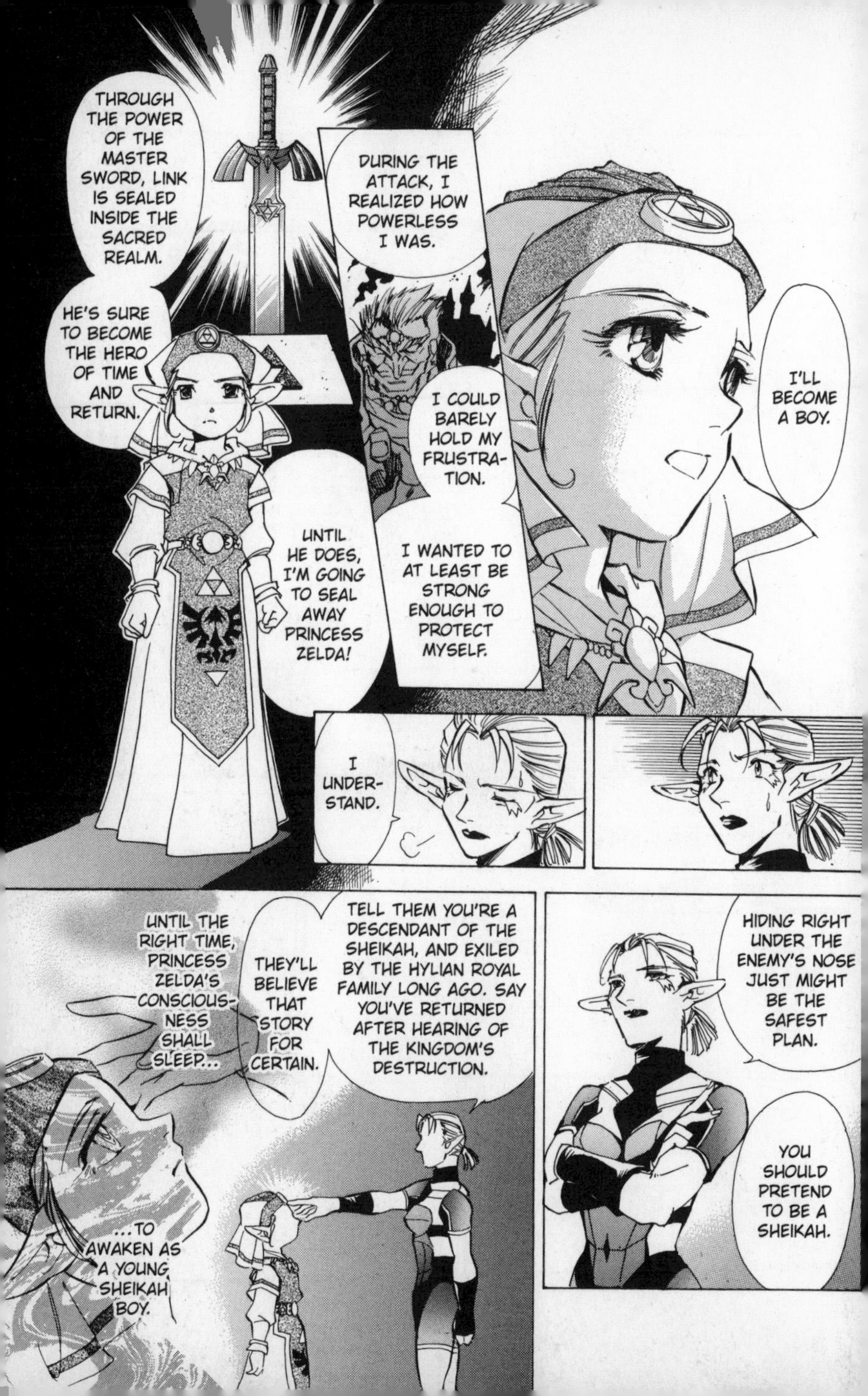
THROUGH THE POWER OF THE MASTER SWORD, LINK IS SEALED INSIDE THE SACRED REALM.
HE'S SURE TO BECOME THE HERO OF TIME AND RETURN.
UNTIL HE DOES, I'M GOING TO SEAL AWAY PRINCESS ZELDA!
DURING THE ATTACK, I REALIZED HOW POWERLESS I WAS.
I COULD BARELY HOLD MY FRUSTRA-TION.
I WANTED TO AT LEAST BE STRONG ENOUGH TO PROTECT MYSELF.
I'LL BECOME A BOY.
I UNDER-STAND.
HIDING RIGHT UNDER THE ENEMY'S NOSE JUST MIGHT BE THE SAFEST PLAN.
YOU SHOULD PRETEND TO BE A SHEIKAH.
TELL THEM YOU'RE A DESCENDANT OF THE SHEIKAH, AND EXILED BY THE HYLIAN ROYAL FAMILY LONG AGO. SAY YOU'VE RETURNED AFTER HEARING OF THE KINGDOM'S DESTRUCTION.
THEY'LL BELIEVE THAT STORY FOR CERTAIN.
UNTIL THE RIGHT TIME, PRINCESS ZELDA'S CONSCIOUS-NESS SHALL SLEEP...
...TO AWAKEN AS A YOUNG SHEIKAH BOY.

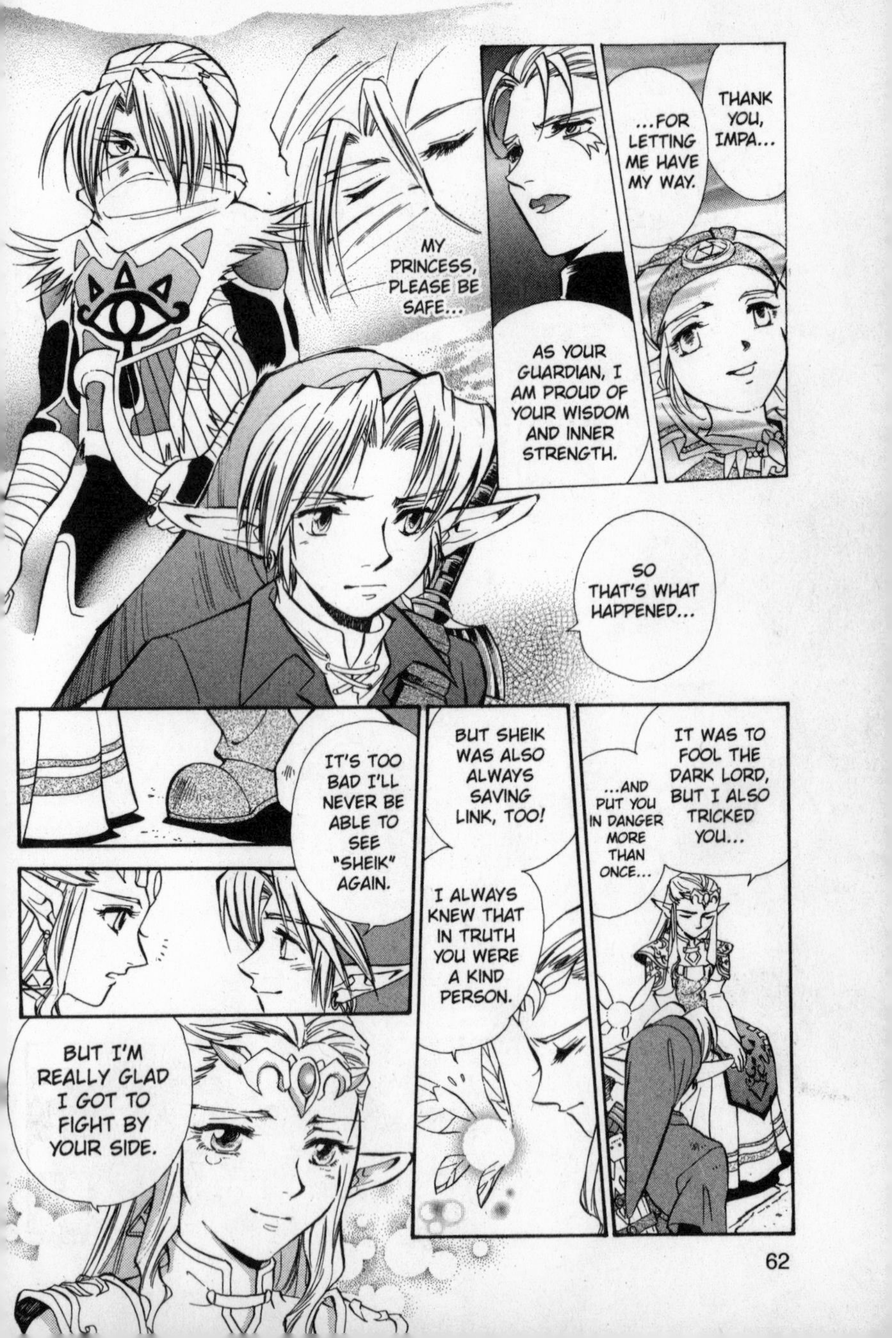
THANK YOU, IMPA...
...FOR LETTING ME HAVE MY WAY.
AS YOUR GUARDIAN, I AM PROUD OF YOUR WISDOM AND INNER STRENGTH.
MY PRINCESS, PLEASE BE SAFE...
SO THAT'S WHAT HAPPENED...
IT WAS TO FOOL THE DARK LORD, BUT I ALSO TRICKED YOU...
...AND PUT YOU IN DANGER MORE THAN ONCE...
BUT SHEIK WAS ALSO ALWAYS SAVING LINK, TOO!
I ALWAYS KNEW THAT IN TRUTH YOU WERE A KIND PERSON.
IT'S TOO BAD I'LL NEVER BE ABLE TO SEE "SHEIK" AGAIN.
BUT I'M REALLY GLAD I GOT TO FIGHT BY YOUR SIDE.

BONUS ILLUSTRATION 4

A ROUGH SKETCH HIMEKAWA-SENSEI DREW BEFORE
BEGINNING WORK ON THE SERIES.

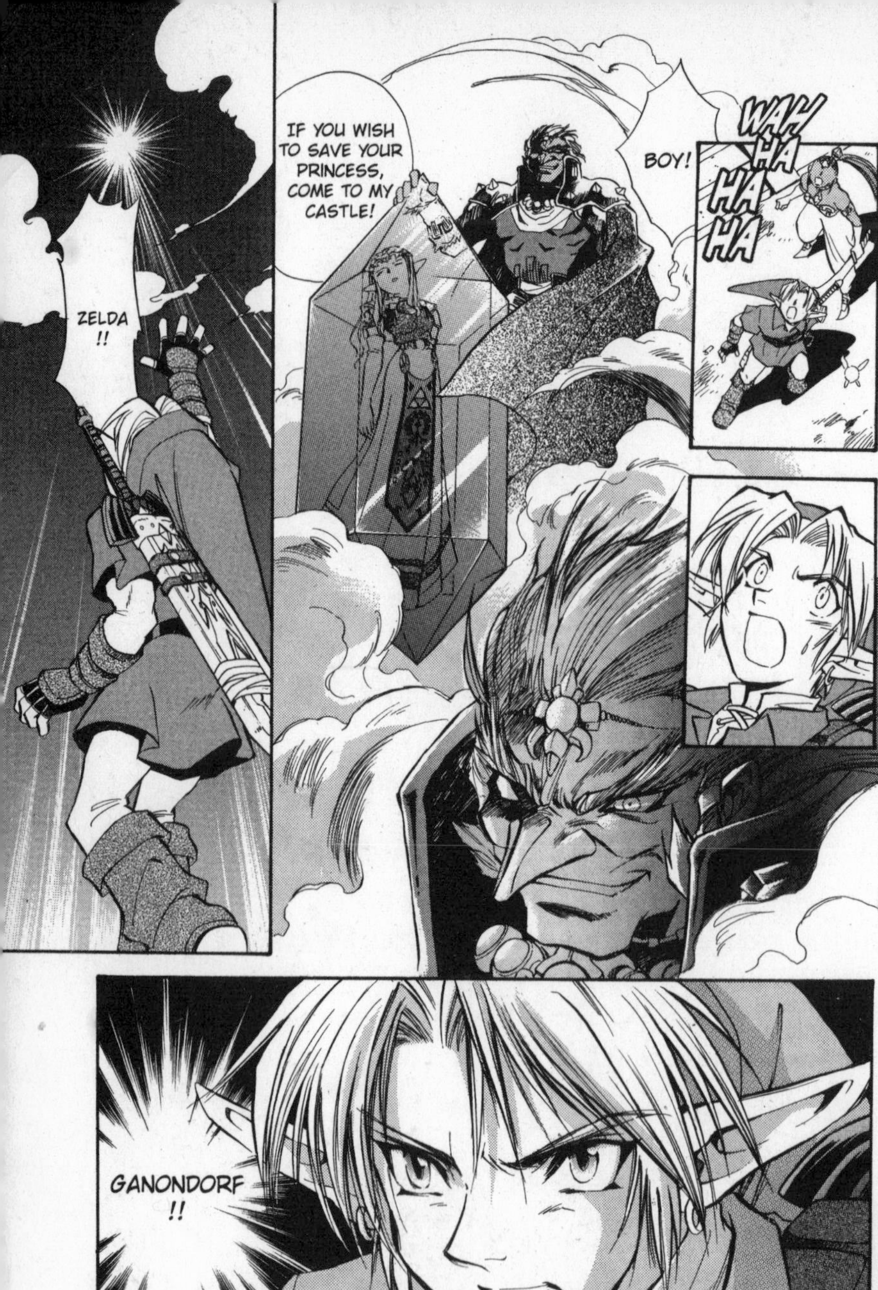
BOY!
IF YOU WISH TO SAVE YOUR PRINCESS, COME TO MY CASTLE!
WAH HA HA HA
ZELDA !!
GANONDORF !!

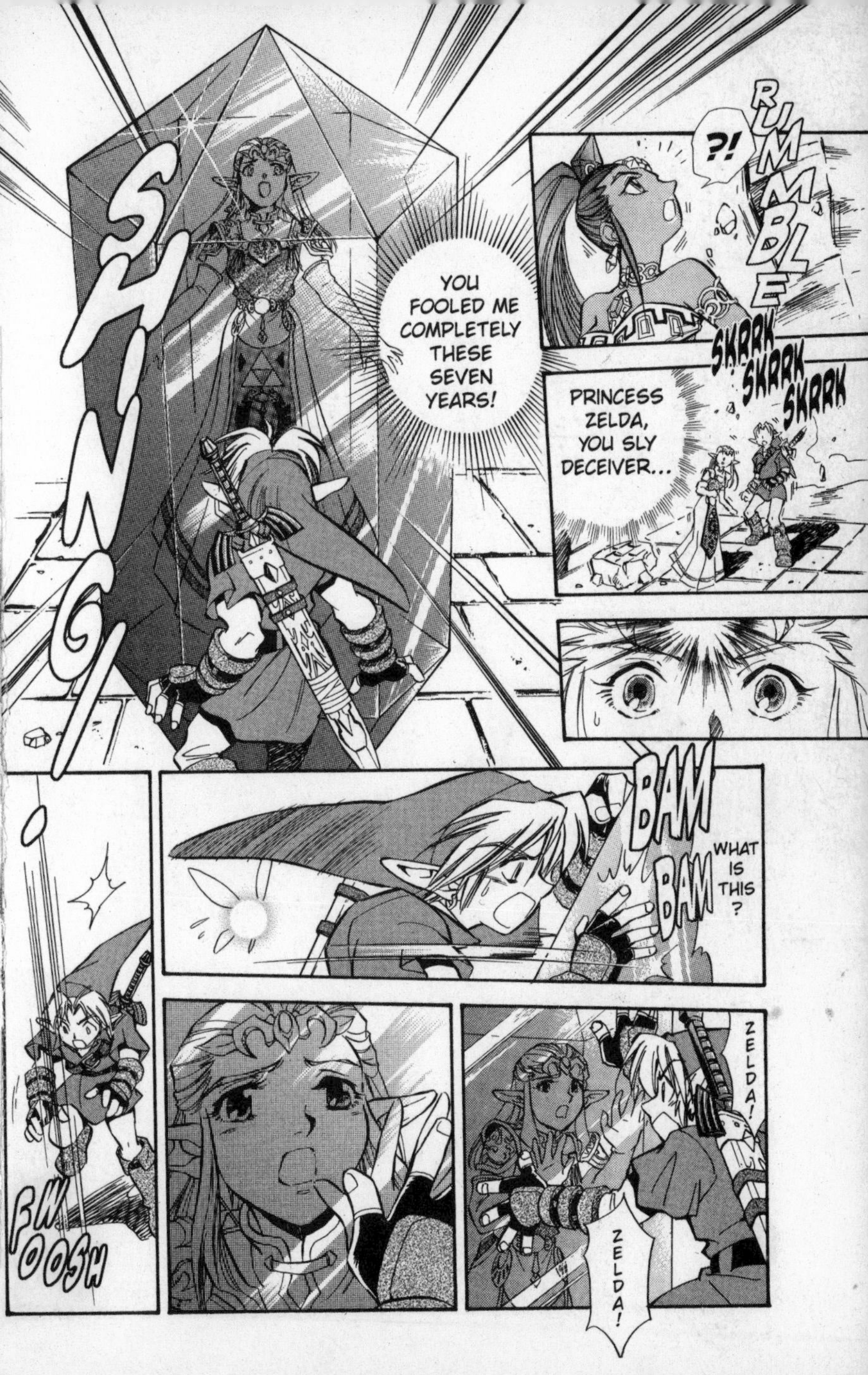
?!
RUMMBLE
SKRRK SKRRK SKRRK
PRINCESS ZELDA, YOU SLY DECEIVER...
SHING!
YOU FOOLED ME COMPLETELY THESE SEVEN YEARS!
BAM BAM
WHAT IS THIS?
ZELDA!
ZELDA!
FWOOSH

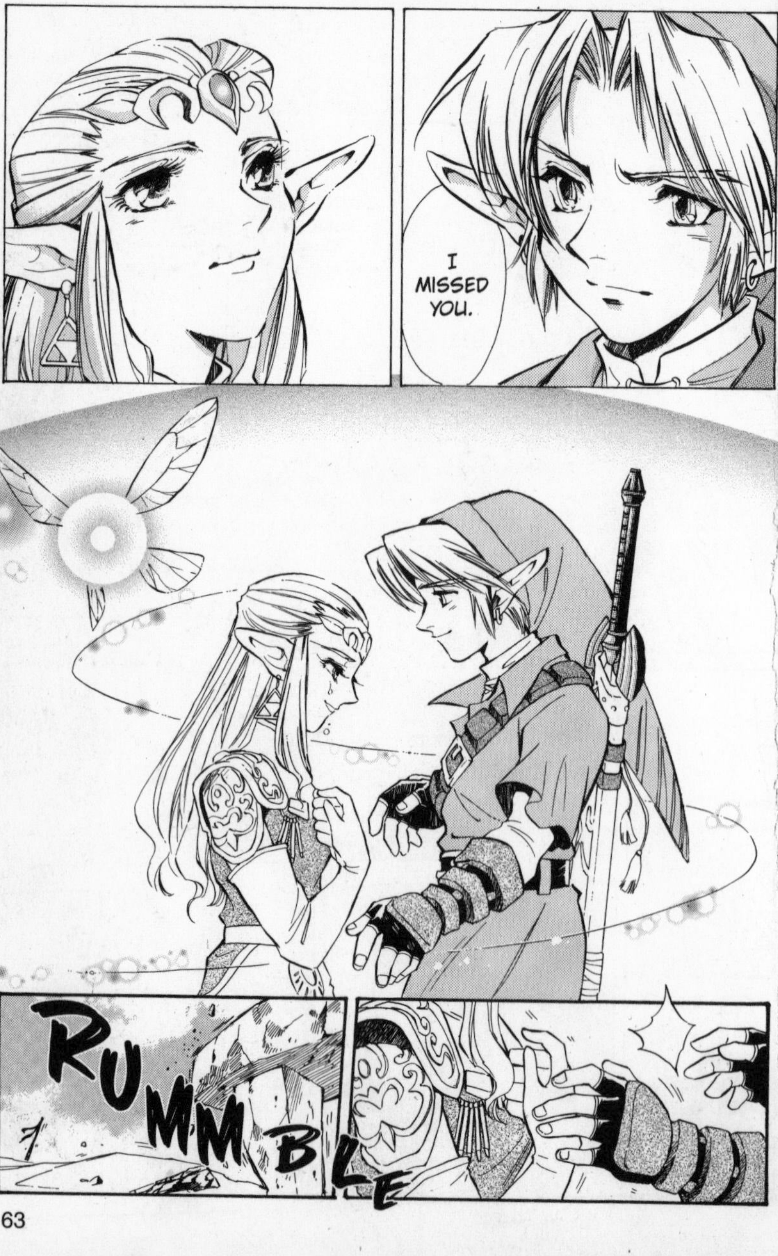
I MISSED YOU.
RUMMBLE

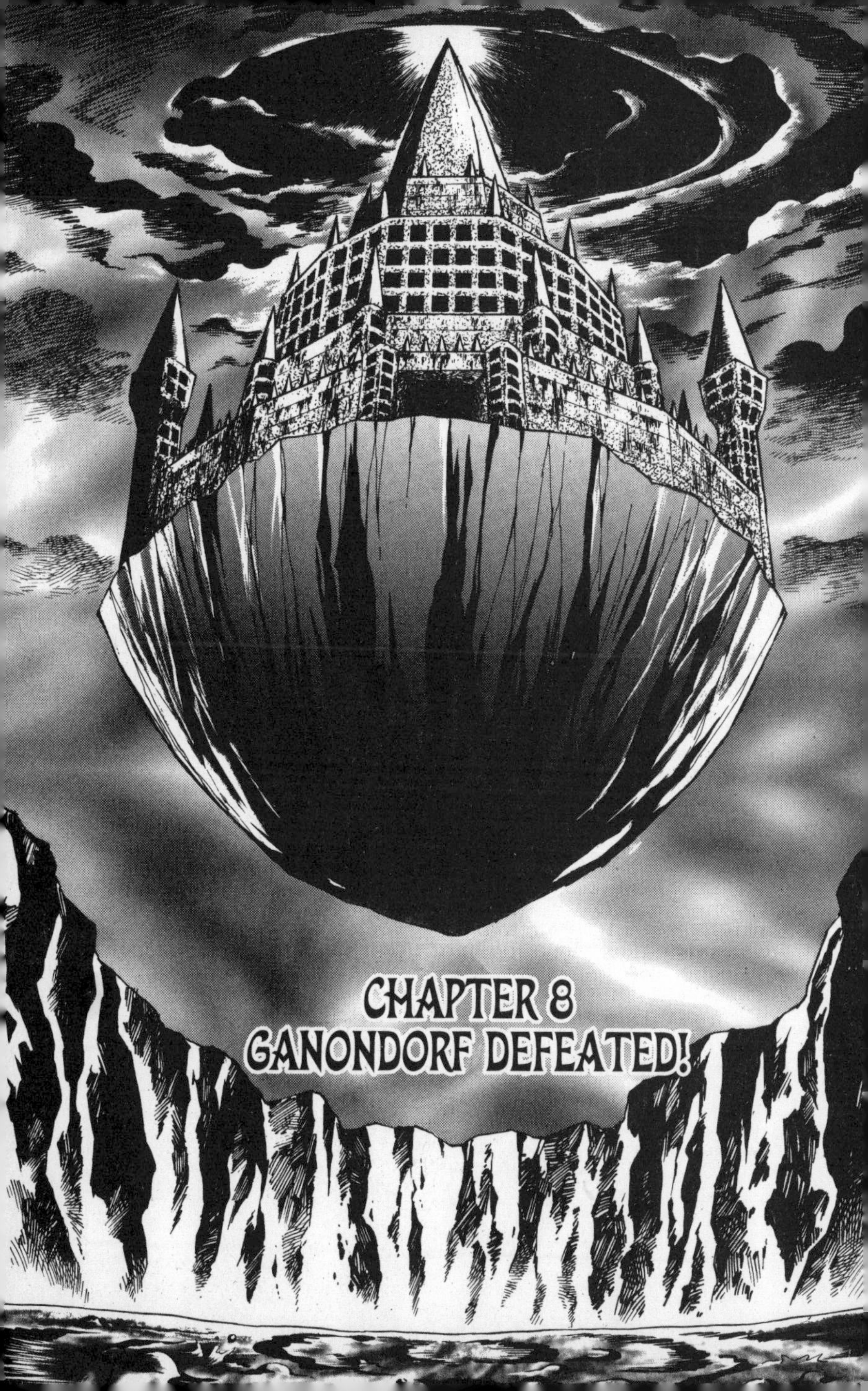
CHAPTER 8
GANONDORF DEFEATED!

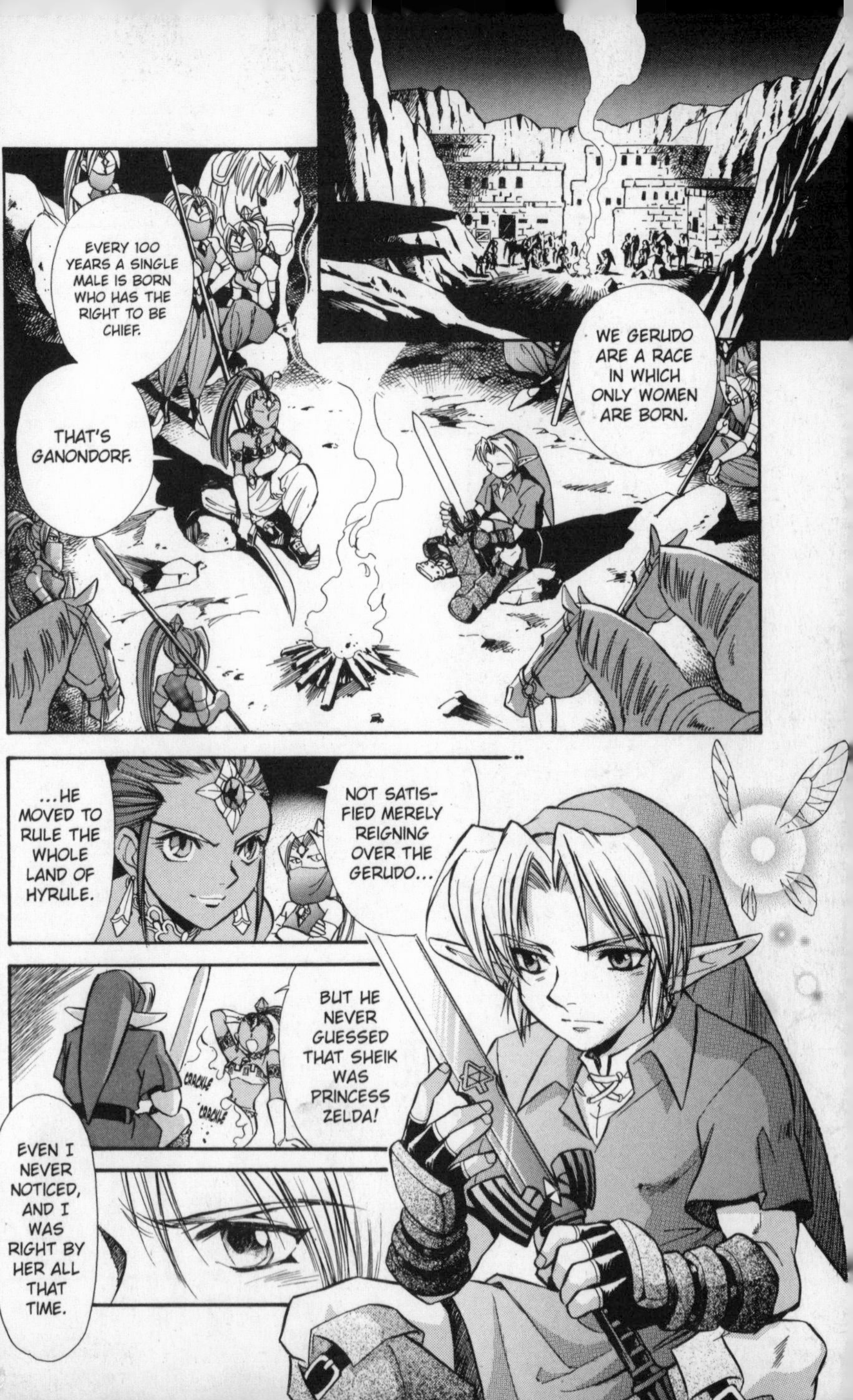
WE GERUDO ARE A RACE IN WHICH ONLY WOMEN ARE BORN.
EVERY 100 YEARS A SINGLE MALE IS BORN WHO HAS THE RIGHT TO BE CHIEF.
THAT'S GANONDORF.
NOT SATIS-FIED MERELY REIGNING OVER THE GERUDO...
...HE MOVED TO RULE THE WHOLE LAND OF HYRULE.
BUT HE NEVER GUESSED THAT SHEIK WAS PRINCESS ZELDA!
CRACKLE
CRACKLE
EVEN I NEVER NOTICED, AND I WAS RIGHT BY HER ALL THAT TIME.

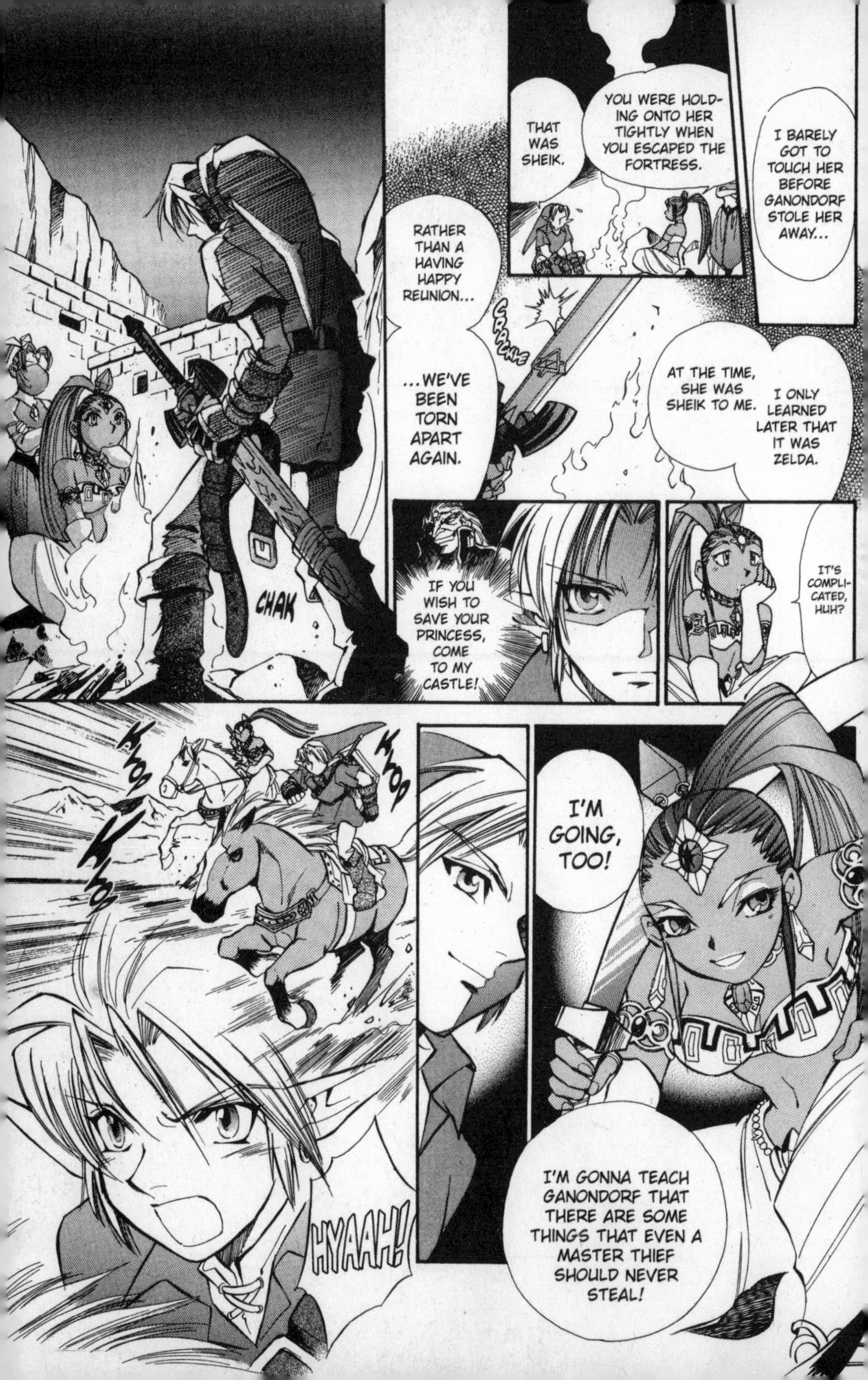
I BARELY GOT TO TOUCH HER BEFORE GANONDORF STOLE HER AWAY...
YOU WERE HOLDING ONTO HER TIGHTLY WHEN YOU ESCAPED THE FORTRESS.
THAT WAS SHEIK.
AT THE TIME, SHE WAS SHEIK TO ME.
I ONLY LEARNED LATER THAT IT WAS ZELDA.
CRACKLE
RATHER THAN A HAVING HAPPY REUNION...
...WE'VE BEEN TORN APART AGAIN.
IT'S COMPLICATED, HUH?
IF YOU WISH TO SAVE YOUR PRINCESS, COME TO MY CASTLE!
CHAK
I'M GOING, TOO!
I'M GONNA TEACH GANONDORF THAT THERE ARE SOME THINGS THAT EVEN A MASTER THIEF SHOULD NEVER STEAL!
HYAAH!

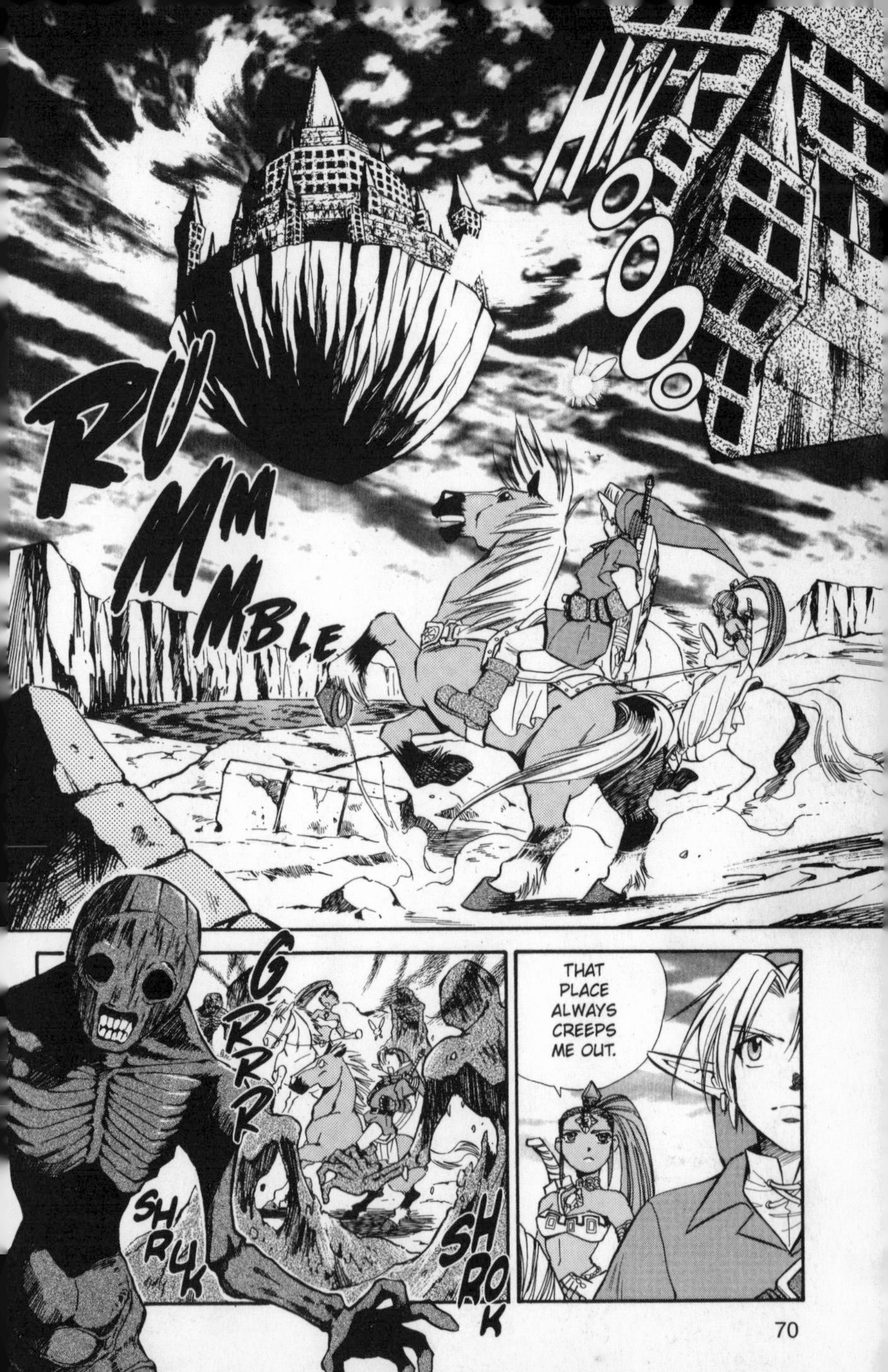
HWOOOOOO
RUMMMMMBLE
THAT PLACE ALWAYS CREEPS ME OUT.
GRRRR
SHRUK
SHROK

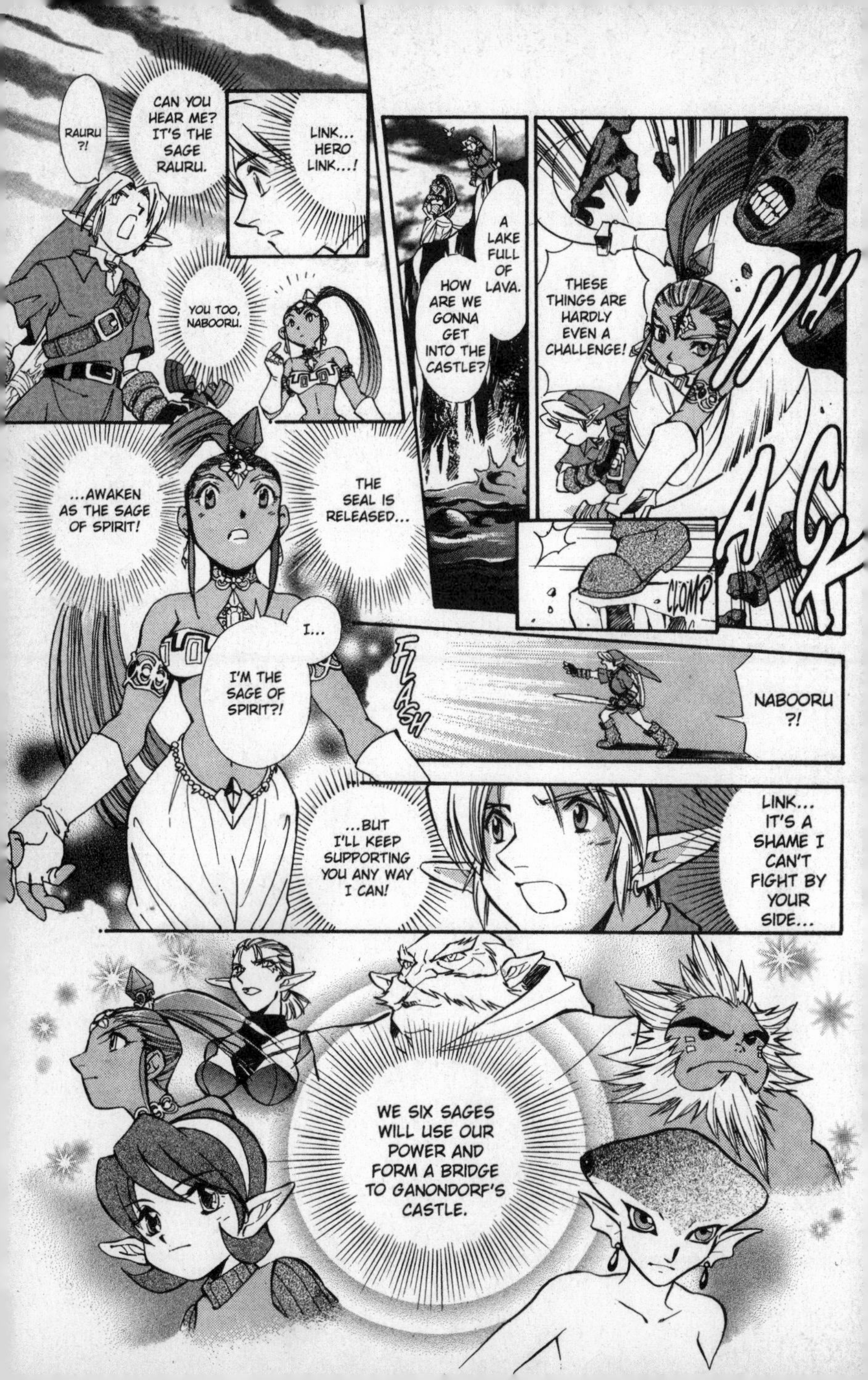
THESE THINGS ARE HARDLY EVEN A CHALLENGE!
WHACK
CLOMP
A LAKE FULL OF LAVA.
HOW ARE WE GONNA GET INTO THE CASTLE?
LINK... HERO LINK...!
CAN YOU HEAR ME? IT'S THE SAGE RAURU.
RAURU ?!
YOU TOO, NABOORU.
THE SEAL IS RELEASED...
...AWAKEN AS THE SAGE OF SPIRIT!
I...
I'M THE SAGE OF SPIRIT?!
FLASH
NABOORU ?!
LINK... IT'S A SHAME I CAN'T FIGHT BY YOUR SIDE...
...BUT I'LL KEEP SUPPORTING YOU ANY WAY I CAN!
WE SIX SAGES WILL USE OUR POWER AND FORM A BRIDGE TO GANONDORF'S CASTLE.

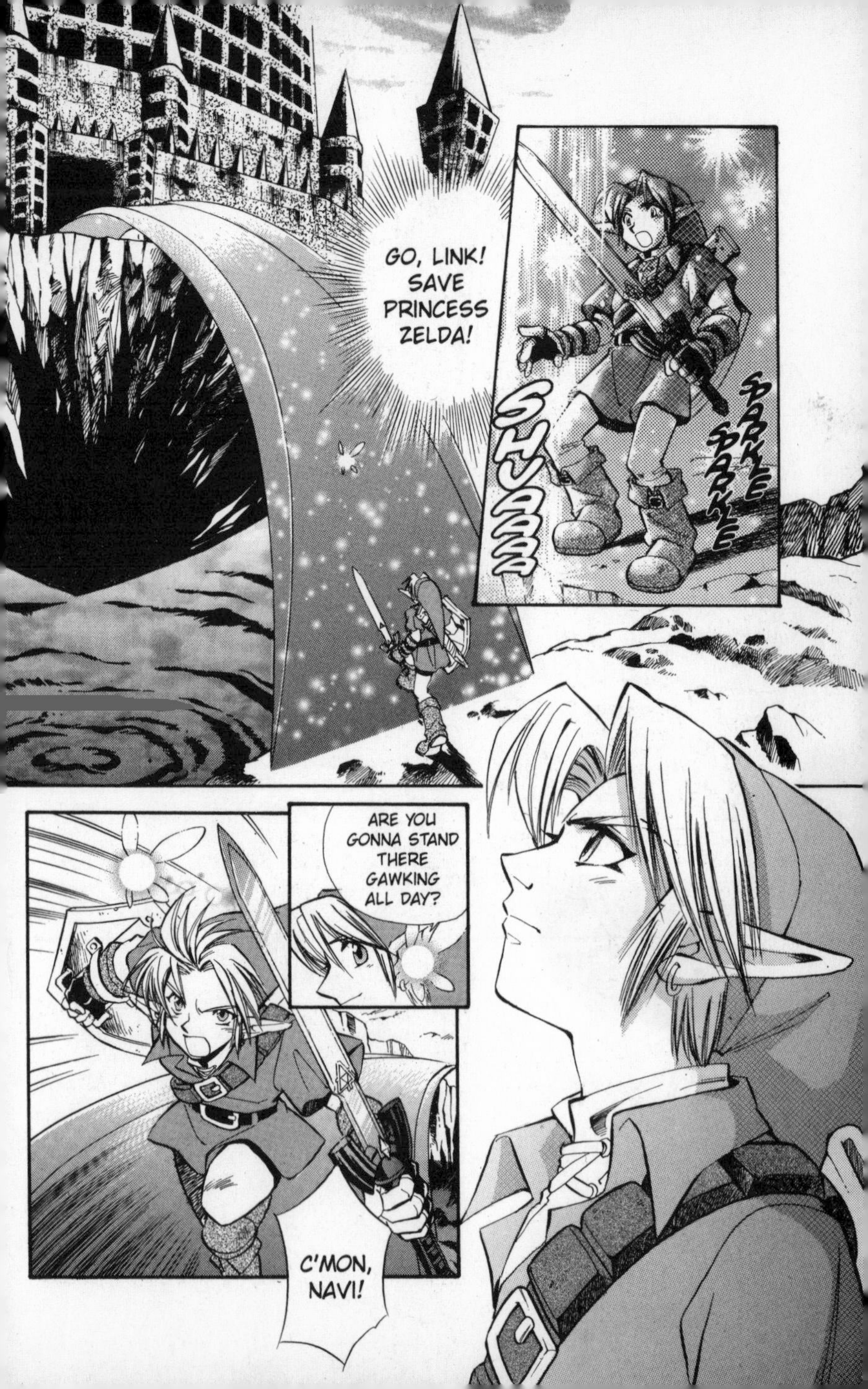
GO, LINK! SAVE PRINCESS ZELDA!
SHUAAAA
SPARKLE SPARKLE
ARE YOU GONNA STAND THERE GAWKING ALL DAY?
C'MON, NAVI!

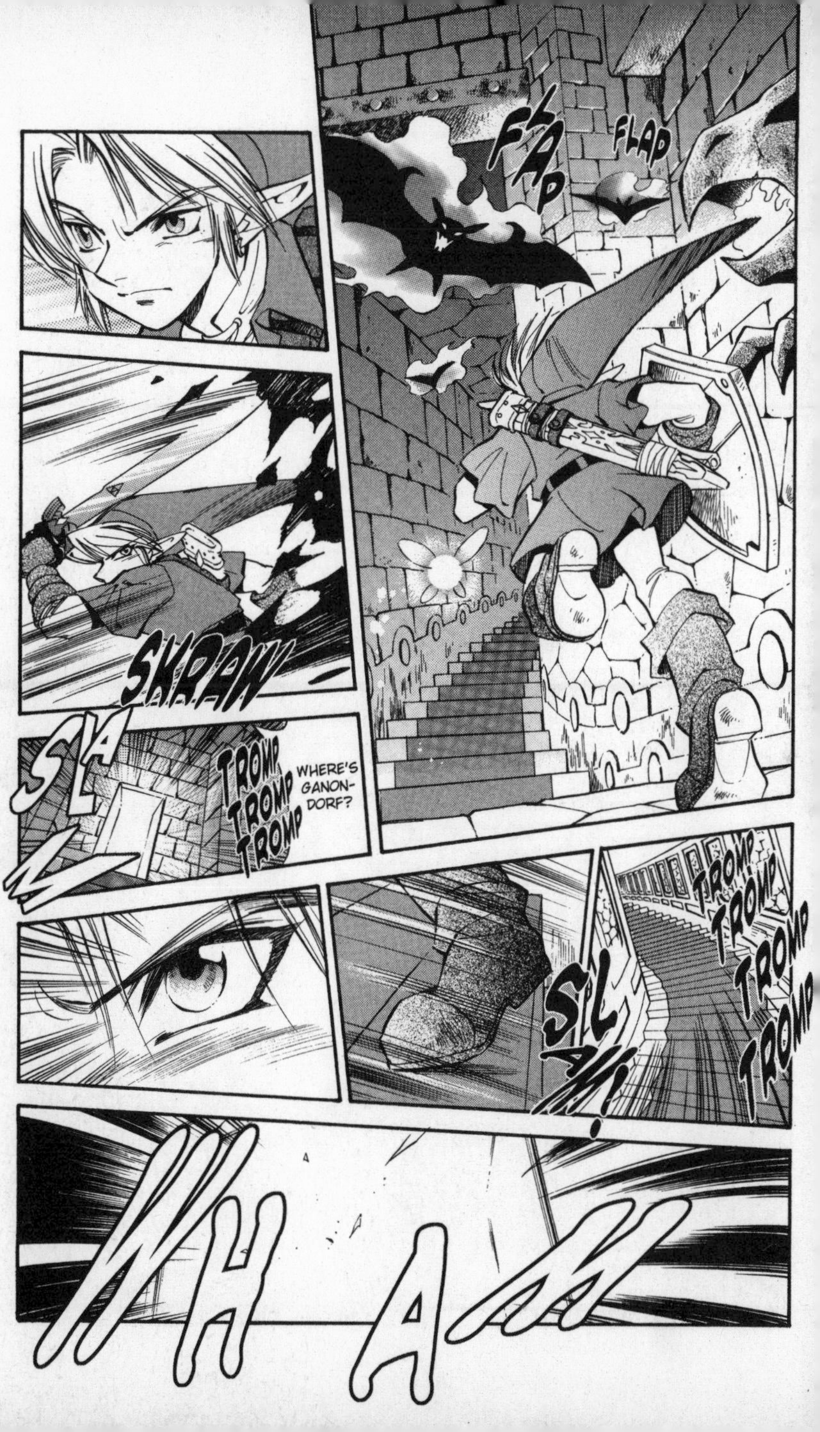
FLAP
FLAP
SKRAW
TROMP TROMP TROMP
WHERE'S GANON-DORF?
SLAM
TROMP TROMP TROMP TROMP
SLAM!
WHAM

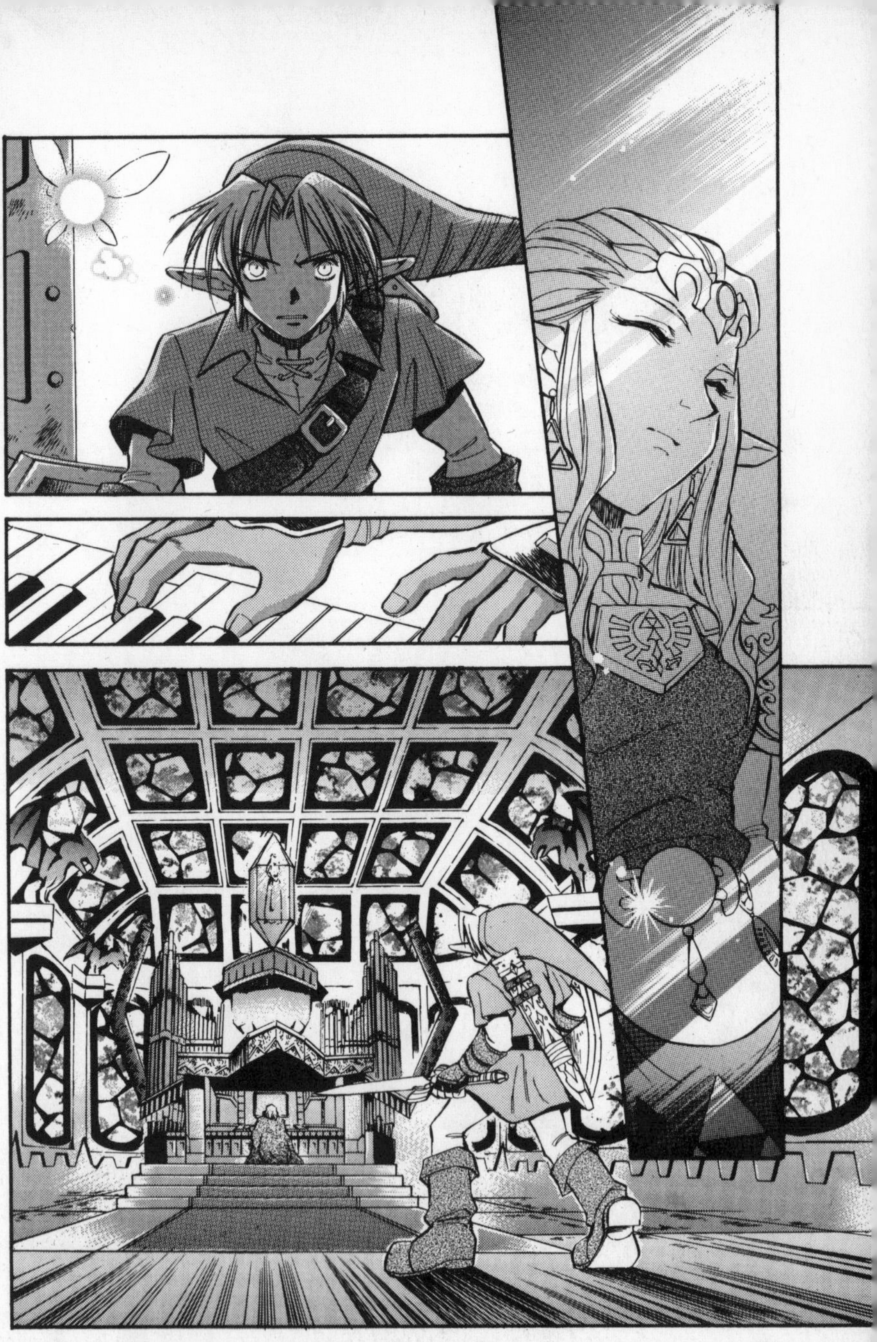

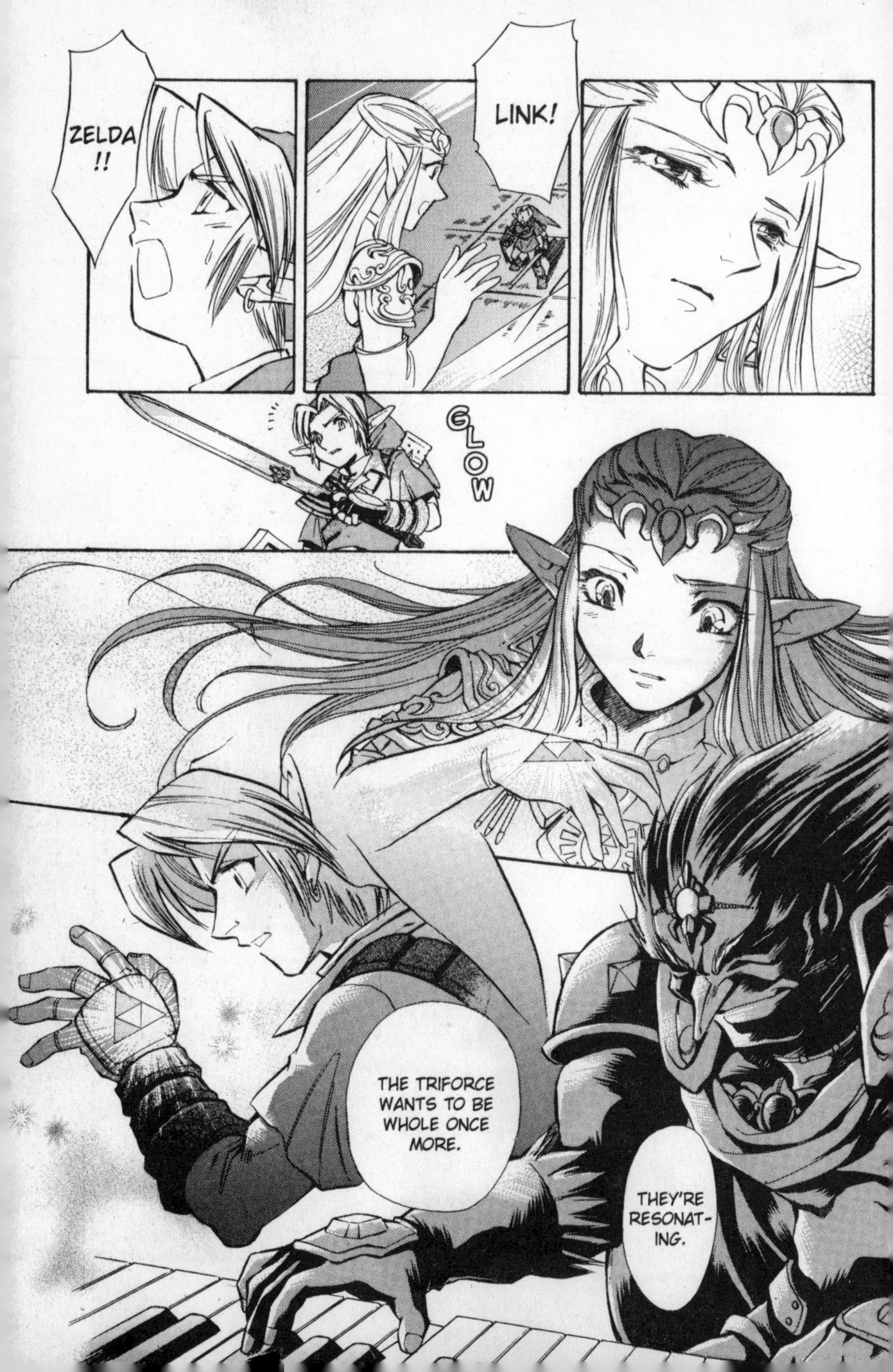
LINK!
ZELDA !!
GLOW
THE TRIFORCE WANTS TO BE WHOLE ONCE MORE.
THEY'RE RESONAT-ING.

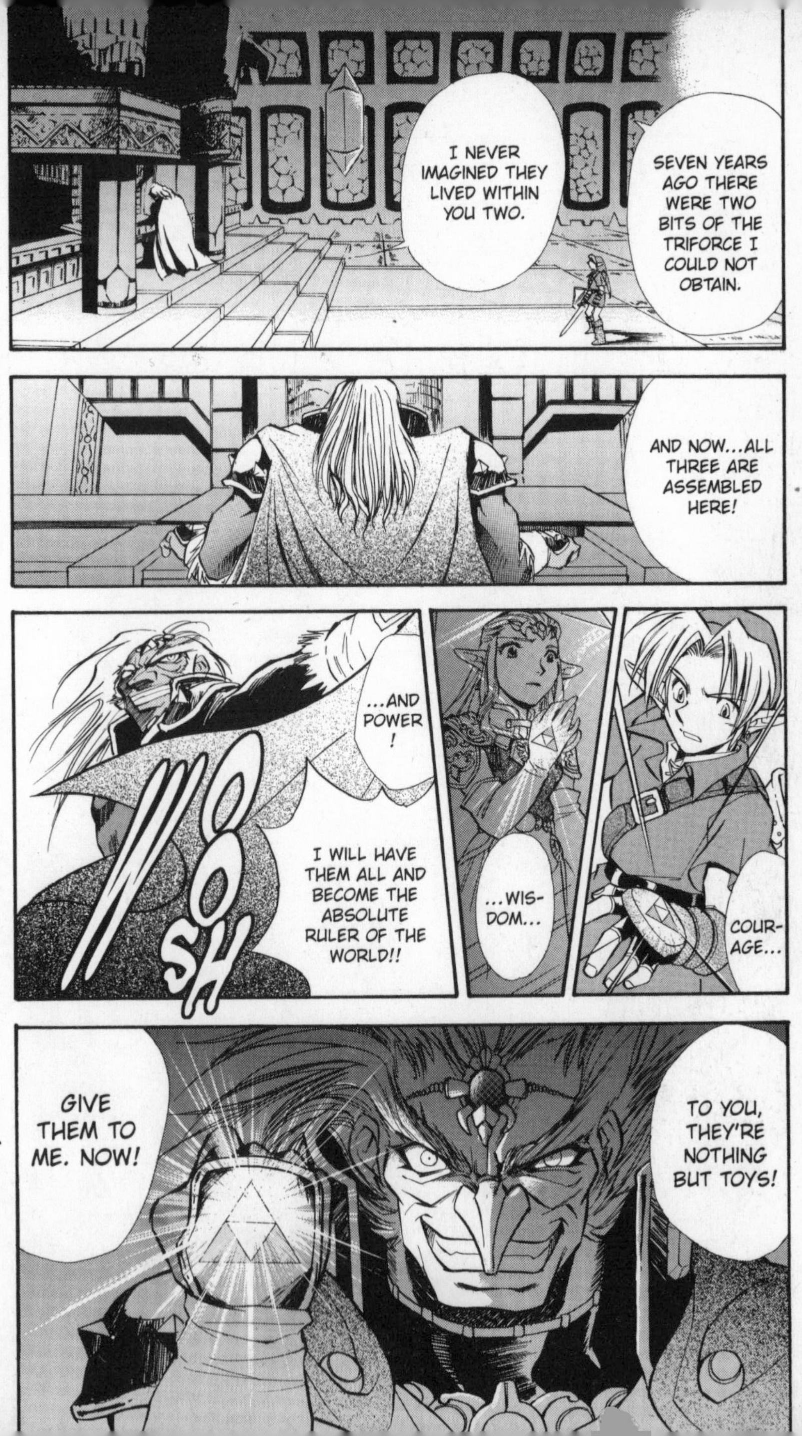
SEVEN YEARS AGO THERE WERE TWO BITS OF THE TRIFORCE I COULD NOT OBTAIN.
I NEVER IMAGINED THEY LIVED WITHIN YOU TWO.
AND NOW...ALL THREE ARE ASSEMBLED HERE!
COURAGE...
...WISDOM...
...AND POWER!
I WILL HAVE THEM ALL AND BECOME THE ABSOLUTE RULER OF THE WORLD!!
WOOSH
TO YOU, THEY'RE NOTHING BUT TOYS!
GIVE THEM TO ME. NOW!

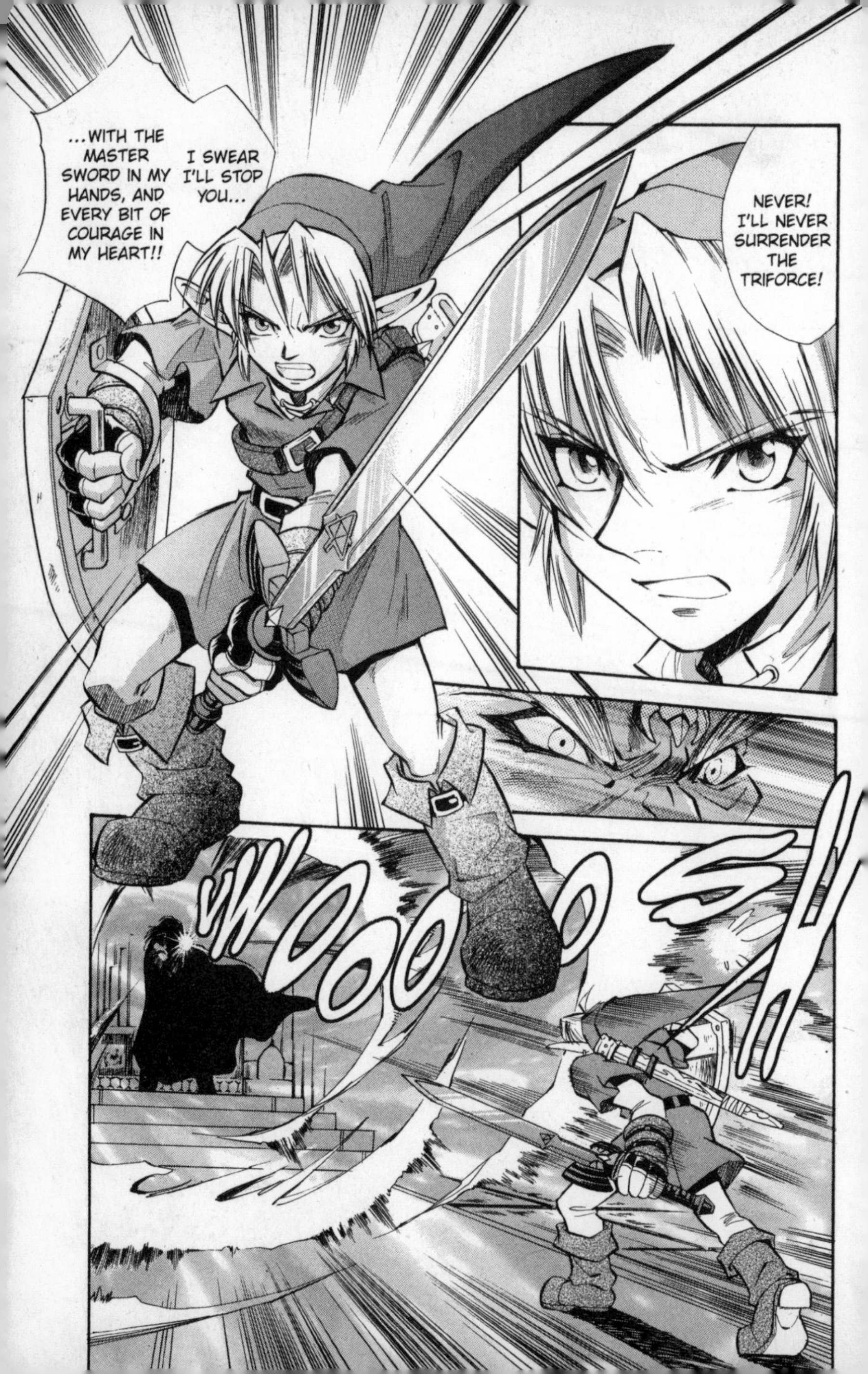
NEVER! I'LL NEVER SURRENDER THE TRIFORCE!
I SWEAR I'LL STOP YOU...
...WITH THE MASTER SWORD IN MY HANDS, AND EVERY BIT OF COURAGE IN MY HEART!!
WOOOOOSH

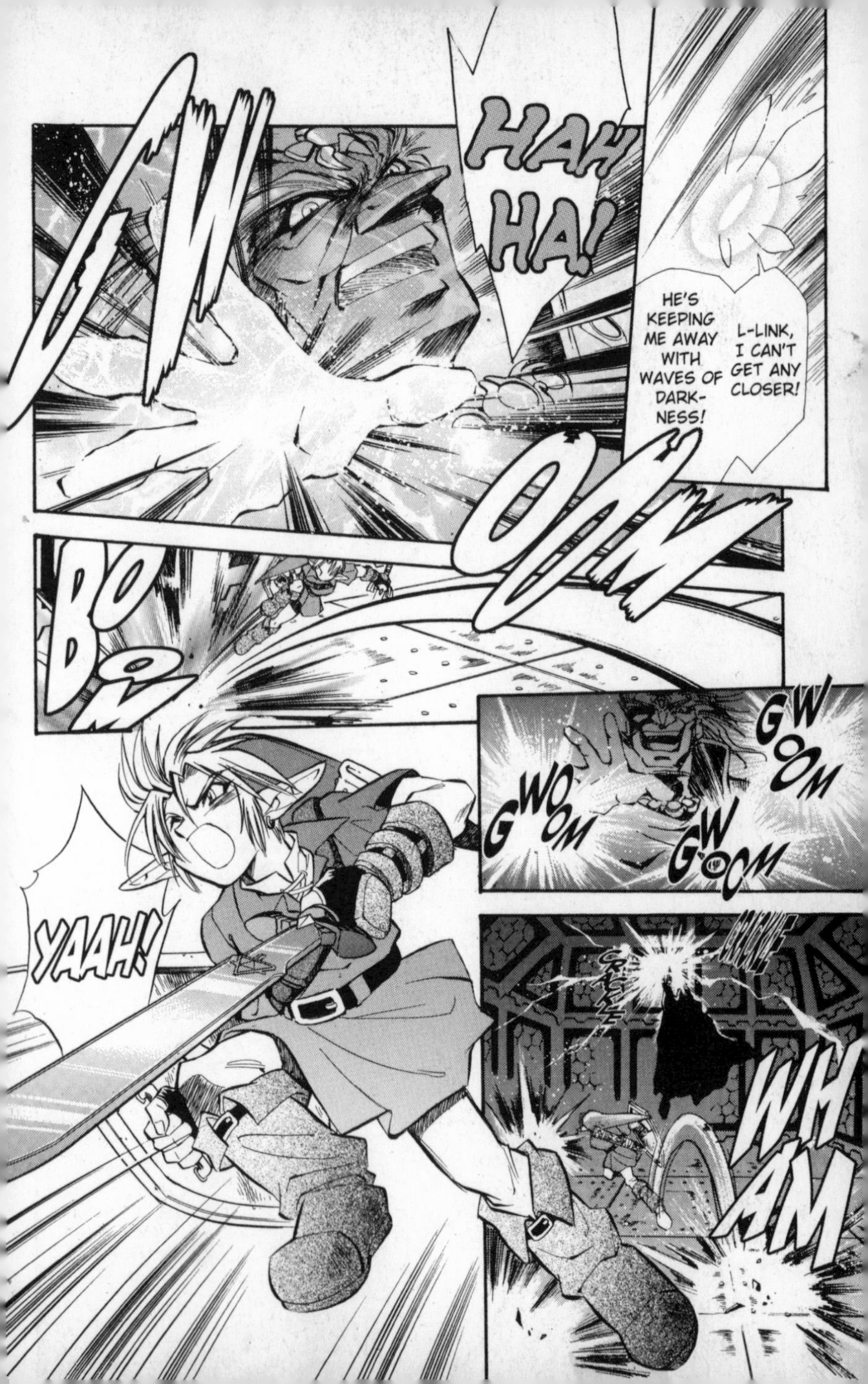
L-LINK, I CAN'T GET ANY CLOSER!
HE'S KEEPING ME AWAY WITH WAVES OF DARKNESS!
HAH HA!
GWOOM
GWOOM
GWOOM
YAAH!
CRACKLE
CRACKLE
WHAM

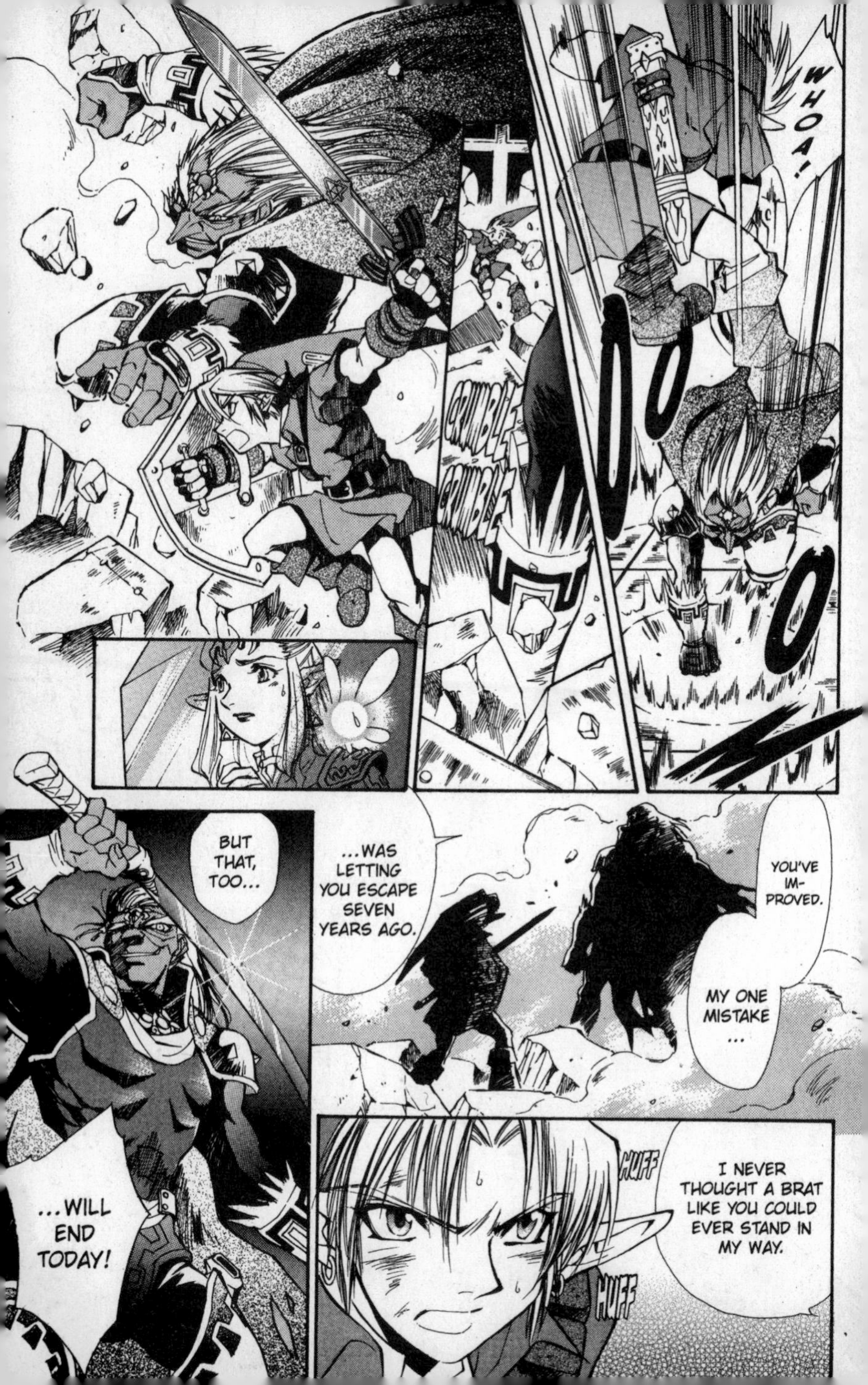
WHOA!
CRUMBLE
CRUMBLE
YOU'VE IM-PROVED.
MY ONE MISTAKE ...
...WAS LETTING YOU ESCAPE SEVEN YEARS AGO.
I NEVER THOUGHT A BRAT LIKE YOU COULD EVER STAND IN MY WAY.
HUFF
HUFF
BUT THAT, TOO...
...WILL END TODAY!

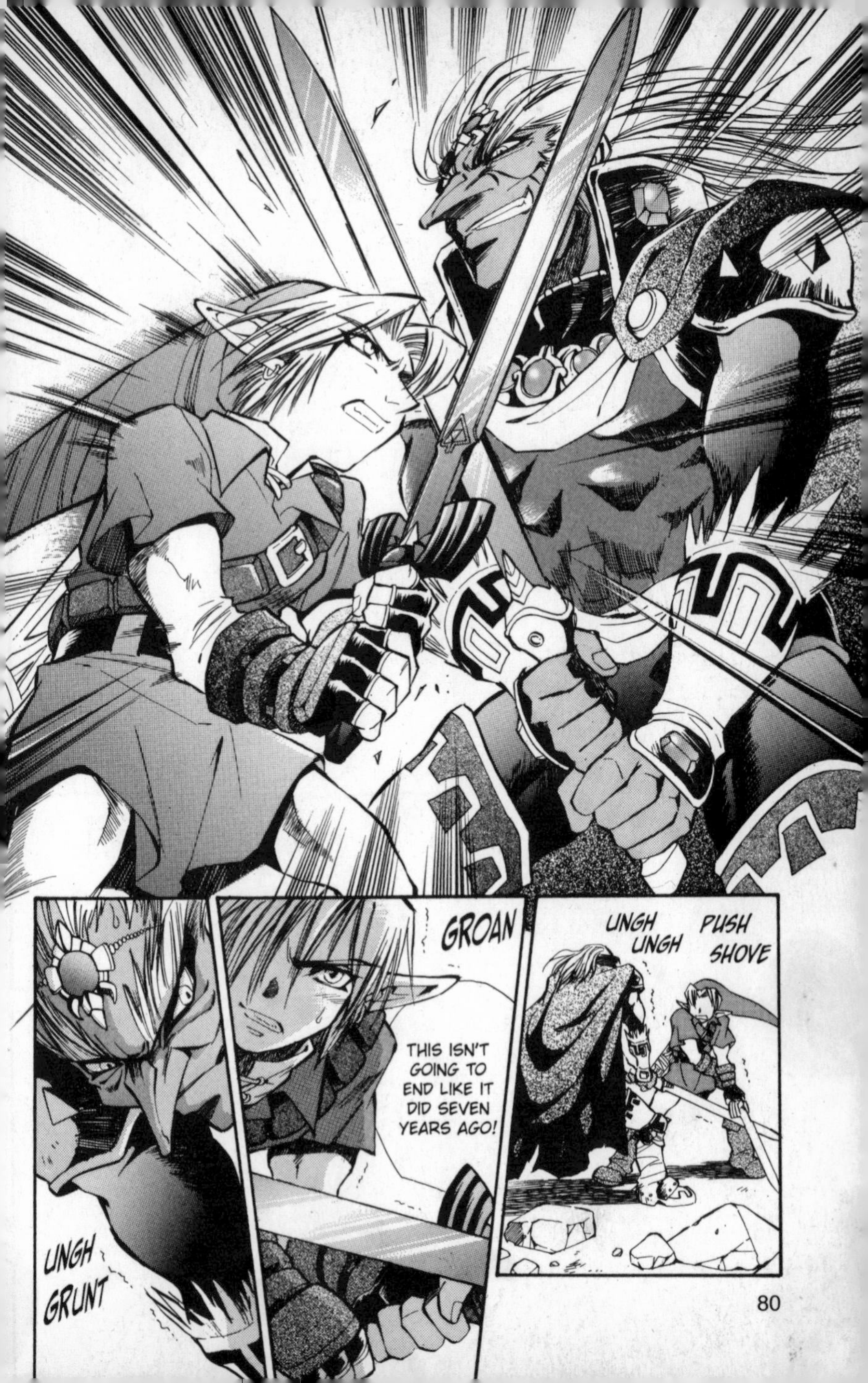
PUSH SHOVE
UNGH UNGH
GROAN
THIS ISN'T GOING TO END LIKE IT DID SEVEN YEARS AGO!
UNGH GRUNT

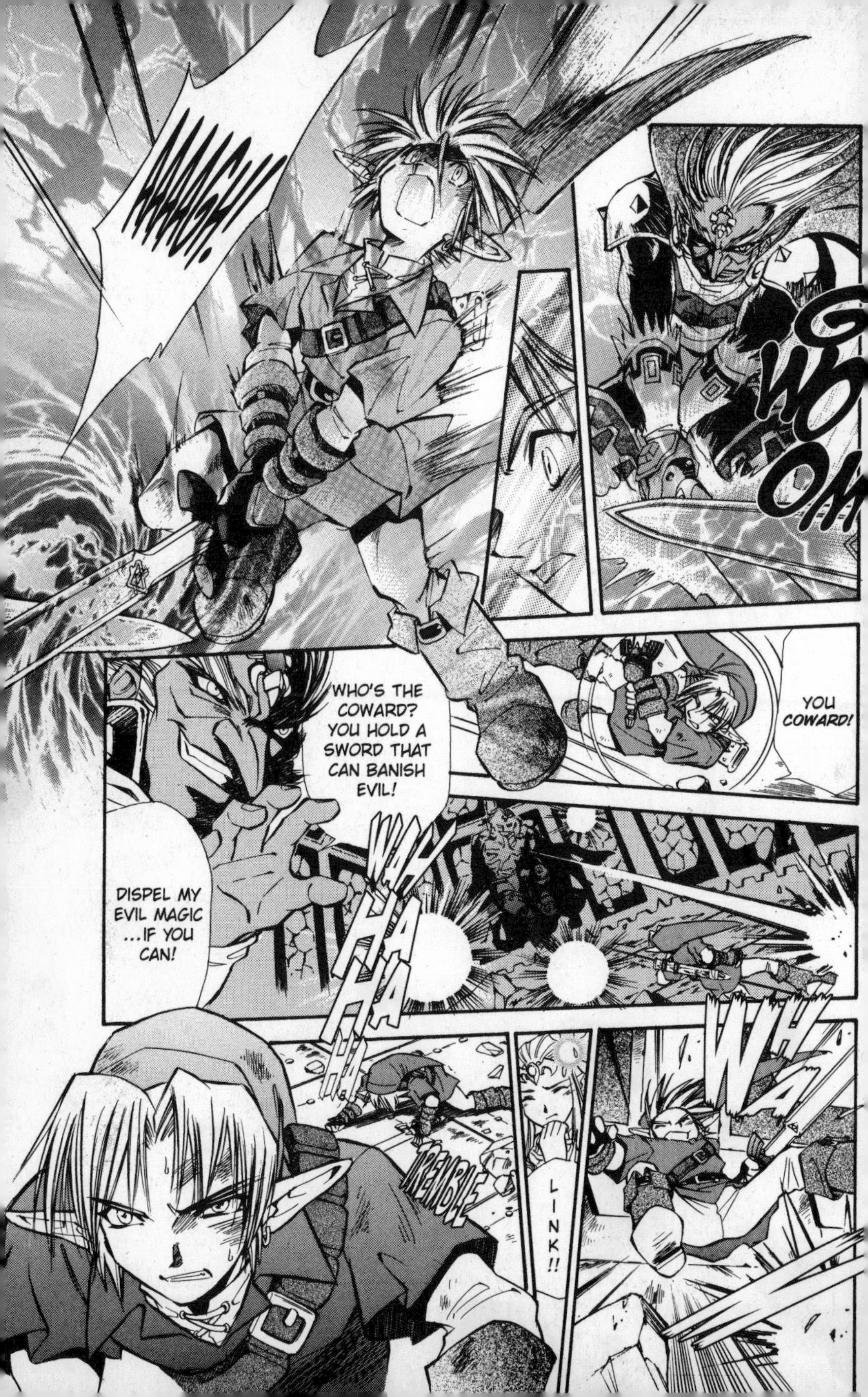
GWOOM
KRAASH!
YOU COWARD!
WHO'S THE COWARD? YOU HOLD A SWORD THAT CAN BANISH EVIL!
DISPEL MY EVIL MAGIC ...IF YOU CAN!
WAH HA HA HA
WHA
LINK!!
TREMBLE

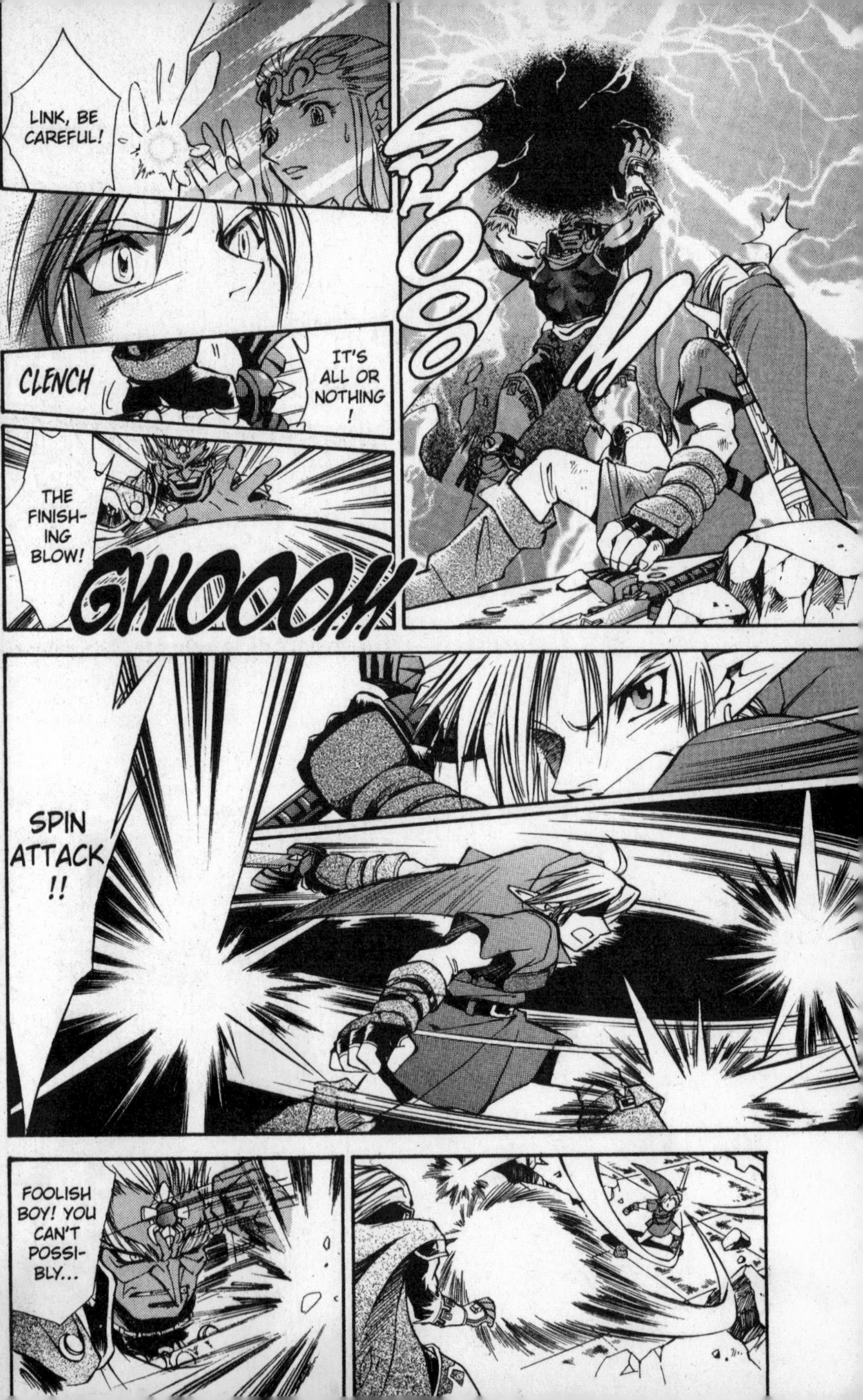
WHOOOM
LINK, BE CAREFUL!
CLENCH
IT'S ALL OR NOTHING!
THE FINISHING BLOW!
GWOOOM
SPIN ATTACK!!
FOOLISH BOY! YOU CAN'T POSSIBLY...

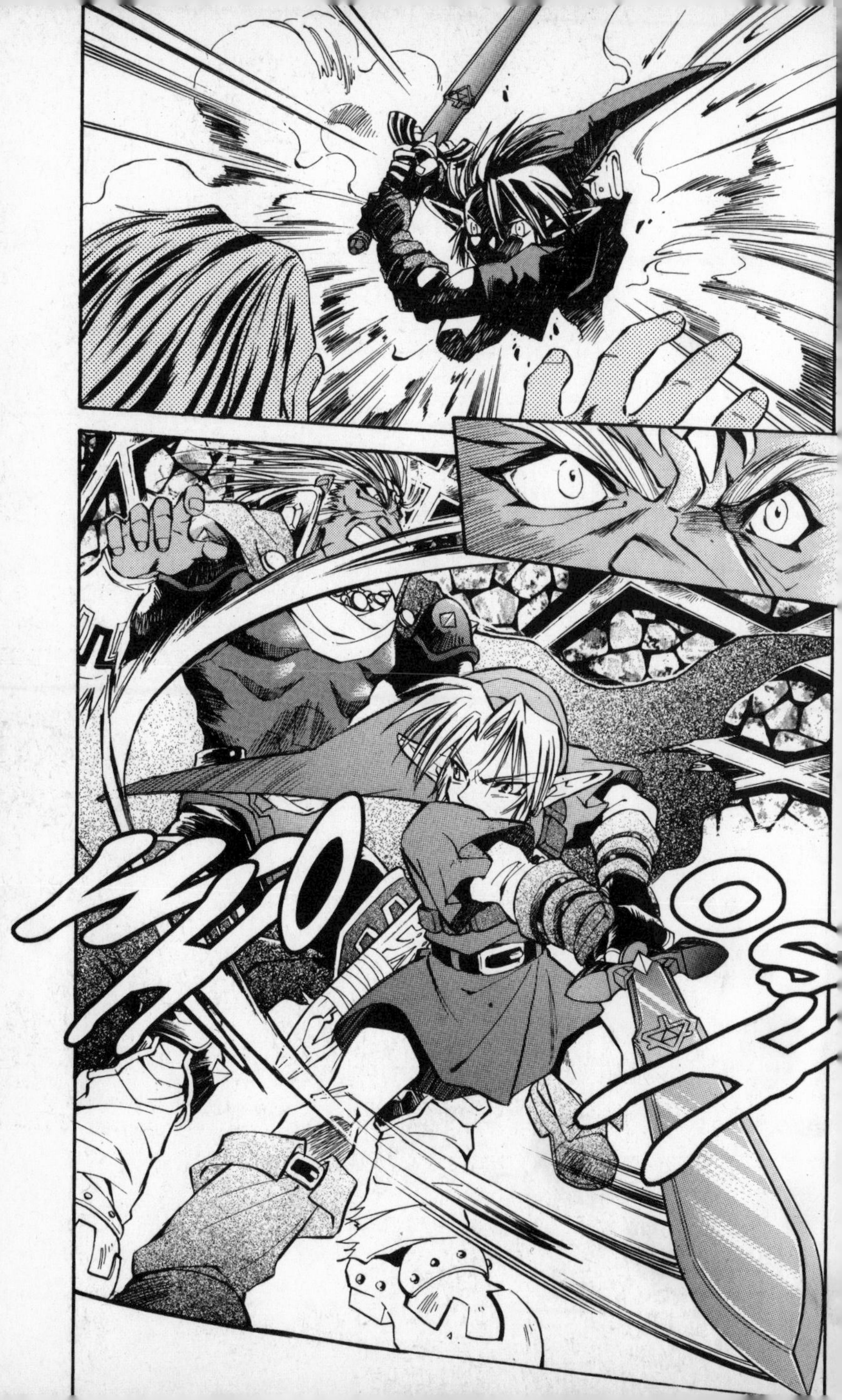

BONUS ILLUSTRATION
A ROUGH SKETCH HIMEKAWA-SENSEI DREW
BEFORE WORKING ON THE SERIES.

CHAPTER 9
A NEW JOURNEY BEGINS

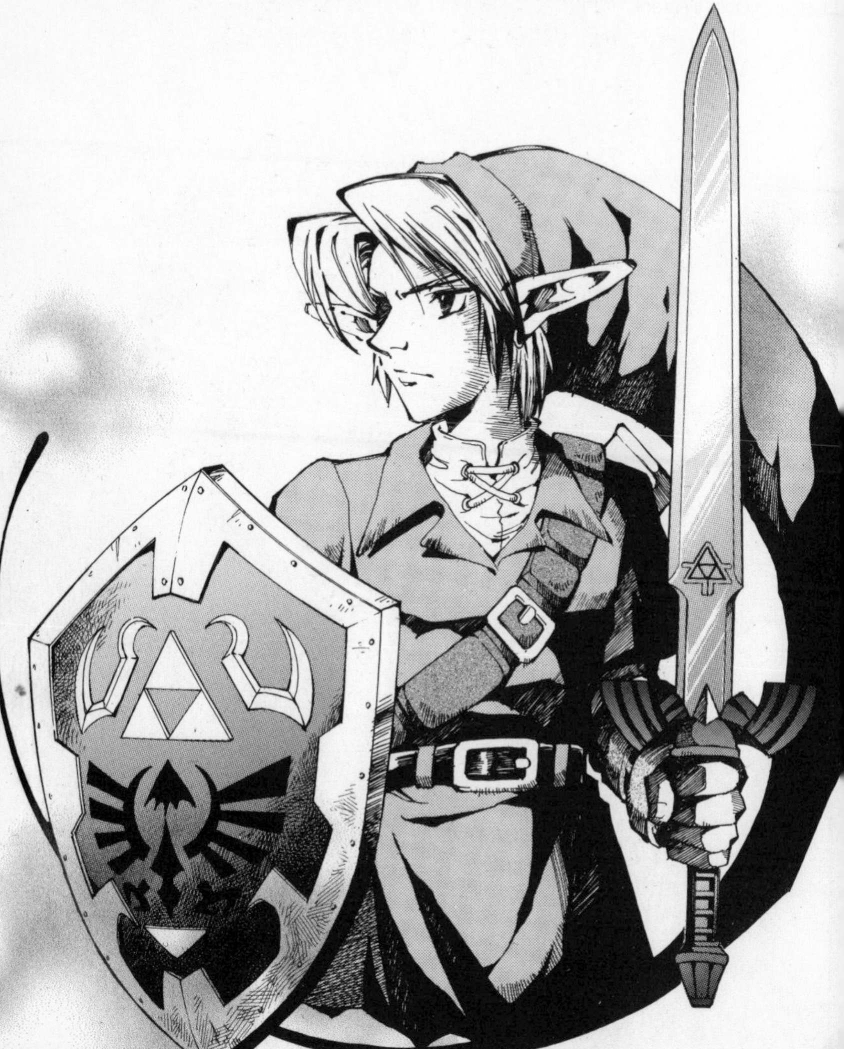

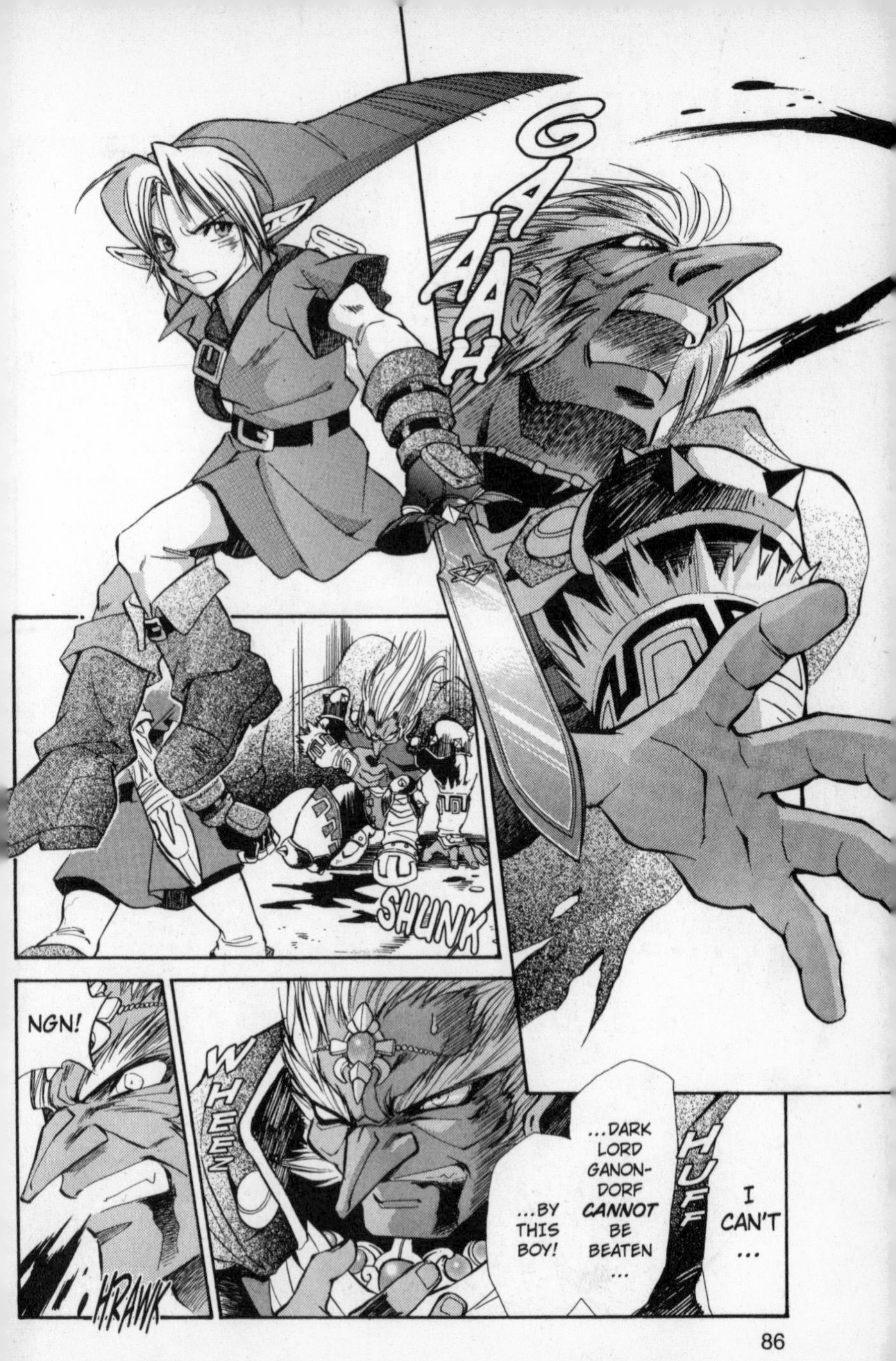
GAAAH
SHUNK
I CAN'T ...
HUFF
...DARK LORD GANON-DORF **CANNOT** BE BEATEN ...
...BY THIS BOY!
WHEEZ
NGN!
HRAWK

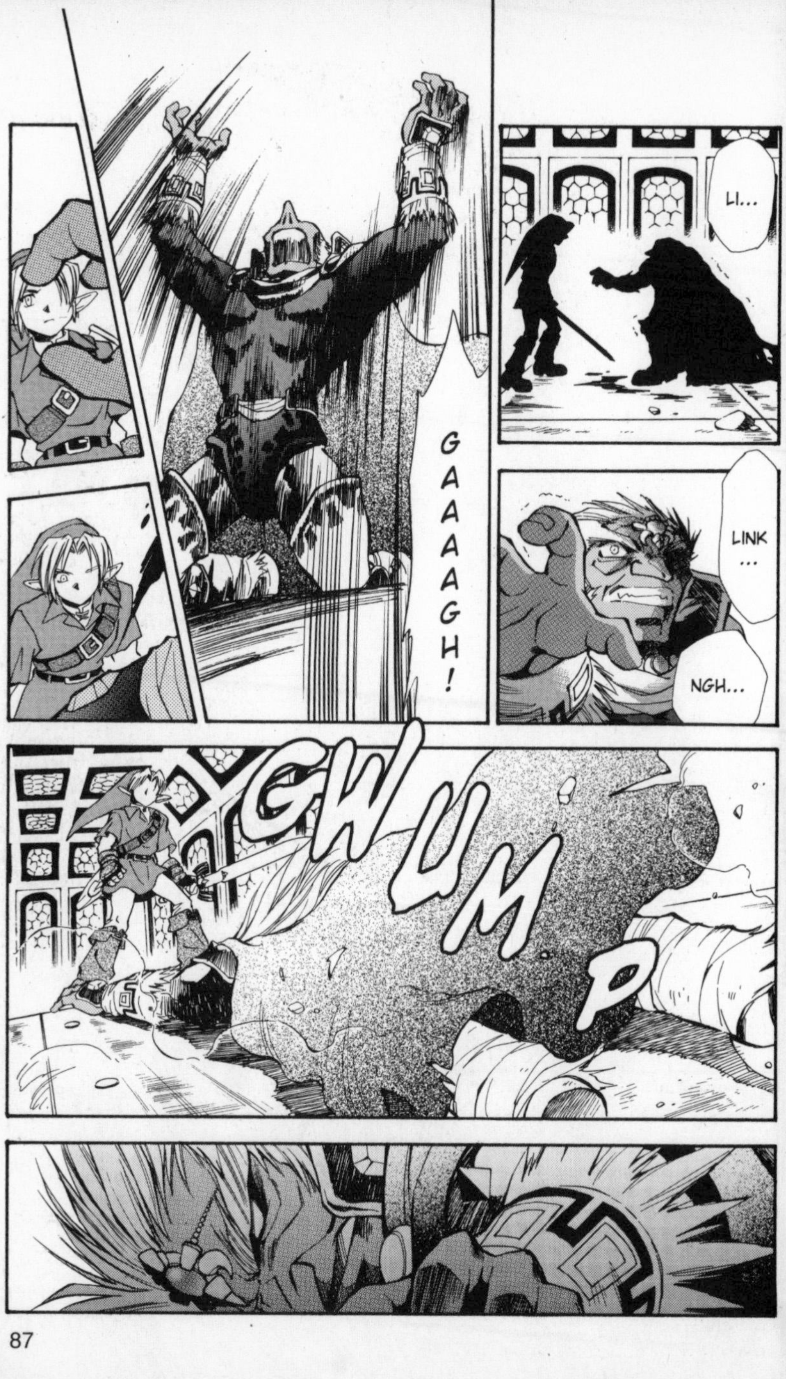
LI...
LINK ...
NGH...
GAAAAAGH!
GWUMP

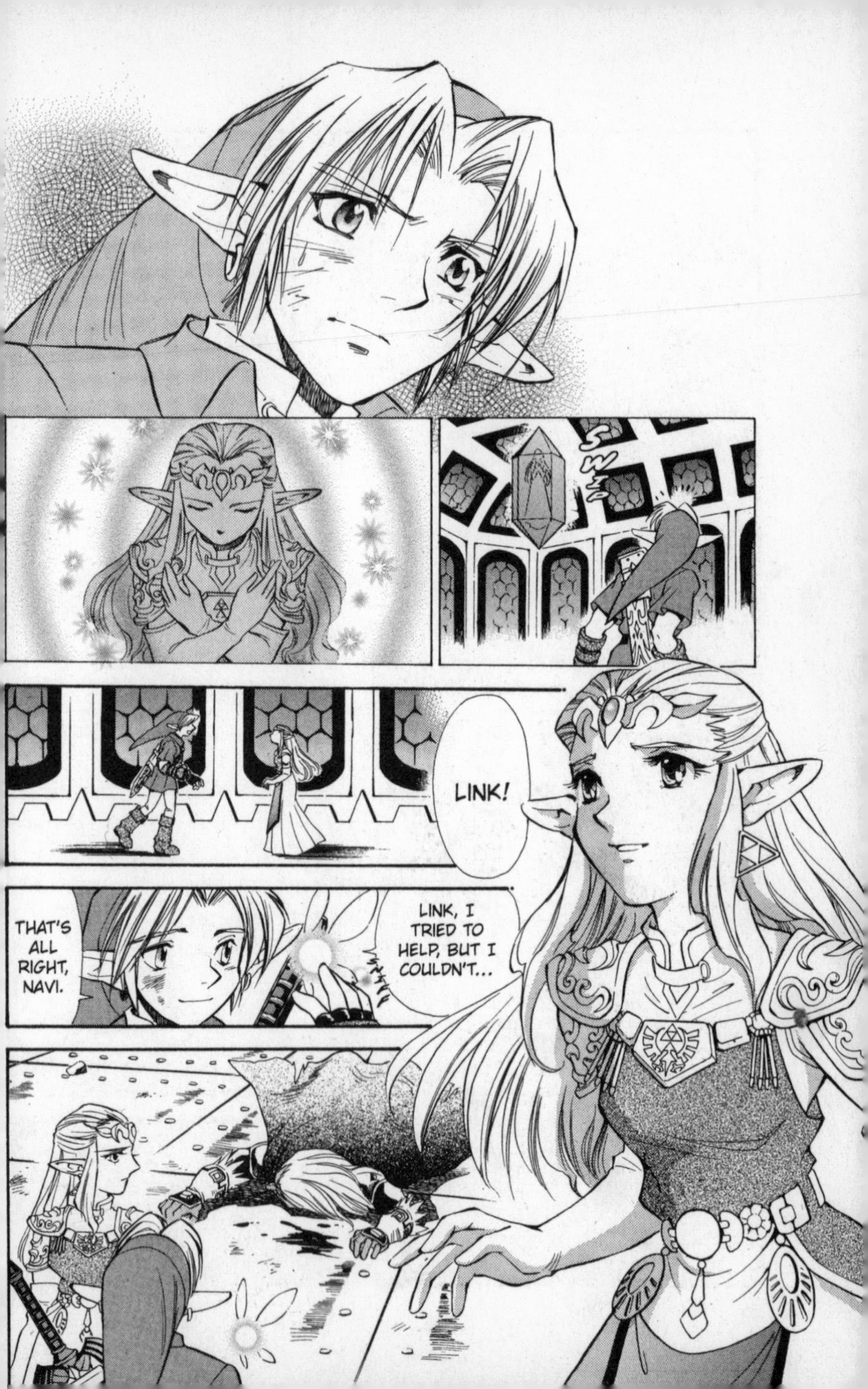
SWIP
LINK!
LINK, I TRIED TO HELP, BUT I COULDN'T...
THAT'S ALL RIGHT, NAVI.

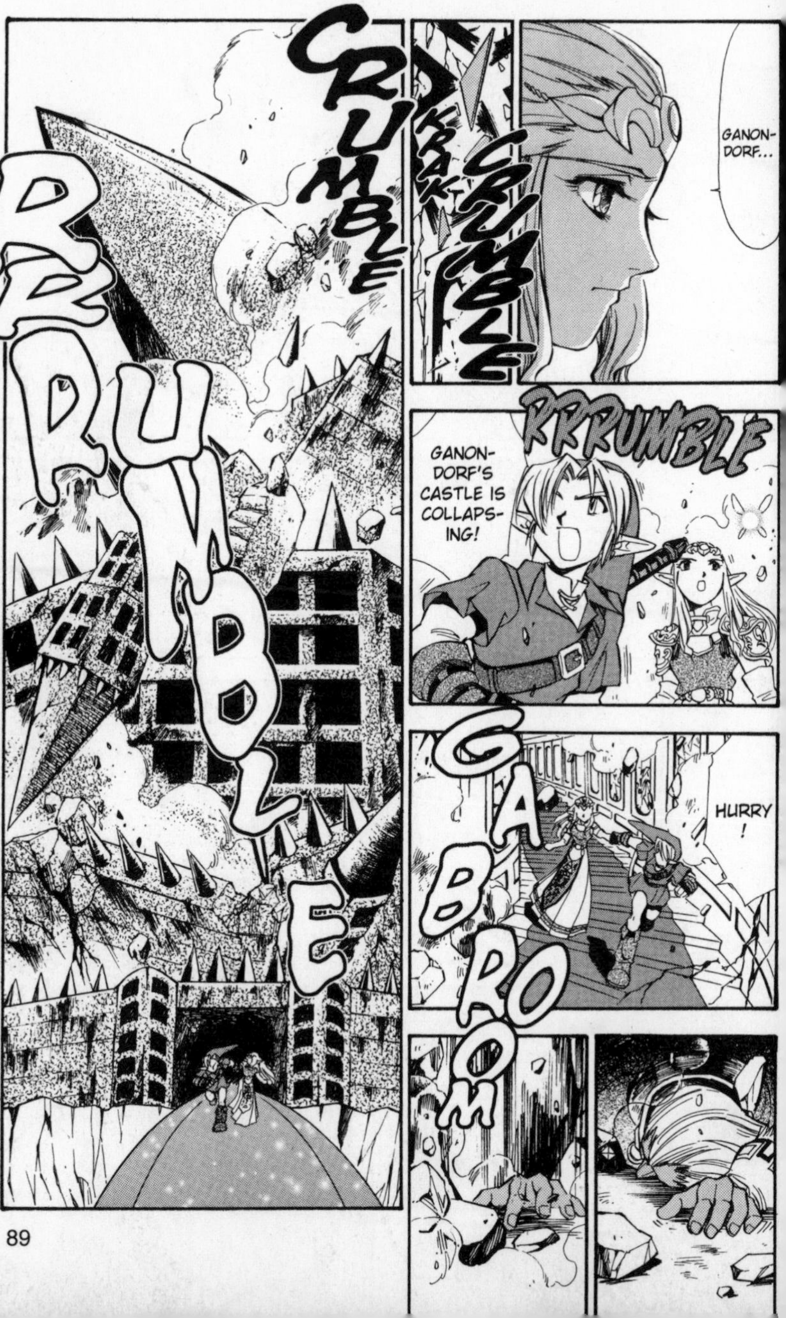
GANON-DORF...
KRAK
CRUMBLE
RRRUMBLE
GANON-DORF'S CASTLE IS COLLAPS-ING!
HURRY!
GABBROOM
CRUMBLE
RRUMBLE

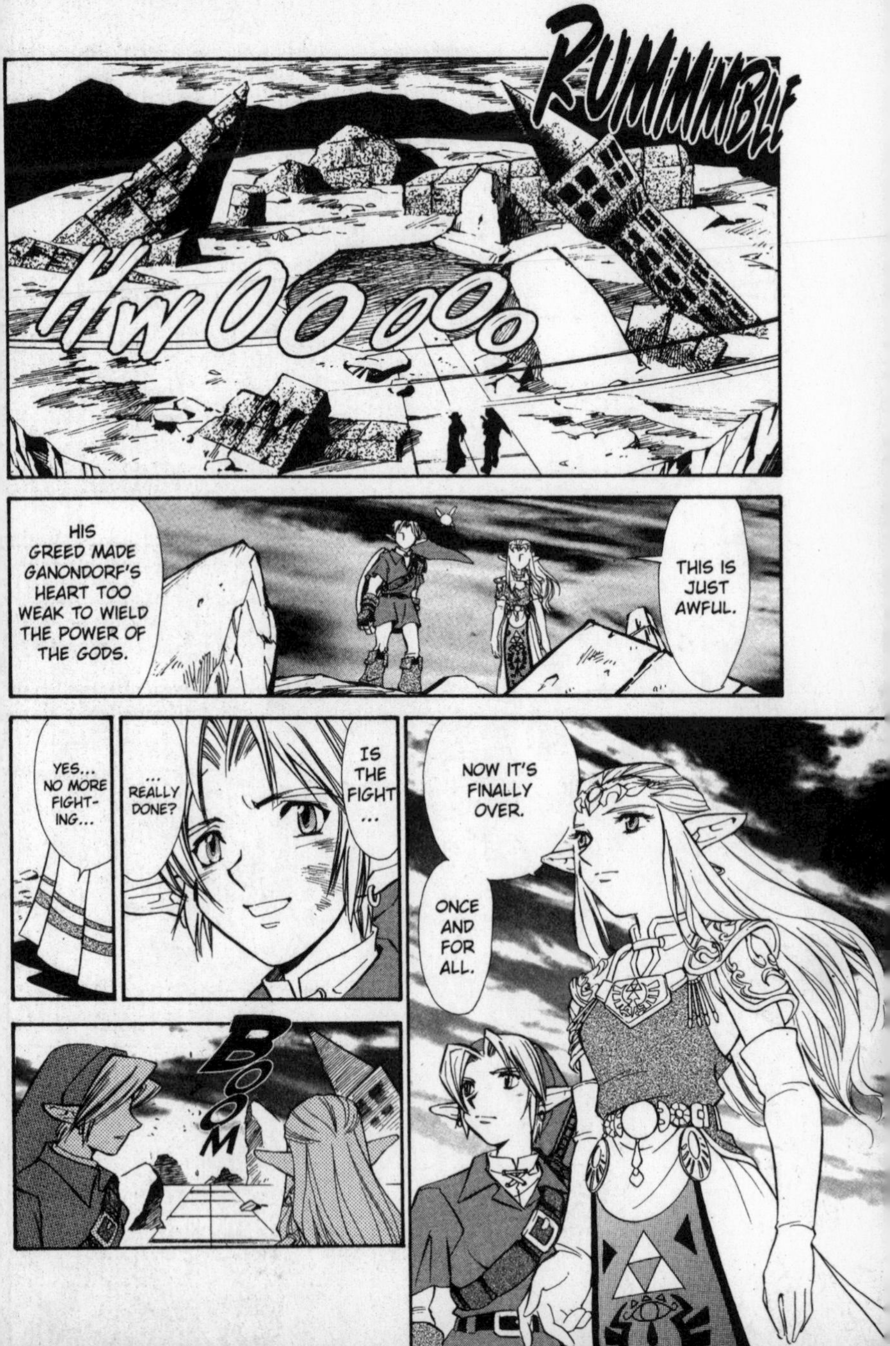
RUMMMBLE
HWOOOOOO
THIS IS JUST AWFUL.
HIS GREED MADE GANONDORF'S HEART TOO WEAK TO WIELD THE POWER OF THE GODS.
NOW IT'S FINALLY OVER.
ONCE AND FOR ALL.
IS THE FIGHT ...
... REALLY DONE?
YES... NO MORE FIGHT-ING...
BOOOM

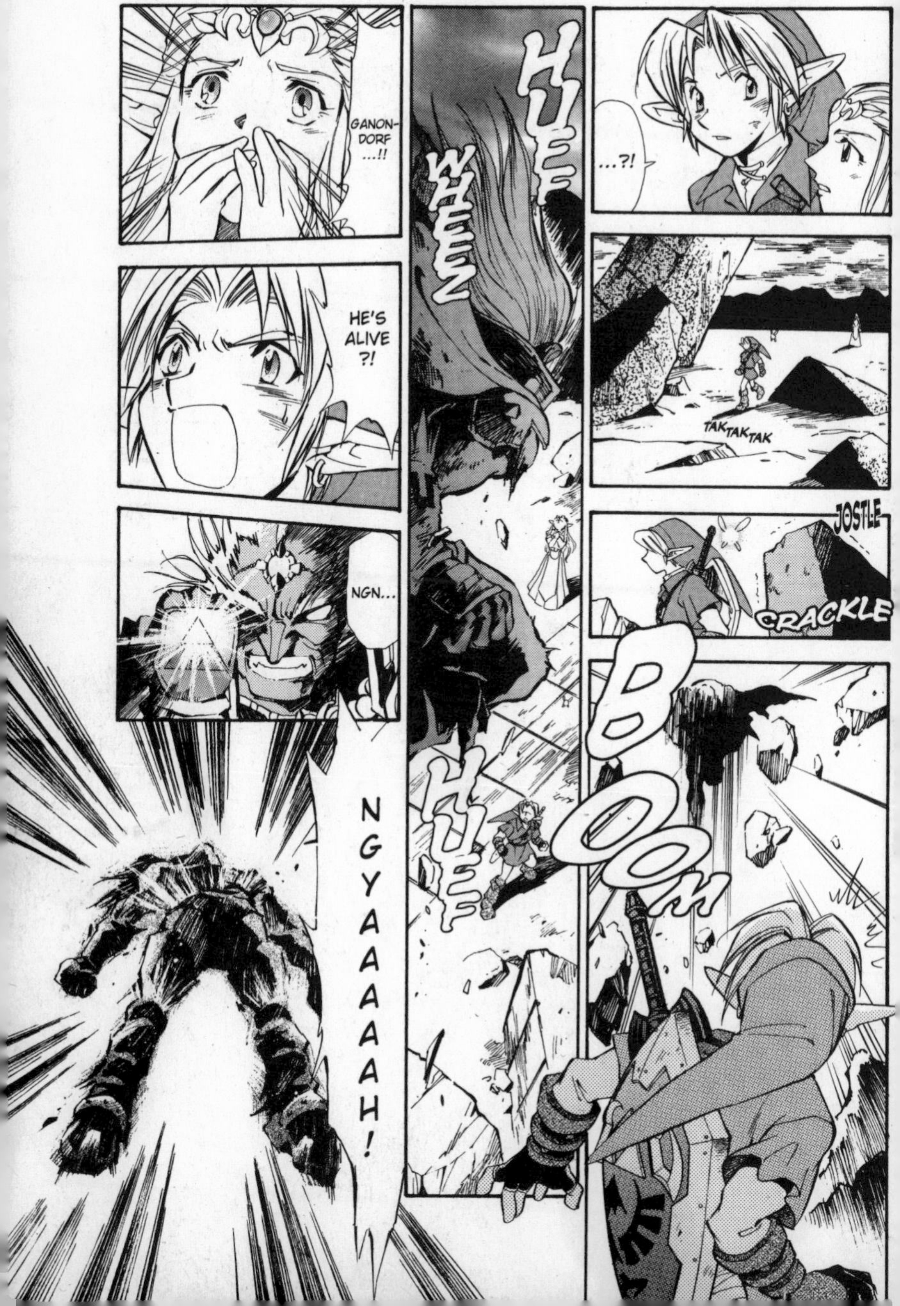
...?!
TAKTAKTAK
JOSTLE
CRACKLE
BOOM
HUFF
WHEEZ
HUFF
GANONDORF ...!!
HE'S ALIVE ?!
NGN...
NGYAAAAAAAH!

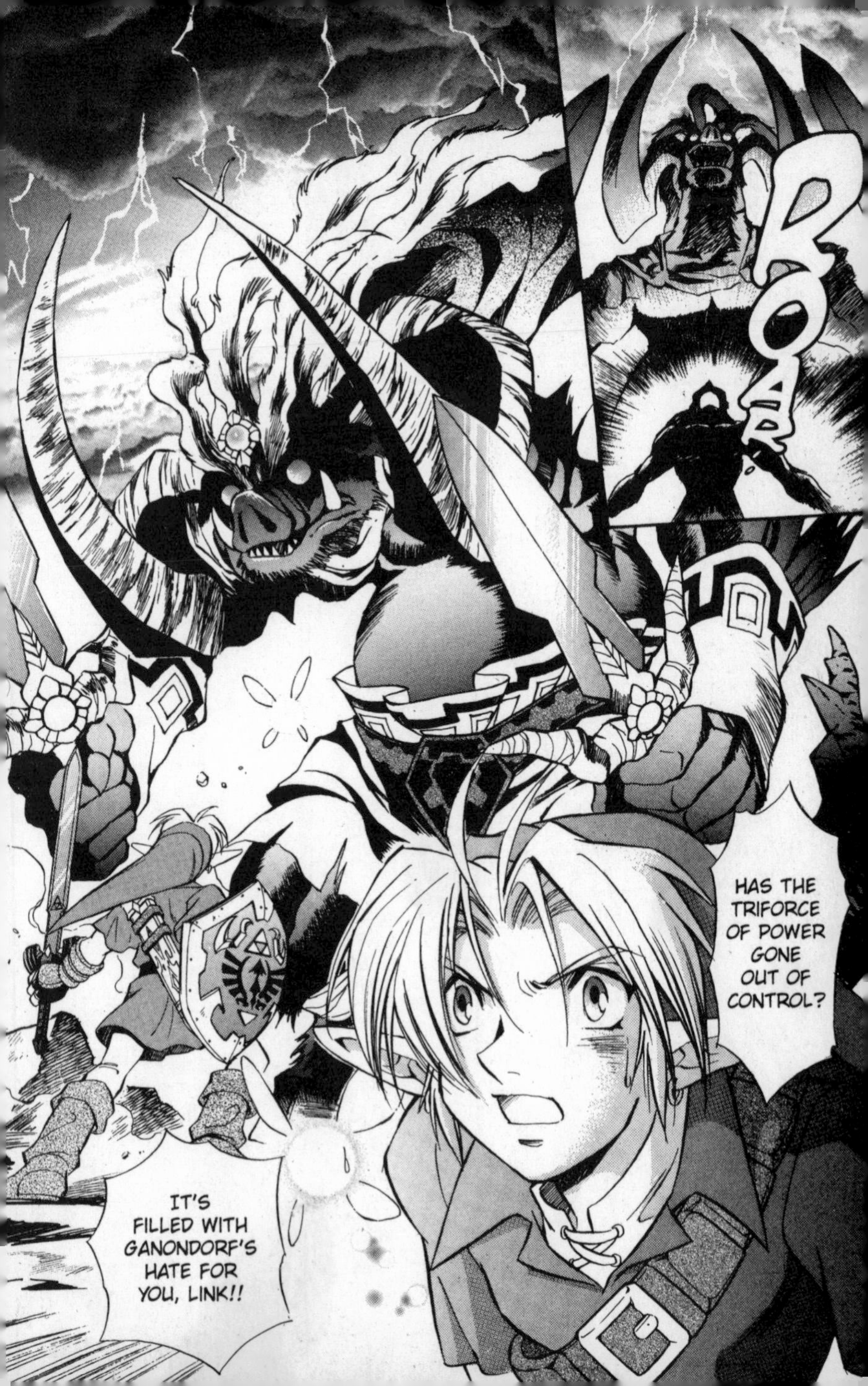
ROAR
HAS THE TRIFORCE OF POWER GONE OUT OF CONTROL?
IT'S FILLED WITH GANONDORF'S HATE FOR YOU, LINK!!

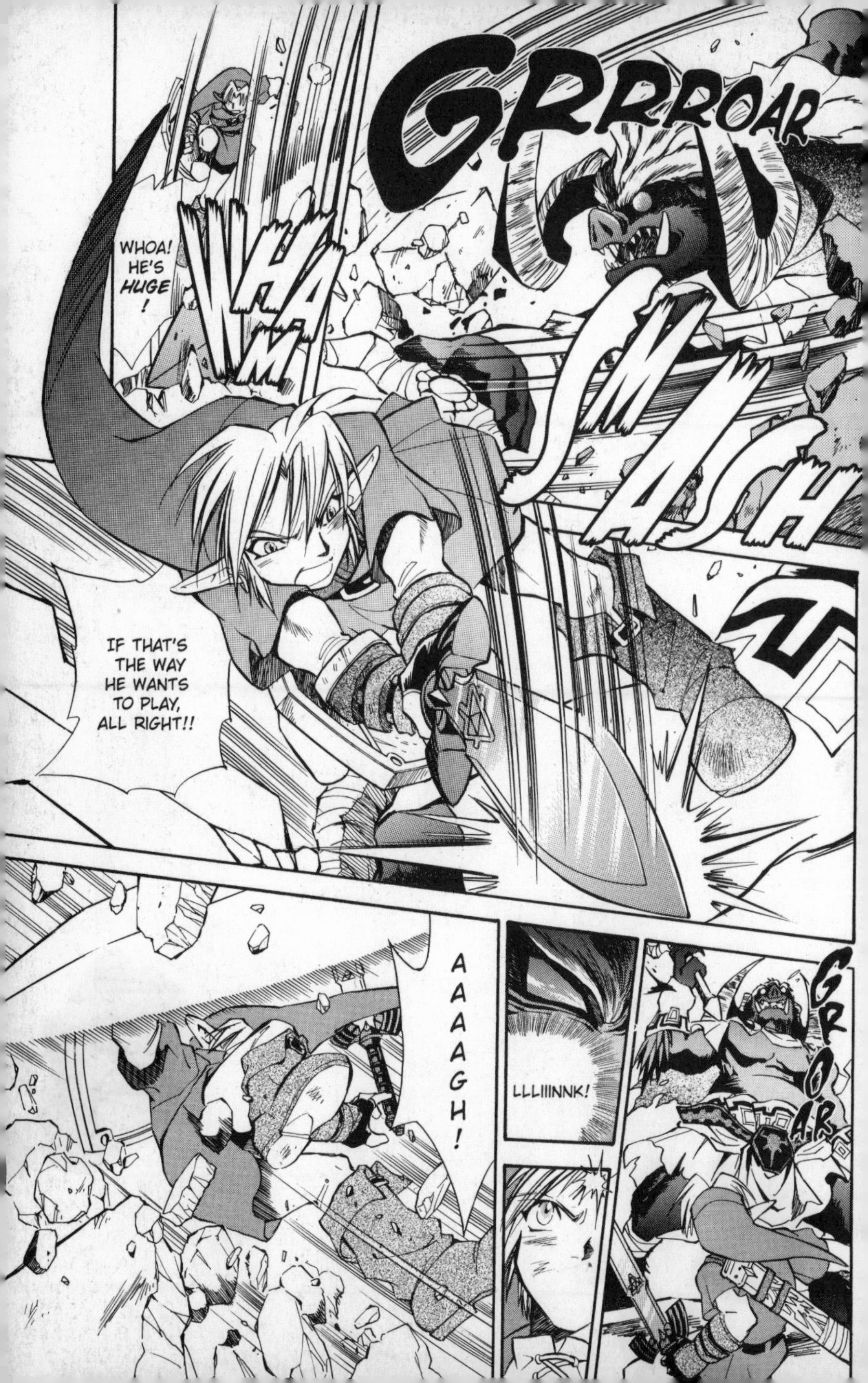
GRRROAR
SMASH
WHAM
WHOA! HE'S HUGE!
IF THAT'S THE WAY HE WANTS TO PLAY, ALL RIGHT!!
GROAR
LLLIIINNK!
AAAAAGH!

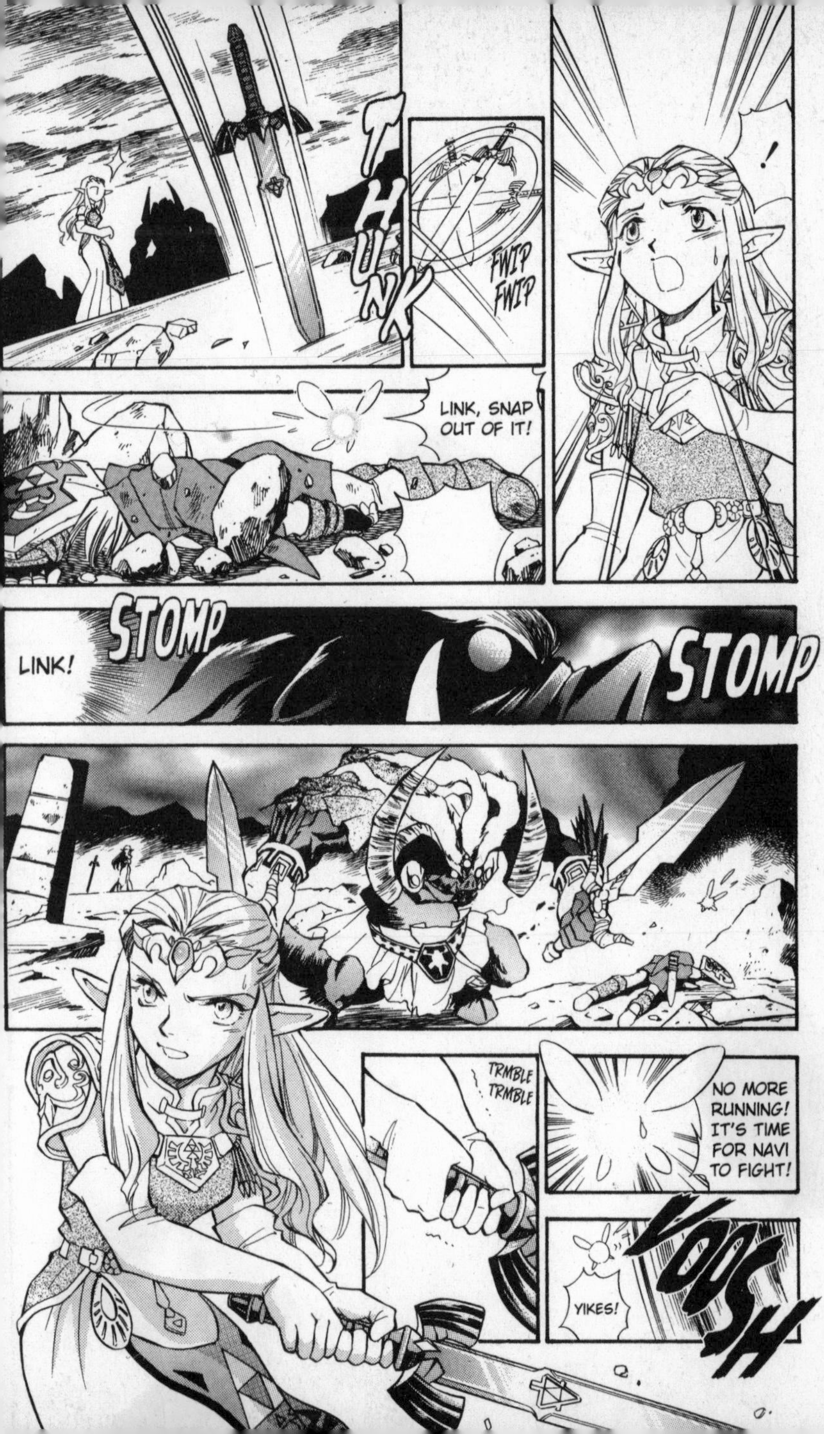
!
FWIP FWIP
THUNK
LINK, SNAP OUT OF IT!
STOMP
STOMP
LINK!
TRMBLE TRMBLE
NO MORE RUNNING! IT'S TIME FOR NAVI TO FIGHT!
VOOSH
YIKES!

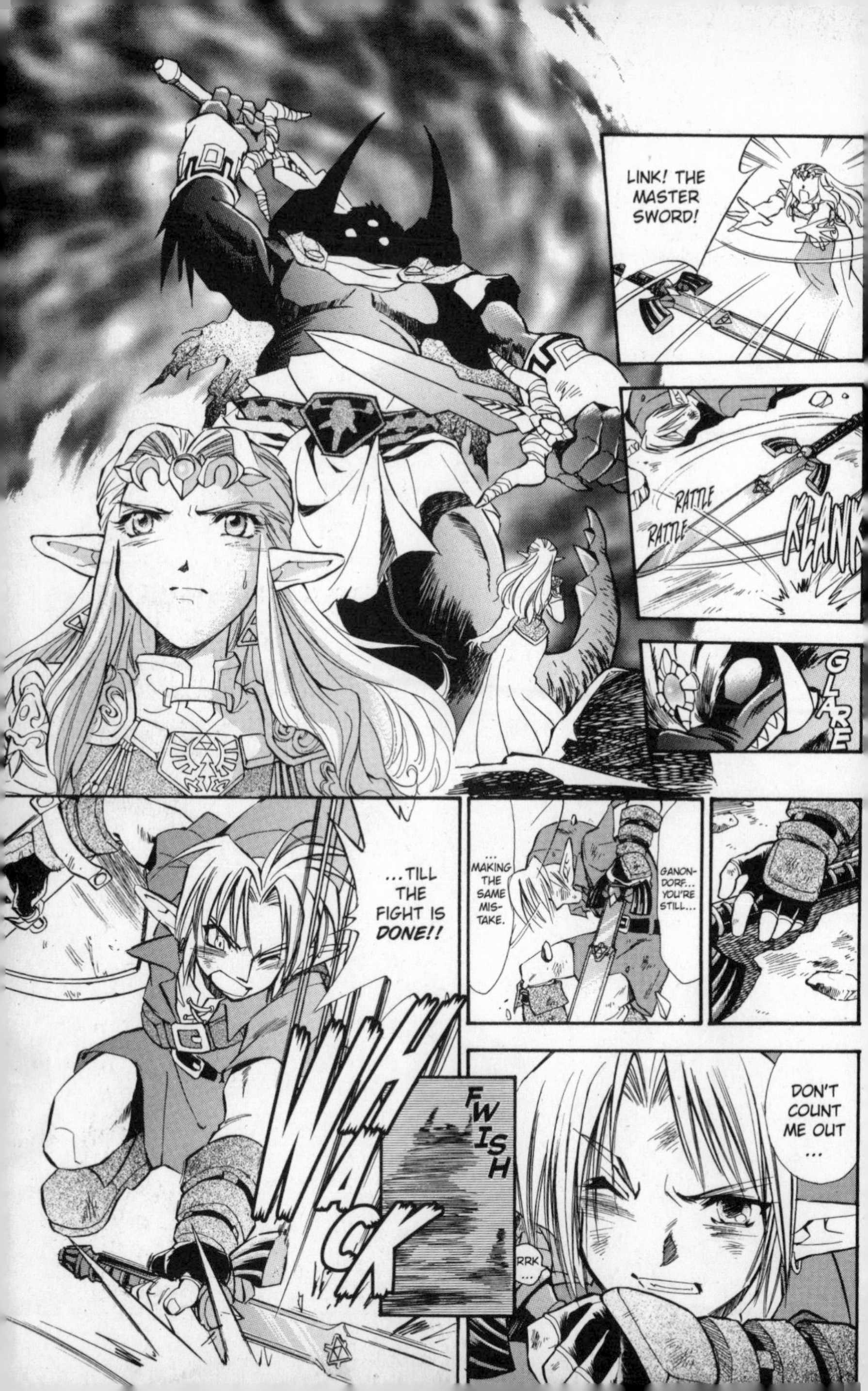
LINK! THE MASTER SWORD!
RATTLE RATTLE
KLANK
GLARE
GANONDORF... YOU'RE STILL...
... MAKING THE SAME MISTAKE.
DON'T COUNT ME OUT ...
RRK ...
...TILL THE FIGHT IS *DONE!!*
FWISH
WHACK

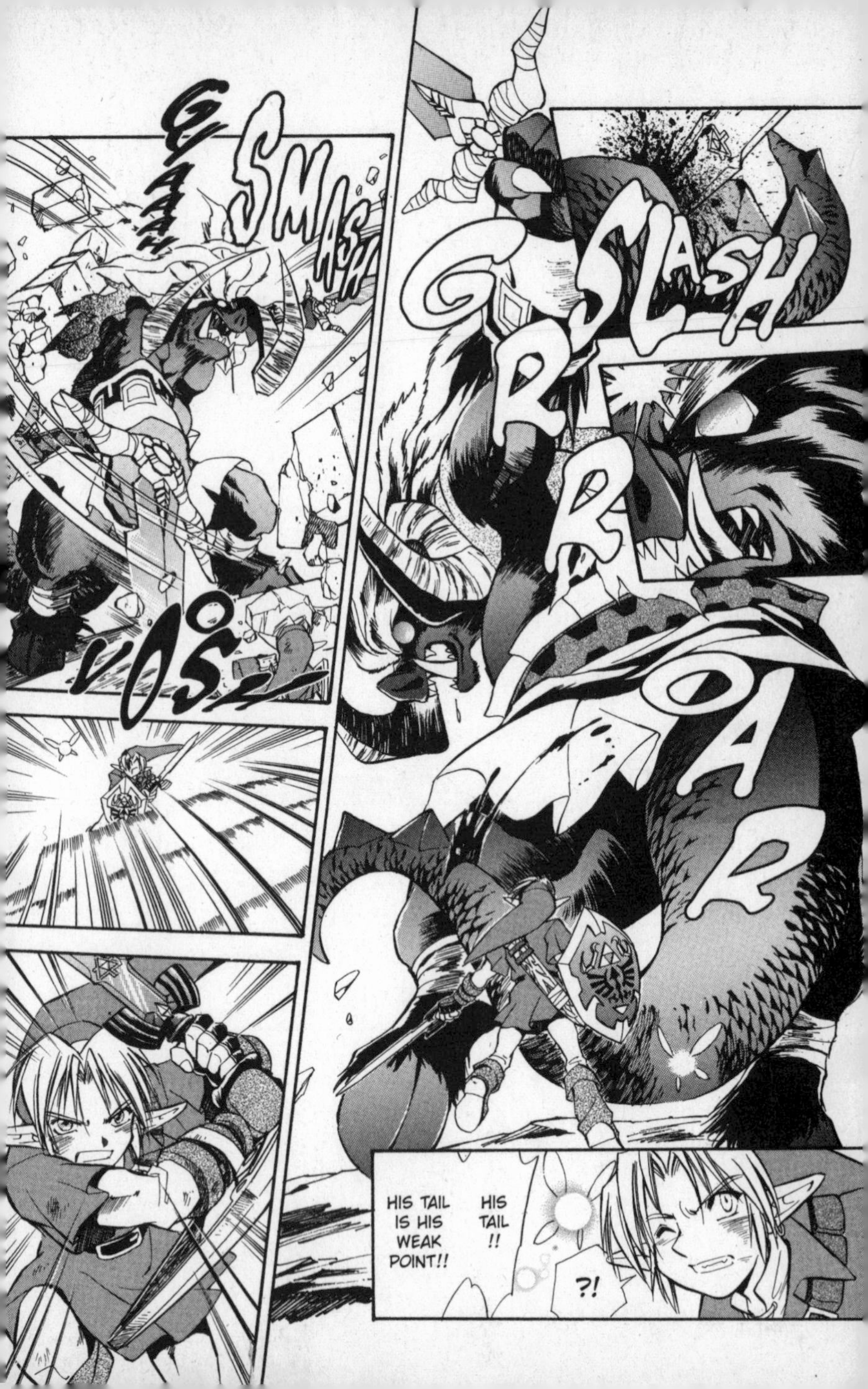
SLASH
GRRROAR
HIS TAIL !!
HIS TAIL IS HIS WEAK POINT!!
?!
GYAAAH
SMASH
VOOSH

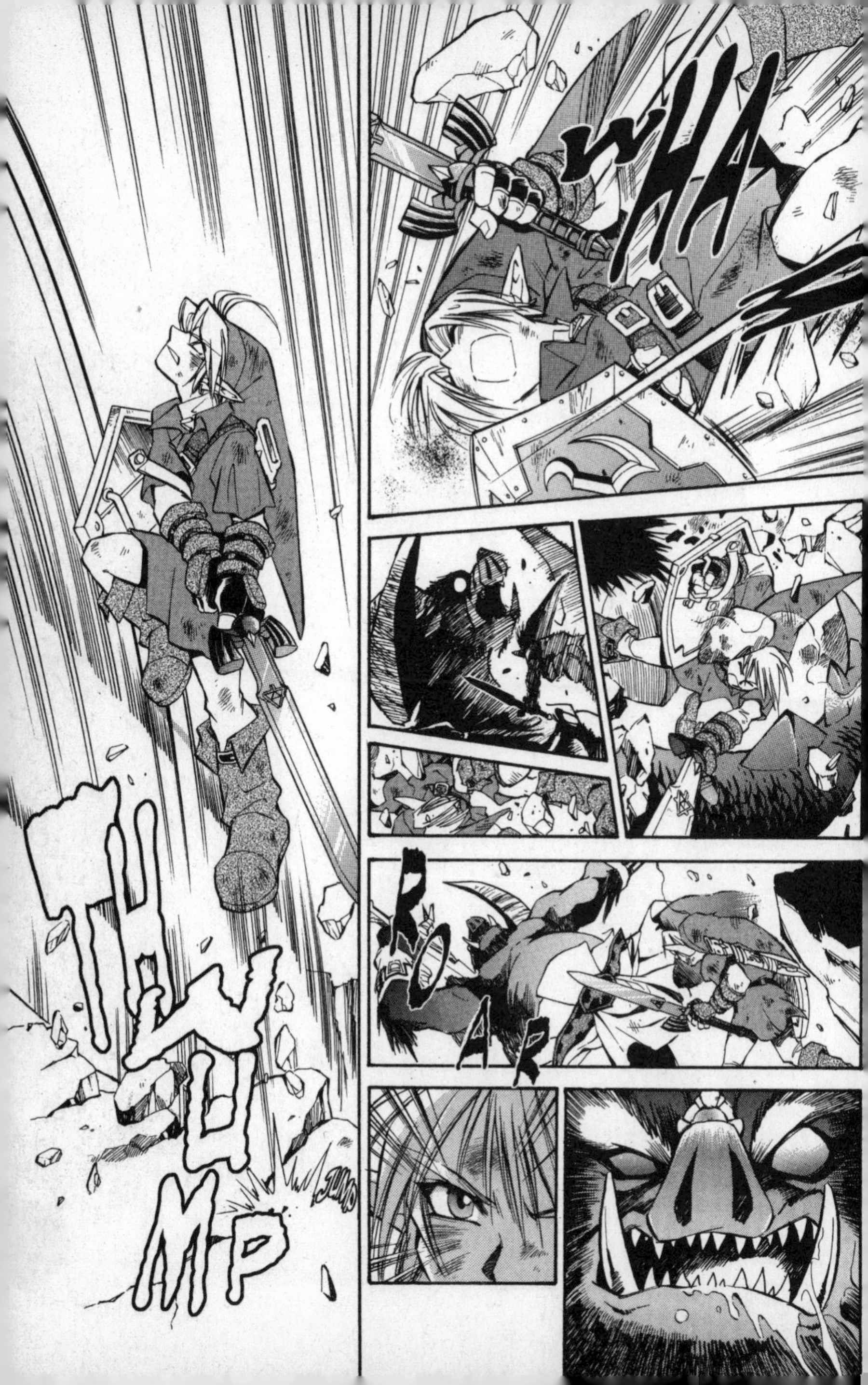
WHAM
ROAR
THUMP

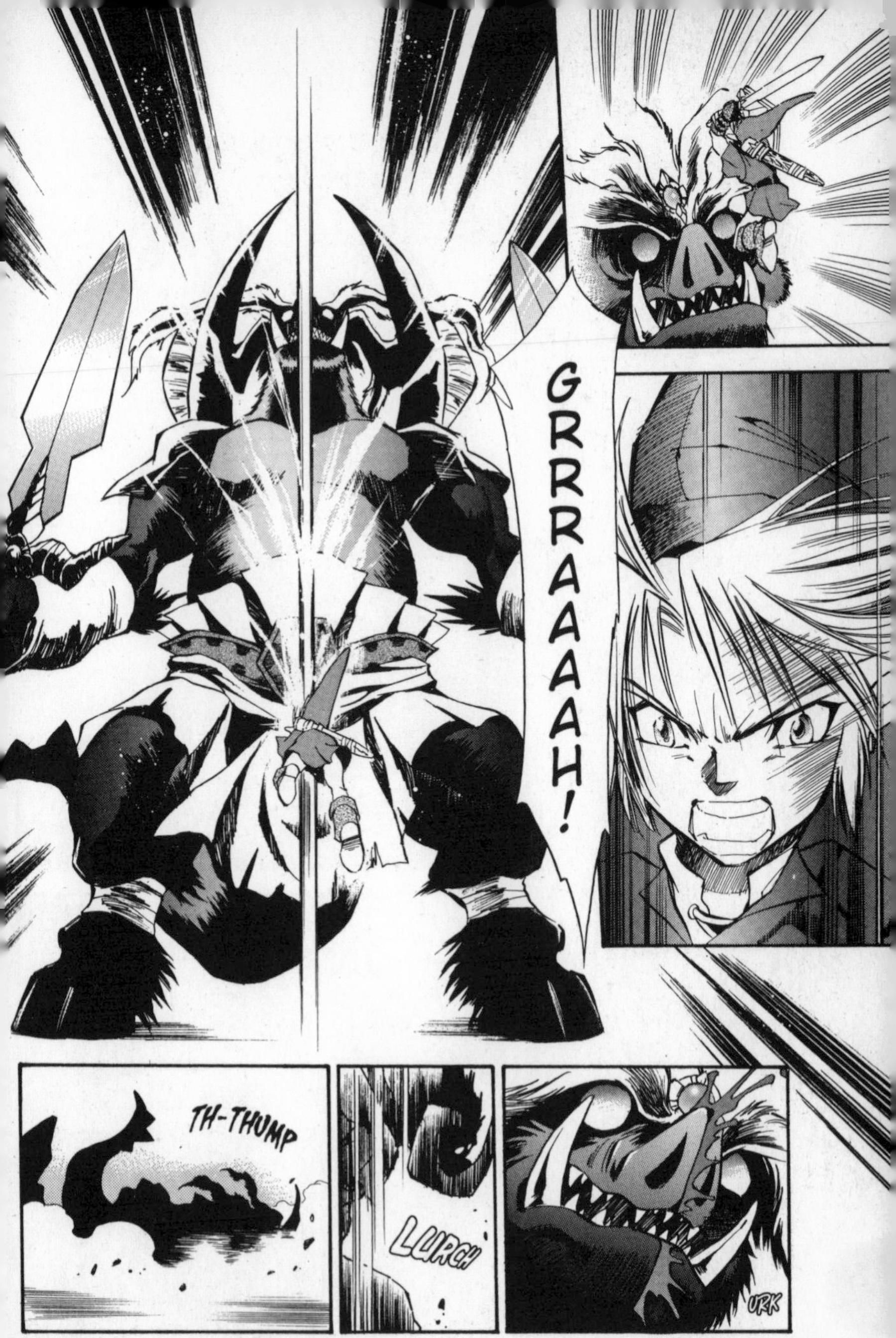
GRRRAAAAAH!
URK
LURCH
TH-THUMP

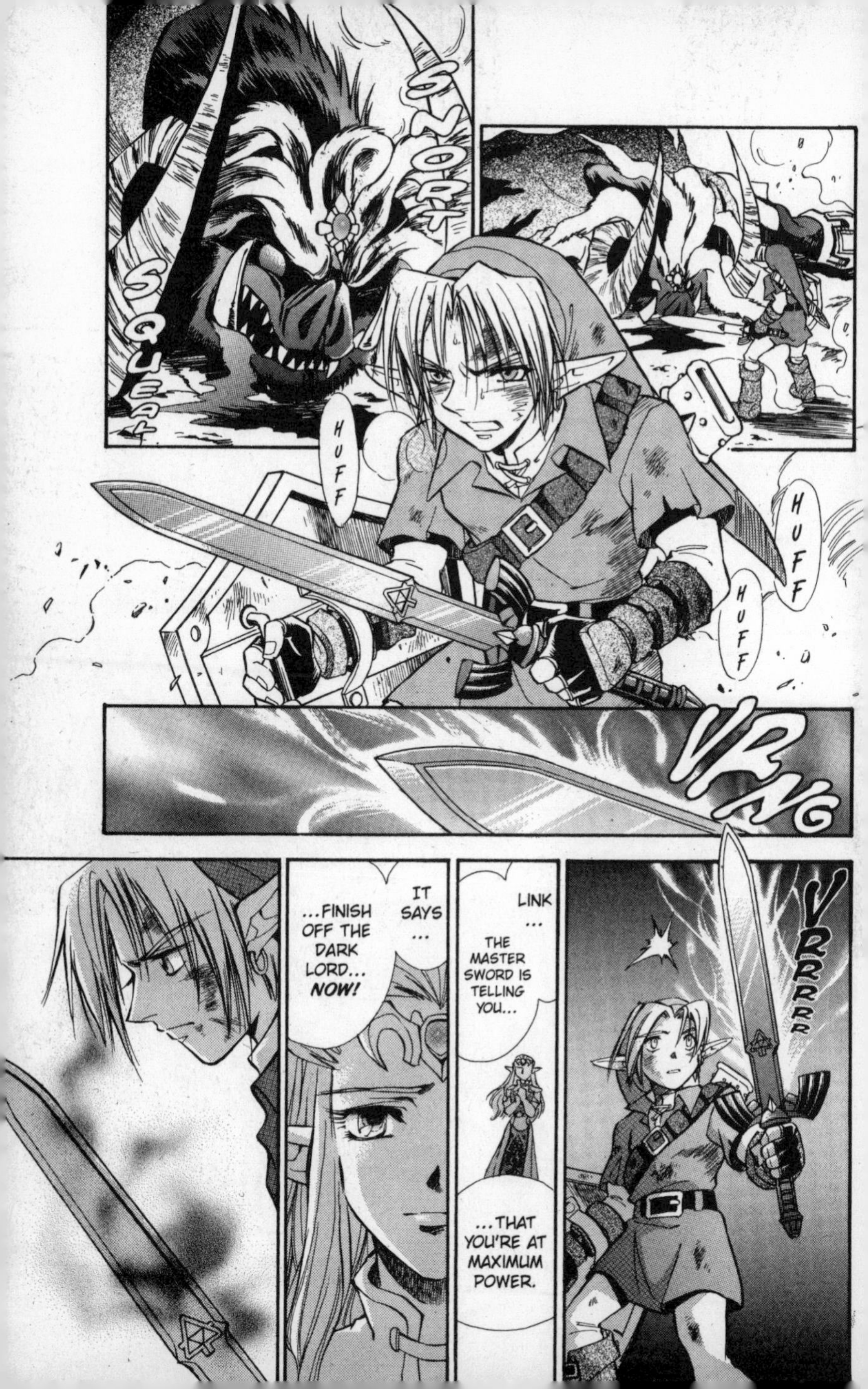
SNORT
SQUEAL
HUFF
HUFF
HUFF
VRING
VRRRRR
LINK...
THE MASTER SWORD IS TELLING YOU...
...THAT YOU'RE AT MAXIMUM POWER.
IT SAYS...
...FINISH OFF THE DARK LORD... **NOW!**

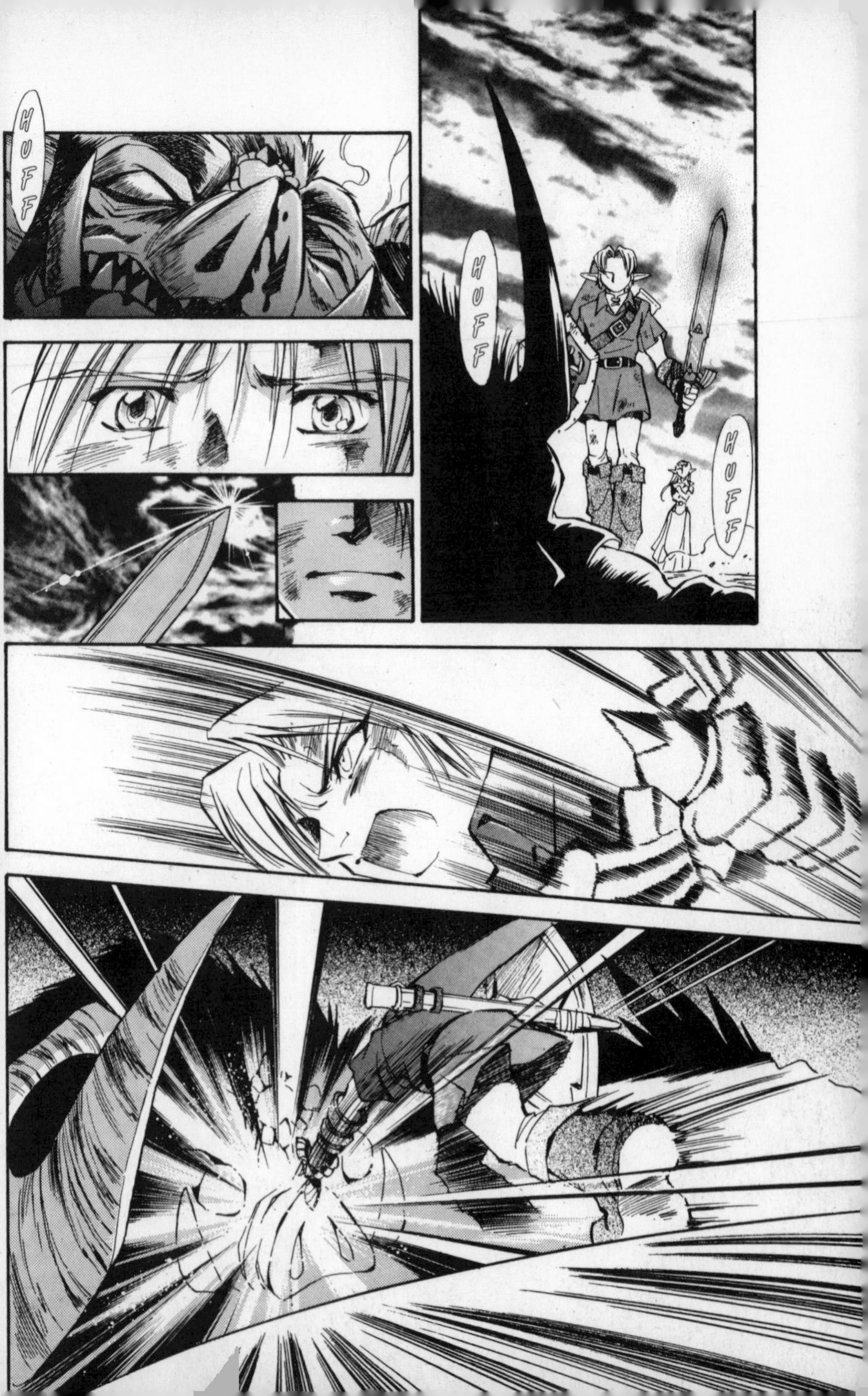
HUFF
HUFF
HUFF

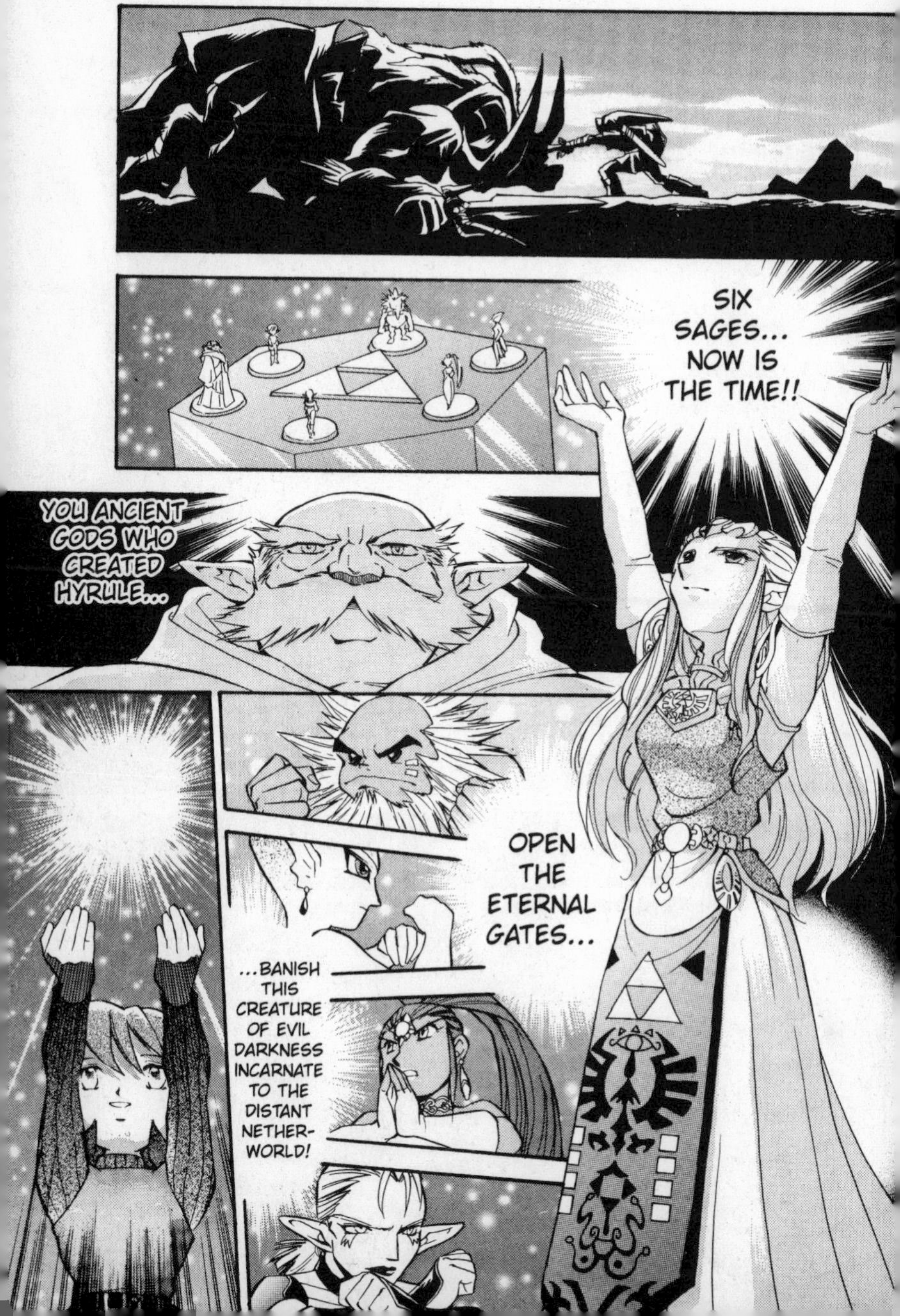
SIX SAGES... NOW IS THE TIME!!
YOU! ANCIENT GODS WHO CREATED HYRULE...
OPEN THE ETERNAL GATES...
...BANISH THIS CREATURE OF EVIL DARKNESS INCARNATE TO THE DISTANT NETHER-WORLD!

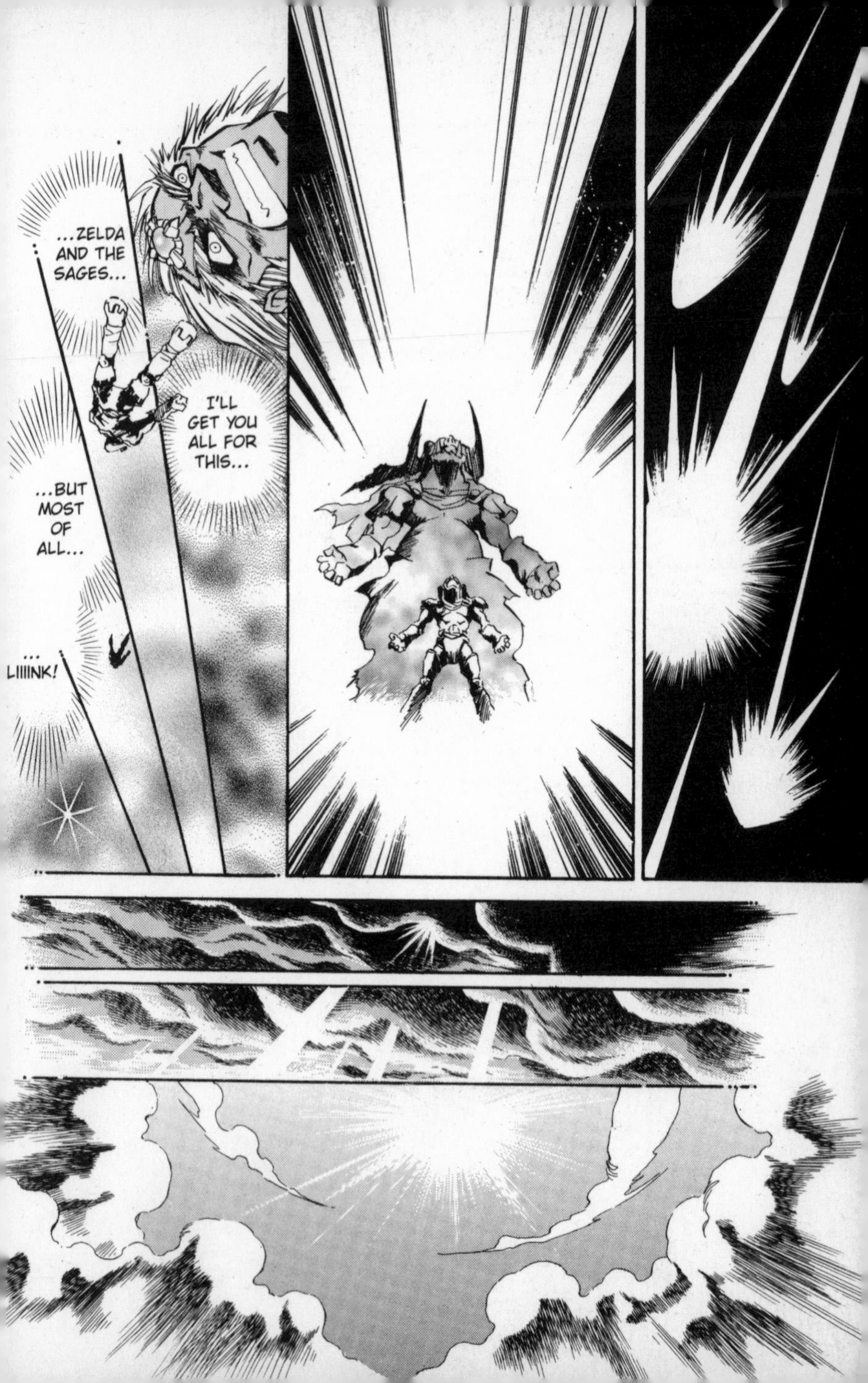
I'LL GET YOU ALL FOR THIS...
...ZELDA AND THE SAGES...
...BUT MOST OF ALL...
... LIIIINK!

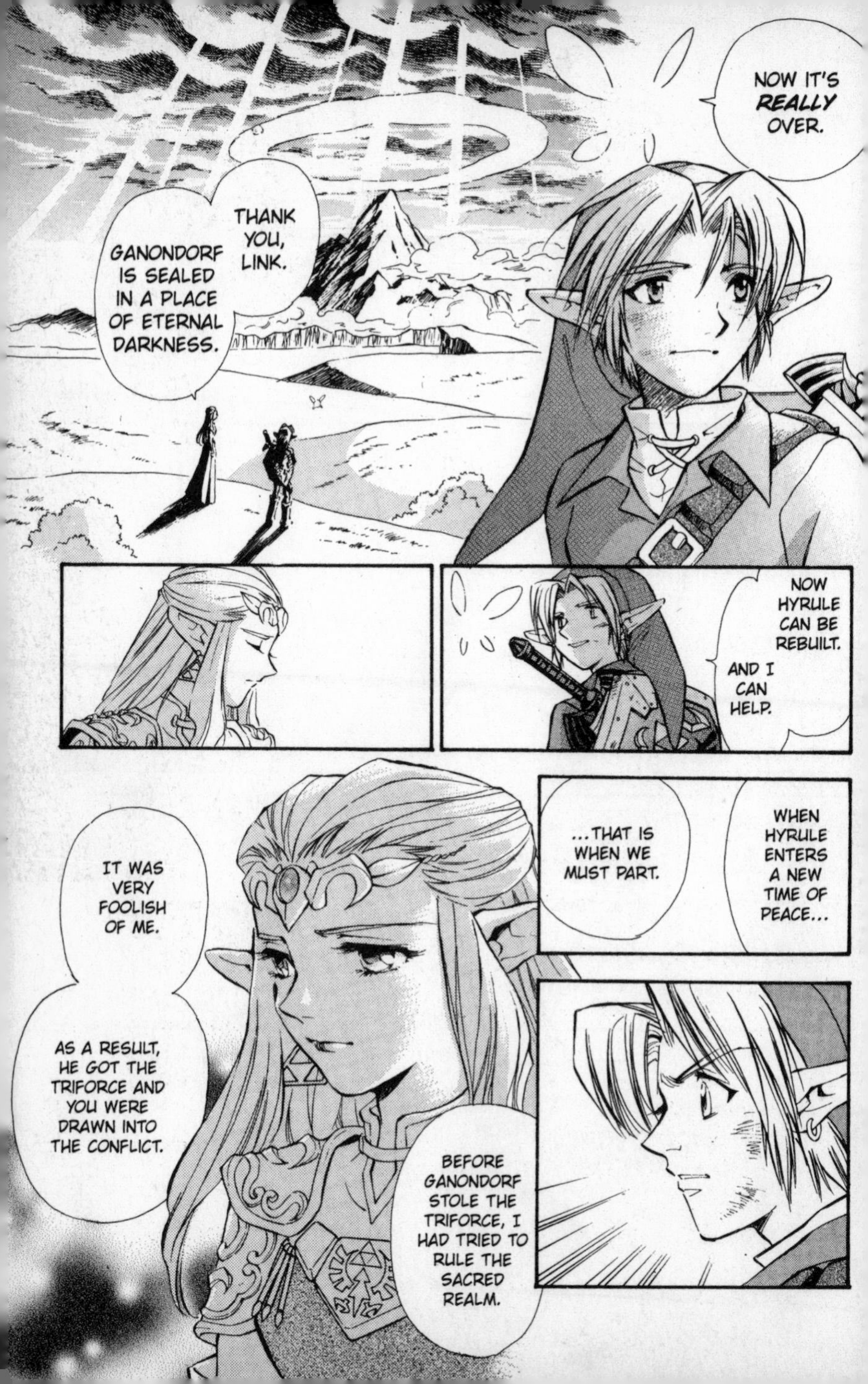
NOW IT'S *REALLY* OVER.
THANK YOU, LINK.
GANONDORF IS SEALED IN A PLACE OF ETERNAL DARKNESS.
NOW HYRULE CAN BE REBUILT.
AND I CAN HELP.
WHEN HYRULE ENTERS A NEW TIME OF PEACE...
...THAT IS WHEN WE MUST PART.
BEFORE GANONDORF STOLE THE TRIFORCE, I HAD TRIED TO RULE THE SACRED REALM.
IT WAS VERY FOOLISH OF ME.
AS A RESULT, HE GOT THE TRIFORCE AND YOU WERE DRAWN INTO THE CONFLICT.

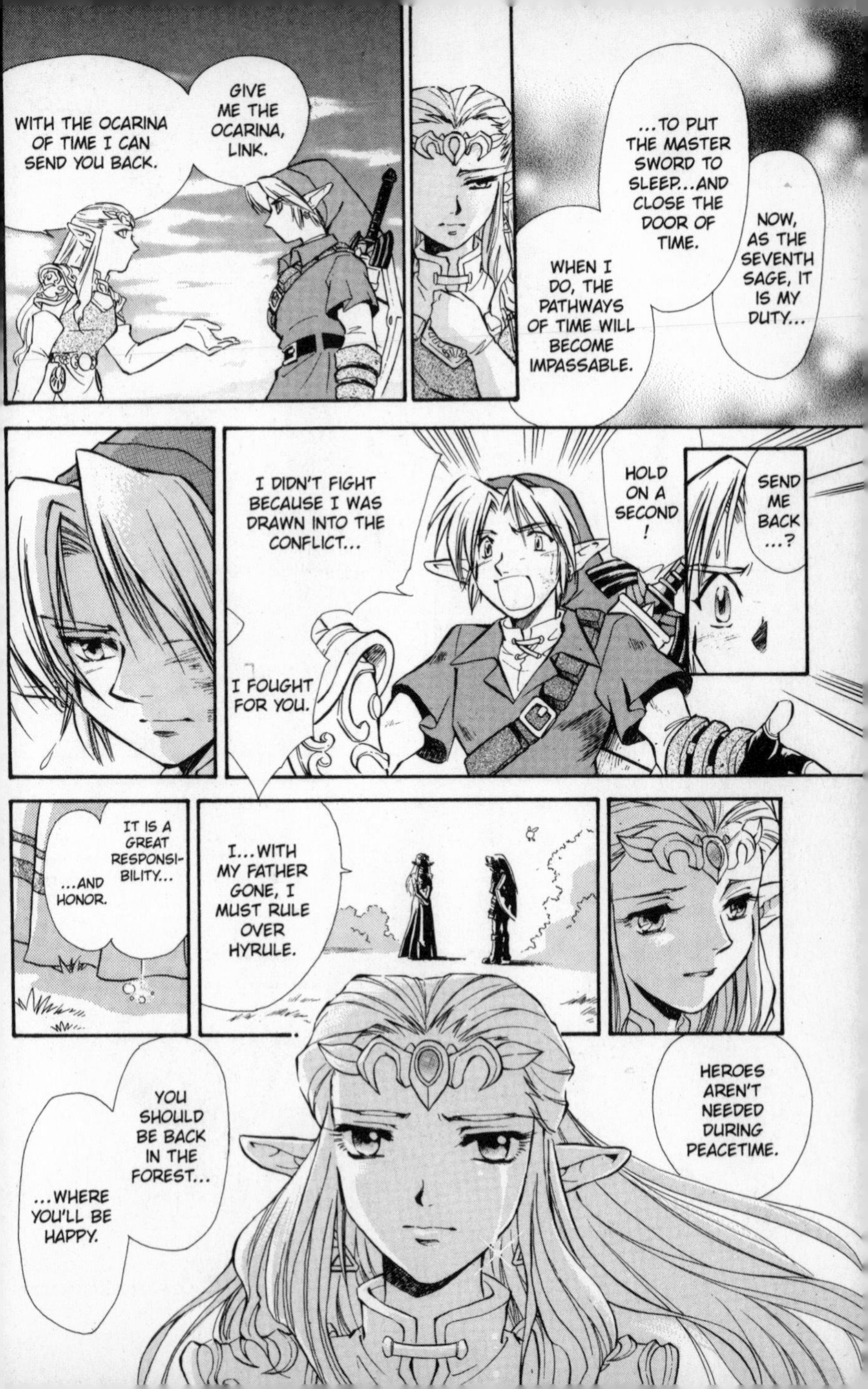
NOW, AS THE SEVENTH SAGE, IT IS MY DUTY...
...TO PUT THE MASTER SWORD TO SLEEP...AND CLOSE THE DOOR OF TIME.
WHEN I DO, THE PATHWAYS OF TIME WILL BECOME IMPASSABLE.
GIVE ME THE OCARINA, LINK.
WITH THE OCARINA OF TIME I CAN SEND YOU BACK.
SEND ME BACK...?
HOLD ON A SECOND!
I DIDN'T FIGHT BECAUSE I WAS DRAWN INTO THE CONFLICT...
I FOUGHT FOR YOU.
I...WITH MY FATHER GONE, I MUST RULE OVER HYRULE.
IT IS A GREAT RESPONSIBILITY...
...AND HONOR.
HEROES AREN'T NEEDED DURING PEACETIME.
YOU SHOULD BE BACK IN THE FOREST...
...WHERE YOU'LL BE HAPPY.

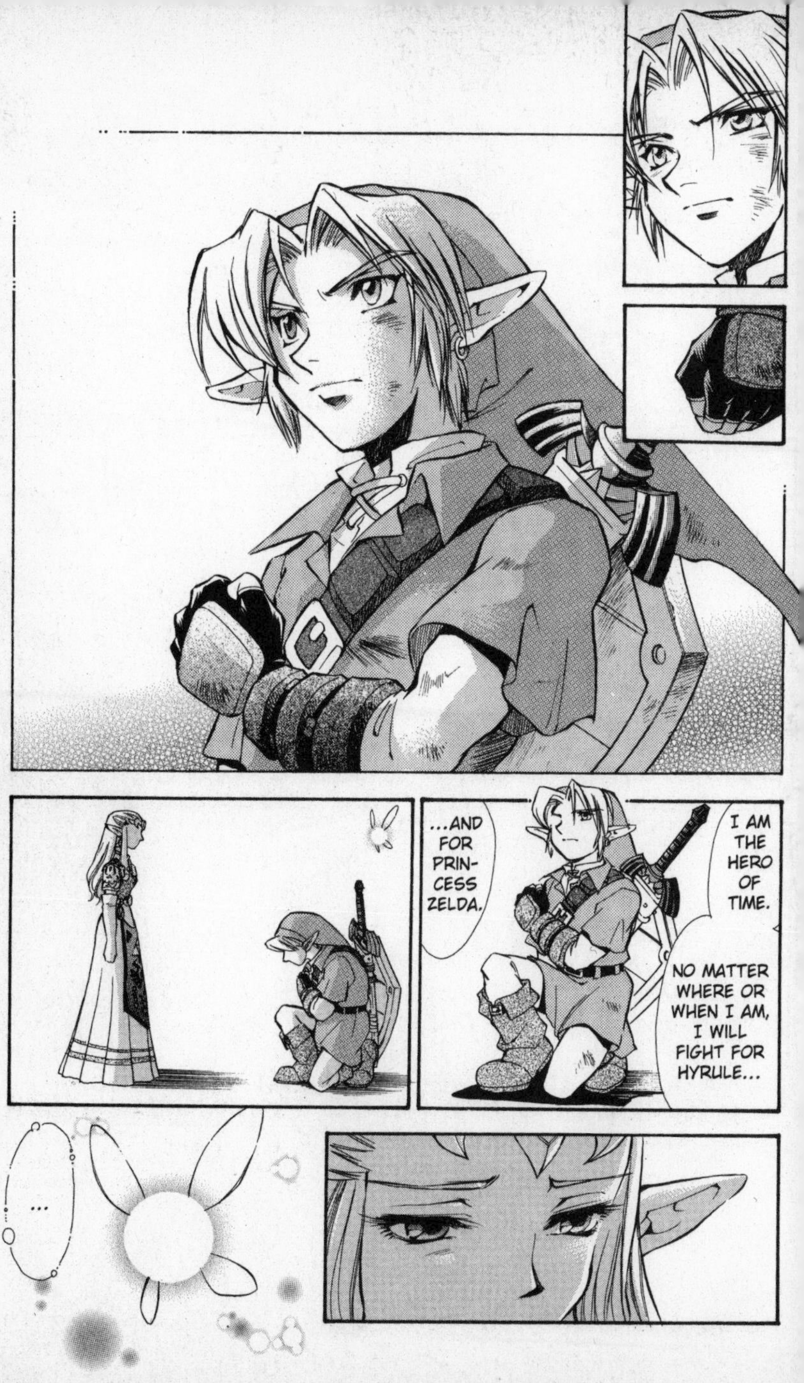
I AM THE HERO OF TIME.
NO MATTER WHERE OR WHEN I AM, I WILL FIGHT FOR HYRULE...
...AND FOR PRINCESS ZELDA.
...

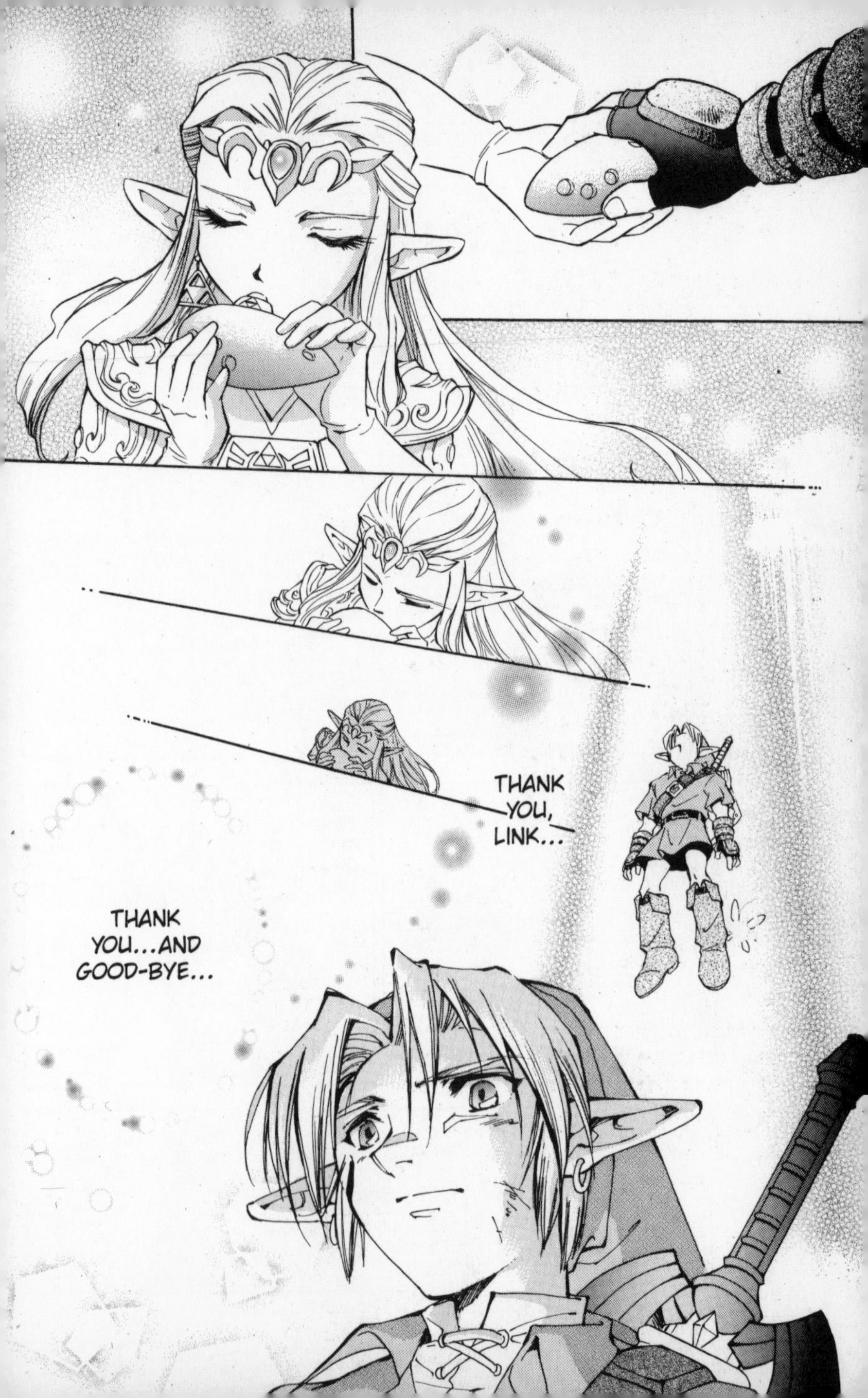
THANK YOU, LINK...
THANK YOU...AND GOOD-BYE...

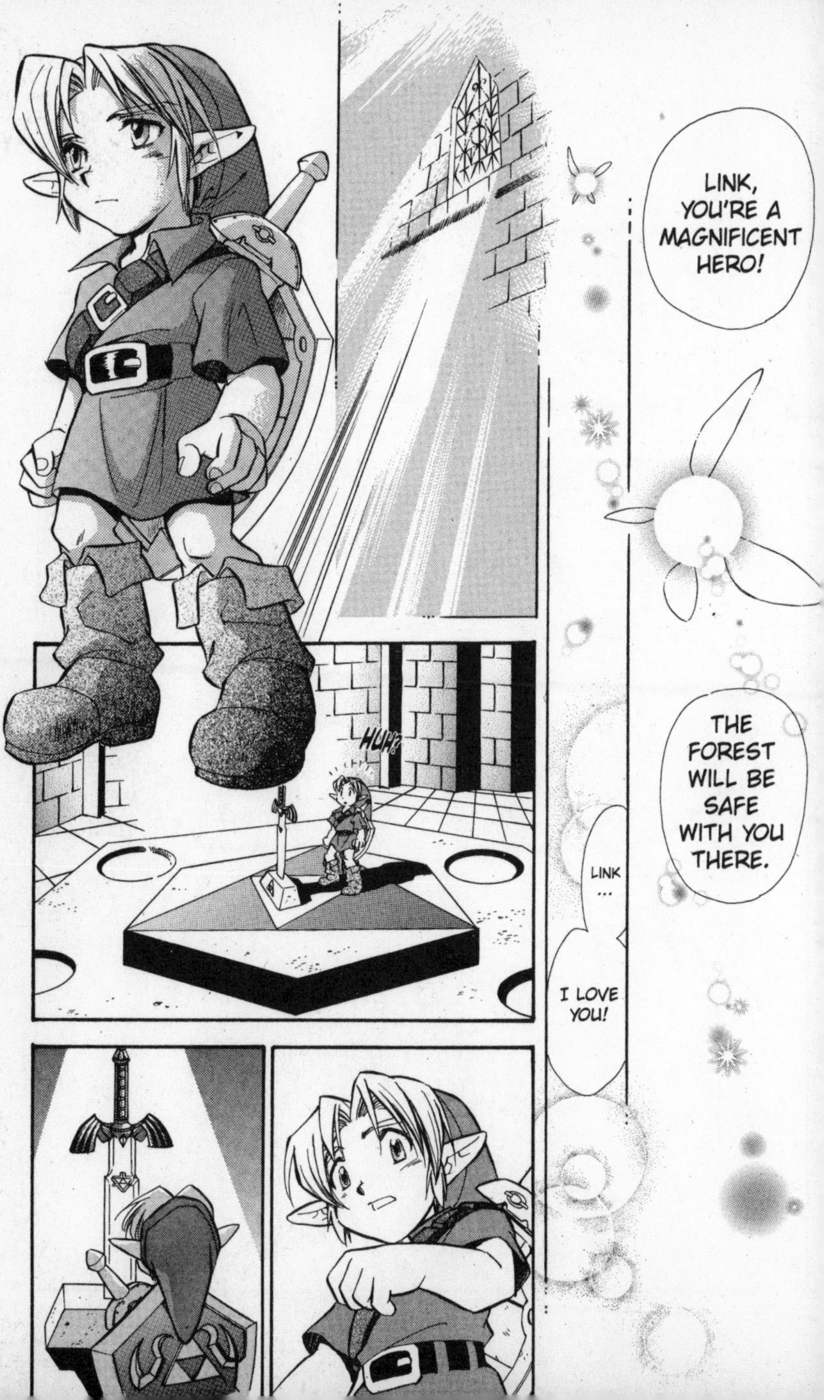
LINK, YOU'RE A MAGNIFICENT HERO!
THE FOREST WILL BE SAFE WITH YOU THERE.
LINK ...
I LOVE YOU!
HUH?

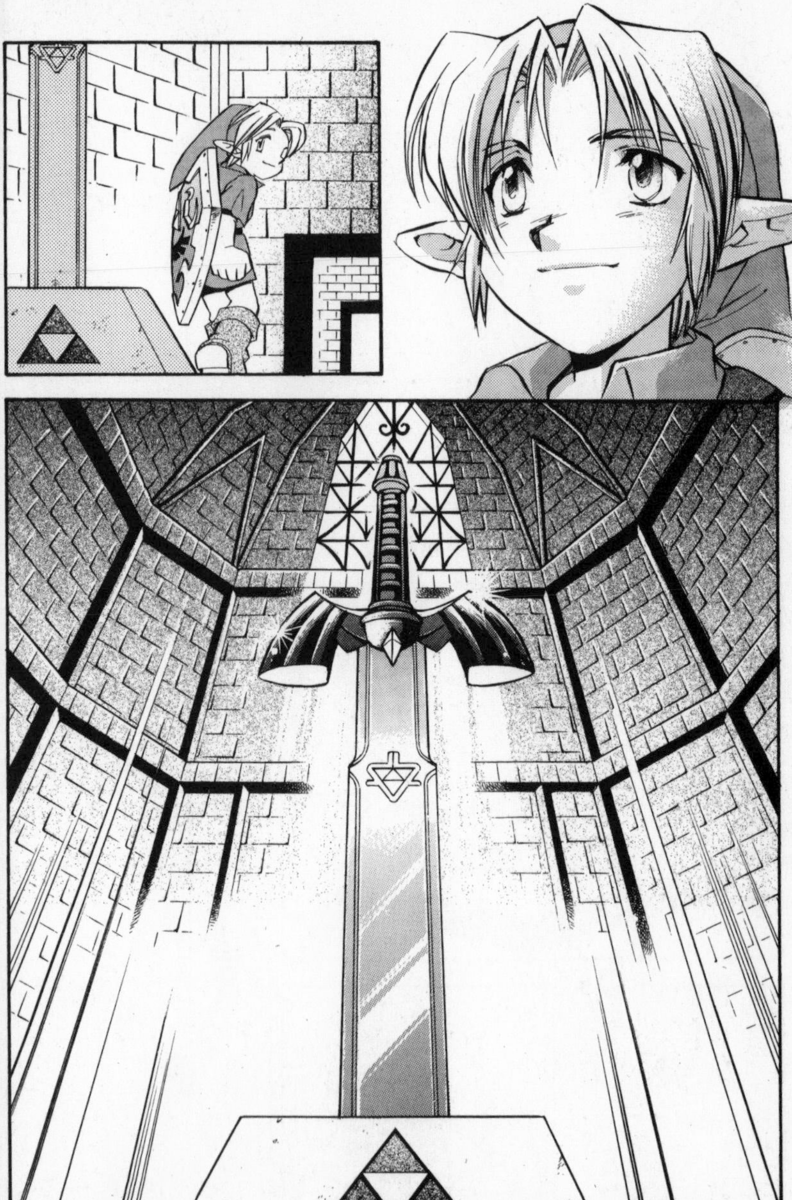

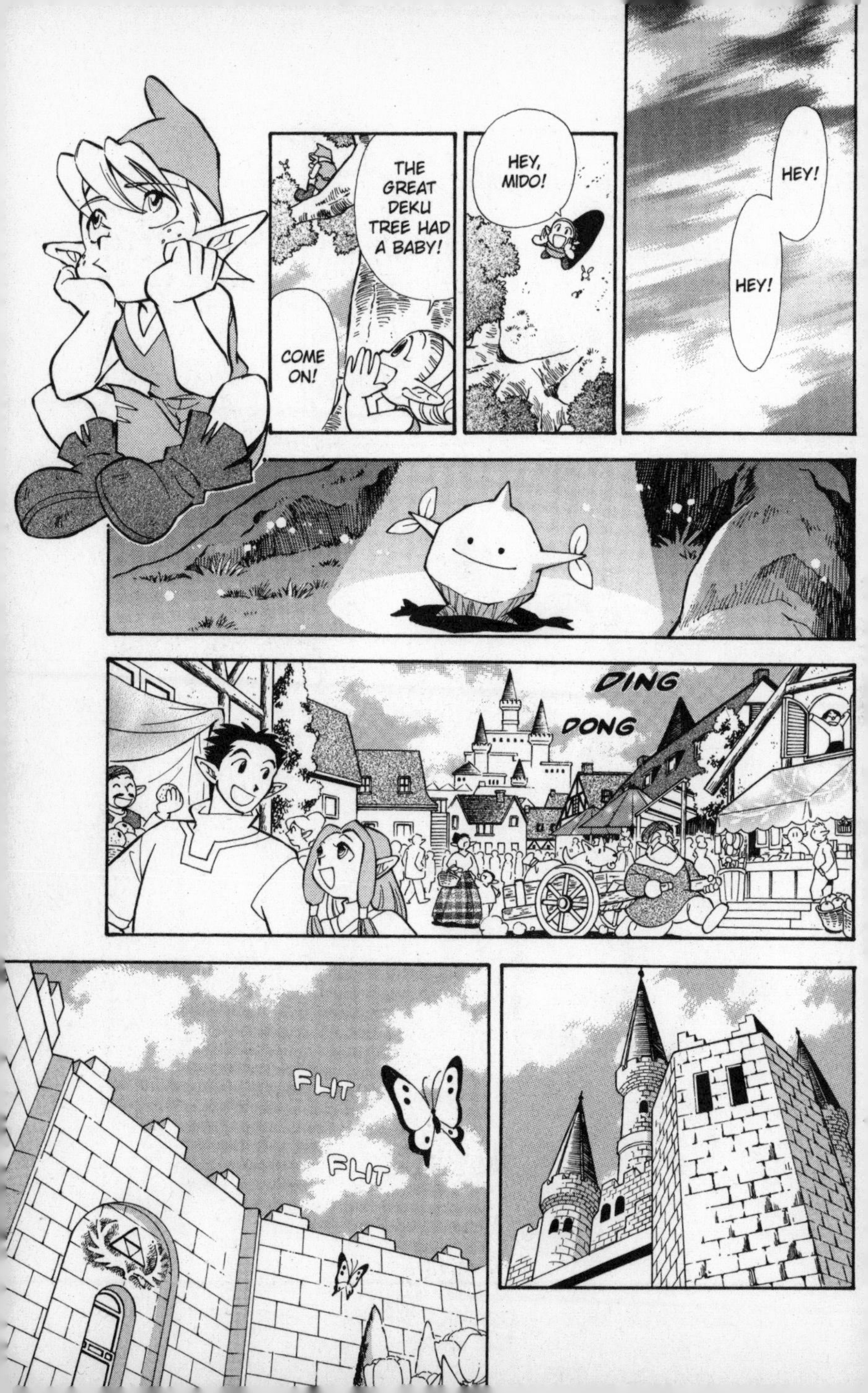
HEY!
HEY!
HEY, MIDO!
THE GREAT DEKU TREE HAD A BABY!
COME ON!
DING
DONG
FLIT
FLIT

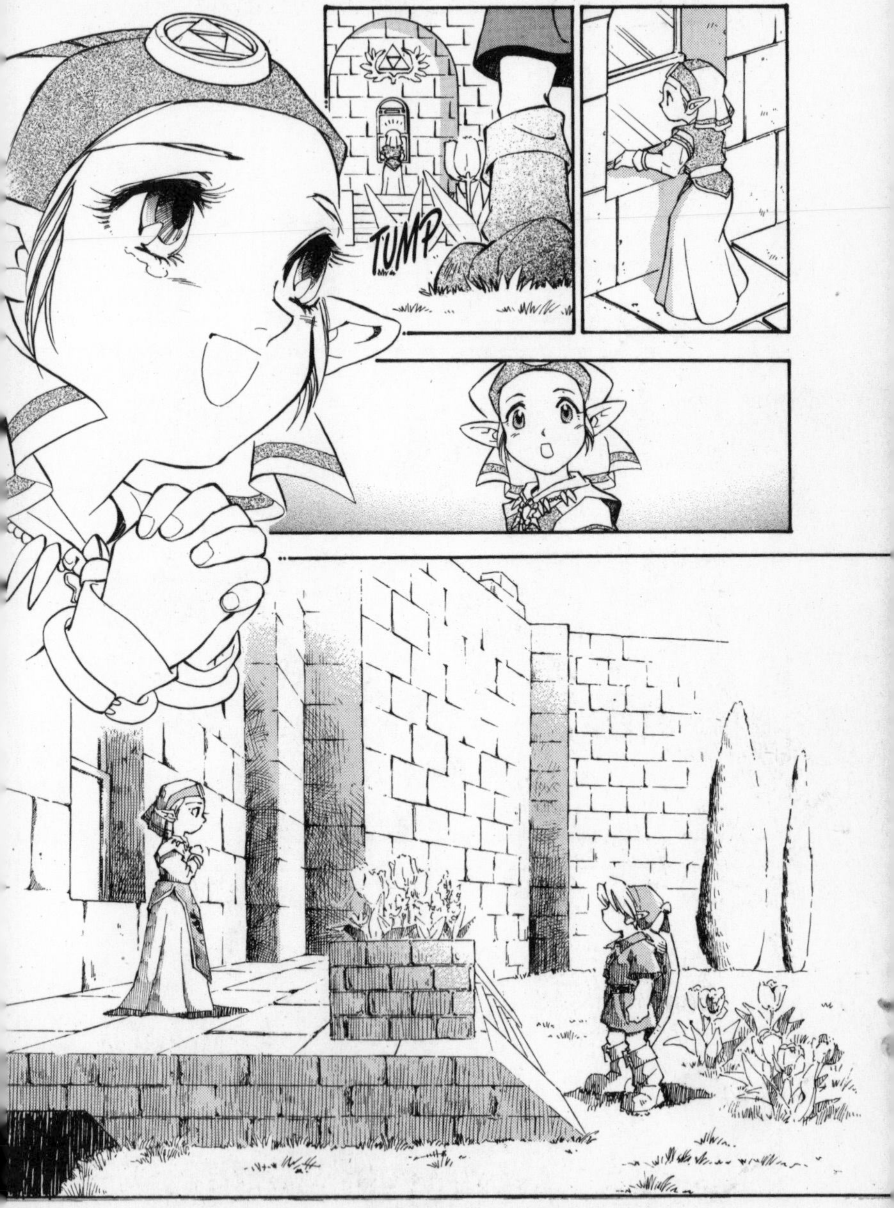
TUMP

THE LEGEND OF ZELDA - OCARINA OF TIME - HERO OF TIME 110
THE END

OCARINA OF TIME ~ BONUS STORY
THE SKULL KID AND THE MASK ~ PART 1

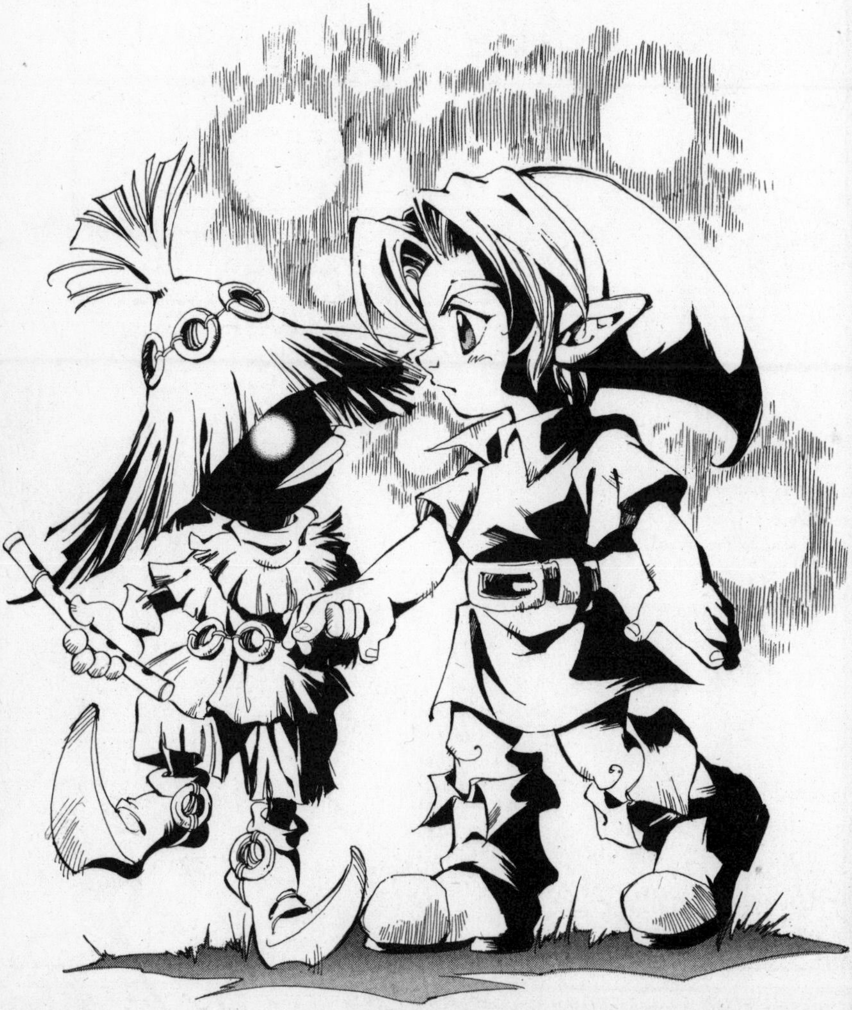

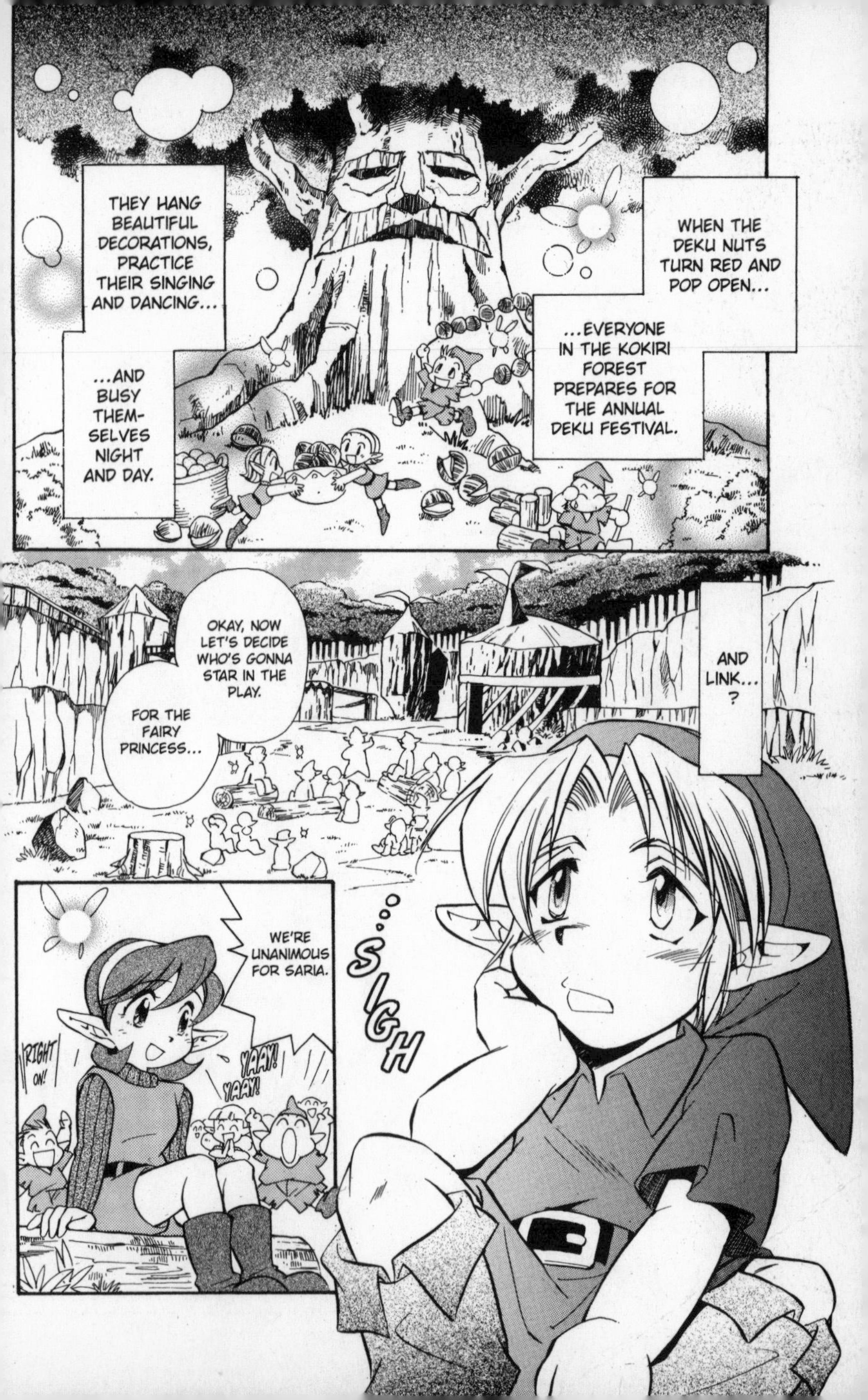
WHEN THE DEKU NUTS TURN RED AND POP OPEN...
...EVERYONE IN THE KOKIRI FOREST PREPARES FOR THE ANNUAL DEKU FESTIVAL.
THEY HANG BEAUTIFUL DECORATIONS, PRACTICE THEIR SINGING AND DANCING...
...AND BUSY THEM-SELVES NIGHT AND DAY.
OKAY, NOW LET'S DECIDE WHO'S GONNA STAR IN THE PLAY.
FOR THE FAIRY PRINCESS...
WE'RE UNANIMOUS FOR SARIA.
YAAY! YAAY!
RIGHT ON!
AND LINK...?
SIGH

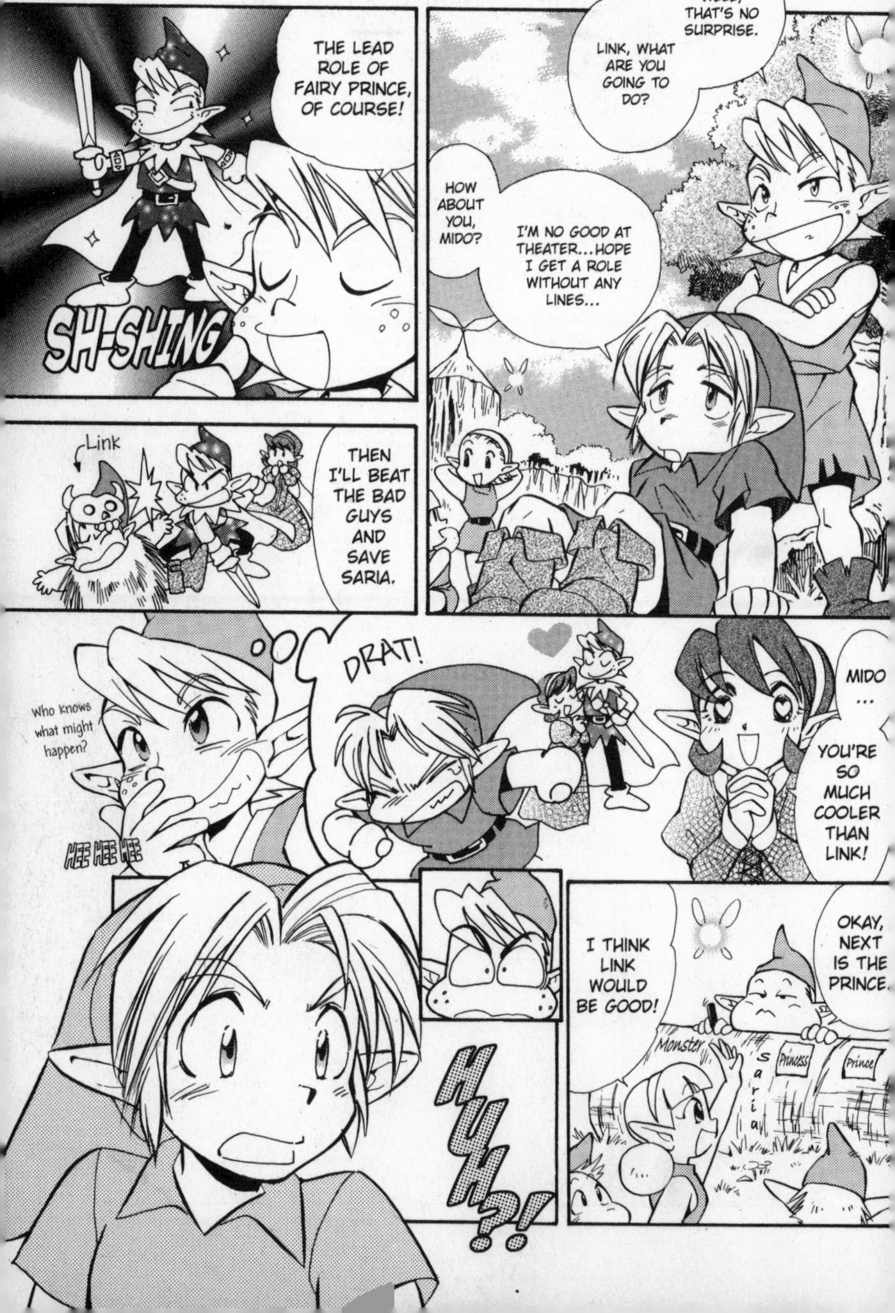
WELL, THAT'S NO SURPRISE.
LINK, WHAT ARE YOU GOING TO DO?
I'M NO GOOD AT THEATER...HOPE I GET A ROLE WITHOUT ANY LINES...
HOW ABOUT YOU, MIDO?
THE LEAD ROLE OF FAIRY PRINCE, OF COURSE!
SH-SHING
THEN I'LL BEAT THE BAD GUYS AND SAVE SARIA.
Link
MIDO...
YOU'RE SO MUCH COOLER THAN LINK!
DRAT!
Who knows what might happen?
HEE HEE HEE
OKAY, NEXT IS THE PRINCE.
I THINK LINK WOULD BE GOOD!
Prince
Princess
Saria
Monster
...
HUH?!

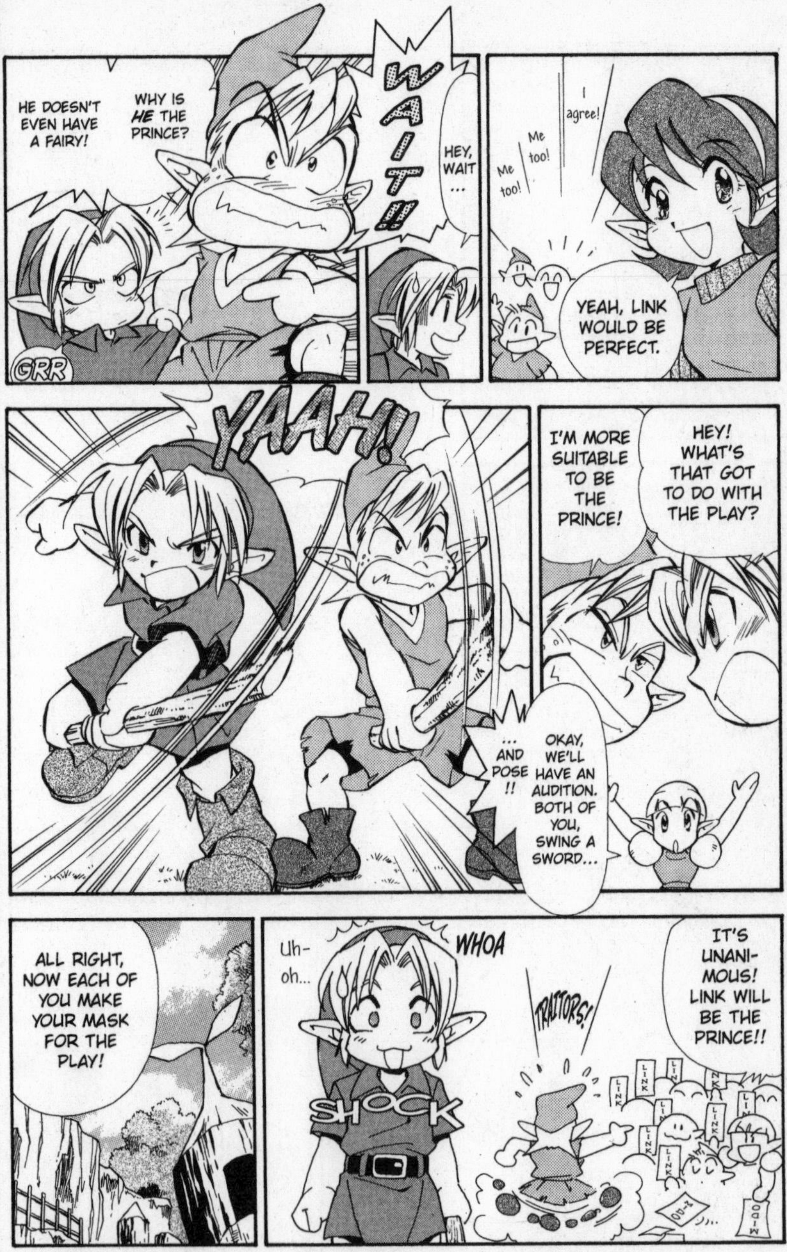
I agree!
Me too!
Me too!
YEAH, LINK WOULD BE PERFECT.
HEY, WAIT...
WAIT!!
WHY IS HE THE PRINCE?
HE DOESN'T EVEN HAVE A FAIRY!
GRR
HEY! WHAT'S THAT GOT TO DO WITH THE PLAY?
I'M MORE SUITABLE TO BE THE PRINCE!
OKAY, WE'LL HAVE AN AUDITION. BOTH OF YOU, SWING A SWORD...
... AND POSE!!
YAAH!
IT'S UNANI-MOUS! LINK WILL BE THE PRINCE!!
TRAITORS!
WHOA
Uh-oh...
SHOCK
ALL RIGHT, NOW EACH OF YOU MAKE YOUR MASK FOR THE PLAY!

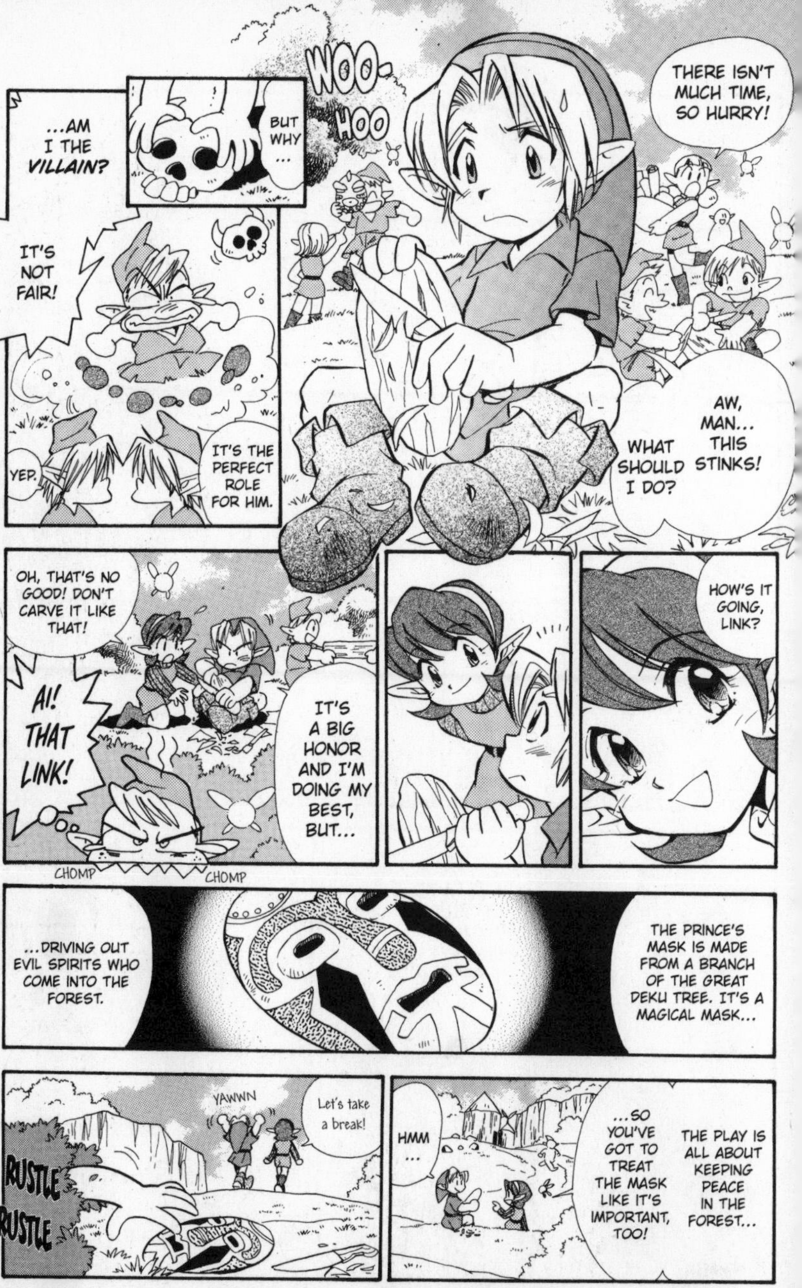
THERE ISN'T MUCH TIME, SO HURRY!
WOO-HOO
AW, MAN... THIS STINKS!
WHAT SHOULD I DO?
BUT WHY ...
...AM I THE *VILLAIN?*
IT'S NOT FAIR!
IT'S THE PERFECT ROLE FOR HIM.
YEP.
HOW'S IT GOING, LINK?
IT'S A BIG HONOR AND I'M DOING MY BEST, BUT...
OH, THAT'S NO GOOD! DON'T CARVE IT LIKE THAT!
AI! THAT LINK!
CHOMP
CHOMP
THE PRINCE'S MASK IS MADE FROM A BRANCH OF THE GREAT DEKU TREE. IT'S A MAGICAL MASK...
...DRIVING OUT EVIL SPIRITS WHO COME INTO THE FOREST.
THE PLAY IS ALL ABOUT KEEPING PEACE IN THE FOREST...
...SO YOU'VE GOT TO TREAT THE MASK LIKE IT'S IMPORTANT, TOO!
HMM ...
Let's take a break!
YAWWN
RUSTLE
RUSTLE

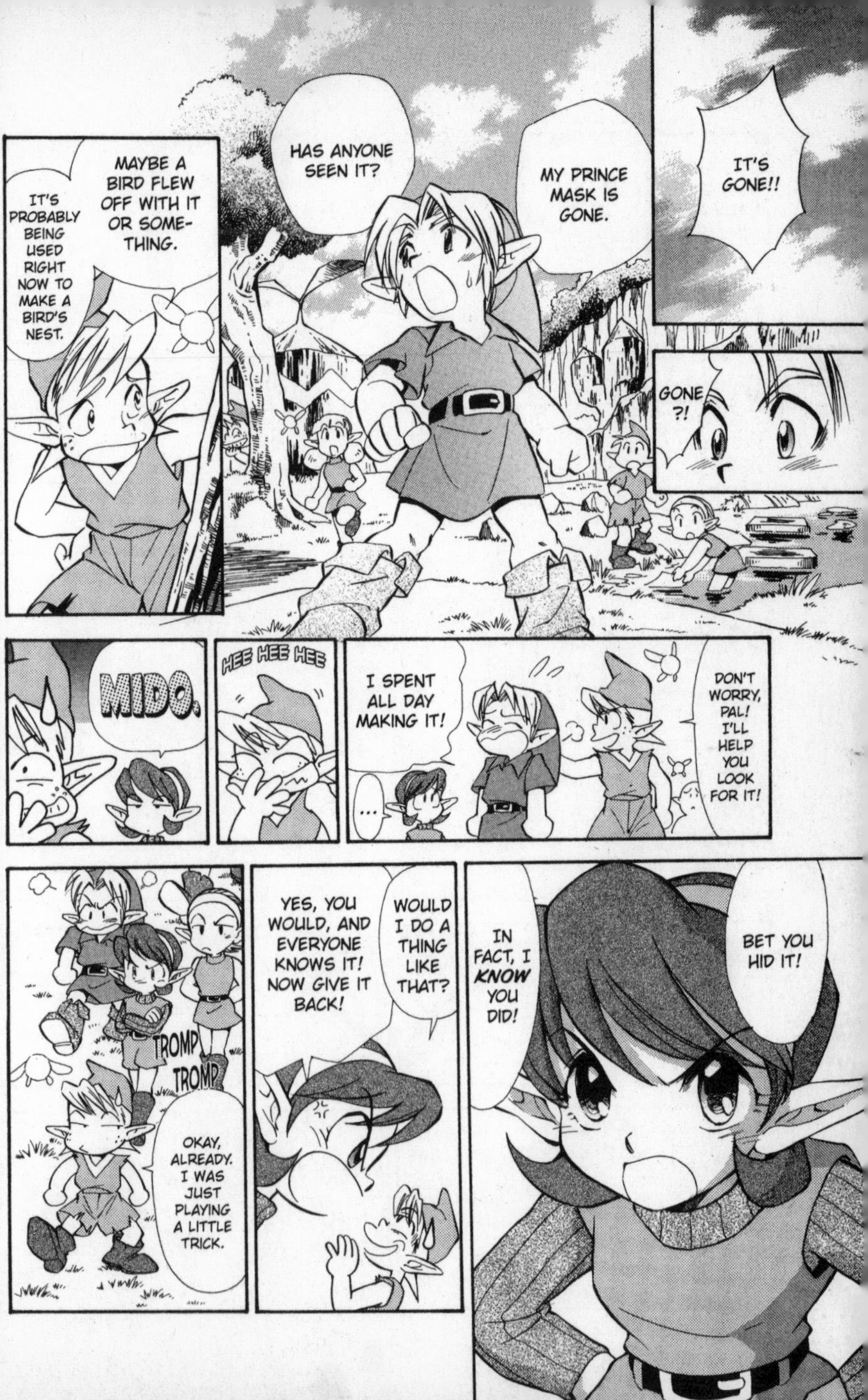
IT'S GONE!!
GONE ?!
MY PRINCE MASK IS GONE.
HAS ANYONE SEEN IT?
MAYBE A BIRD FLEW OFF WITH IT OR SOME-THING.
IT'S PROBABLY BEING USED RIGHT NOW TO MAKE A BIRD'S NEST.
DON'T WORRY, PAL! I'LL HELP YOU LOOK FOR IT!
I SPENT ALL DAY MAKING IT!
...
HEE HEE HEE
MIDO.
BET YOU HID IT!
IN FACT, I *KNOW* YOU DID!
WOULD I DO A THING LIKE THAT?
YES, YOU WOULD, AND EVERYONE KNOWS IT! NOW GIVE IT BACK!
TROMP TROMP
OKAY, ALREADY. I WAS JUST PLAYING A LITTLE TRICK.

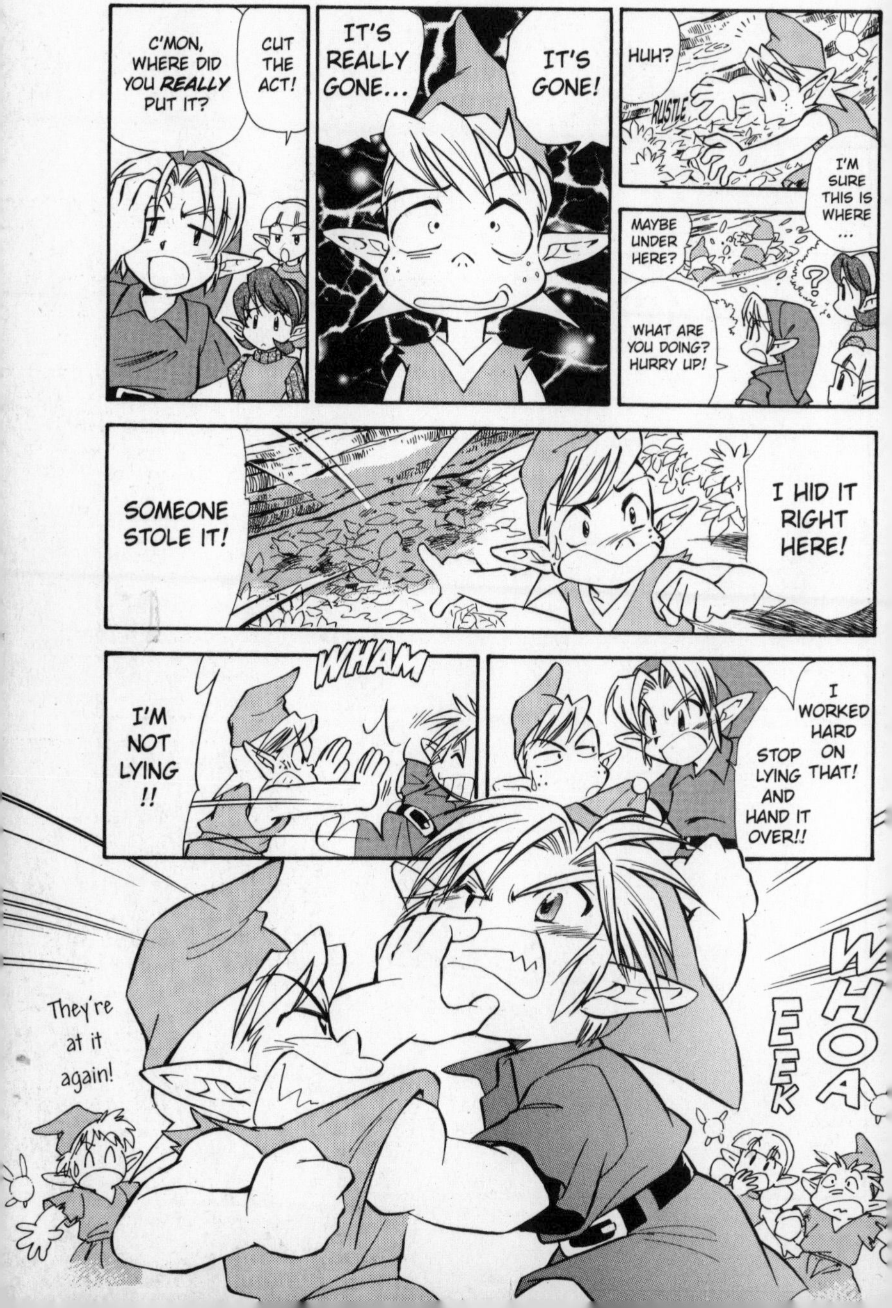
HUH?
RUSTLE
I'M SURE THIS IS WHERE ...
MAYBE UNDER HERE?
WHAT ARE YOU DOING? HURRY UP!
IT'S GONE!
IT'S REALLY GONE...
CUT THE ACT!
C'MON, WHERE DID YOU REALLY PUT IT?
I HID IT RIGHT HERE!
SOMEONE STOLE IT!
I WORKED HARD ON THAT!
STOP LYING AND HAND IT OVER!!
WHAM
I'M NOT LYING!!
WHOA
EEEK
They're at it again!

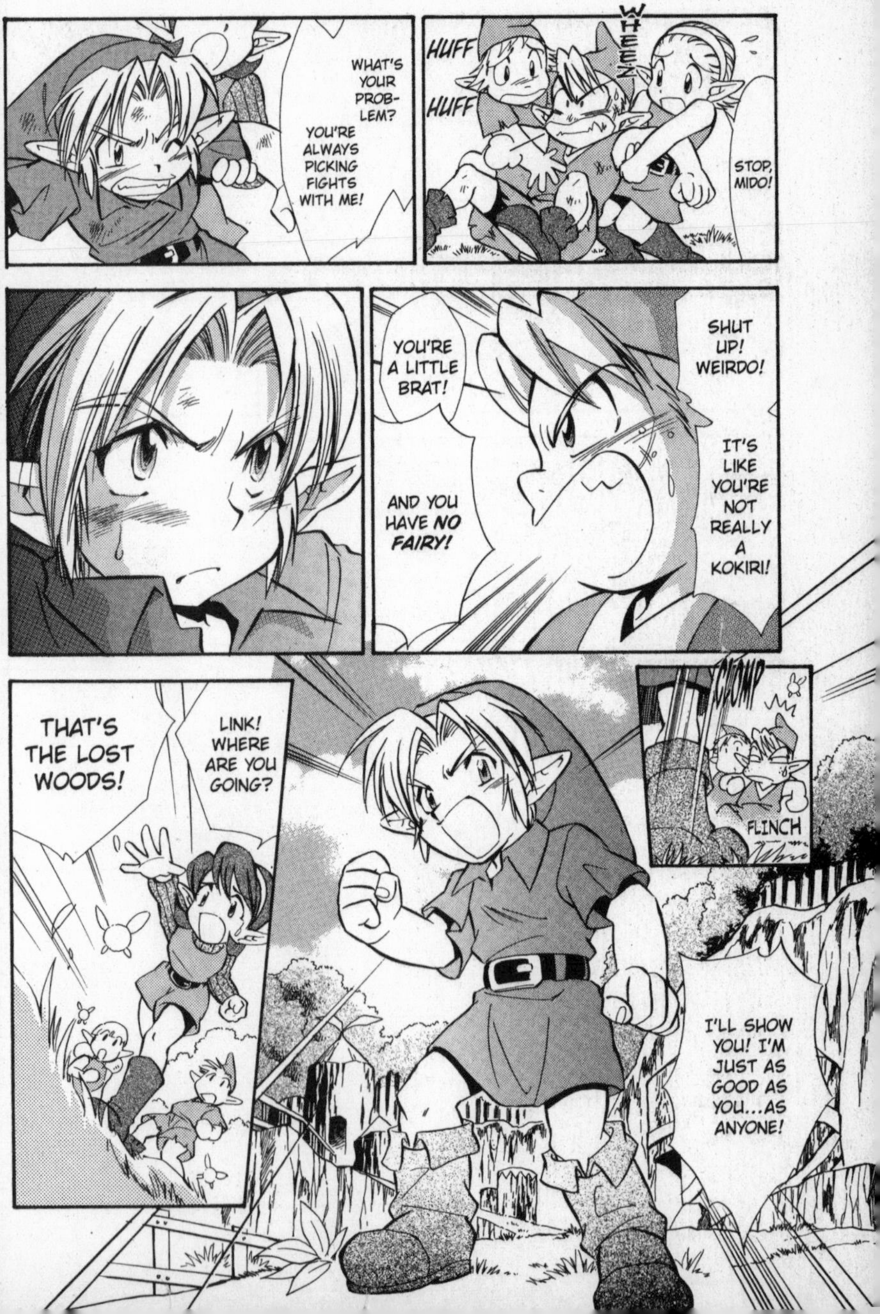
WHEEZ
HUFF
HUFF
STOP, MIDO!
WHAT'S YOUR PROBLEM?
YOU'RE ALWAYS PICKING FIGHTS WITH ME!
SHUT UP! WEIRDO!
IT'S LIKE YOU'RE NOT REALLY A KOKIRI!
YOU'RE A LITTLE BRAT!
AND YOU HAVE *NO FAIRY!*
CHOMP
FLINCH
I'LL SHOW YOU! I'M JUST AS GOOD AS YOU...AS ANYONE!
LINK! WHERE ARE YOU GOING?
THAT'S THE LOST WOODS!

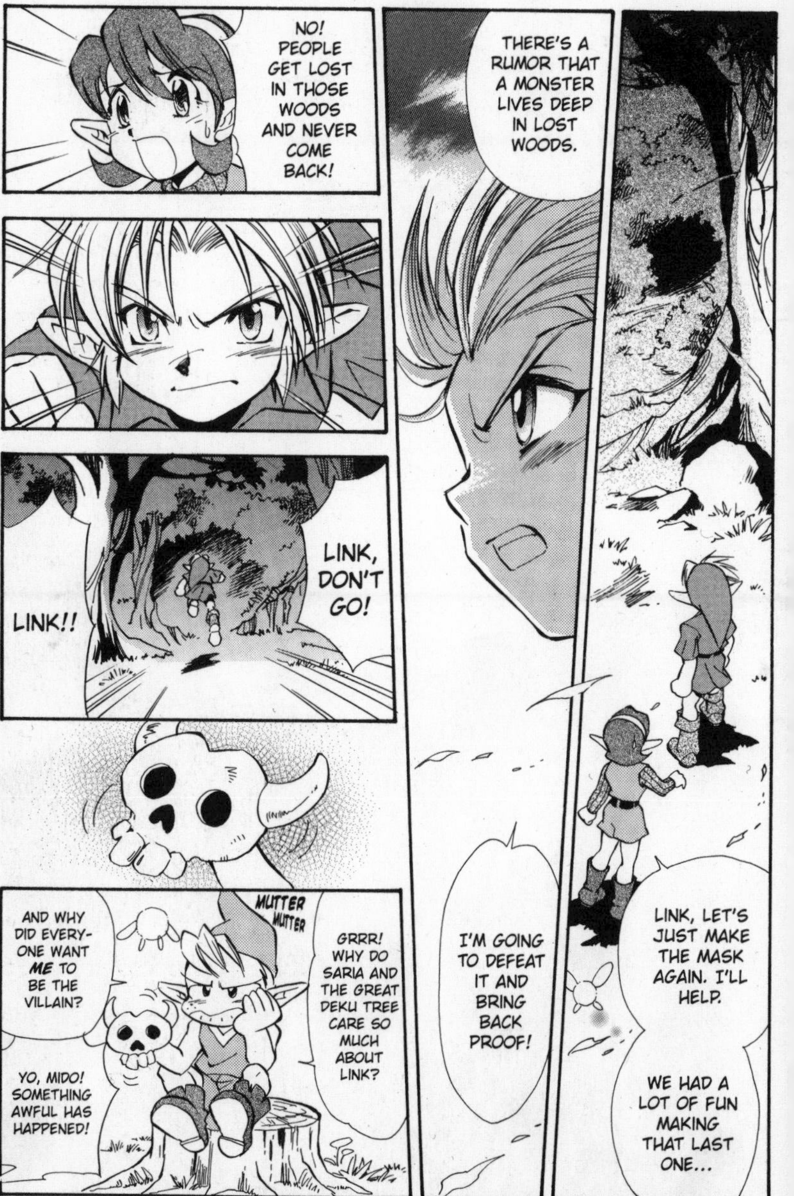
LINK, LET'S JUST MAKE THE MASK AGAIN. I'LL HELP.
WE HAD A LOT OF FUN MAKING THAT LAST ONE...
THERE'S A RUMOR THAT A MONSTER LIVES DEEP IN LOST WOODS.
I'M GOING TO DEFEAT IT AND BRING BACK PROOF!
NO! PEOPLE GET LOST IN THOSE WOODS AND NEVER COME BACK!
LINK, DON'T GO!
LINK!!
MUTTER MUTTER
GRRR! WHY DO SARIA AND THE GREAT DEKU TREE CARE SO MUCH ABOUT LINK?
AND WHY DID EVERY-ONE WANT *ME* TO BE THE VILLAIN?
YO, MIDO! SOMETHING AWFUL HAS HAPPENED!

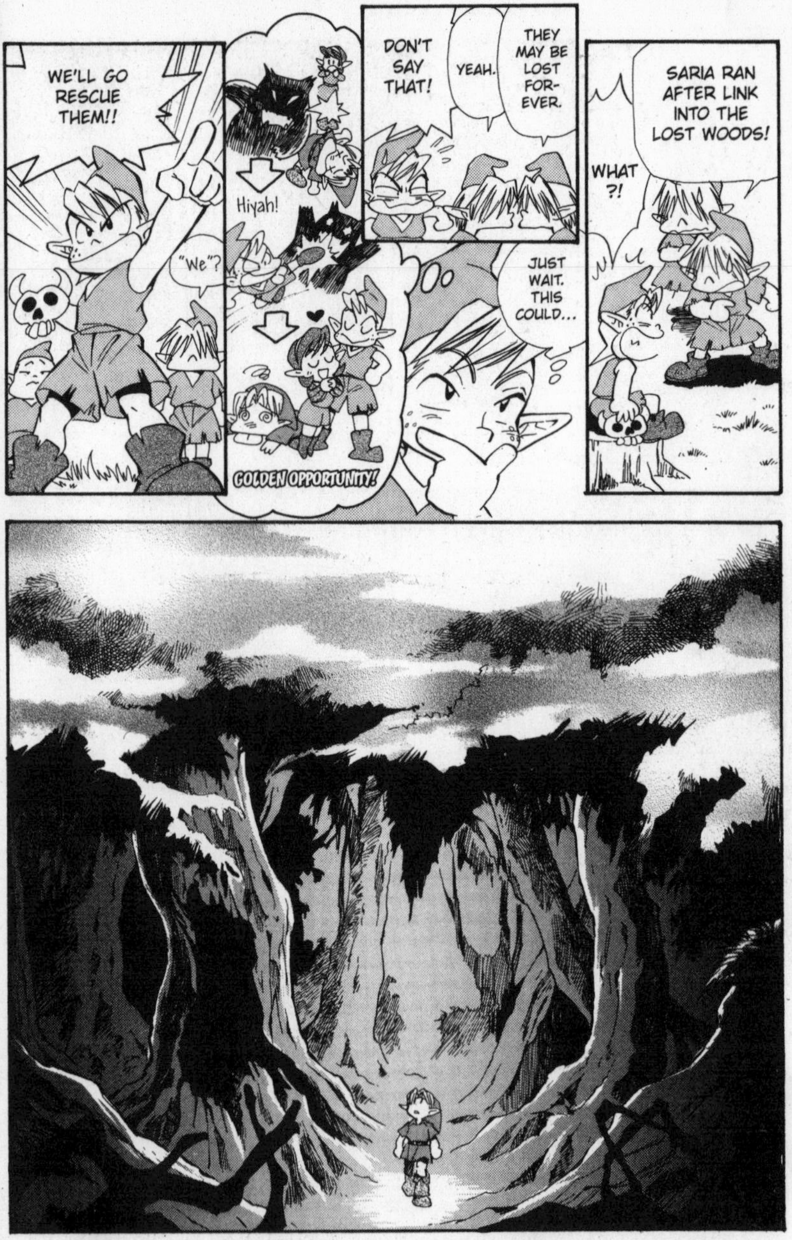
SARIA RAN AFTER LINK INTO THE LOST WOODS!
WHAT ?!
THEY MAY BE LOST FOR- EVER.
YEAH.
DON'T SAY THAT!
JUST WAIT. THIS COULD...
Hiyah!
GOLDEN OPPORTUNITY!
WE'LL GO RESCUE THEM!!
"We"?

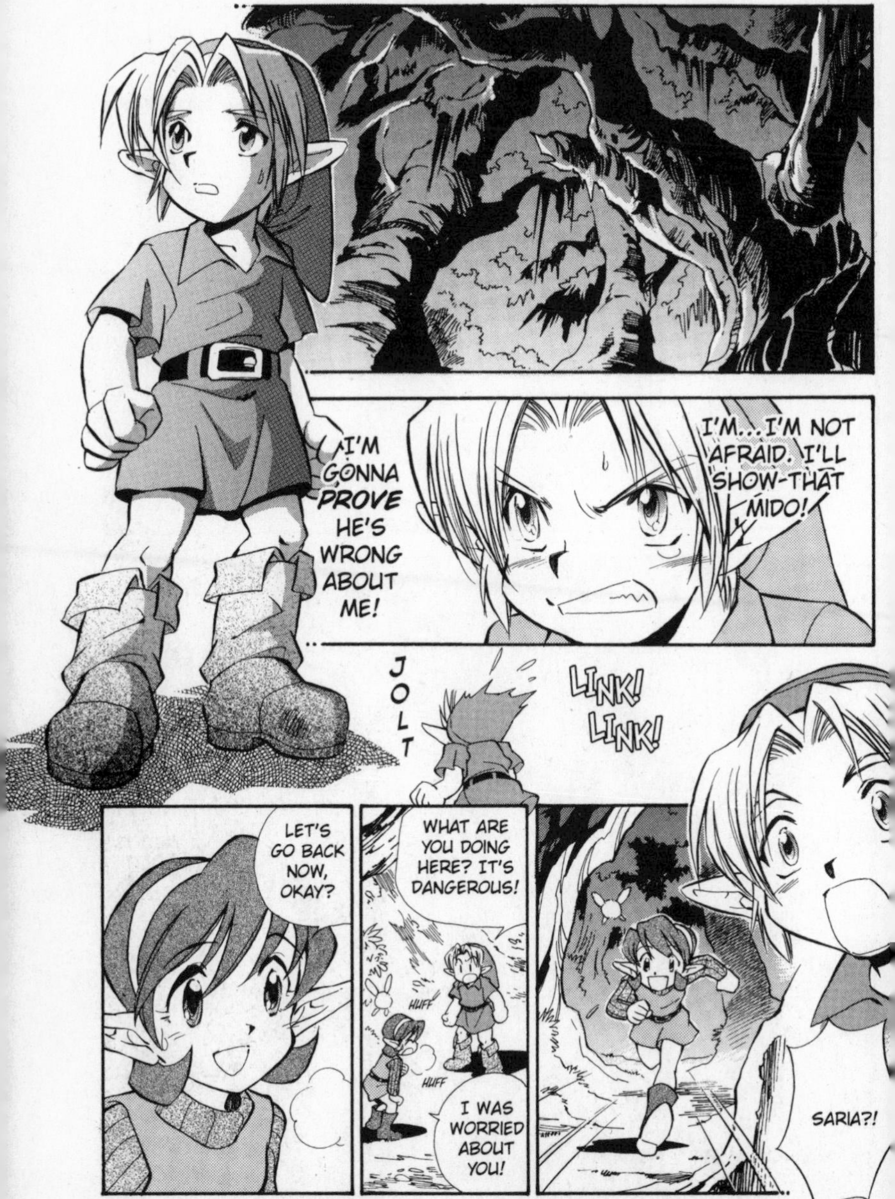

I'M... I'M NOT AFRAID. I'LL SHOW THAT MIDO!
I'M GONNA PROVE HE'S WRONG ABOUT ME!
LINK! LINK!
JOLT
SARIA?!
WHAT ARE YOU DOING HERE? IT'S DANGEROUS!
HUFF
HUFF
I WAS WORRIED ABOUT YOU!
LET'S GO BACK NOW, OKAY?

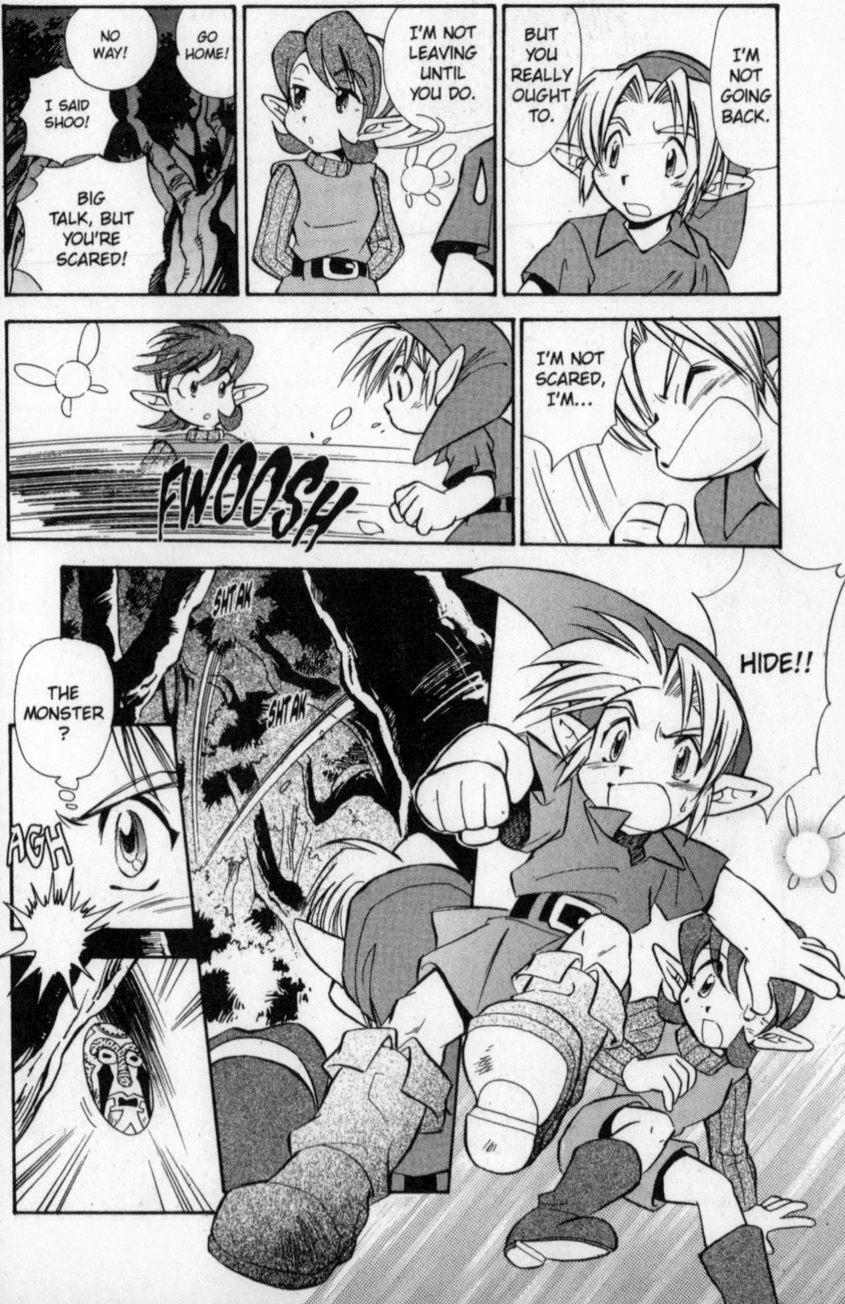
I'M NOT GOING BACK.
BUT YOU REALLY OUGHT TO.
I'M NOT LEAVING UNTIL YOU DO.
GO HOME!
NO WAY!
I SAID SHOO!
BIG TALK, BUT YOU'RE SCARED!
I'M NOT SCARED, I'M...
FWOOSH
HIDE!!
SHTAK
SHTAK
THE MONSTER?
AGH

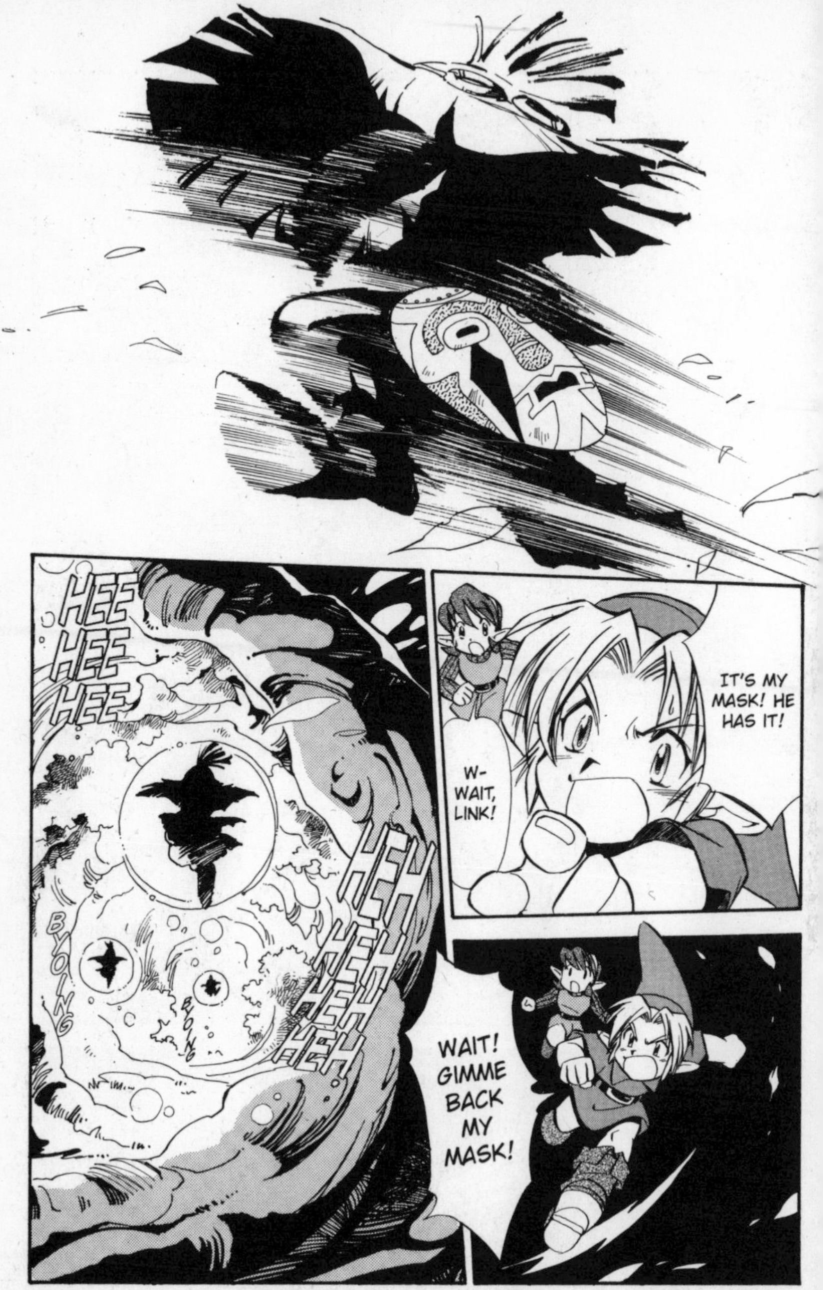

IT'S MY MASK! HE HAS IT!
W-WAIT, LINK!
WAIT! GIMME BACK MY MASK!
HEE HEE HEE
HEH HEH HEH HEH
BYOING
BYOING

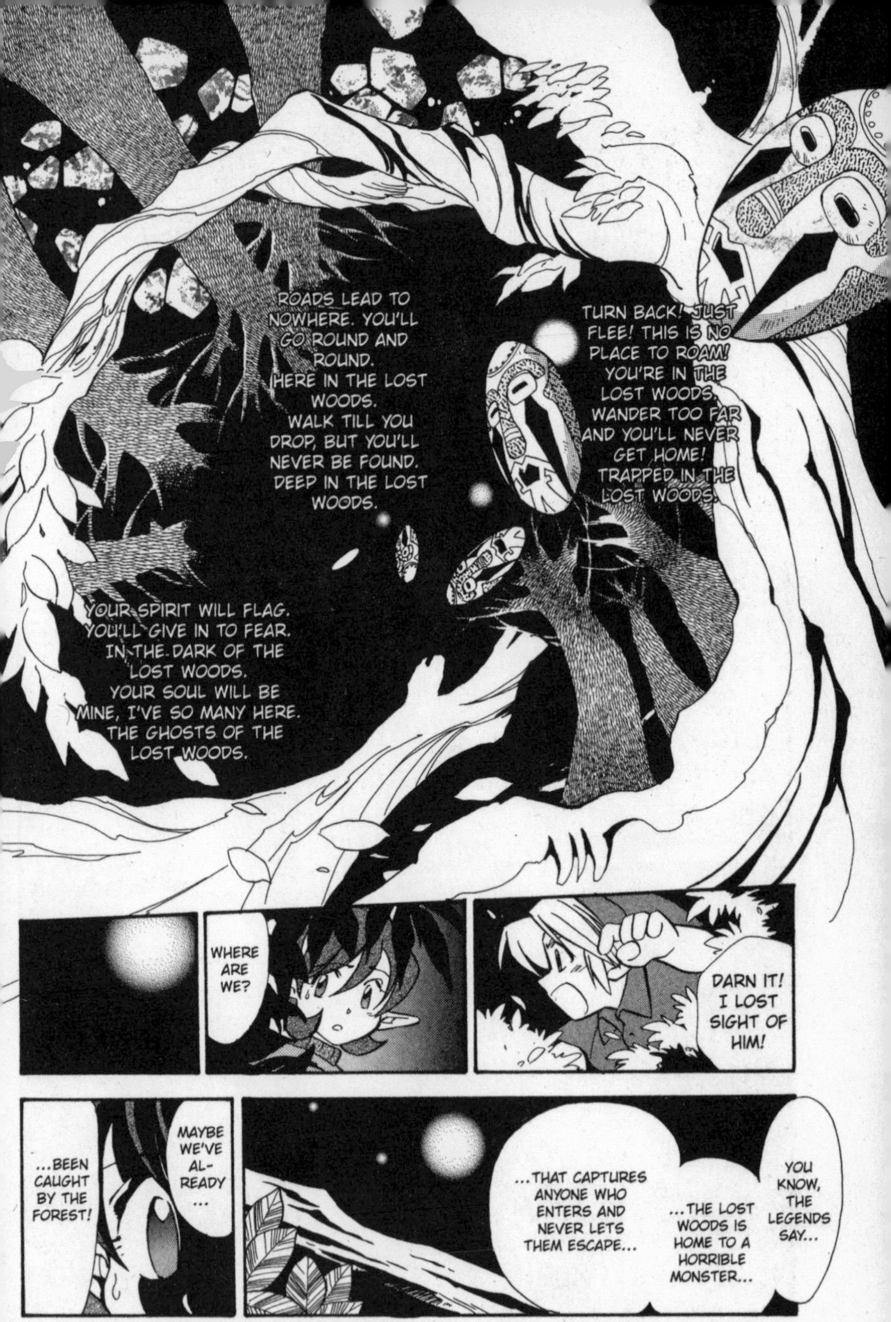
TURN BACK! JUST FLEE! THIS IS NO PLACE TO ROAM! YOU'RE IN THE LOST WOODS. WANDER TOO FAR AND YOU'LL NEVER GET HOME! TRAPPED IN THE LOST WOODS.
ROADS LEAD TO NOWHERE. YOU'LL GO ROUND AND ROUND. HERE IN THE LOST WOODS. WALK TILL YOU DROP, BUT YOU'LL NEVER BE FOUND. DEEP IN THE LOST WOODS.
YOUR SPIRIT WILL FLAG. YOU'LL GIVE IN TO FEAR. IN THE DARK OF THE LOST WOODS. YOUR SOUL WILL BE MINE, I'VE SO MANY HERE. THE GHOSTS OF THE LOST WOODS.
DARN IT! I LOST SIGHT OF HIM!
WHERE ARE WE?
YOU KNOW, THE LEGENDS SAY...
...THE LOST WOODS IS HOME TO A HORRIBLE MONSTER...
...THAT CAPTURES ANYONE WHO ENTERS AND NEVER LETS THEM ESCAPE...
MAYBE WE'VE AL-READY ...
...BEEN CAUGHT BY THE FOREST!

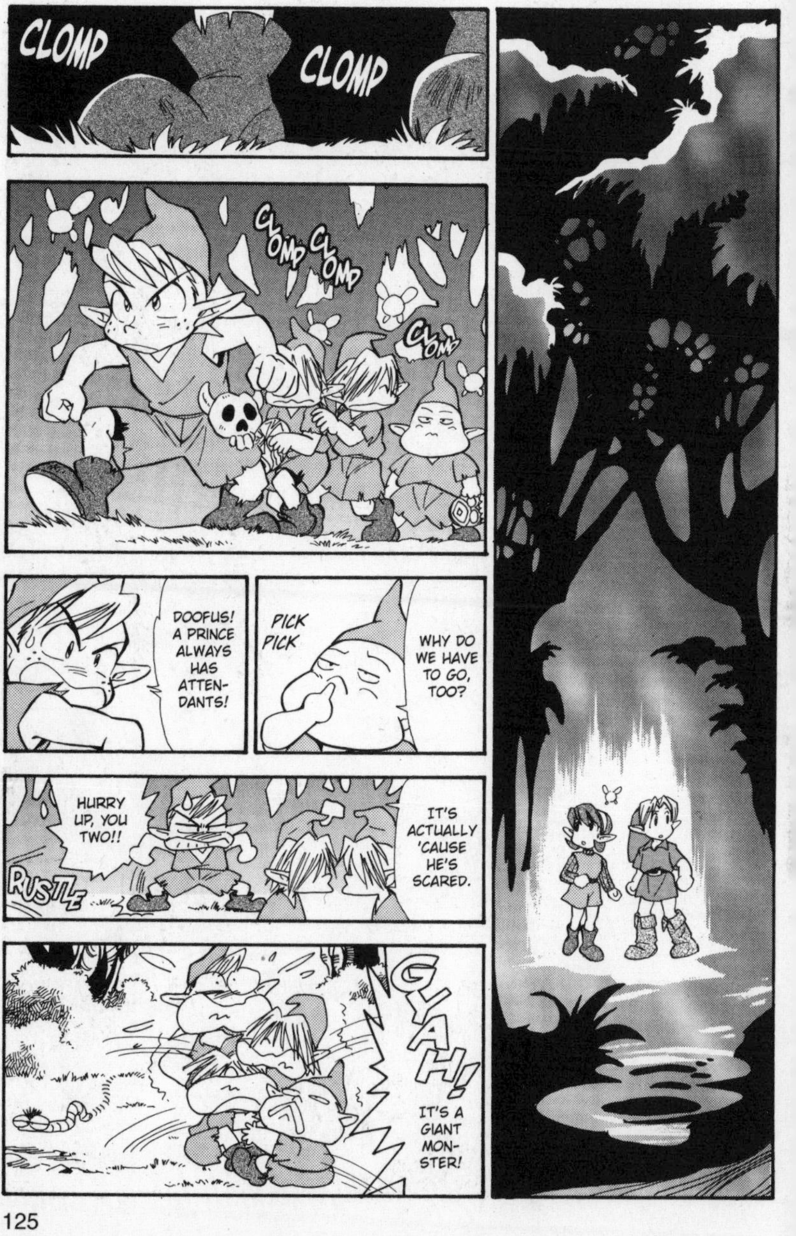
CLOMP
CLOMP
CLOMP CLOMP
CLOMP
PICK PICK
WHY DO WE HAVE TO GO, TOO?
DOOFUS! A PRINCE ALWAYS HAS ATTEN-DANTS!
IT'S ACTUALLY 'CAUSE HE'S SCARED.
HURRY UP, YOU TWO!!
RUSTLE
GYAH!
IT'S A GIANT MON-STER!

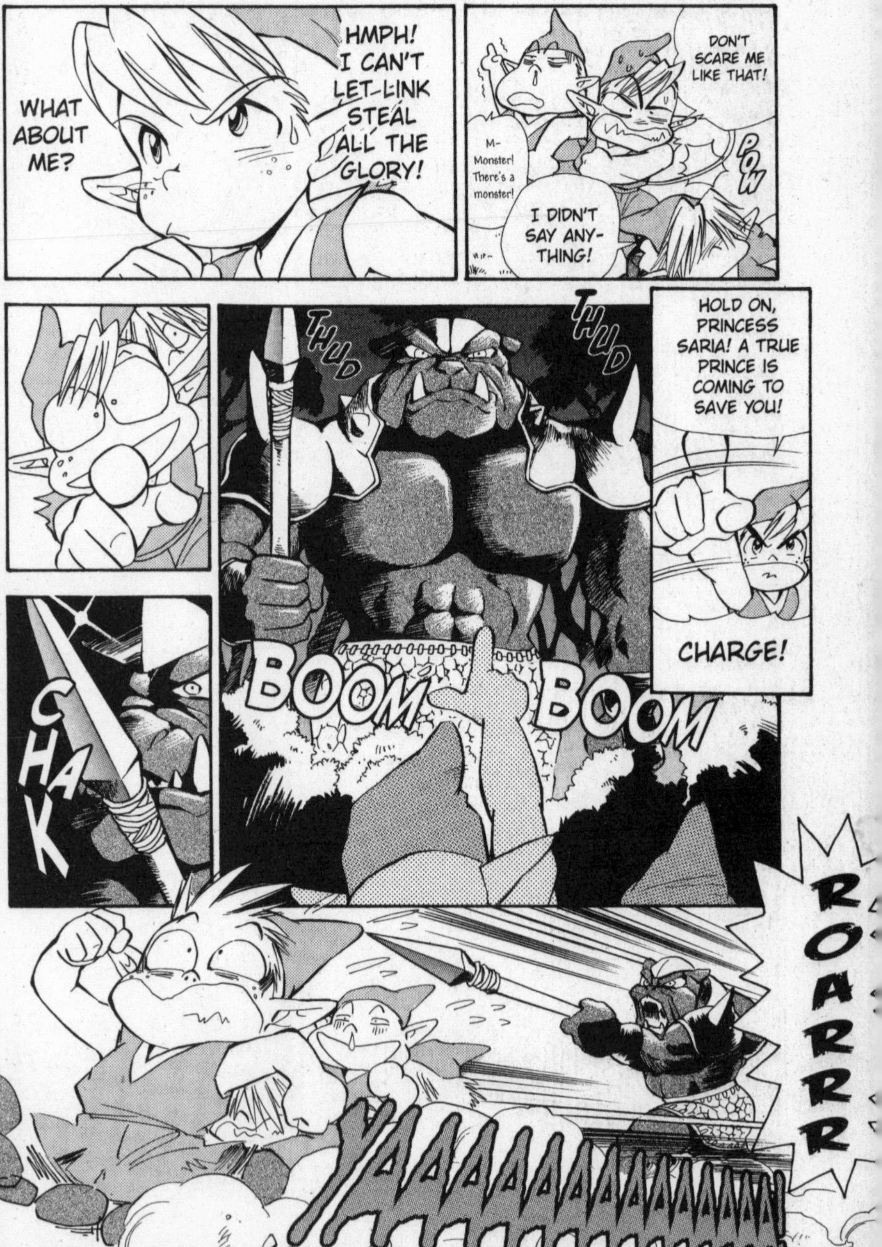
DON'T SCARE ME LIKE THAT!
POW
M- Monster! There's a monster!
I DIDN'T SAY ANY-THING!
HMPH! I CAN'T LET LINK STEAL ALL THE GLORY!
WHAT ABOUT ME?
HOLD ON, PRINCESS SARIA! A TRUE PRINCE IS COMING TO SAVE YOU!
CHARGE!
THUD
THUD
BOOM
BOOM
CHAK
ROARRR
YAAAAAAAAAAAAAA!

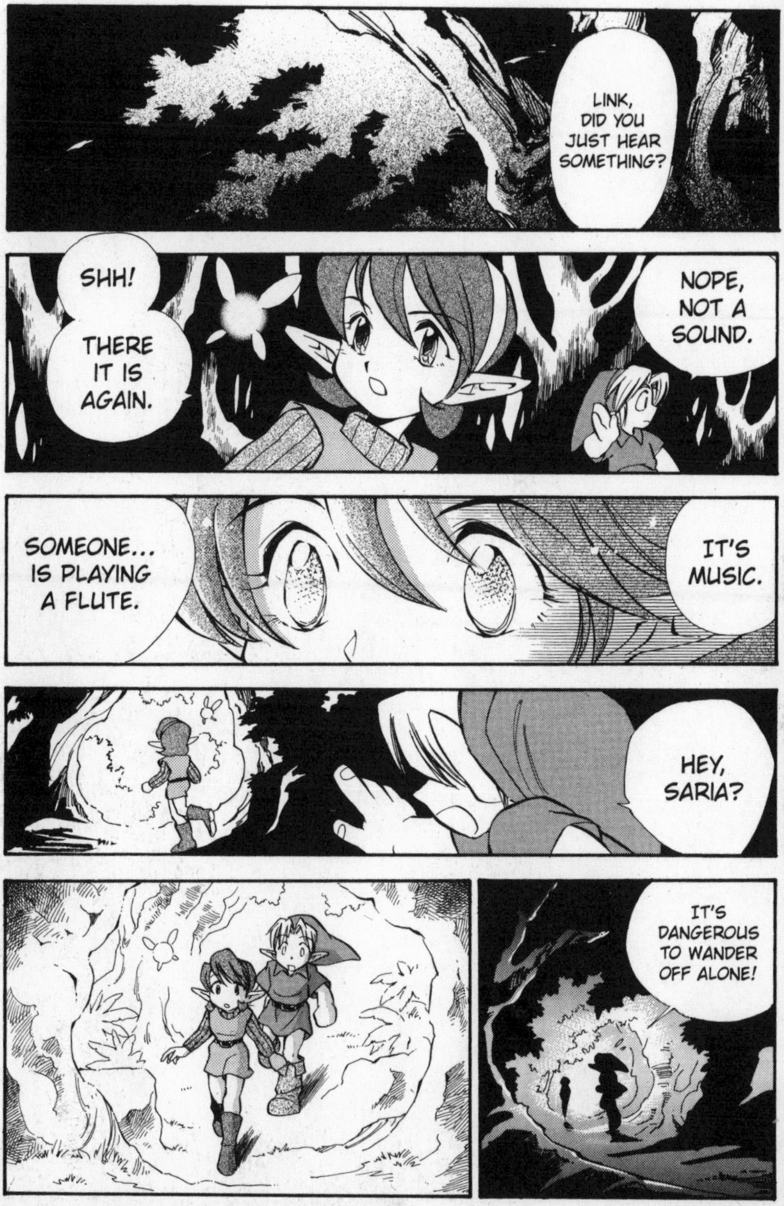
LINK, DID YOU JUST HEAR SOMETHING?
NOPE, NOT A SOUND.
SHH!
THERE IT IS AGAIN.
IT'S MUSIC.
SOMEONE... IS PLAYING A FLUTE.
HEY, SARIA?
IT'S DANGEROUS TO WANDER OFF ALONE!

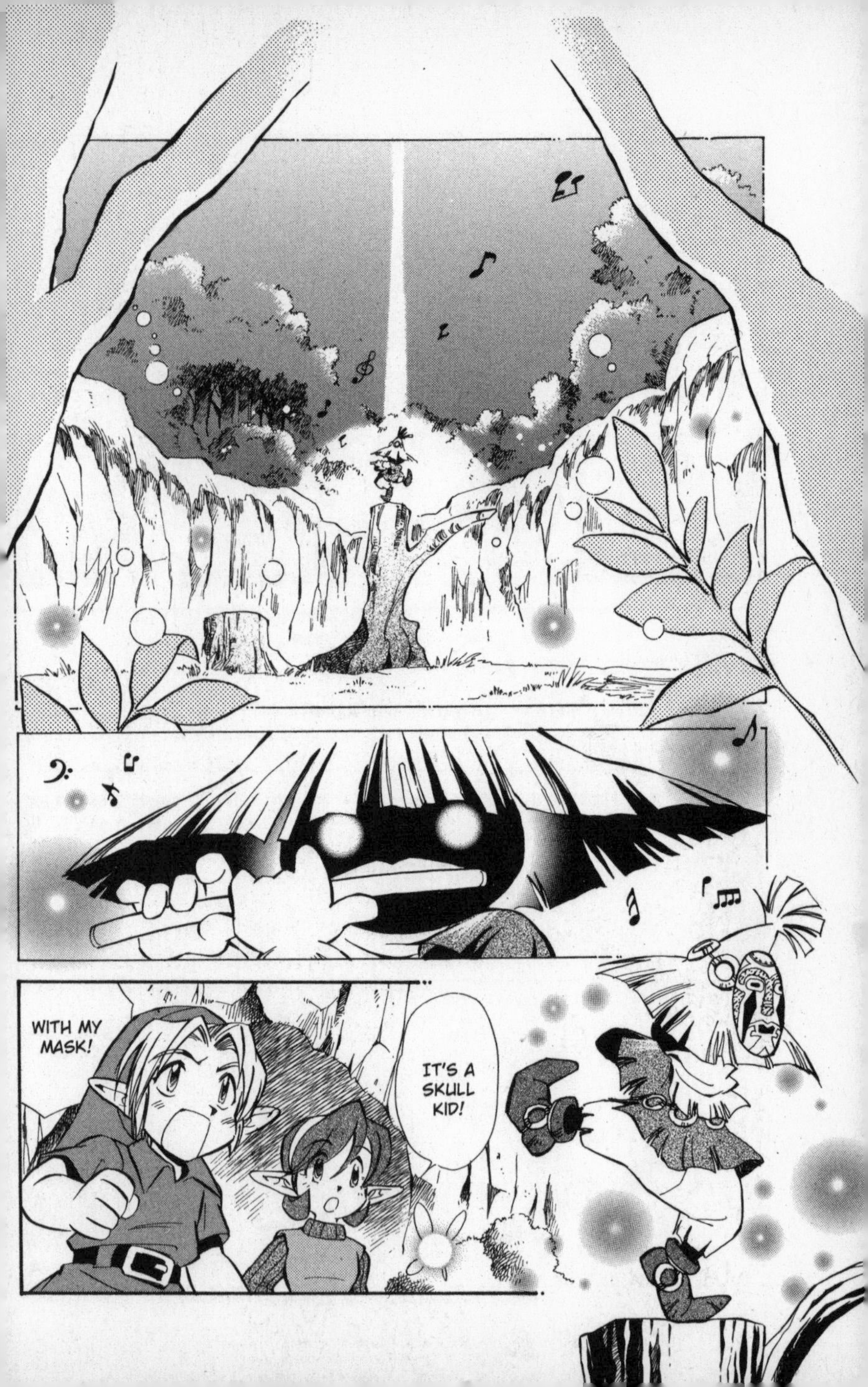
IT'S A SKULL KID!
WITH MY MASK!

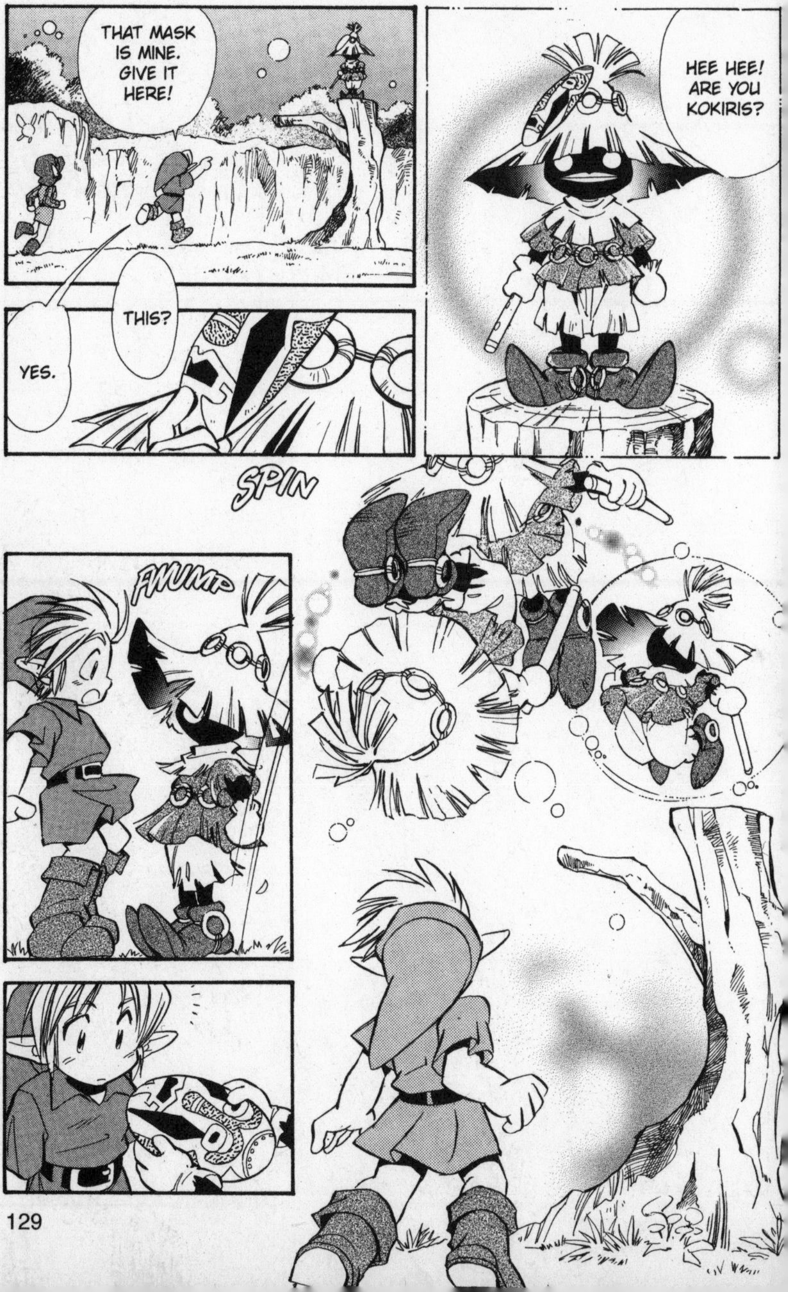
HEE HEE! ARE YOU KOKIRIS?
THAT MASK IS MINE. GIVE IT HERE!
THIS?
YES.
SPIN
FWUMP

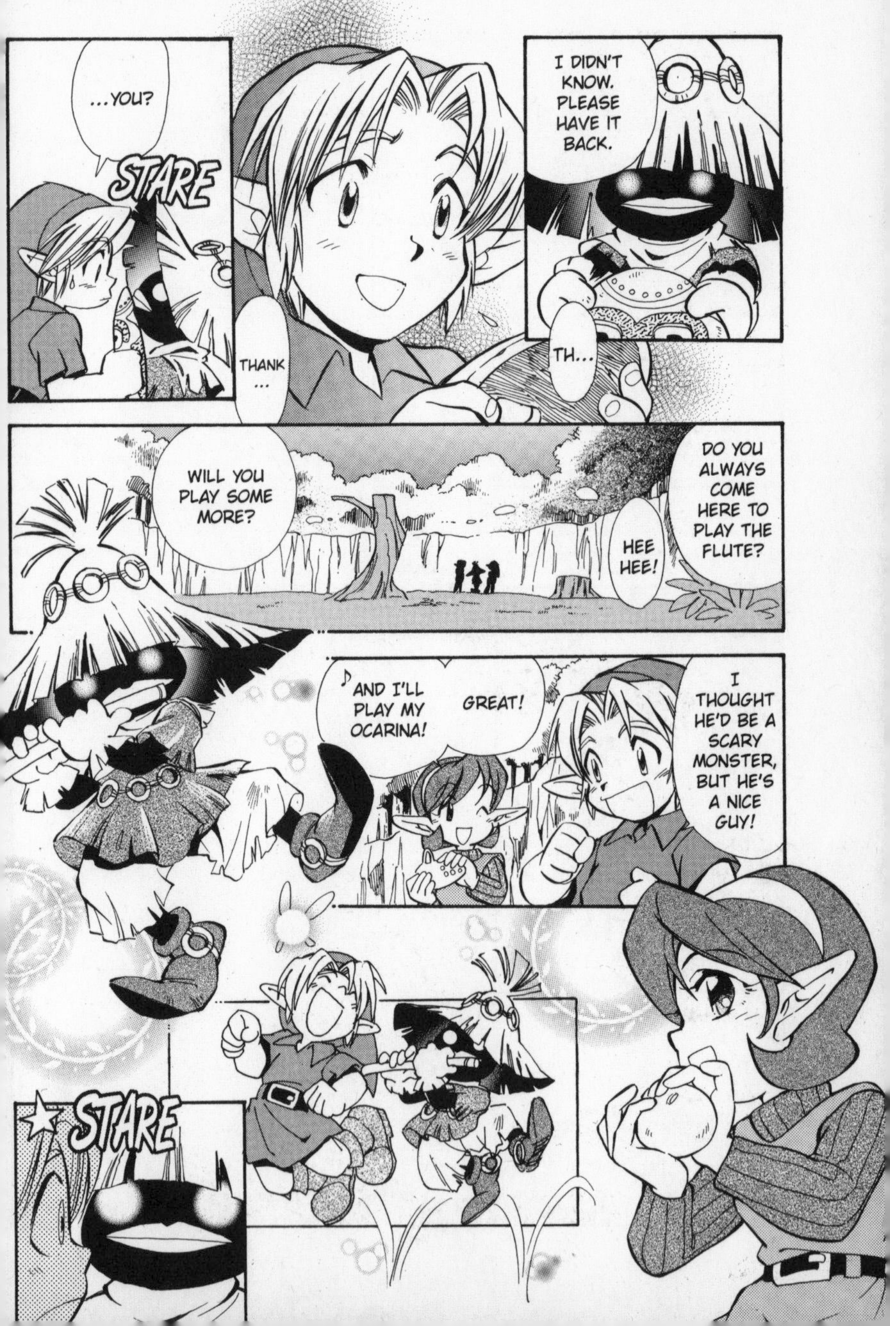
I DIDN'T KNOW. PLEASE HAVE IT BACK.
TH...
THANK ...
...YOU?
STARE
DO YOU ALWAYS COME HERE TO PLAY THE FLUTE?
HEE HEE!
WILL YOU PLAY SOME MORE?
I THOUGHT HE'D BE A SCARY MONSTER, BUT HE'S A NICE GUY!
GREAT!
♪ AND I'LL PLAY MY OCARINA!
STARE

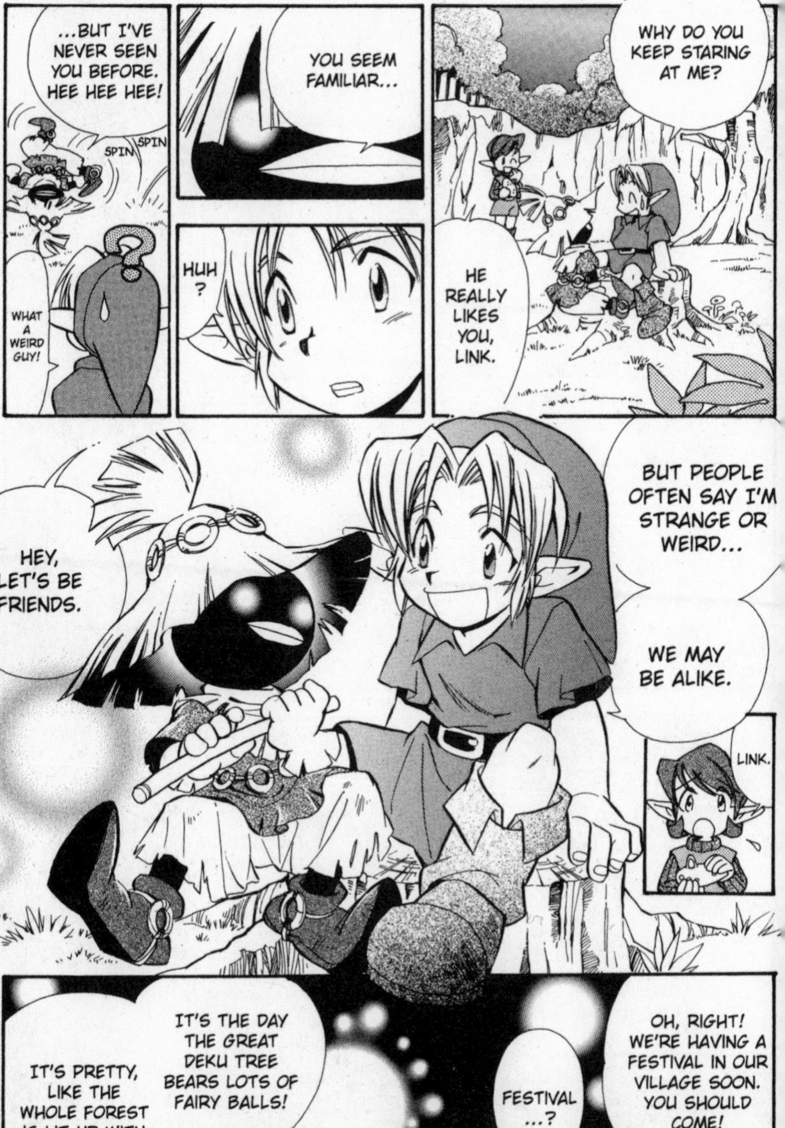
WHY DO YOU KEEP STARING AT ME?
HE REALLY LIKES YOU, LINK.
YOU SEEM FAMILIAR...
HUH?
...BUT I'VE NEVER SEEN YOU BEFORE. HEE HEE HEE!
SPIN
SPIN
WHAT A WEIRD GUY!
BUT PEOPLE OFTEN SAY I'M STRANGE OR WEIRD...
WE MAY BE ALIKE.
LINK.
HEY, LET'S BE FRIENDS.
OH, RIGHT! WE'RE HAVING A FESTIVAL IN OUR VILLAGE SOON. YOU SHOULD COME!
FESTIVAL ...?
IT'S THE DAY THE GREAT DEKU TREE BEARS LOTS OF FAIRY BALLS!
IT'S PRETTY, LIKE THE WHOLE FOREST IS LIT UP WITH LAMPS.

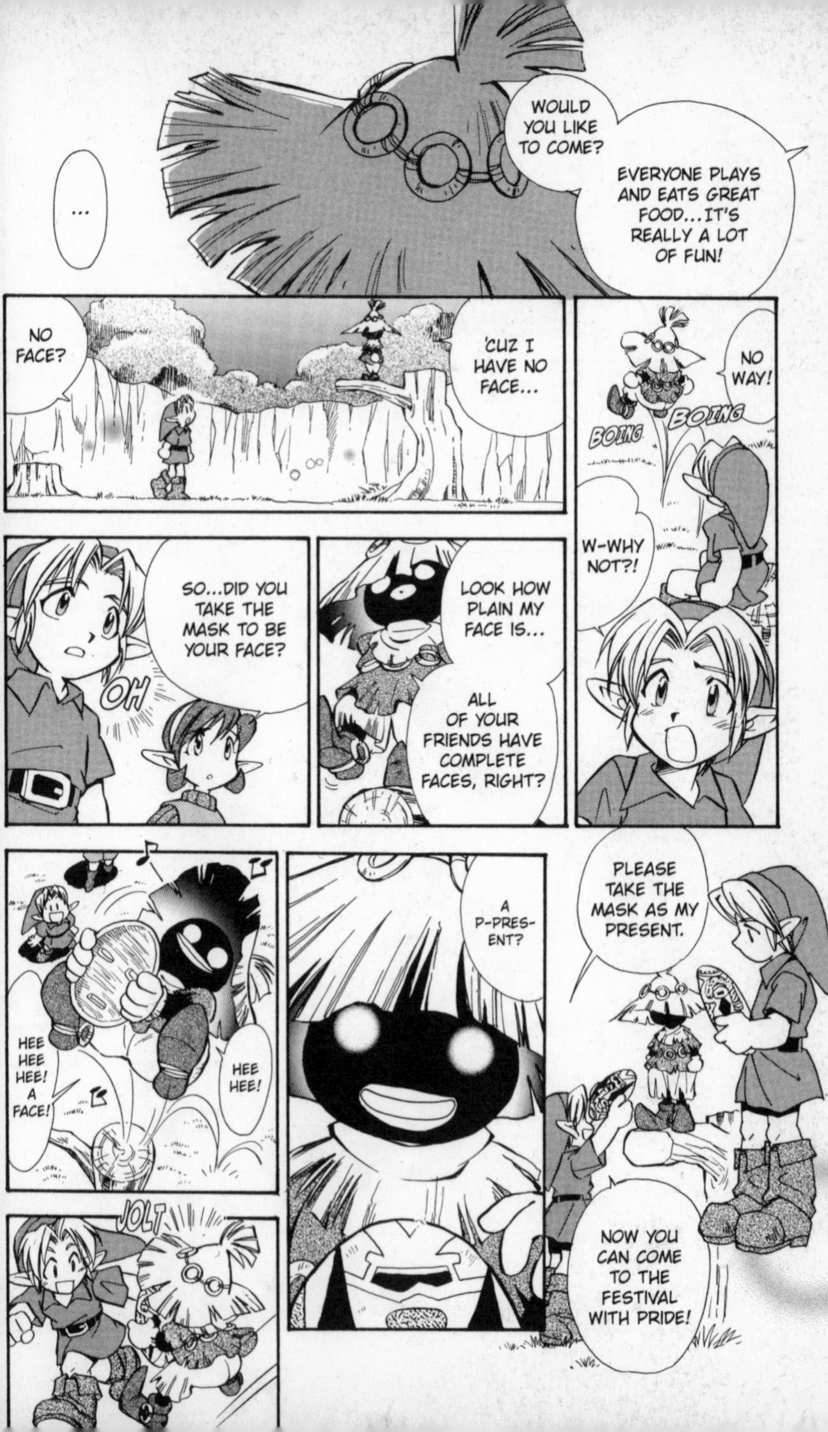
WOULD YOU LIKE TO COME?
EVERYONE PLAYS AND EATS GREAT FOOD...IT'S REALLY A LOT OF FUN!
...
NO WAY!
BOING
BOING
W-WHY NOT?!
'CUZ I HAVE NO FACE...
NO FACE?
LOOK HOW PLAIN MY FACE IS...
ALL OF YOUR FRIENDS HAVE COMPLETE FACES, RIGHT?
SO...DID YOU TAKE THE MASK TO BE YOUR FACE?
OH
PLEASE TAKE THE MASK AS MY PRESENT.
NOW YOU CAN COME TO THE FESTIVAL WITH PRIDE!
A P-PRES-ENT?
HEE HEE!
HEE HEE HEE! A FACE!
JOLT

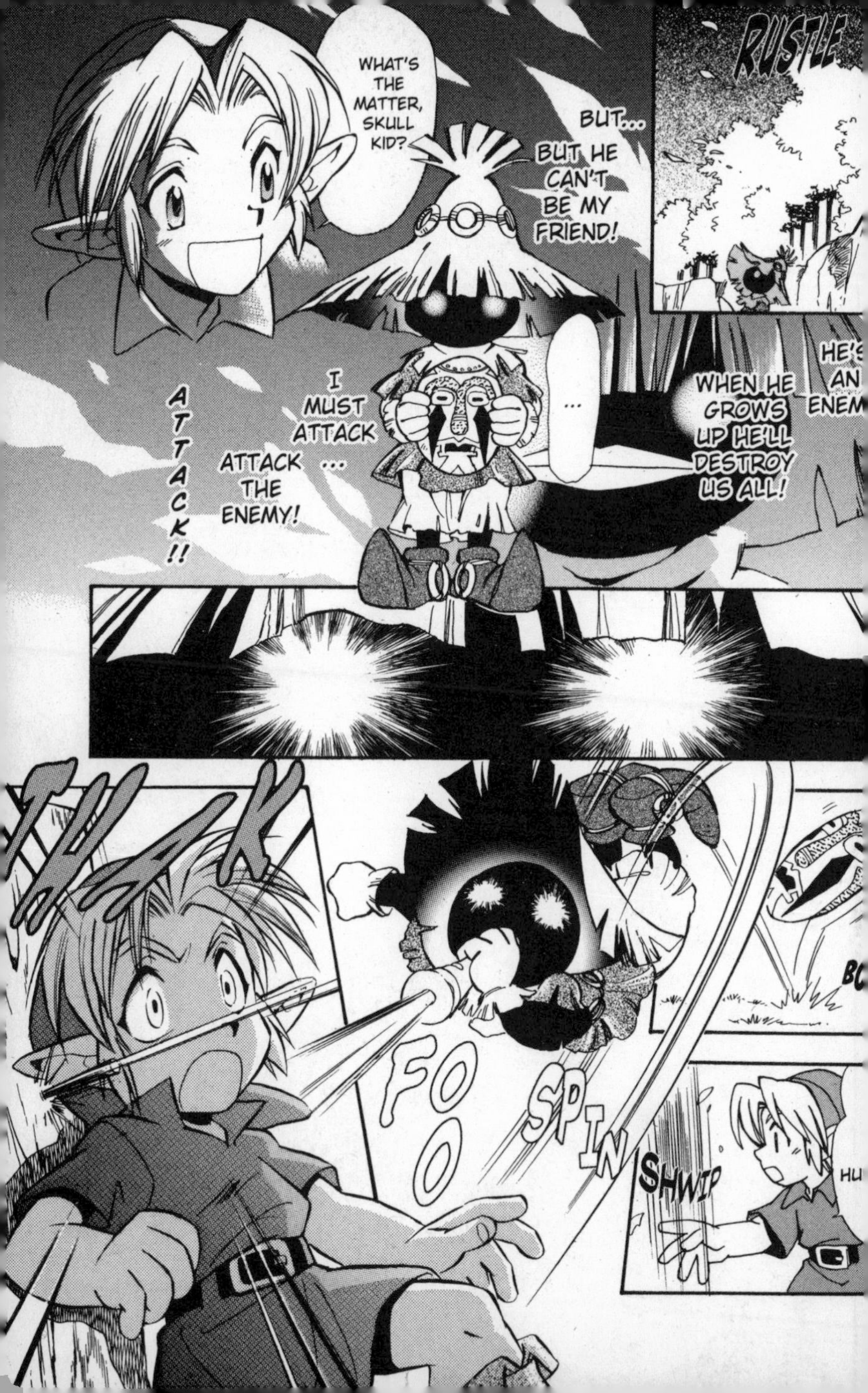
RUSTLE
WHAT'S THE MATTER, SKULL KID?
BUT...
BUT HE CAN'T BE MY FRIEND!
HE'S AN ENEM
WHEN HE GROWS UP HE'LL DESTROY US ALL!
...
I MUST ATTACK
ATTACK ...
ATTACK THE ENEMY!
ATTACK!!
BO
SHWIP
HU
SPIN
FOO

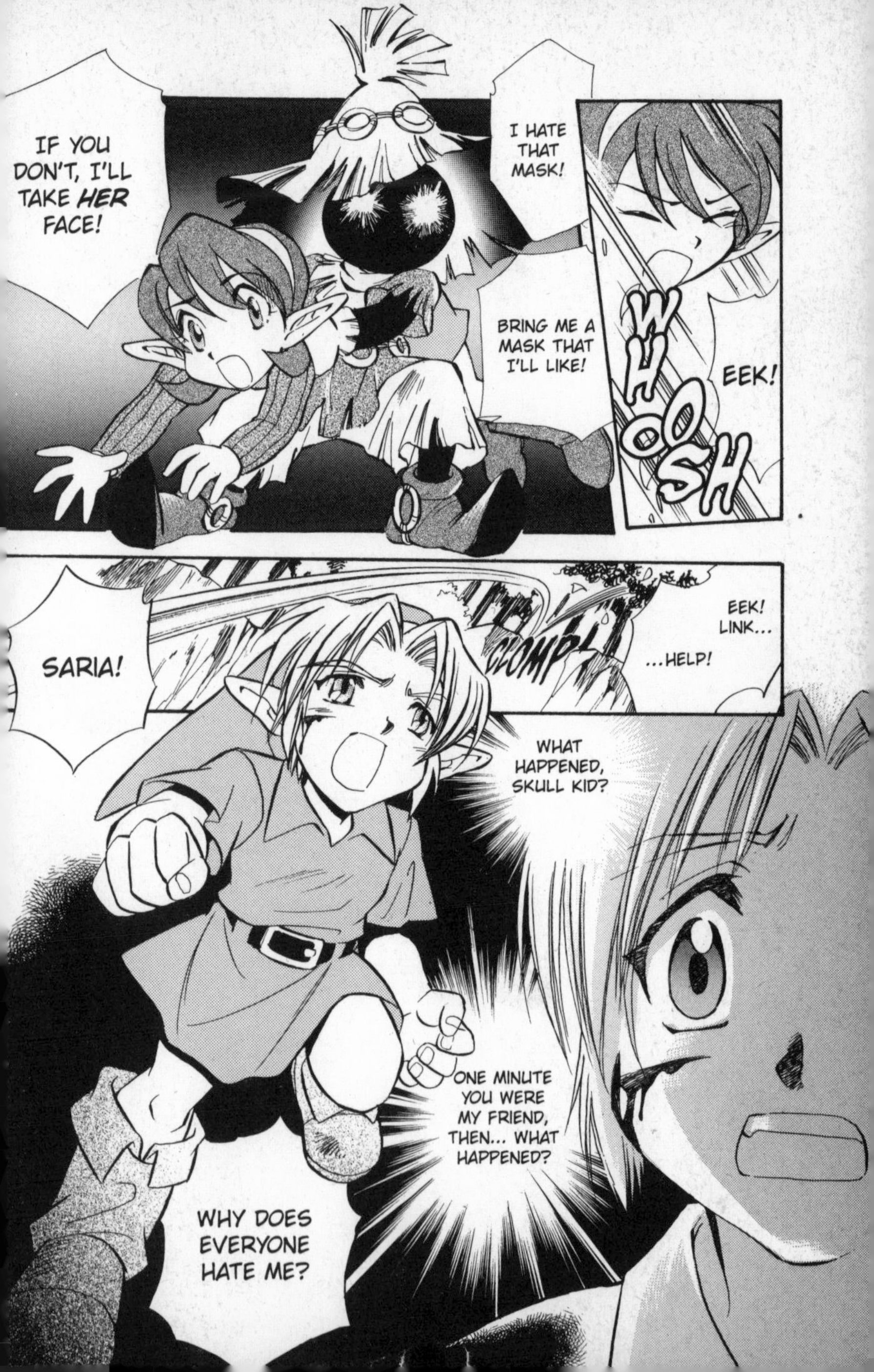
WHOOSH
EEK!
I HATE THAT MASK!
BRING ME A MASK THAT I'LL LIKE!
IF YOU DON'T, I'LL TAKE *HER* FACE!
EEK! LINK...
...HELP!
CLOMP
SARIA!
WHAT HAPPENED, SKULL KID?
ONE MINUTE YOU WERE MY FRIEND, THEN... WHAT HAPPENED?
WHY DOES EVERYONE HATE ME?

OCARINA OF TIME ~ BONUS STORY
THE SKULL KID AND THE MASK ~ PART 2

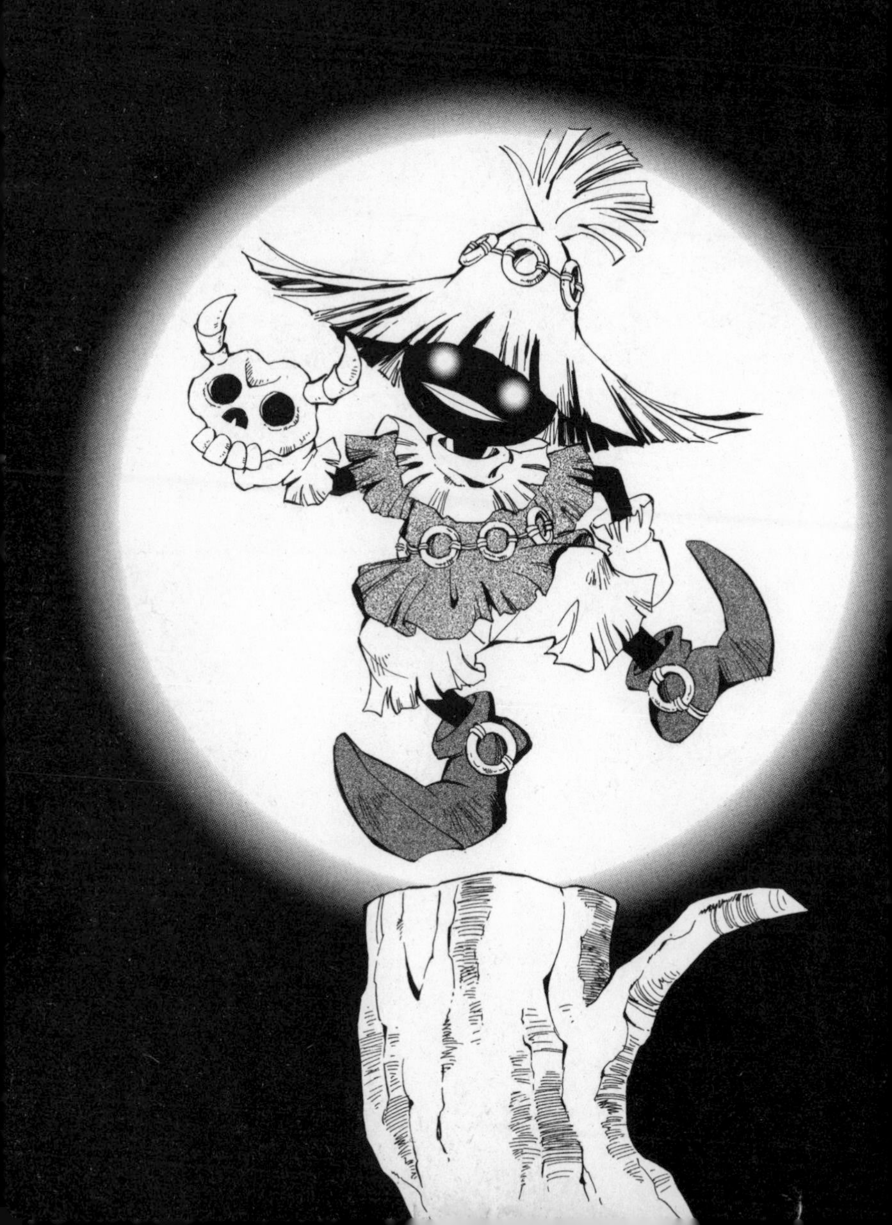

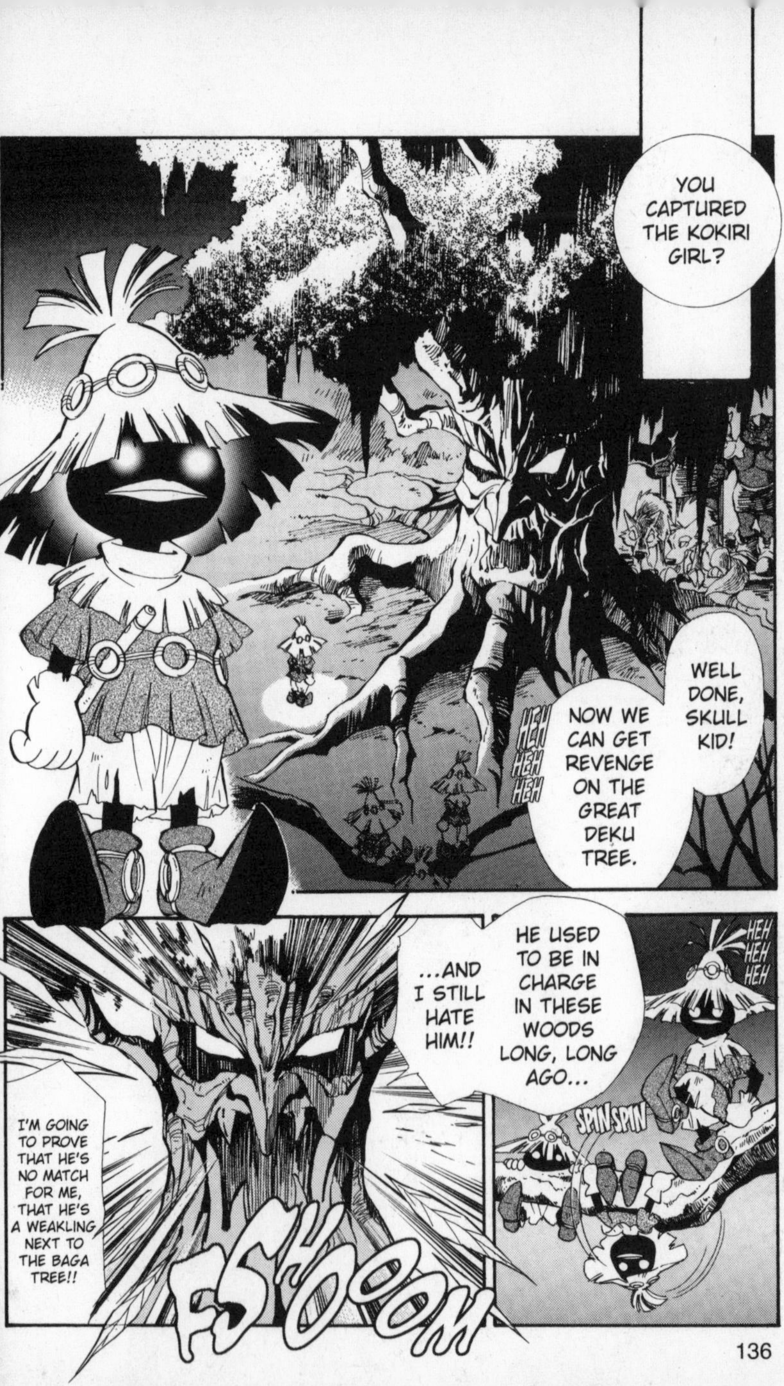
YOU CAPTURED THE KOKIRI GIRL?
WELL DONE, SKULL KID!
NOW WE CAN GET REVENGE ON THE GREAT DEKU TREE.
HEH HEH HEH
HEH HEH HEH
HE USED TO BE IN CHARGE IN THESE WOODS LONG, LONG AGO...
SPIN SPIN
...AND I STILL HATE HIM!!
I'M GOING TO PROVE THAT HE'S NO MATCH FOR ME, THAT HE'S A WEAKLING NEXT TO THE BAGA TREE!!
FSHOOOM

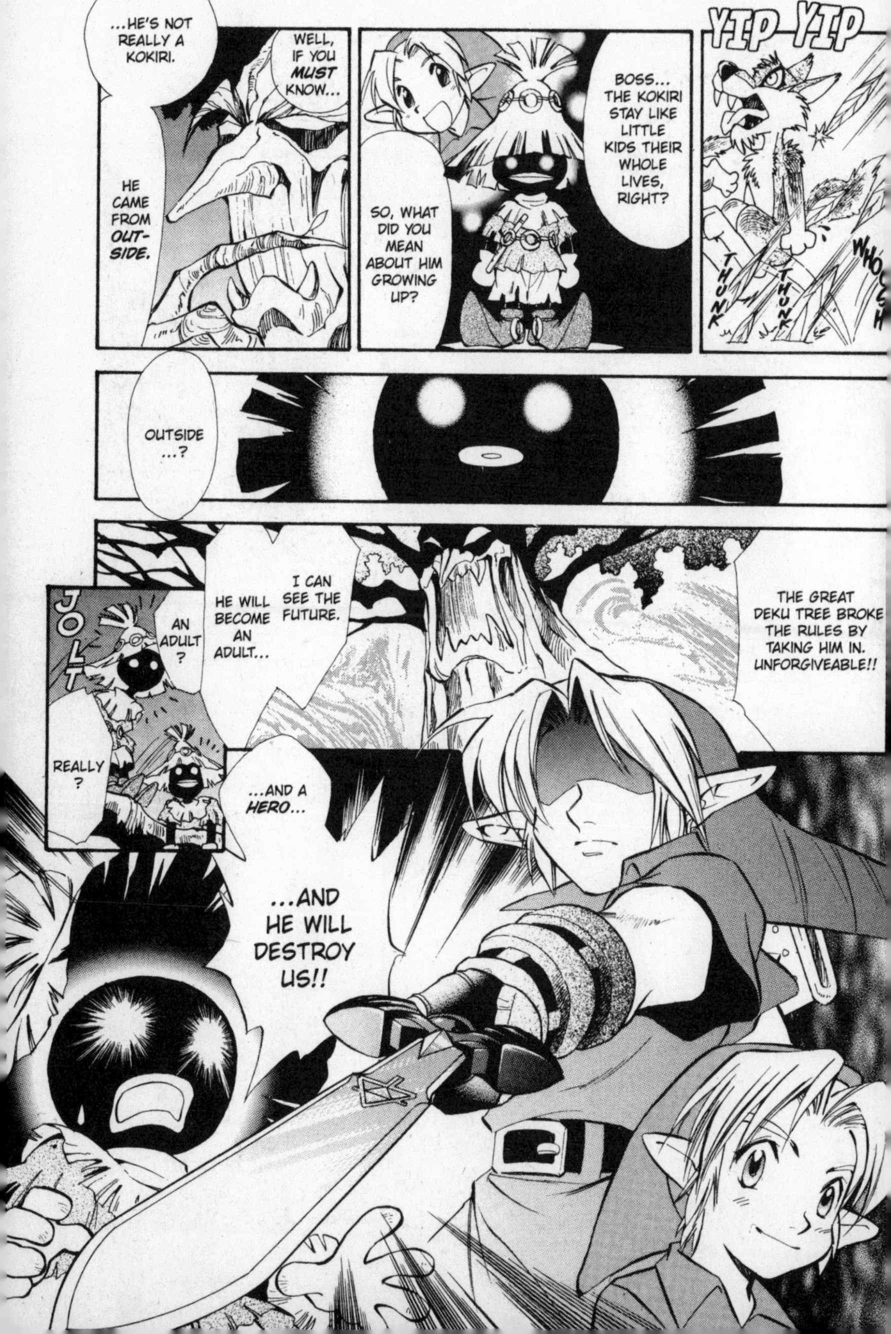
YIP YIP
WHOOSH
THUNK
THUNK
BOSS... THE KOKIRI STAY LIKE LITTLE KIDS THEIR WHOLE LIVES, RIGHT?
SO, WHAT DID YOU MEAN ABOUT HIM GROWING UP?
WELL, IF YOU MUST KNOW...
...HE'S NOT REALLY A KOKIRI.
HE CAME FROM OUT-SIDE.
OUTSIDE ...?
THE GREAT DEKU TREE BROKE THE RULES BY TAKING HIM IN. UNFORGIVEABLE!!
I CAN SEE THE FUTURE.
HE WILL BECOME AN ADULT...
AN ADULT ?
JOLT
REALLY ?
...AND A HERO...
...AND HE WILL DESTROY US!!

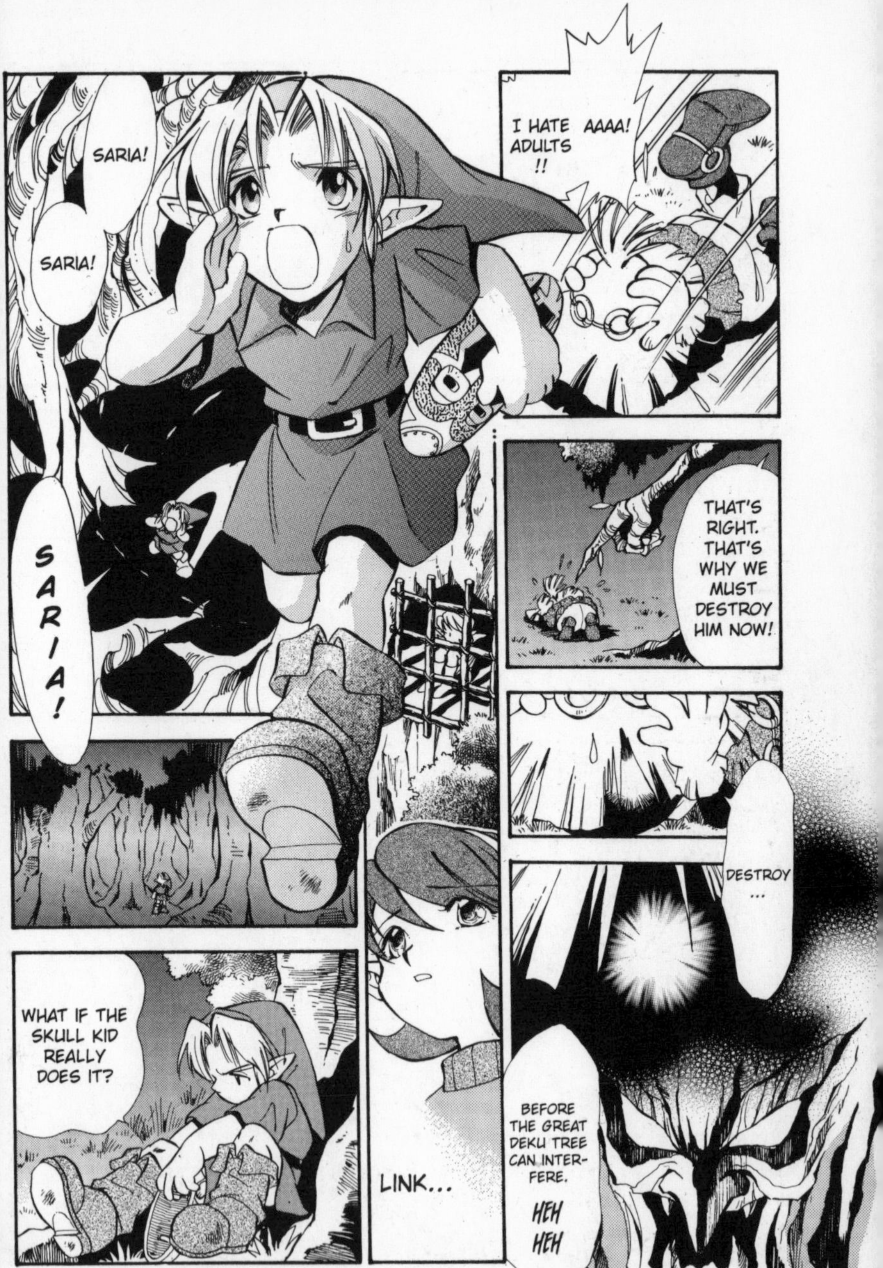

AAAA!
I HATE ADULTS !!
THAT'S RIGHT. THAT'S WHY WE MUST DESTROY HIM NOW!
DESTROY ...
BEFORE THE GREAT DEKU TREE CAN INTER-FERE.
HEH HEH
SARIA!
SARIA!
SARIA!
LINK...
WHAT IF THE SKULL KID REALLY DOES IT?

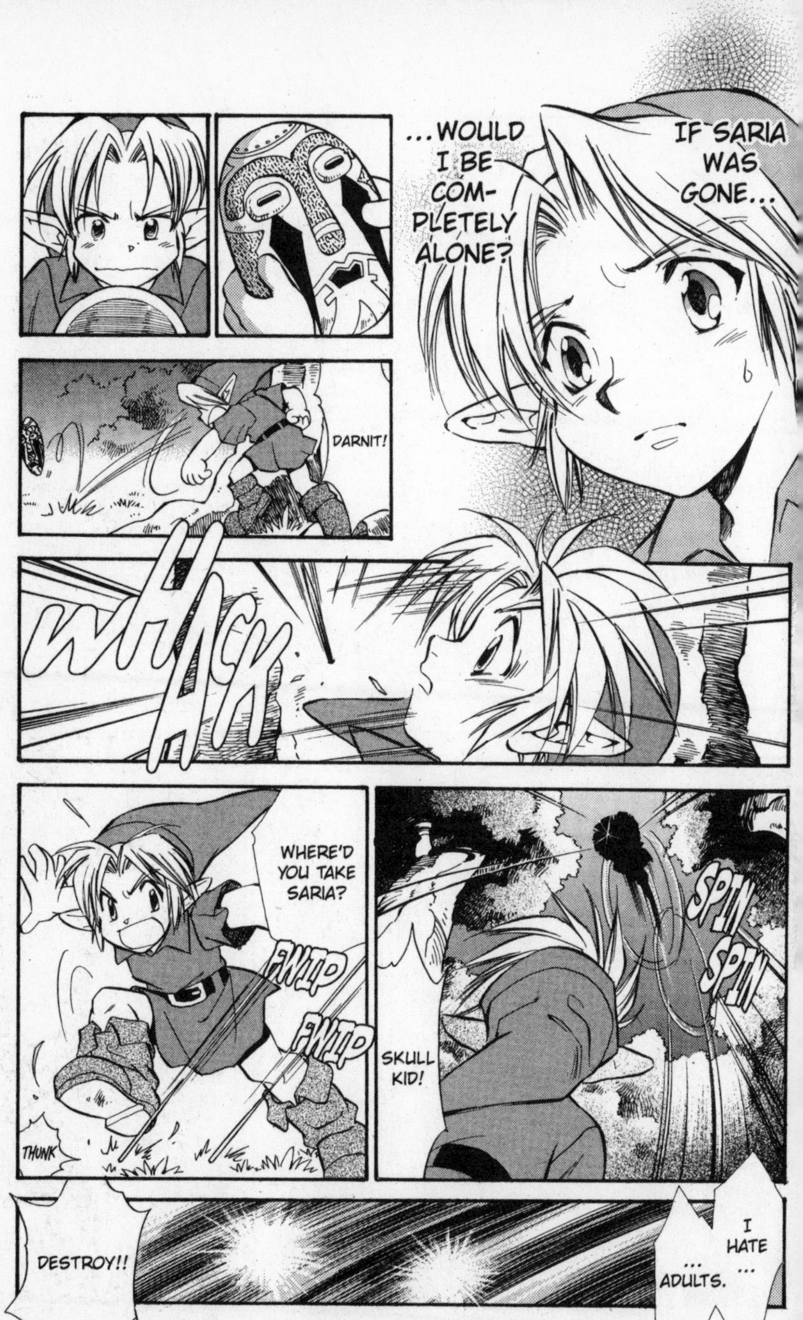
IF SARIA WAS GONE...
...WOULD I BE COM-PLETELY ALONE?
DARNIT!
WHACK
SPIN SPIN
SKULL KID!
WHERE'D YOU TAKE SARIA?
FWIP
FWIP
THUNK
I HATE ... ADULTS. ...
DESTROY!!

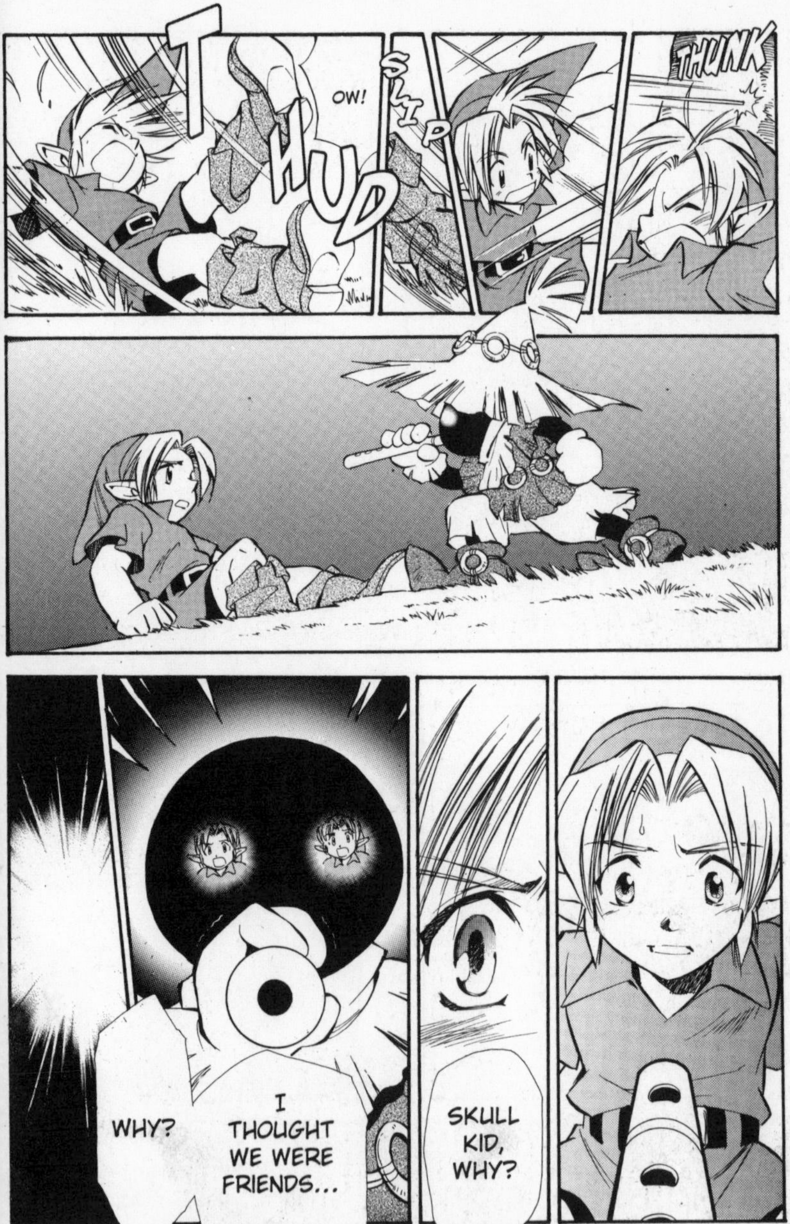
THUNK
SLIP
OW!
THUD
SKULL KID, WHY?
I THOUGHT WE WERE FRIENDS...
WHY?

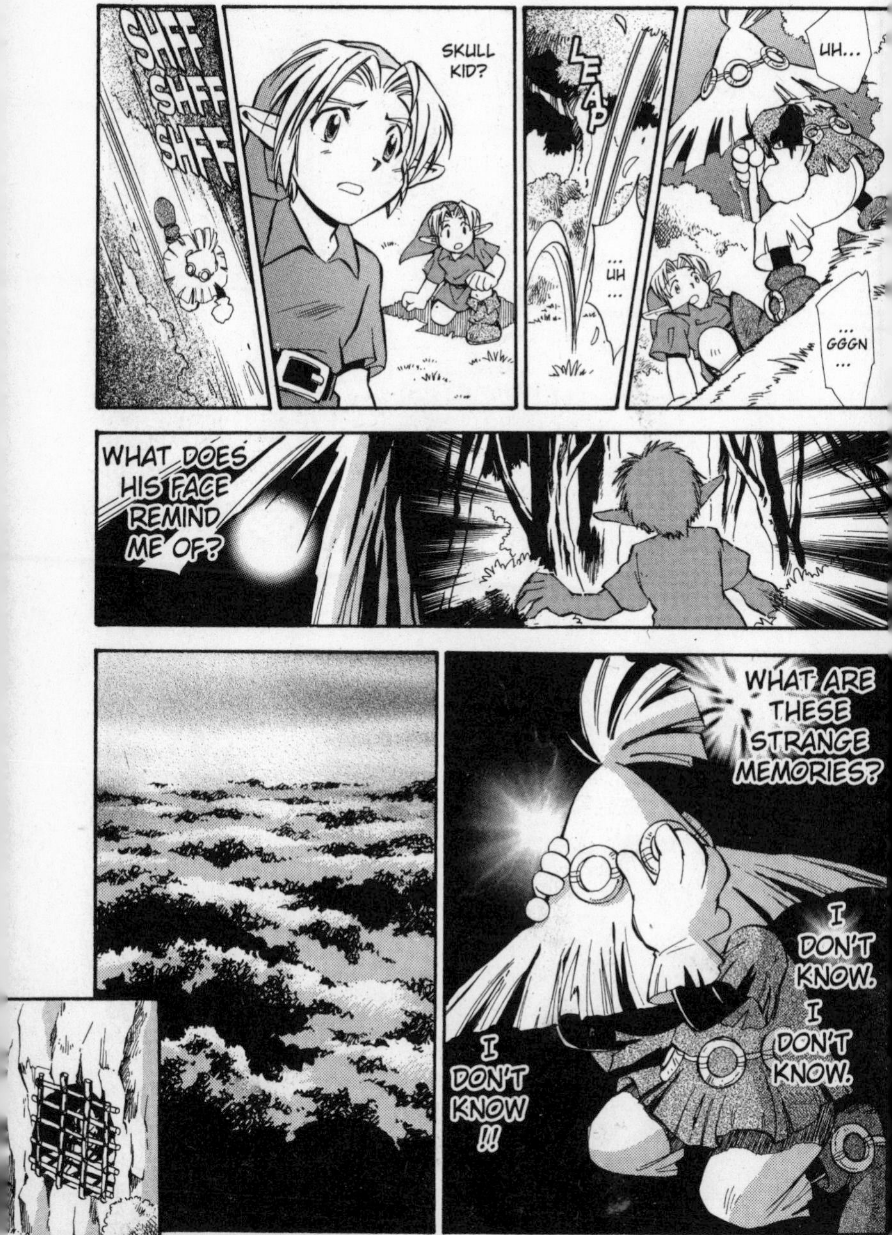

UH...
...GGGN...
LEAP
...UH...
SKULL KID?
SHFF SHFF SHFF
WHAT DOES HIS FACE REMIND ME OF?
WHAT ARE THESE STRANGE MEMORIES?
I DON'T KNOW.
I DON'T KNOW.
I DON'T KNOW!!

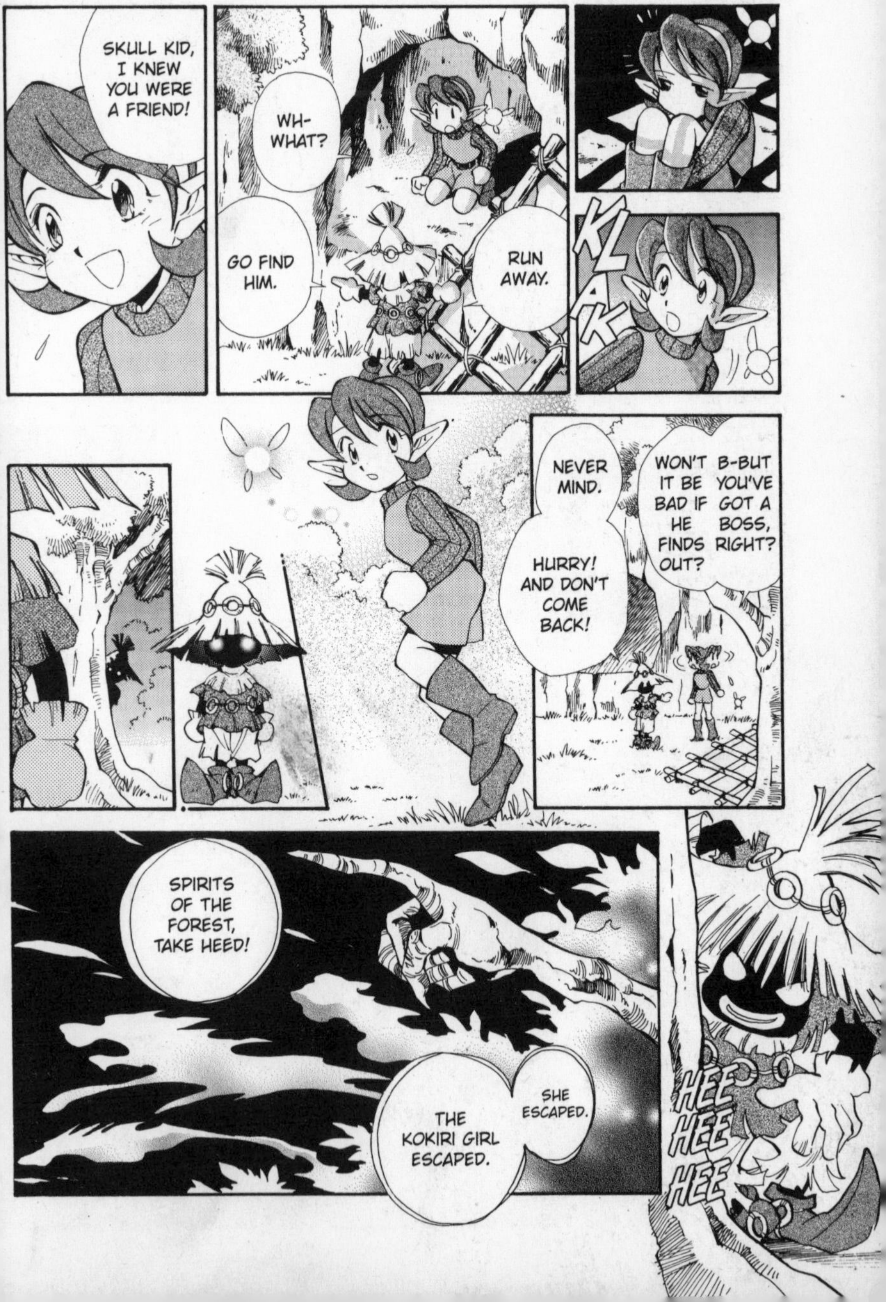
KLAK
WH-WHAT?
RUN AWAY.
GO FIND HIM.
SKULL KID, I KNEW YOU WERE A FRIEND!
B-BUT YOU'VE GOT A BOSS, RIGHT?
WON'T IT BE BAD IF HE FINDS OUT?
NEVER MIND.
HURRY! AND DON'T COME BACK!
HEE HEE HEE
SHE ESCAPED.
THE KOKIRI GIRL ESCAPED.
SPIRITS OF THE FOREST, TAKE HEED!

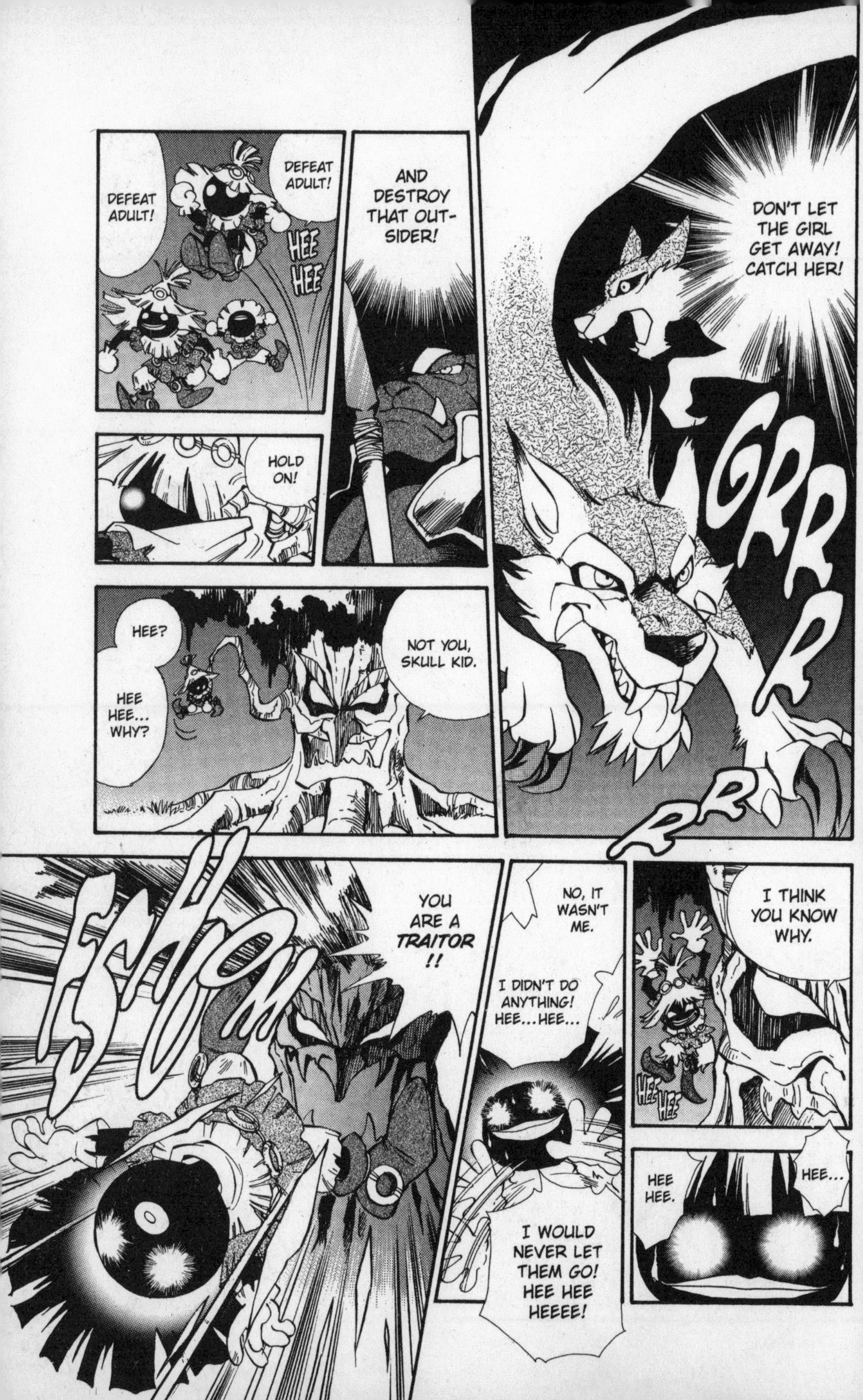
DON'T LET THE GIRL GET AWAY! CATCH HER!
GRRRRR
AND DESTROY THAT OUT-SIDER!
DEFEAT ADULT!
DEFEAT ADULT!
HEE HEE
HOLD ON!
NOT YOU, SKULL KID.
HEE?
HEE HEE... WHY?
I THINK YOU KNOW WHY.
HEE HEE
HEE...
HEE HEE.
NO, IT WASN'T ME.
I DIDN'T DO ANYTHING! HEE...HEE...
I WOULD NEVER LET THEM GO! HEE HEE HEEEE!
YOU ARE A *TRAITOR* !!

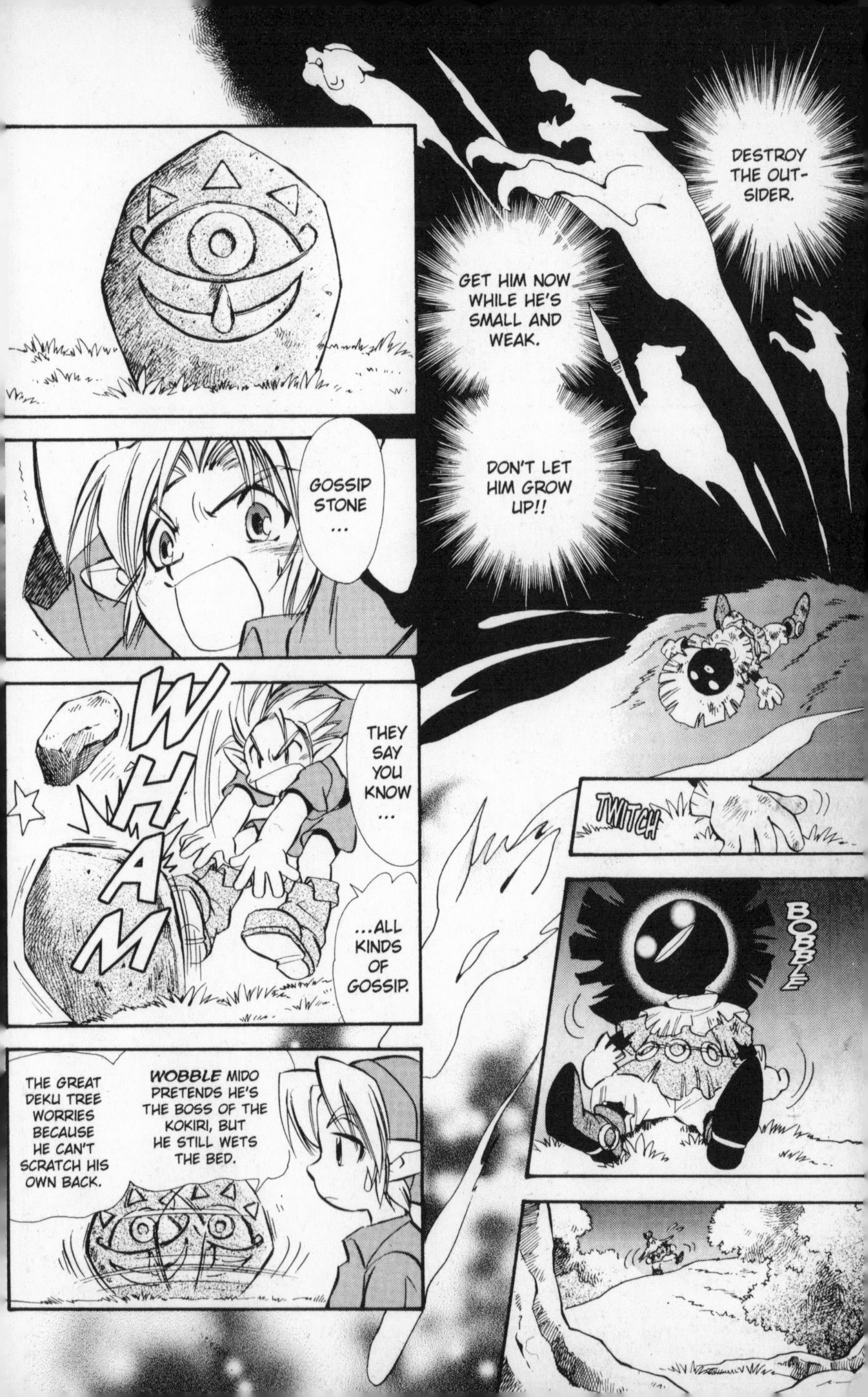
DESTROY THE OUT-SIDER.
GET HIM NOW WHILE HE'S SMALL AND WEAK.
DON'T LET HIM GROW UP!!
TWITCH
BOBBLE
GOSSIP STONE ...
WHAM
THEY SAY YOU KNOW ...
...ALL KINDS OF GOSSIP.
WOBBLE MIDO PRETENDS HE'S THE BOSS OF THE KOKIRI, BUT HE STILL WETS THE BED.
THE GREAT DEKU TREE WORRIES BECAUSE HE CAN'T SCRATCH HIS OWN BACK.

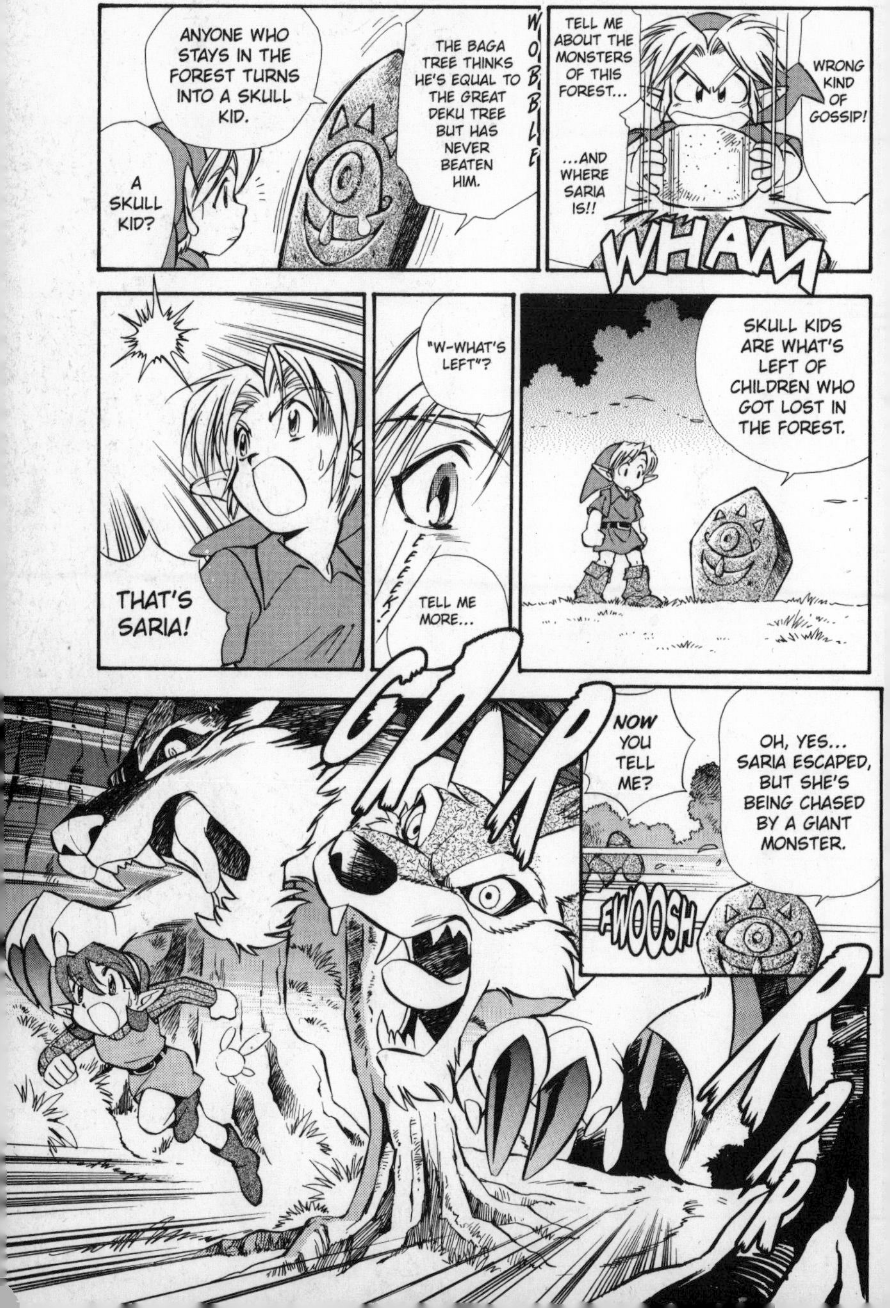
TELL ME ABOUT THE MONSTERS OF THIS FOREST...
...AND WHERE SARIA IS!!
WRONG KIND OF GOSSIP!
WHAM
WOBBLE
THE BAGA TREE THINKS HE'S EQUAL TO THE GREAT DEKU TREE BUT HAS NEVER BEATEN HIM.
ANYONE WHO STAYS IN THE FOREST TURNS INTO A SKULL KID.
A SKULL KID?
SKULL KIDS ARE WHAT'S LEFT OF CHILDREN WHO GOT LOST IN THE FOREST.
"W-WHAT'S LEFT"?
EEEEEK!
TELL ME MORE...
THAT'S SARIA!
OH, YES... SARIA ESCAPED, BUT SHE'S BEING CHASED BY A GIANT MONSTER.
NOW YOU TELL ME?
FWOOSH

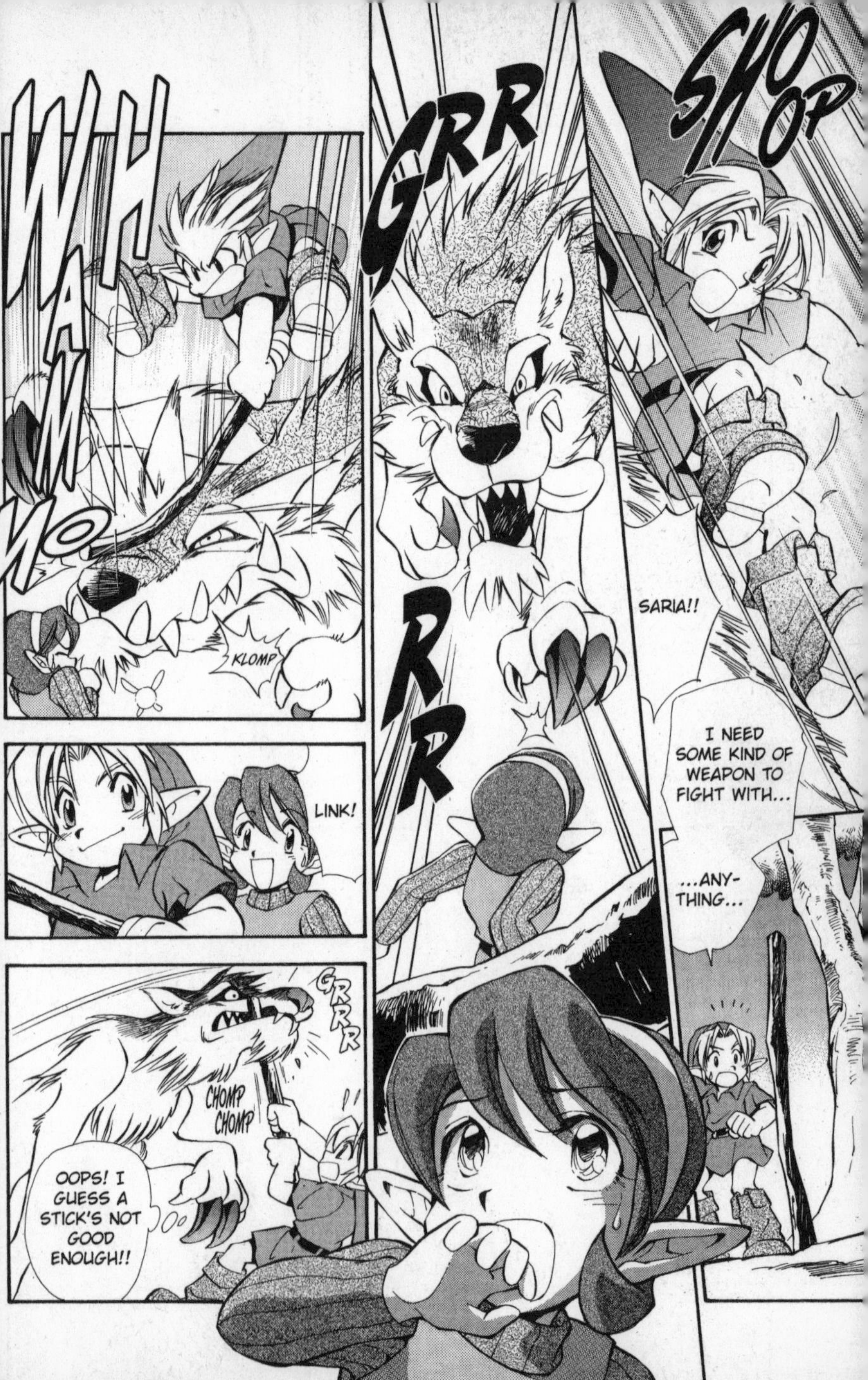
SHOOOP
SARIA!!
I NEED SOME KIND OF WEAPON TO FIGHT WITH...
...ANY-THING...
GRR
RRR
KLOMP
LINK!
GRRR
CHOMP CHOMP
OOPS! I GUESS A STICK'S NOT GOOD ENOUGH!!

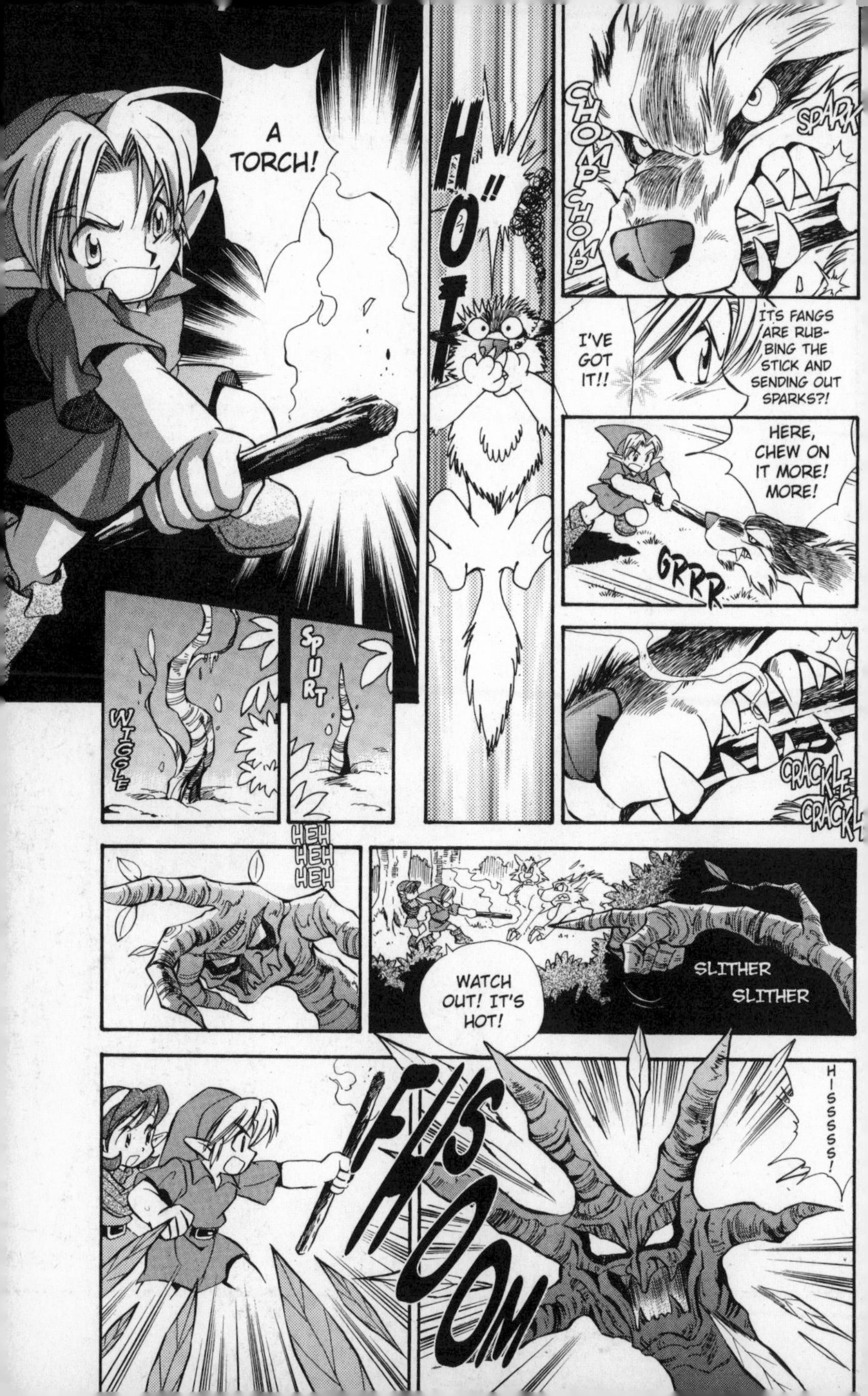
CHOMP CHOMP
SPARK
ITS FANGS ARE RUB-BING THE STICK AND SENDING OUT SPARKS?!
I'VE GOT IT!!
HERE, CHEW ON IT MORE! MORE!
GRRR
CRACKLE CRACKLE
HOT!!
A TORCH!
SPURT
WIGGLE
SLITHER SLITHER
HEH HEH HEH
WATCH OUT! IT'S HOT!
HISSSSS!

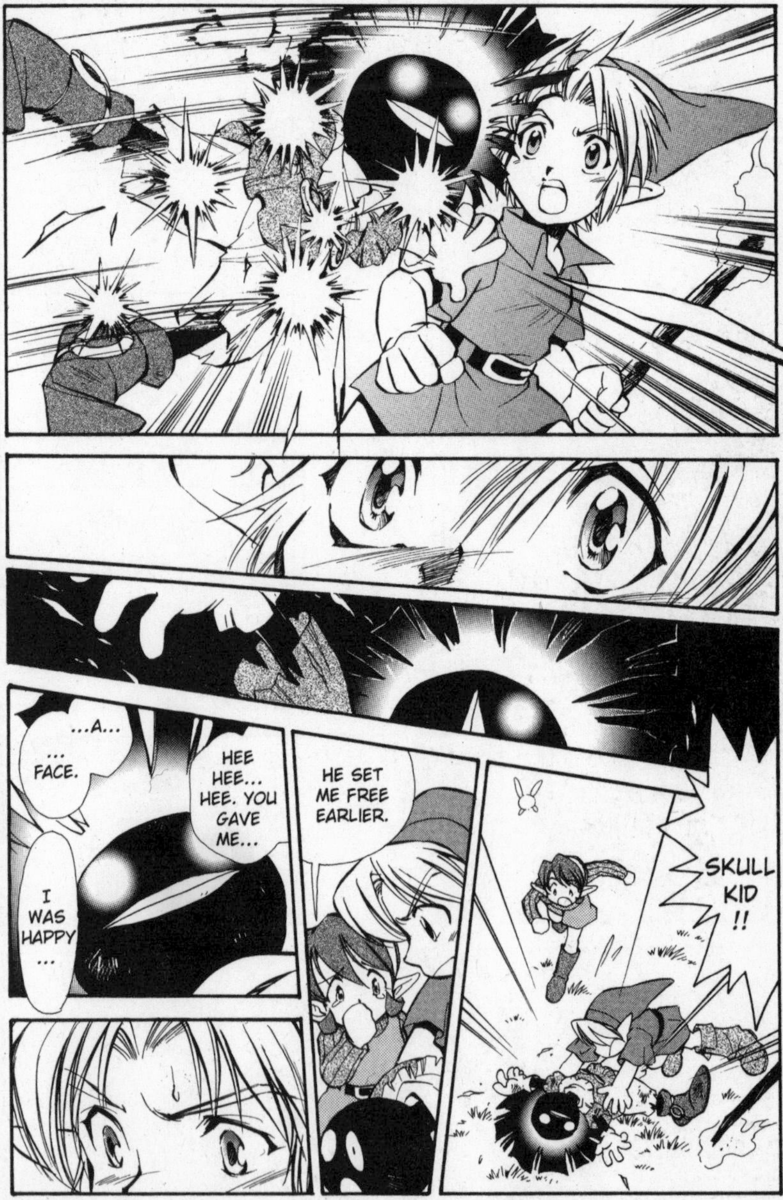
SKULL KID !!
HE SET ME FREE EARLIER.
HEE HEE... HEE. YOU GAVE ME...
...A... ... FACE.
I WAS HAPPY ...

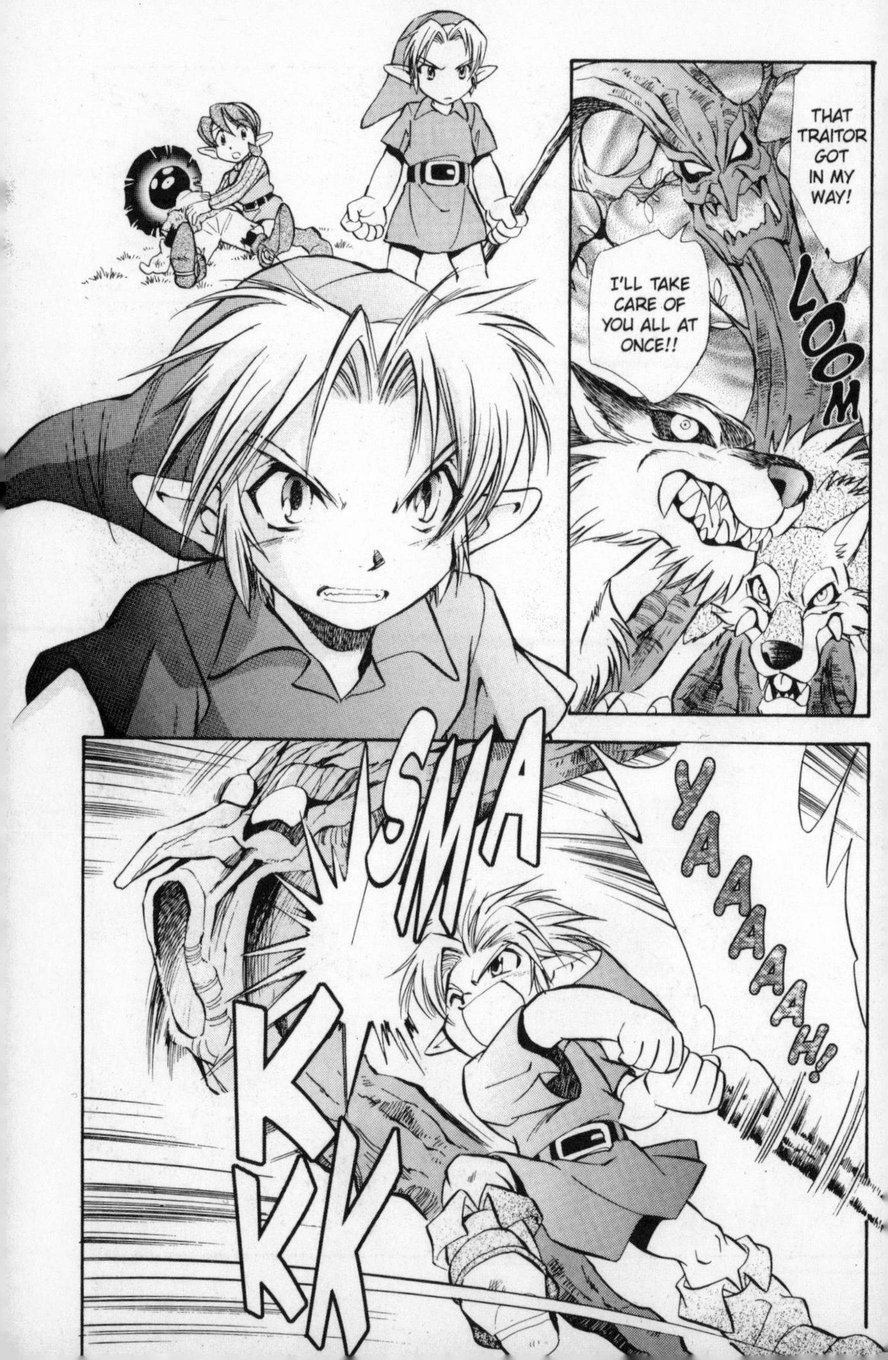
THAT TRAITOR GOT IN MY WAY!
I'LL TAKE CARE OF YOU ALL AT ONCE!!
LOOM
YAAAAAAH!
SMA
KKK

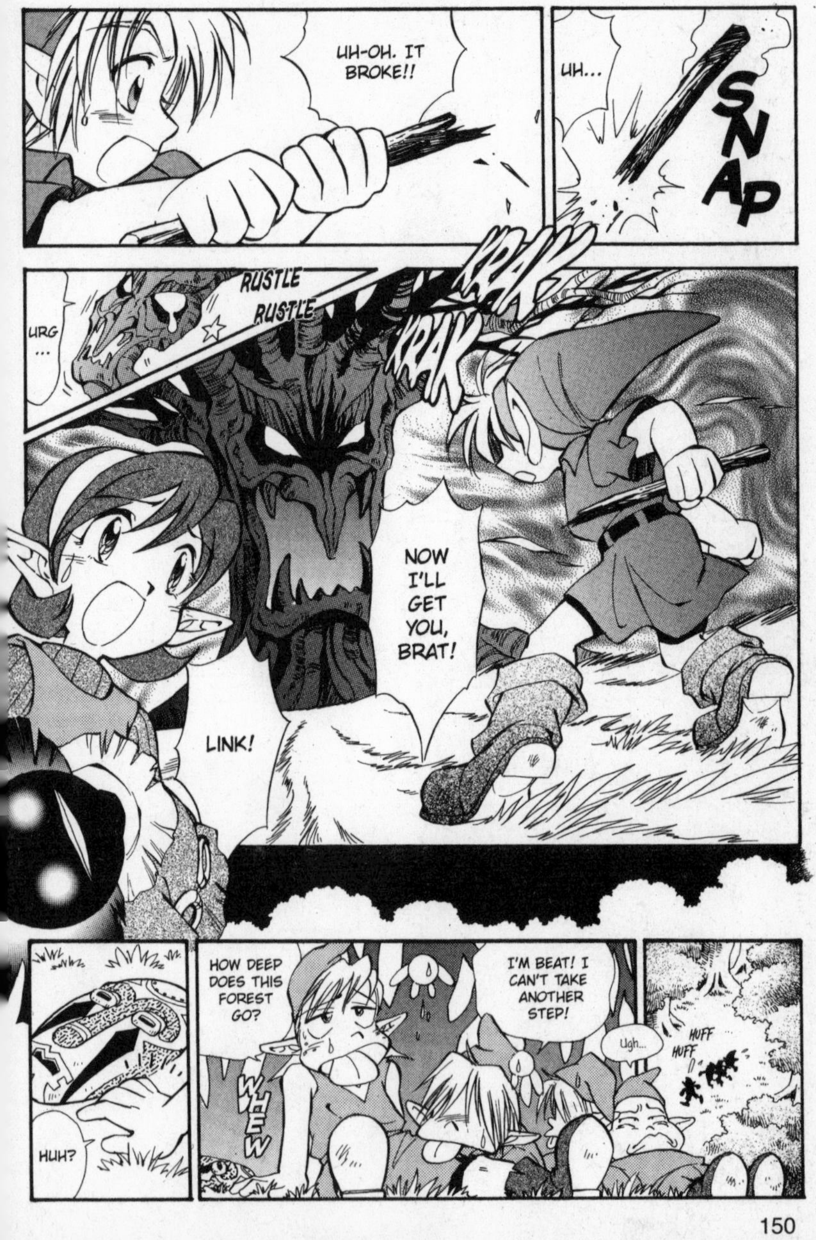
UH...
SNAP
UH-OH. IT BROKE!!
KRAK
KRAK
RUSTLE
RUSTLE
URG...
NOW I'LL GET YOU, BRAT!
LINK!
HUFF HUFF
I'M BEAT! I CAN'T TAKE ANOTHER STEP!
HOW DEEP DOES THIS FOREST GO?
Ugh...
WHEW
HUH?

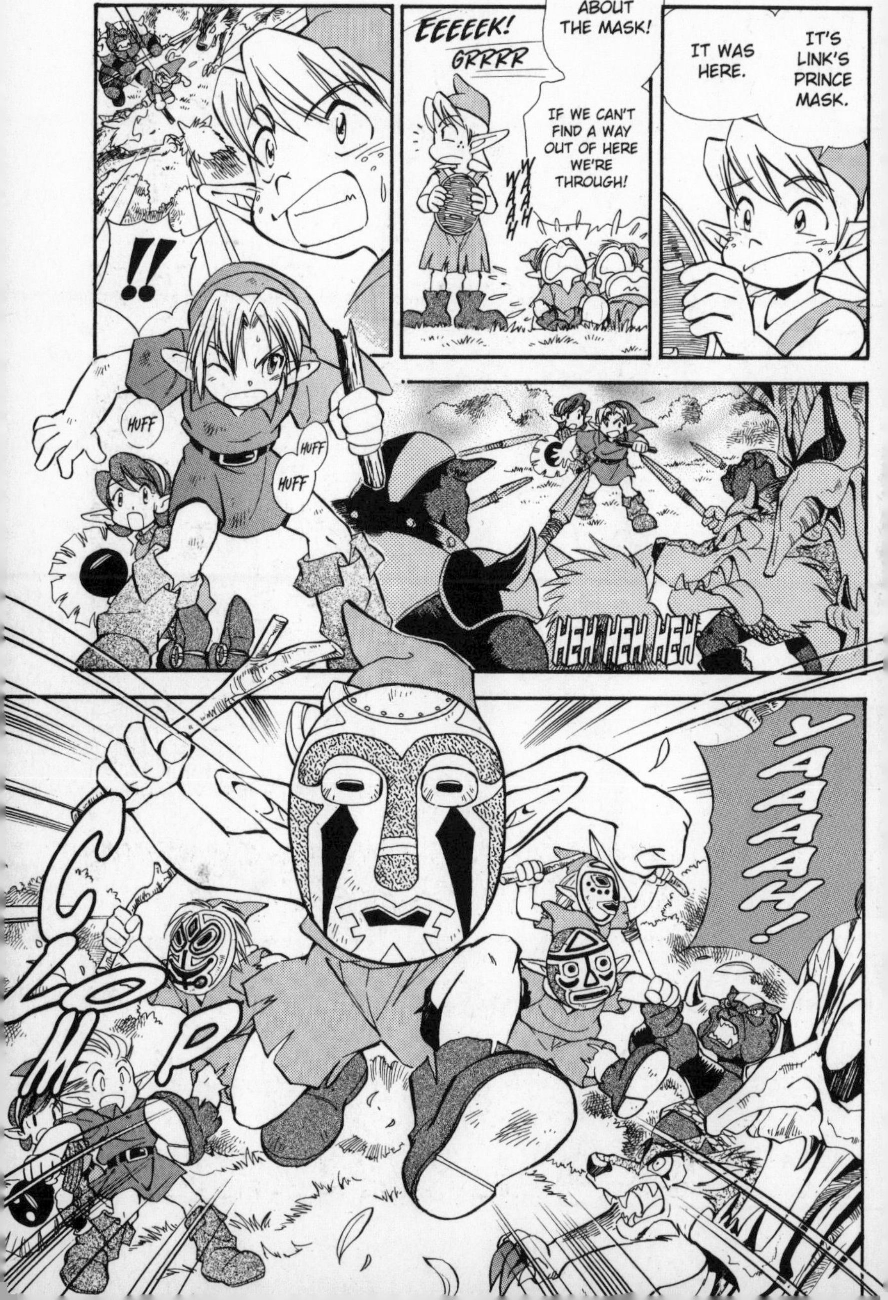
IT'S LINK'S PRINCE MASK.
IT WAS HERE.
FORGET ABOUT THE MASK!
EEEEEK!
GRRRR
IF WE CAN'T FIND A WAY OUT OF HERE WE'RE THROUGH!
WAAAAH
!!
HUFF
HUFF
HUFF
HEH HEH HEH
YAAAAH!
CLOMP

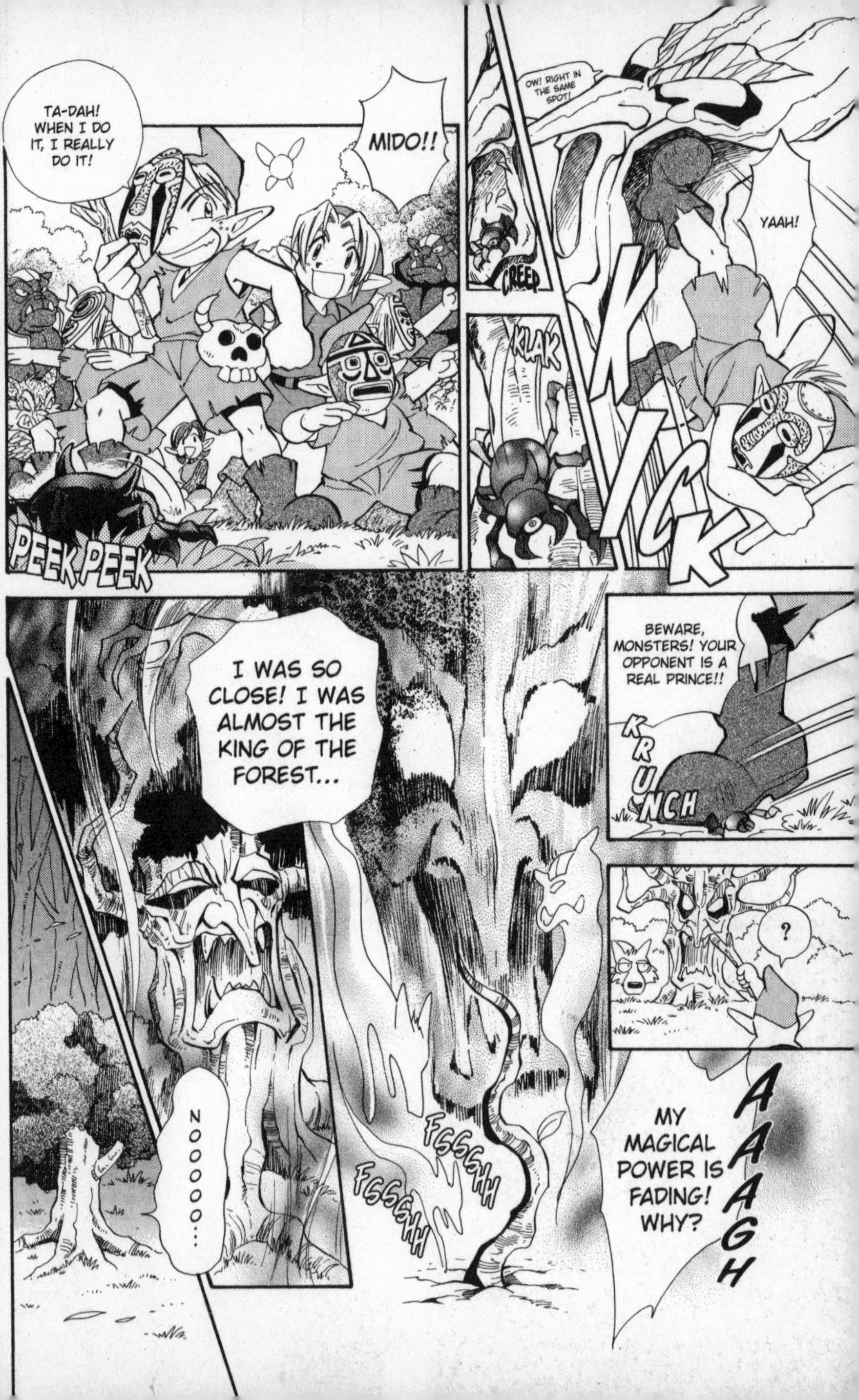
OW! RIGHT IN THE SAME SPOT!
YAAH!
KICK
CREEP
KLAK
MIDO!!
TA-DAH! WHEN I DO IT, I REALLY DO IT!
PEEK PEEK
BEWARE, MONSTERS! YOUR OPPONENT IS A REAL PRINCE!!
KRUNCH
?
AAAAGH
MY MAGICAL POWER IS FADING! WHY?
FSSGHH
FSSGHH
I WAS SO CLOSE! I WAS ALMOST THE KING OF THE FOREST...
NOOOOOO...

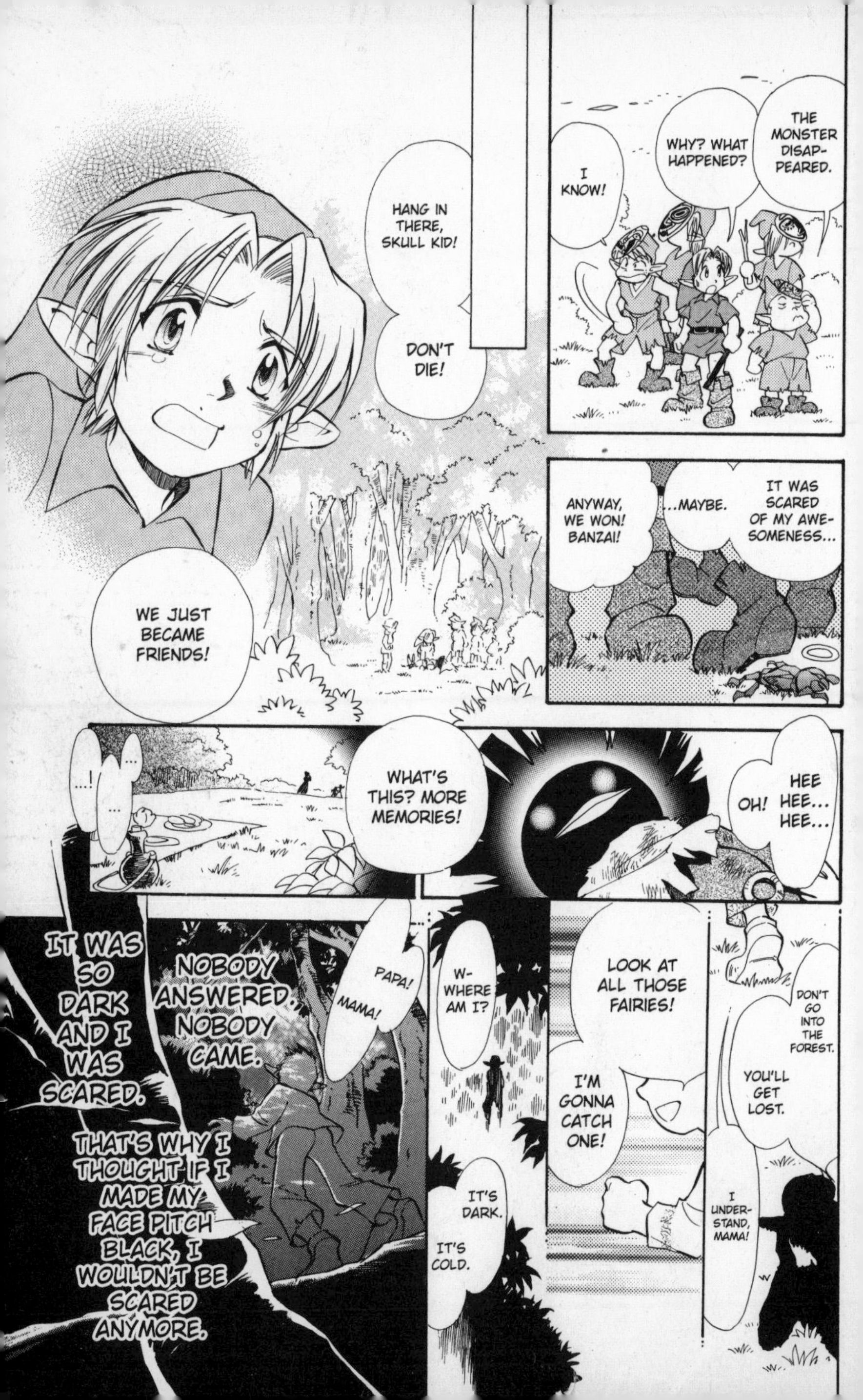
THE MONSTER DISAPPEARED.
WHY? WHAT HAPPENED?
I KNOW!
IT WAS SCARED OF MY AWESOMENESS...
...MAYBE.
ANYWAY, WE WON! BANZAI!
HANG IN THERE, SKULL KID!
DON'T DIE!
WE JUST BECAME FRIENDS!
OH!
HEE HEE... HEE...
WHAT'S THIS? MORE MEMORIES!
...
...!
...
DON'T GO INTO THE FOREST.
YOU'LL GET LOST.
I UNDERSTAND, MAMA!
LOOK AT ALL THOSE FAIRIES!
I'M GONNA CATCH ONE!
W-WHERE AM I?
IT'S DARK.
IT'S COLD.
PAPA!
MAMA!
NOBODY ANSWERED. NOBODY CAME.
IT WAS SO DARK AND I WAS SCARED.
THAT'S WHY I THOUGHT IF I MADE MY FACE PITCH BLACK, I WOULDN'T BE SCARED ANYMORE.

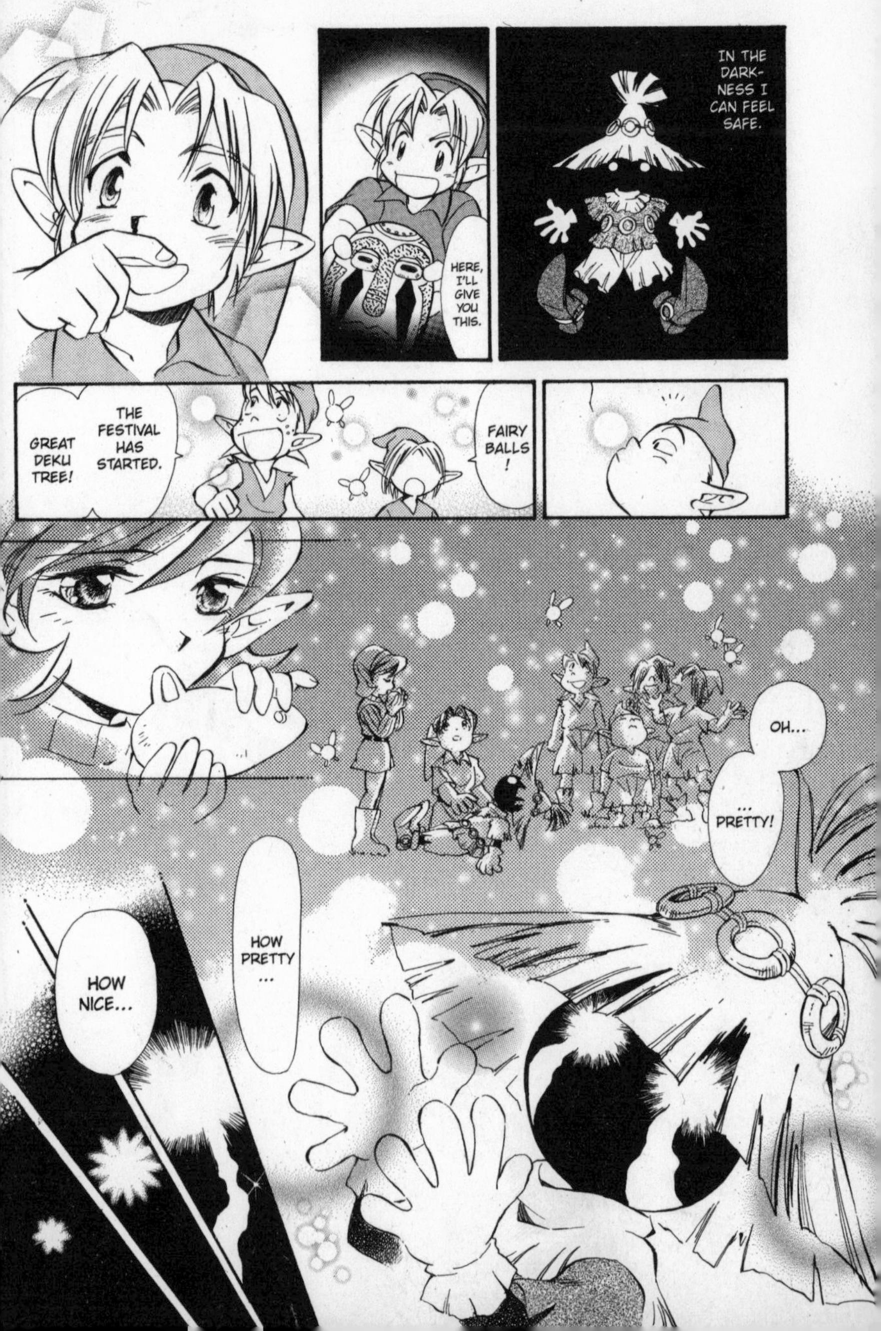
IN THE DARK- NESS I CAN FEEL SAFE.
HERE, I'LL GIVE YOU THIS.
FAIRY BALLS !
THE FESTIVAL HAS STARTED.
GREAT DEKU TREE!
OH...
... PRETTY!
HOW PRETTY ...
HOW NICE...

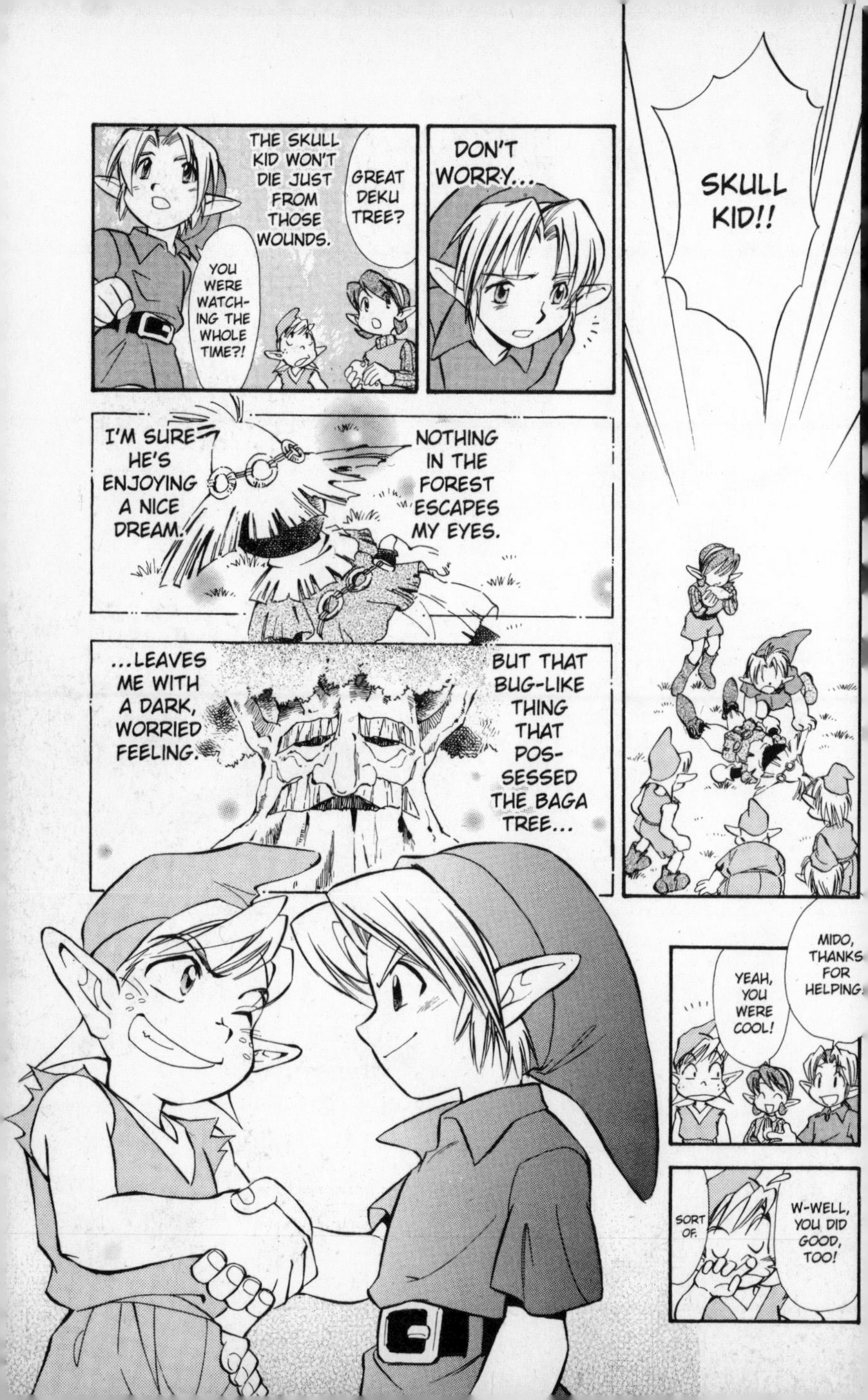

SKULL KID!!
DON'T WORRY...
THE SKULL KID WON'T DIE JUST FROM THOSE WOUNDS.
GREAT DEKU TREE?
YOU WERE WATCHING THE WHOLE TIME?!
NOTHING IN THE FOREST ESCAPES MY EYES.
I'M SURE HE'S ENJOYING A NICE DREAM.
BUT THAT BUG-LIKE THING THAT POS-SESSED THE BAGA TREE...
...LEAVES ME WITH A DARK, WORRIED FEELING.
MIDO, THANKS FOR HELPING.
YEAH, YOU WERE COOL!
W-WELL, YOU DID GOOD, TOO!
SORT OF.

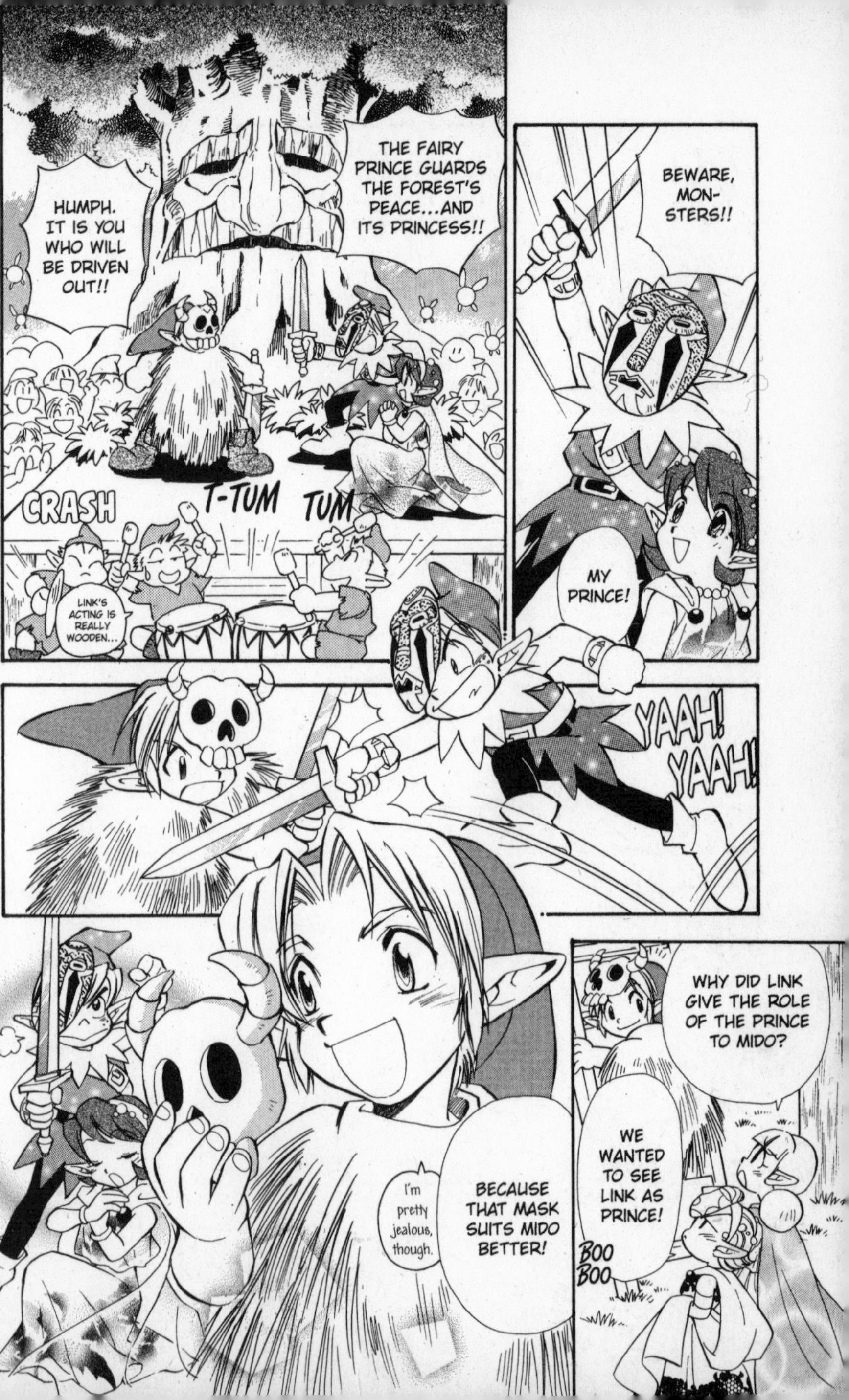
BEWARE, MONSTERS!!
MY PRINCE!
THE FAIRY PRINCE GUARDS THE FOREST'S PEACE...AND ITS PRINCESS!!
HUMPH. IT IS YOU WHO WILL BE DRIVEN OUT!!
TUM
T-TUM
CRASH
LINK'S ACTING IS REALLY WOODEN...
YAAH! YAAH!
WHY DID LINK GIVE THE ROLE OF THE PRINCE TO MIDO?
WE WANTED TO SEE LINK AS PRINCE!
BOO BOO
BECAUSE THAT MASK SUITS MIDO BETTER!
I'm pretty jealous, though.

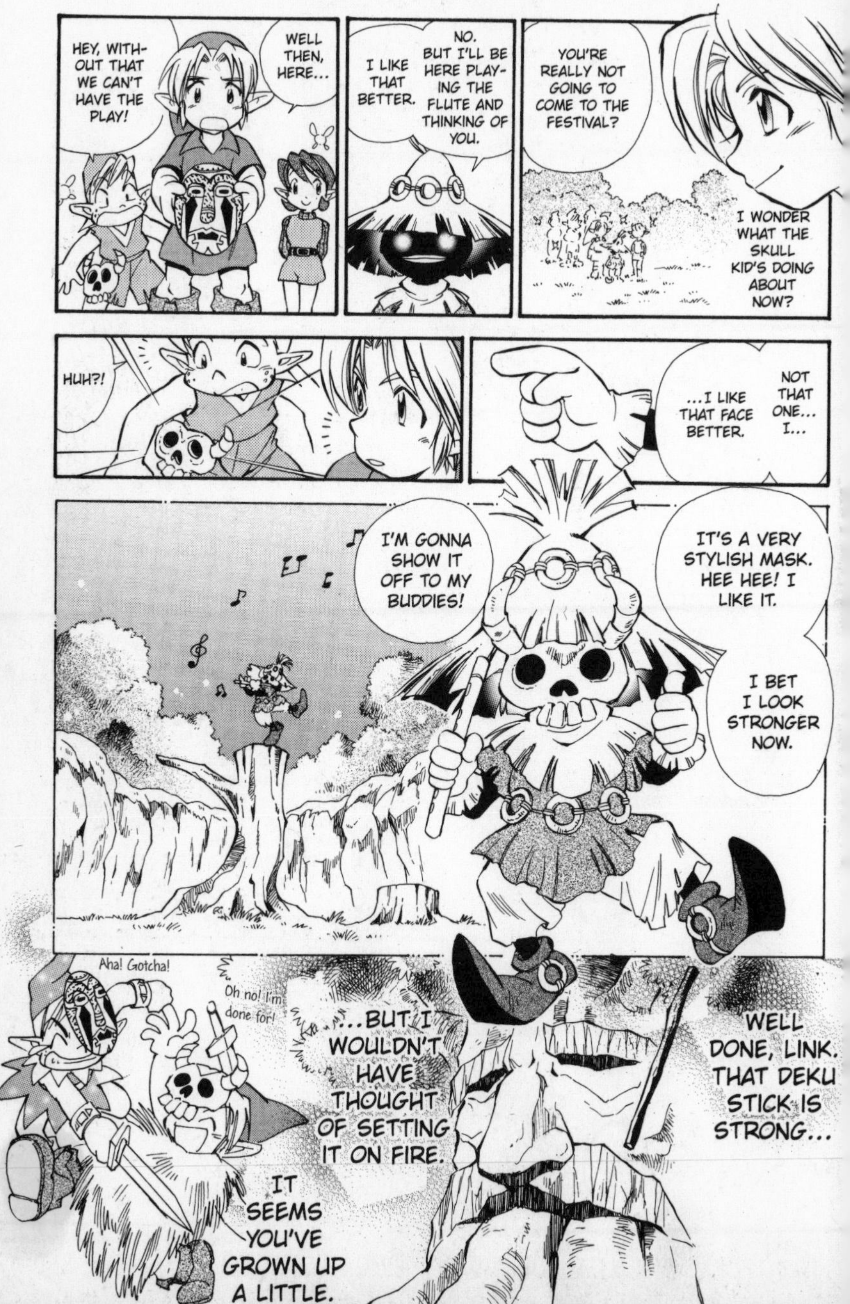
YOU'RE REALLY NOT GOING TO COME TO THE FESTIVAL?
I WONDER WHAT THE SKULL KID'S DOING ABOUT NOW?
NO. BUT I'LL BE HERE PLAYING THE FLUTE AND THINKING OF YOU.
I LIKE THAT BETTER.
WELL THEN, HERE...
HEY, WITHOUT THAT WE CAN'T HAVE THE PLAY!
NOT THAT ONE... I...
...I LIKE THAT FACE BETTER.
HUH?!
IT'S A VERY STYLISH MASK. HEE HEE! I LIKE IT.
I'M GONNA SHOW IT OFF TO MY BUDDIES!
I BET I LOOK STRONGER NOW.
WELL DONE, LINK. THAT DEKU STICK IS STRONG...
...BUT I WOULDN'T HAVE THOUGHT OF SETTING IT ON FIRE.
IT SEEMS YOU'VE GROWN UP A LITTLE.
Aha! Gotcha!
Oh no! I'm done for!

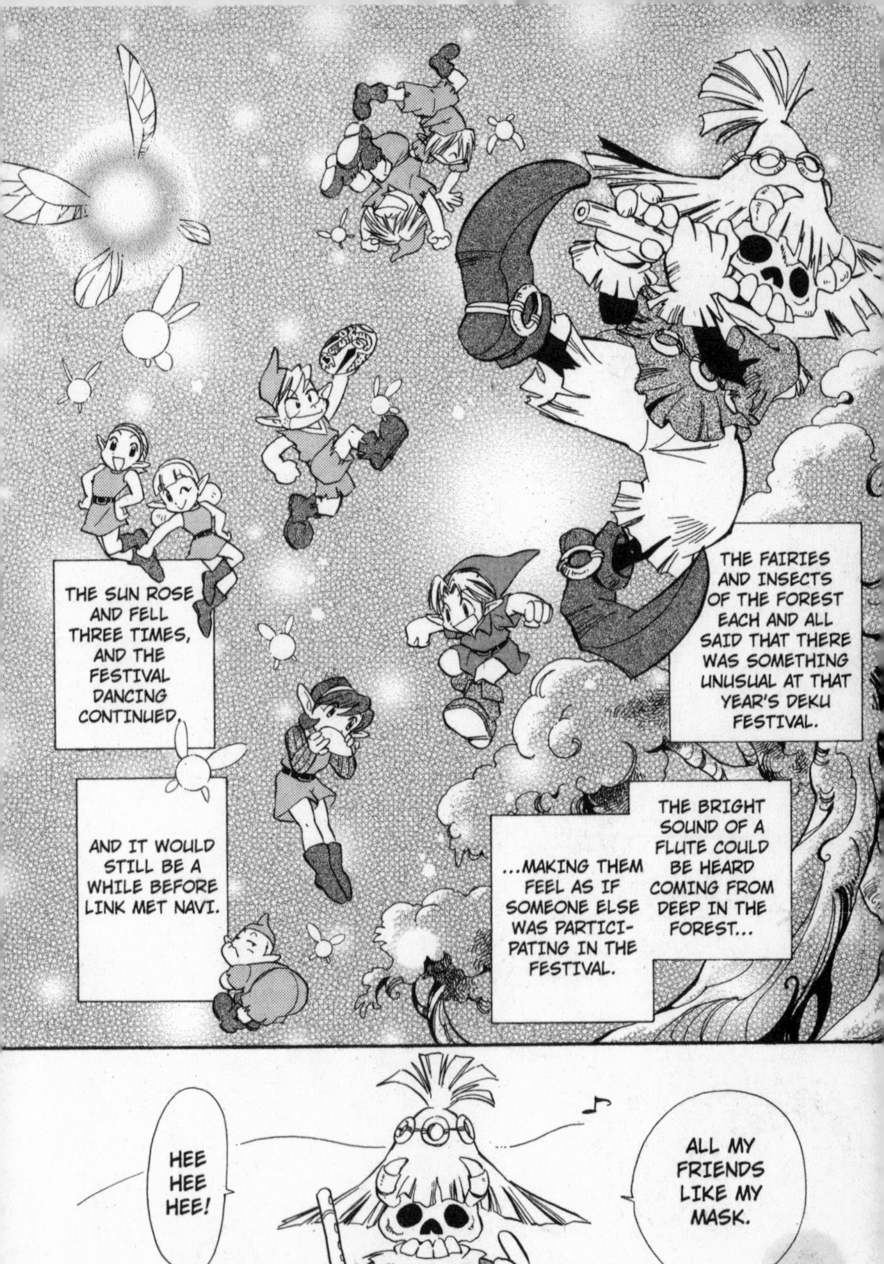
THE FAIRIES AND INSECTS OF THE FOREST EACH AND ALL SAID THAT THERE WAS SOMETHING UNUSUAL AT THAT YEAR'S DEKU FESTIVAL.
THE BRIGHT SOUND OF A FLUTE COULD BE HEARD COMING FROM DEEP IN THE FOREST...
...MAKING THEM FEEL AS IF SOMEONE ELSE WAS PARTICI-PATING IN THE FESTIVAL.
THE SUN ROSE AND FELL THREE TIMES, AND THE FESTIVAL DANCING CONTINUED.
AND IT WOULD STILL BE A WHILE BEFORE LINK MET NAVI.
ALL MY FRIENDS LIKE MY MASK.
HEE HEE HEE!

LEGEND OF ZELDA ~ OCARINA OF TIME ~ BONUS CHAPTER ~ THE END

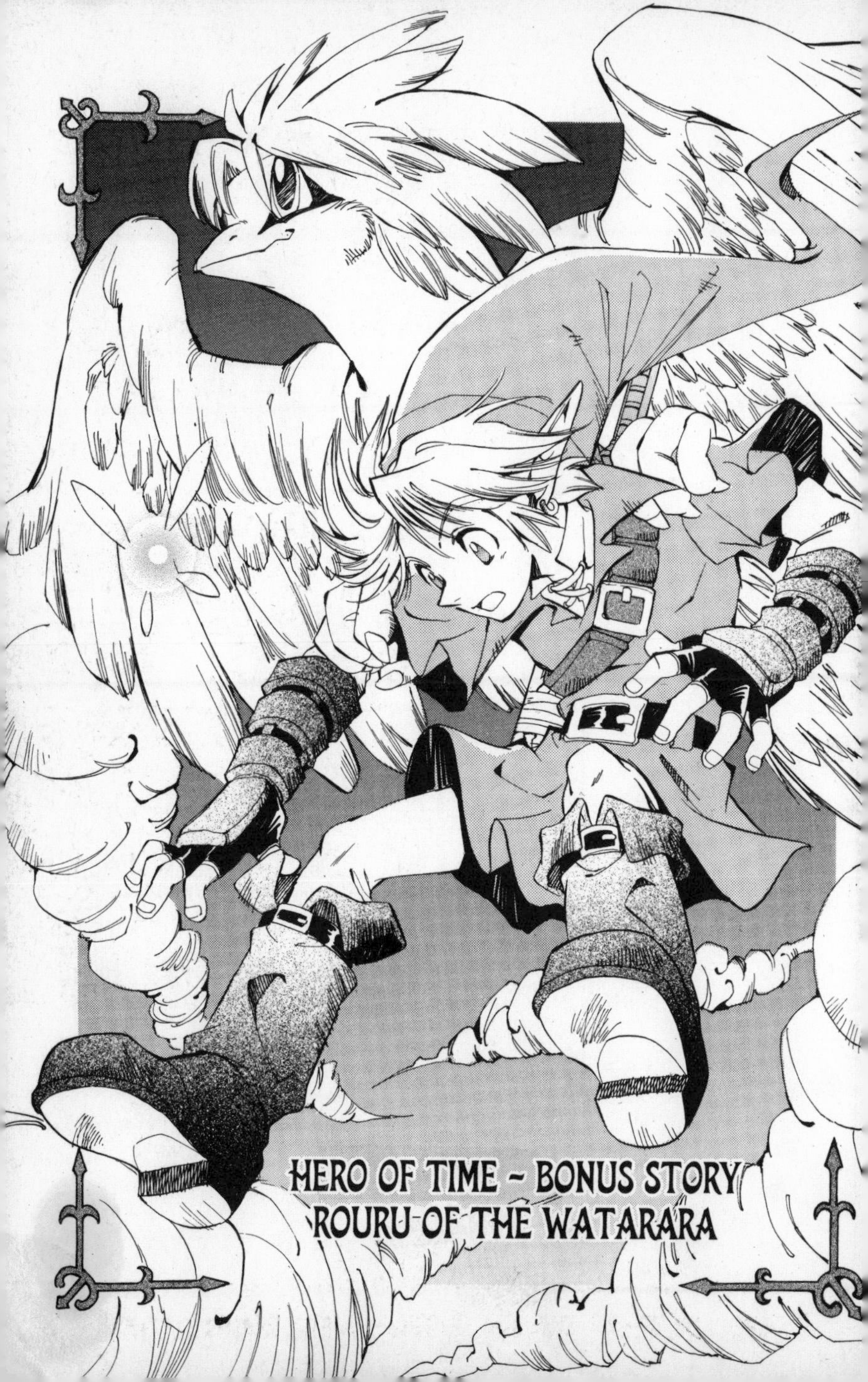
HERO OF TIME ~ BONUS STORY
ROURU OF THE WATARARA

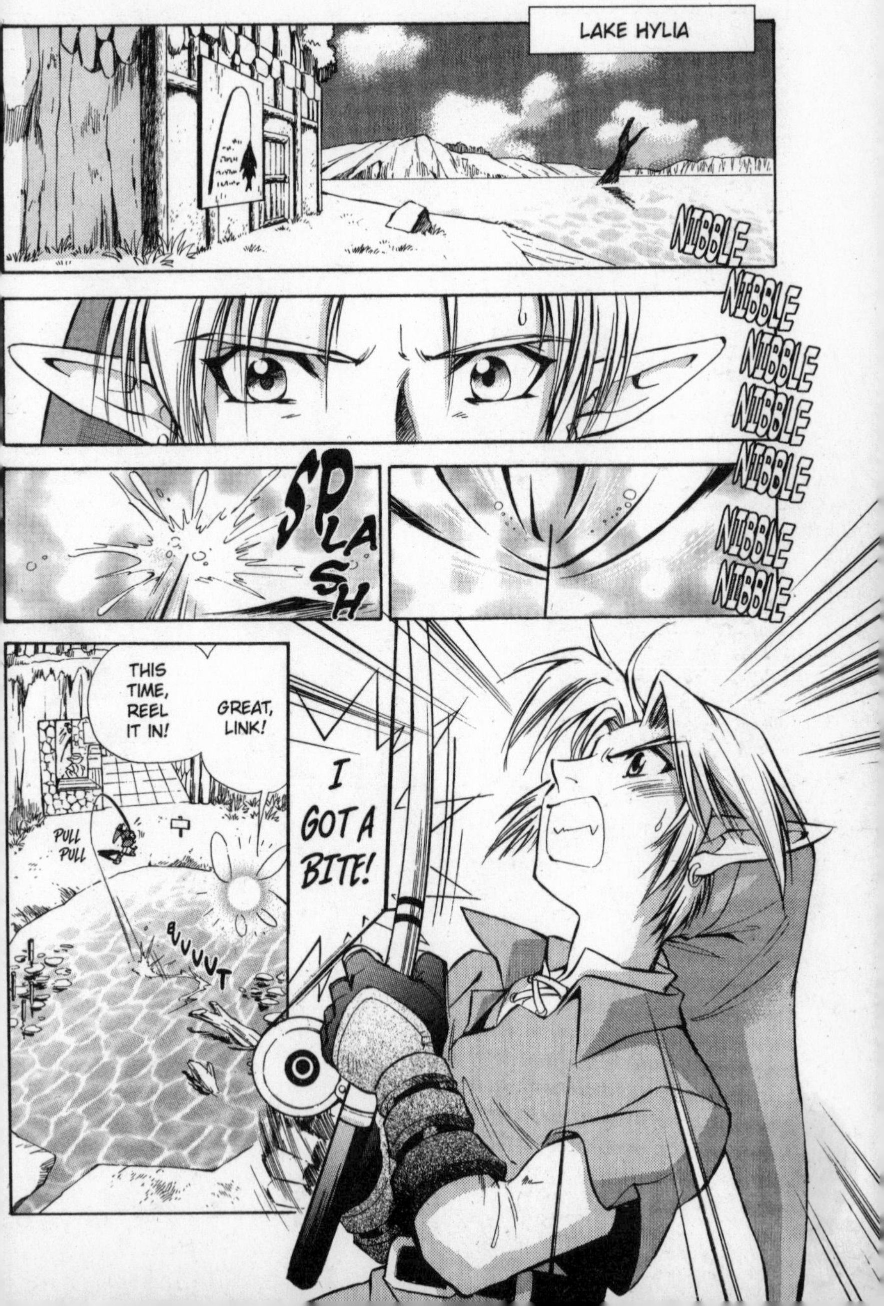

LAKE HYLIA
NIBBLE
NIBBLE
NIBBLE
NIBBLE
NIBBLE
NIBBLE
NIBBLE
SPLASH
I GOT A BITE!
GREAT, LINK!
THIS TIME, REEL IT IN!
PULL PULL
VUUUT

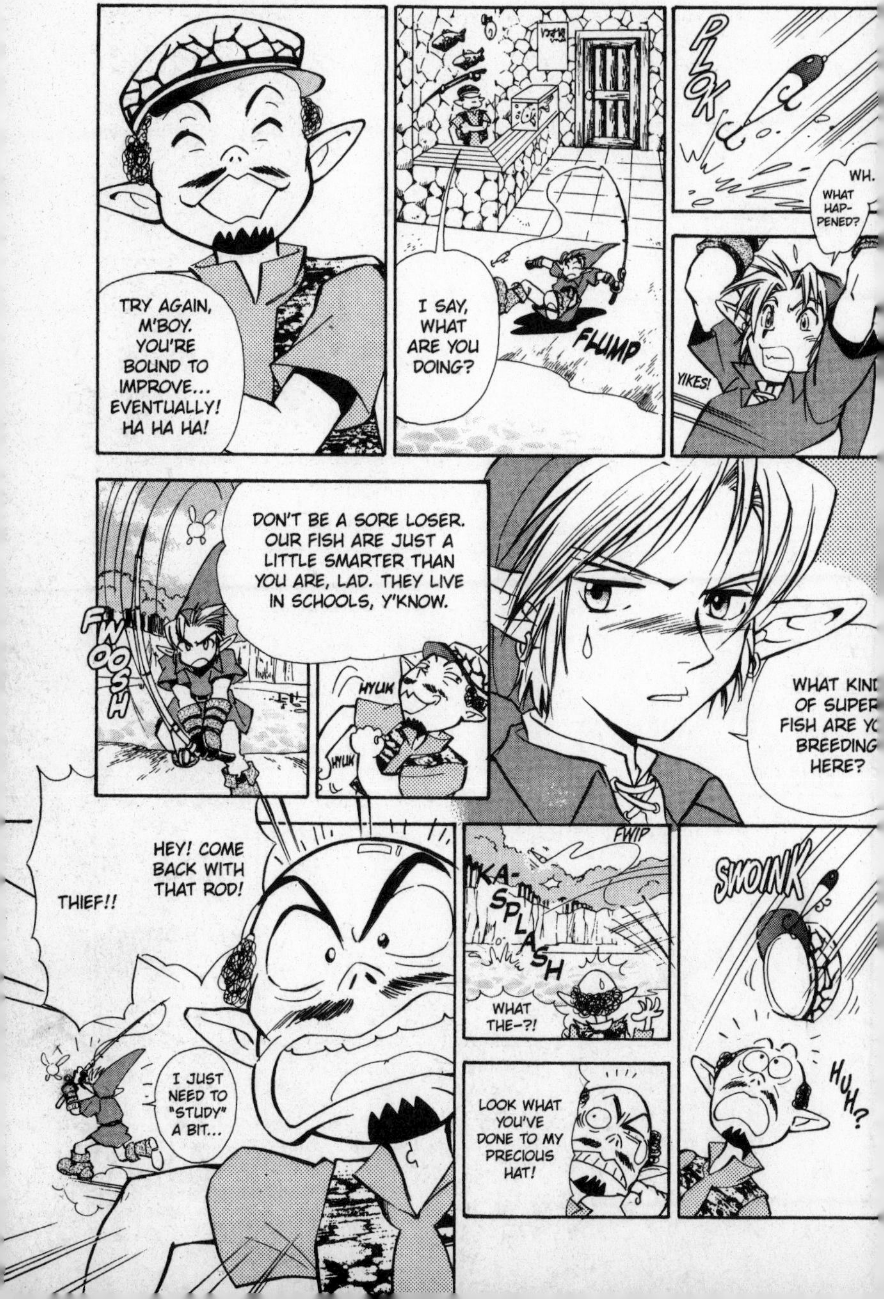
PLOK
WH.
WHAT HAPPENED?
YIKES!
I SAY, WHAT ARE YOU DOING?
FLUMP
TRY AGAIN, M'BOY. YOU'RE BOUND TO IMPROVE... EVENTUALLY! HA HA HA!
WHAT KIND OF SUPER FISH ARE YO BREEDING HERE?
DON'T BE A SORE LOSER. OUR FISH ARE JUST A LITTLE SMARTER THAN YOU ARE, LAD. THEY LIVE IN SCHOOLS, Y'KNOW.
HYUK
HYUK
FWOOSH
SWOINK
HUH?
LOOK WHAT YOU'VE DONE TO MY PRECIOUS HAT!
FWIP
KA-SPLASH
WHAT THE-?!
HEY! COME BACK WITH THAT ROD!
THIEF!!
I JUST NEED TO "STUDY" A BIT...

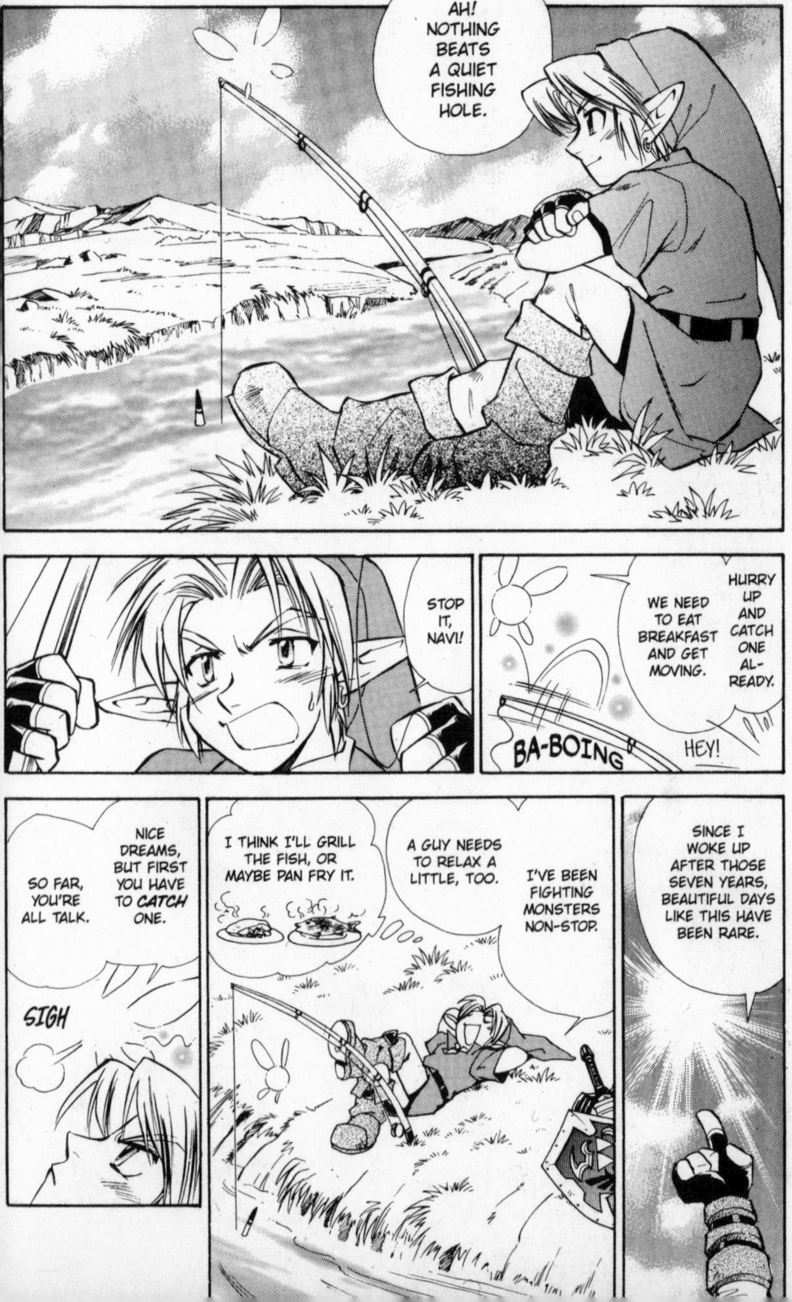
AH! NOTHING BEATS A QUIET FISHING HOLE.
HURRY UP AND CATCH ONE AL-READY.
WE NEED TO EAT BREAKFAST AND GET MOVING.
HEY!
BA-BOING
STOP IT, NAVI!
SINCE I WOKE UP AFTER THOSE SEVEN YEARS, BEAUTIFUL DAYS LIKE THIS HAVE BEEN RARE.
I'VE BEEN FIGHTING MONSTERS NON-STOP.
A GUY NEEDS TO RELAX A LITTLE, TOO.
I THINK I'LL GRILL THE FISH, OR MAYBE PAN FRY IT.
NICE DREAMS, BUT FIRST YOU HAVE TO *CATCH* ONE.
SO FAR, YOU'RE ALL TALK.
SIGH

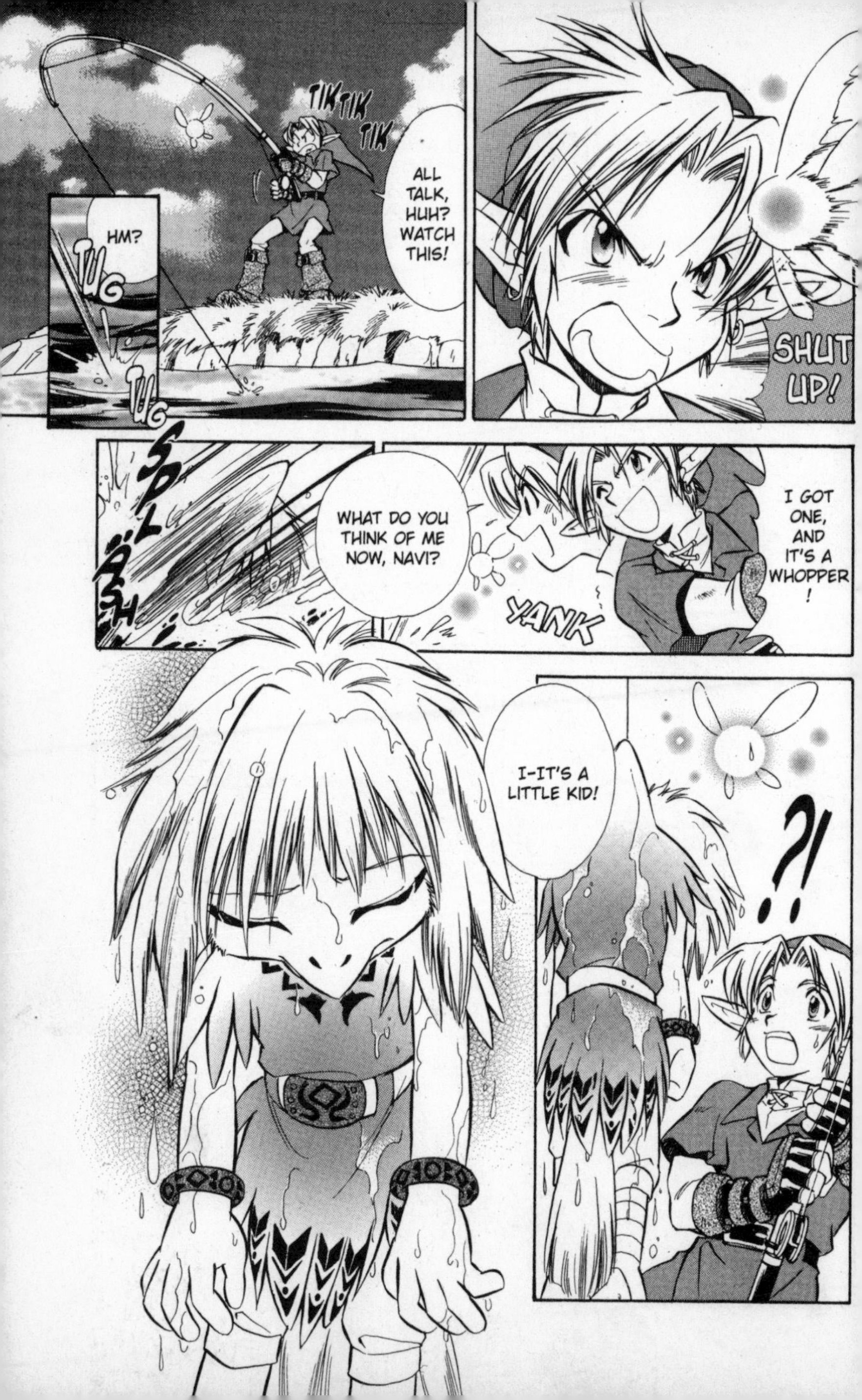
SHUT UP!
ALL TALK, HUH? WATCH THIS!
TIK TIK TIK
HM?
TUG TUG
I GOT ONE, AND IT'S A WHOPPER!
YANK
WHAT DO YOU THINK OF ME NOW, NAVI?
SPLASH
I-IT'S A LITTLE KID!
?!

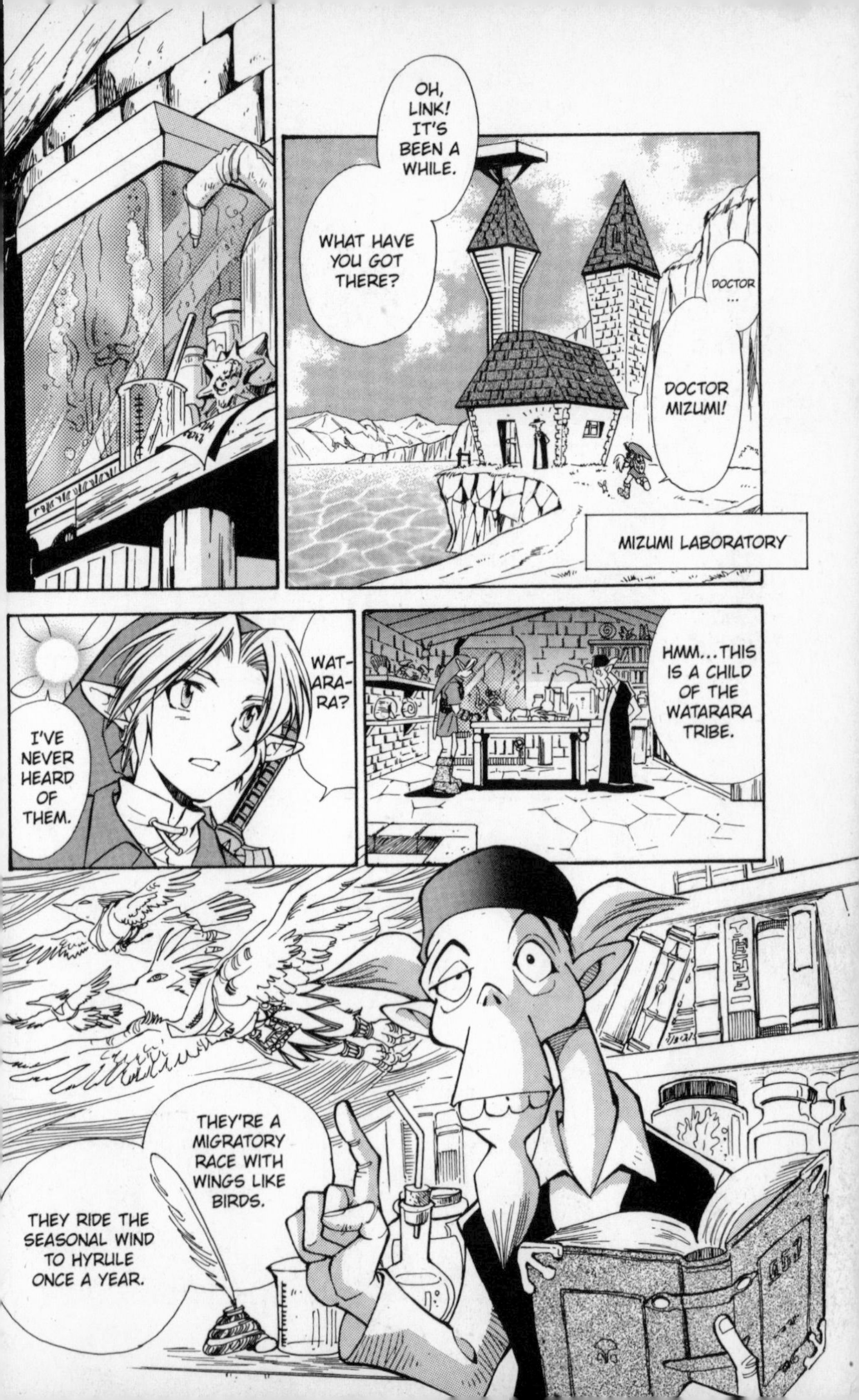
DOCTOR ...
DOCTOR MIZUMI!
MIZUMI LABORATORY
OH, LINK! IT'S BEEN A WHILE.
WHAT HAVE YOU GOT THERE?
HMM...THIS IS A CHILD OF THE WATARARA TRIBE.
WAT-ARA-RA?
I'VE NEVER HEARD OF THEM.
THEY'RE A MIGRATORY RACE WITH WINGS LIKE BIRDS.
THEY RIDE THE SEASONAL WIND TO HYRULE ONCE A YEAR.

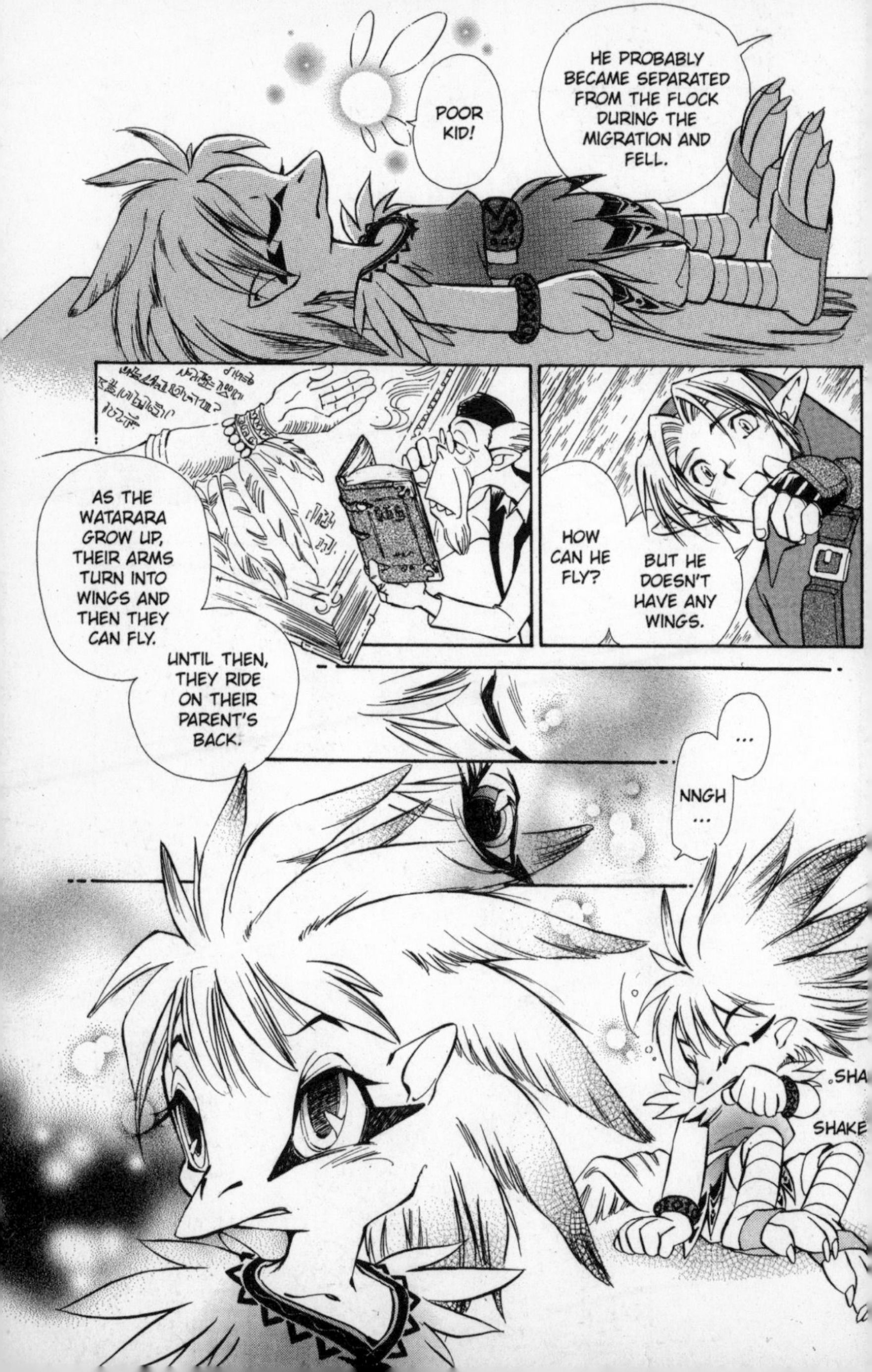
HE PROBABLY BECAME SEPARATED FROM THE FLOCK DURING THE MIGRATION AND FELL.
POOR KID!
BUT HE DOESN'T HAVE ANY WINGS.
HOW CAN HE FLY?
AS THE WATARARA GROW UP, THEIR ARMS TURN INTO WINGS AND THEN THEY CAN FLY.
UNTIL THEN, THEY RIDE ON THEIR PARENT'S BACK.
...
NNGH ...
SHA
SHAKE

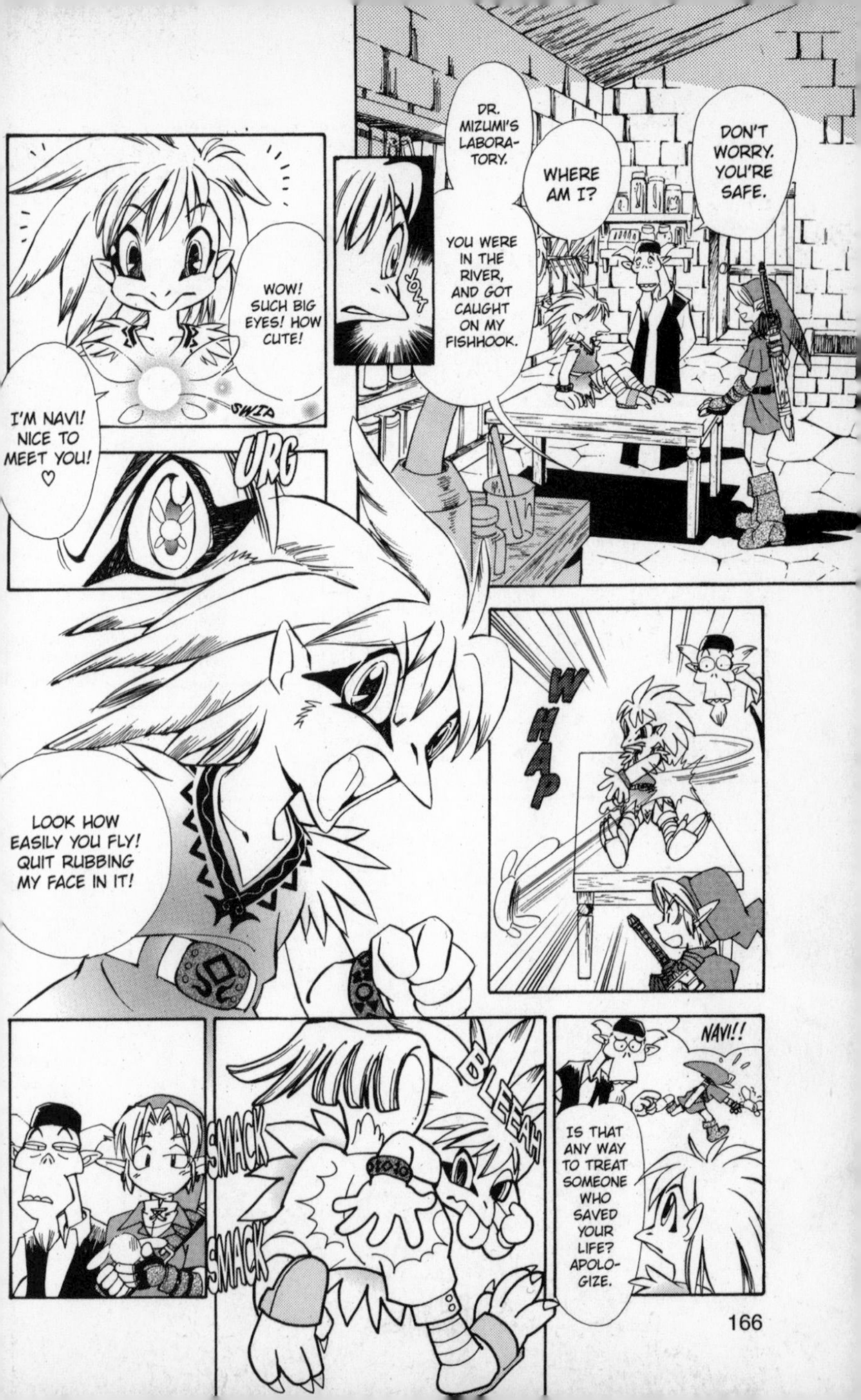
DON'T WORRY. YOU'RE SAFE.
WHERE AM I?
DR. MIZUMI'S LABORA-TORY.
YOU WERE IN THE RIVER, AND GOT CAUGHT ON MY FISHHOOK.
YOW
WOW! SUCH BIG EYES! HOW CUTE!
I'M NAVI! NICE TO MEET YOU! ♡
URG
WHAP
LOOK HOW EASILY YOU FLY! QUIT RUBBING MY FACE IN IT!
NAVI!!
IS THAT ANY WAY TO TREAT SOMEONE WHO SAVED YOUR LIFE? APOLO-GIZE.
BLEEAH
SMACK
SMACK

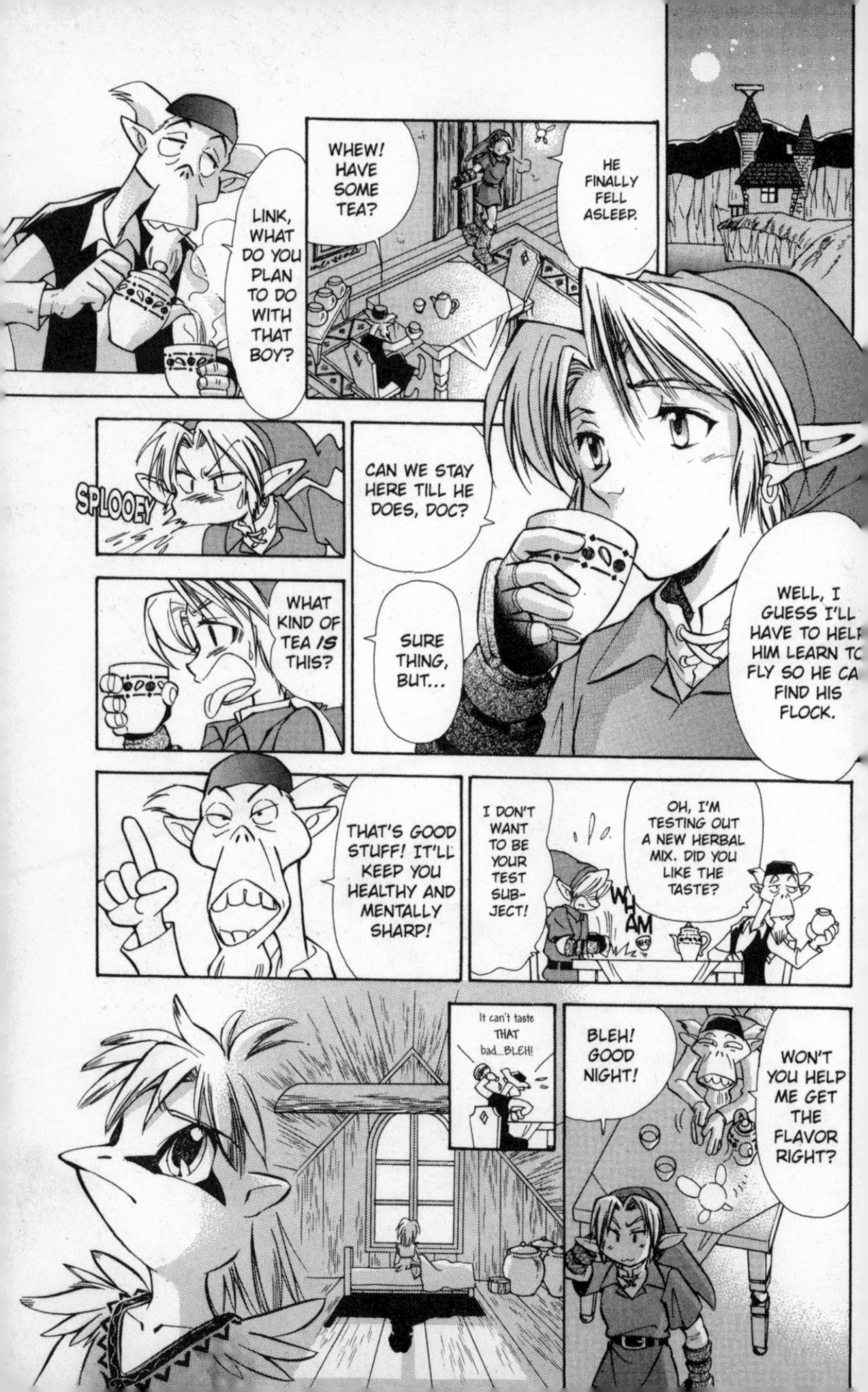
HE FINALLY FELL ASLEEP.
WHEW! HAVE SOME TEA?
LINK, WHAT DO YOU PLAN TO DO WITH THAT BOY?
WELL, I GUESS I'LL HAVE TO HELP HIM LEARN TO FLY SO HE CAN FIND HIS FLOCK.
CAN WE STAY HERE TILL HE DOES, DOC?
SPLOOEY
SURE THING, BUT...
WHAT KIND OF TEA *IS* THIS?
OH, I'M TESTING OUT A NEW HERBAL MIX. DID YOU LIKE THE TASTE?
I DON'T WANT TO BE YOUR TEST SUB-JECT!
WHAM
THAT'S GOOD STUFF! IT'LL KEEP YOU HEALTHY AND MENTALLY SHARP!
WON'T YOU HELP ME GET THE FLAVOR RIGHT?
BLEH! GOOD NIGHT!
It can't taste THAT bad...BLEH!

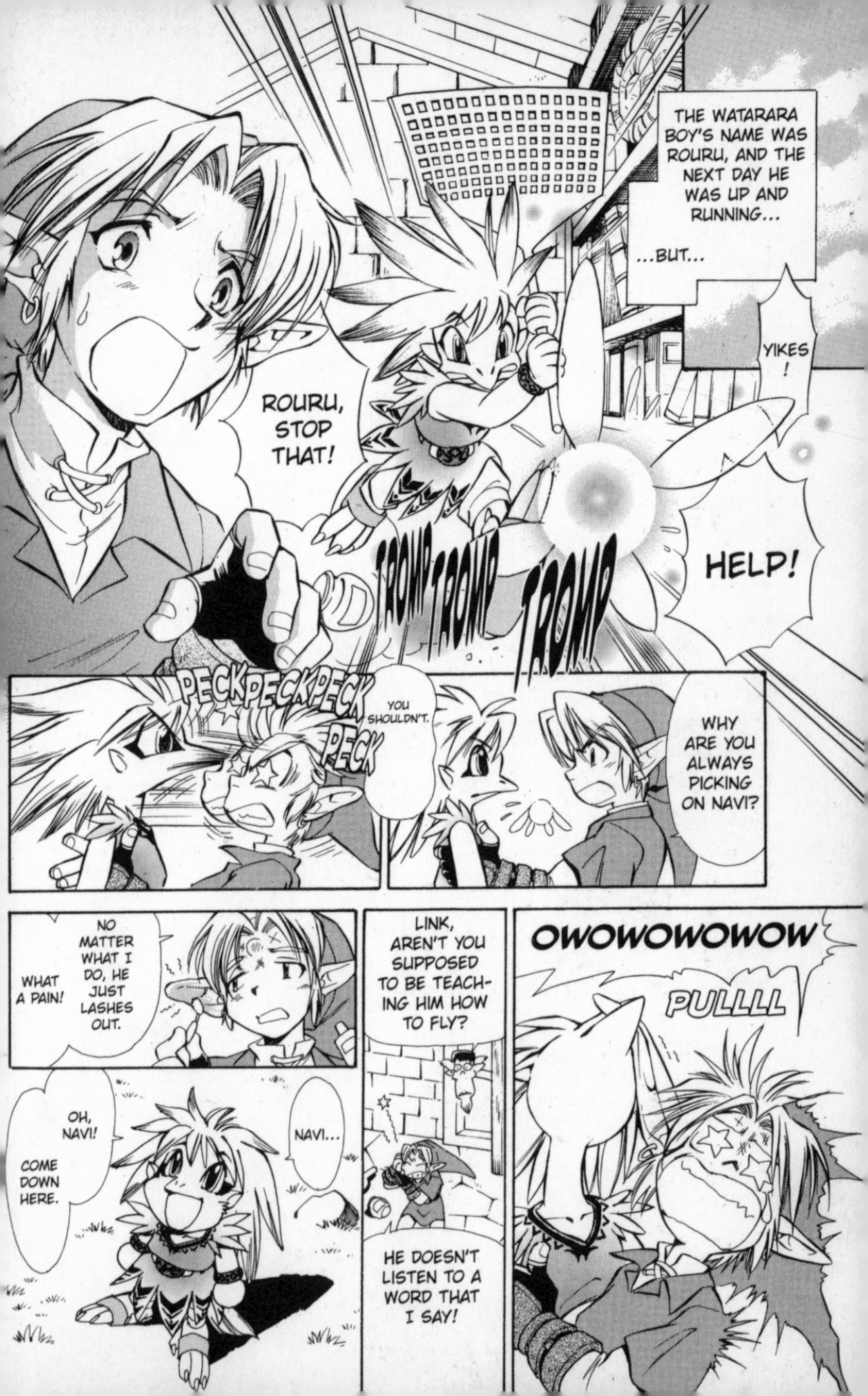
THE WATARARA BOY'S NAME WAS ROURU, AND THE NEXT DAY HE WAS UP AND RUNNING...
...BUT...
YIKES!
HELP!
TROMP TROMP TROMP
ROURU, STOP THAT!
WHY ARE YOU ALWAYS PICKING ON NAVI?
YOU SHOULDN'T.
PECKPECKPECK PECK
OWOWOWOWOWOW
PULLLL
LINK, AREN'T YOU SUPPOSED TO BE TEACHING HIM HOW TO FLY?
HE DOESN'T LISTEN TO A WORD THAT I SAY!
NO MATTER WHAT I DO, HE JUST LASHES OUT.
WHAT A PAIN!
NAVI...
OH, NAVI!
COME DOWN HERE.

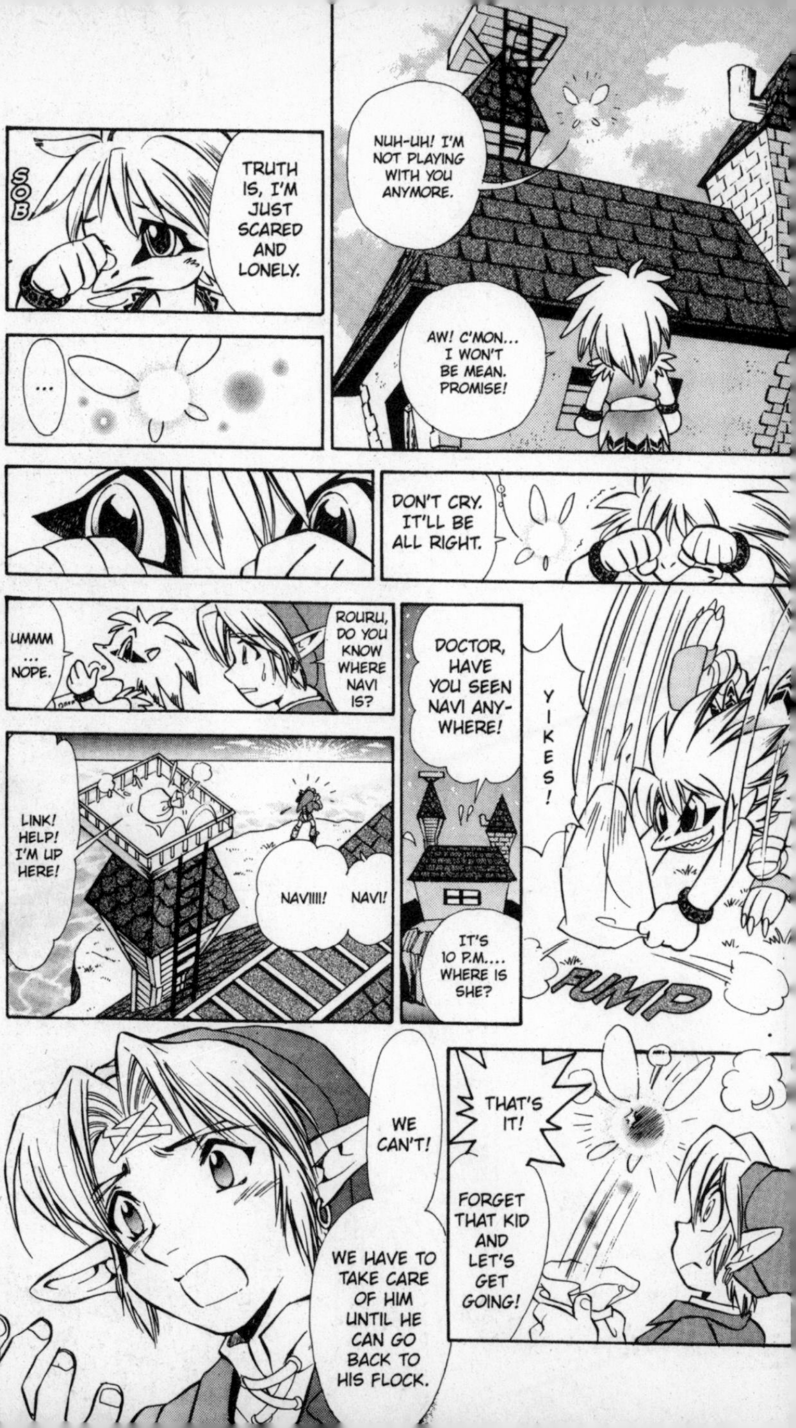
NUH-UH! I'M NOT PLAYING WITH YOU ANYMORE.
AW! C'MON... I WON'T BE MEAN. PROMISE!
SOB
TRUTH IS, I'M JUST SCARED AND LONELY.
...
DON'T CRY. IT'LL BE ALL RIGHT.
YIKES!
FUMP
DOCTOR, HAVE YOU SEEN NAVI ANYWHERE!
IT'S 10 P.M.... WHERE IS SHE?
ROURU, DO YOU KNOW WHERE NAVI IS?
UMMM ... NOPE.
NAVI!
NAVIIII!
LINK! HELP! I'M UP HERE!
THAT'S IT!
FORGET THAT KID AND LET'S GET GOING!
WE CAN'T!
WE HAVE TO TAKE CARE OF HIM UNTIL HE CAN GO BACK TO HIS FLOCK.

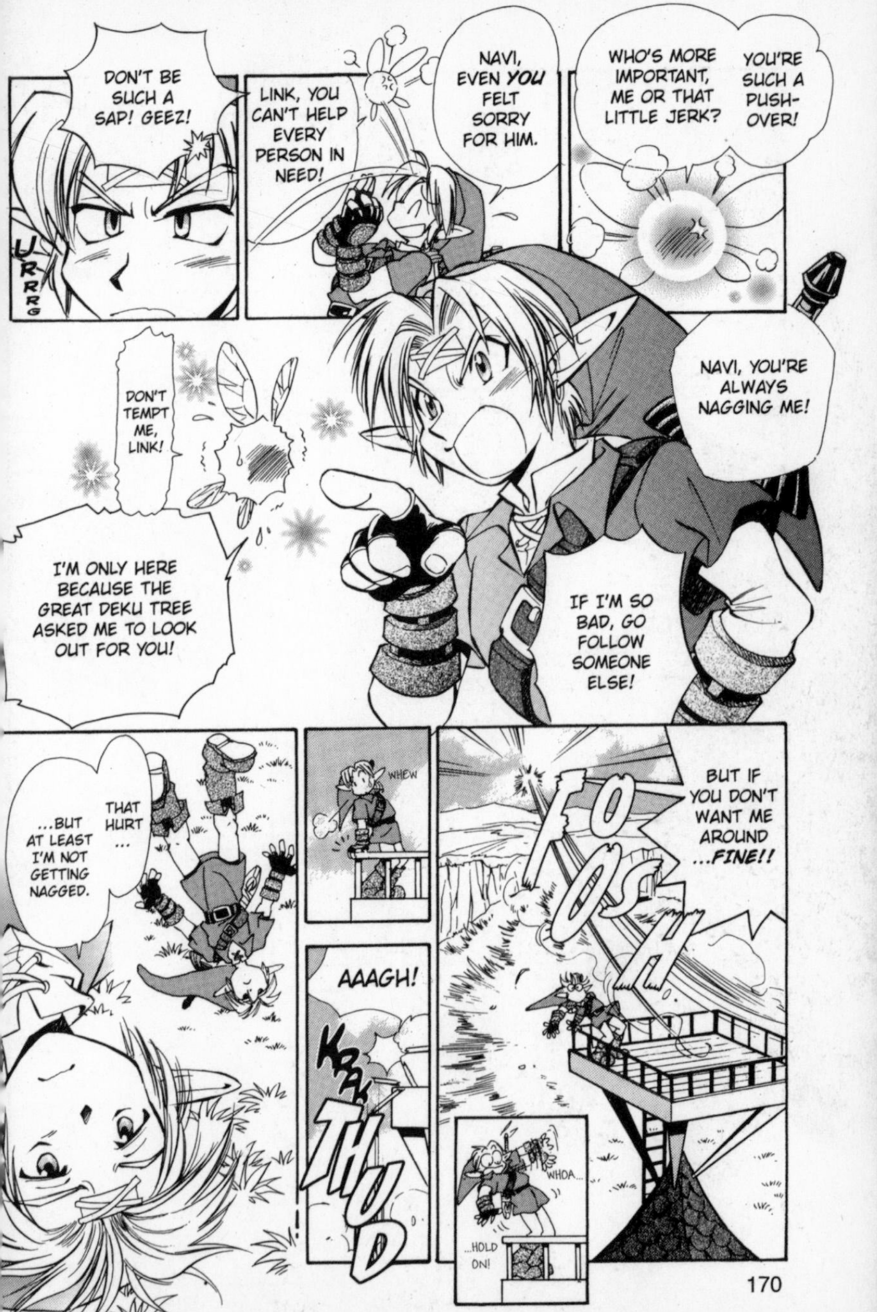
YOU'RE SUCH A PUSH-OVER!
WHO'S MORE IMPORTANT, ME OR THAT LITTLE JERK?
NAVI, EVEN ***YOU*** FELT SORRY FOR HIM.
LINK, YOU CAN'T HELP EVERY PERSON IN NEED!
DON'T BE SUCH A SAP! GEEZ!
URRRG
NAVI, YOU'RE ALWAYS NAGGING ME!
IF I'M SO BAD, GO FOLLOW SOMEONE ELSE!
DON'T TEMPT ME, LINK!
I'M ONLY HERE BECAUSE THE GREAT DEKU TREE ASKED ME TO LOOK OUT FOR YOU!
BUT IF YOU DON'T WANT ME AROUND ...***FINE!!***
FOOSH
WHOA...
...HOLD ON!
WHEW
AAAGH!
KRAK
THUD
THAT HURT...
...BUT AT LEAST I'M NOT GETTING NAGGED.

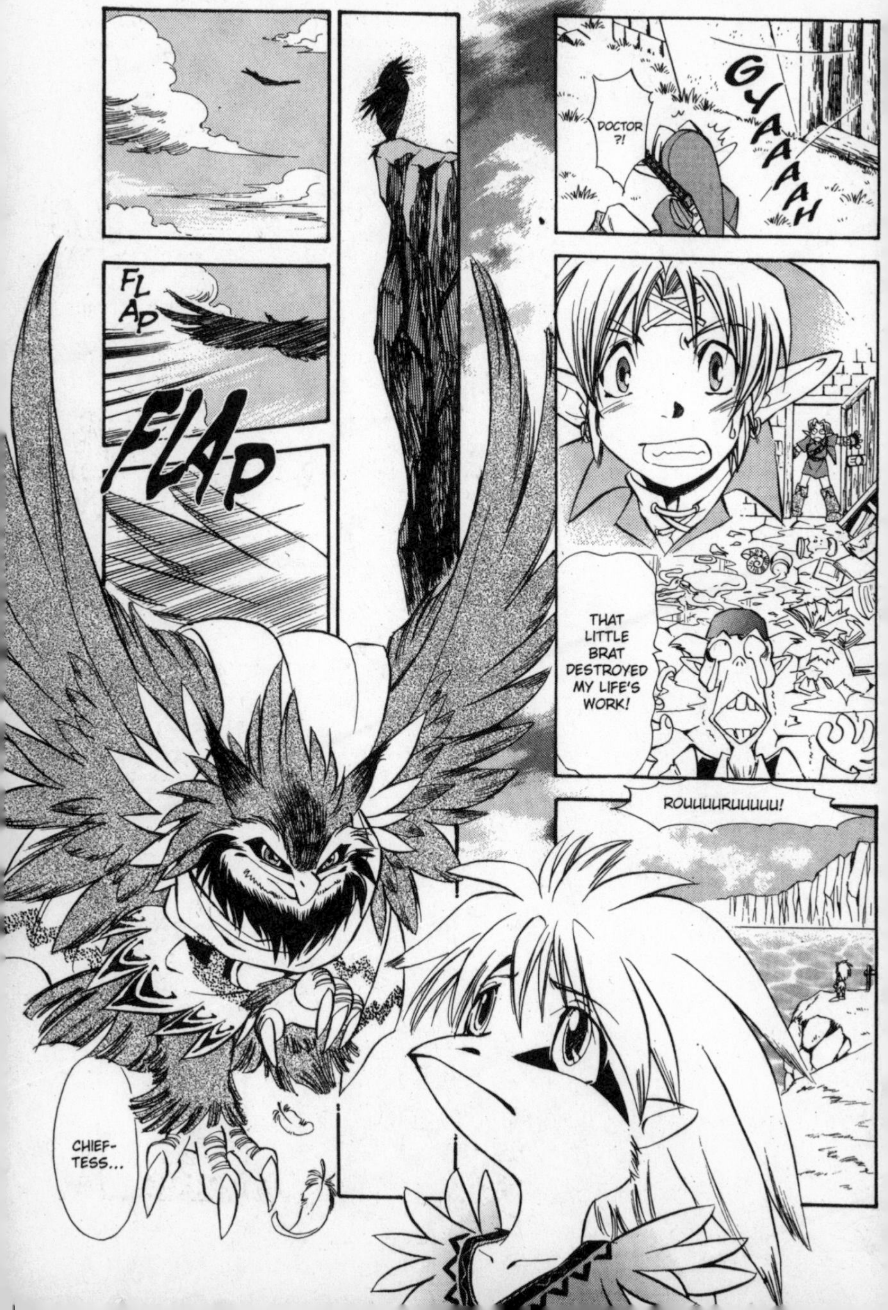
GYAAAAAH
DOCTOR ?!
THAT LITTLE BRAT DESTROYED MY LIFE'S WORK!
ROUUUURUUUUU!
FLAP
FLAP
CHIEF-TESS...

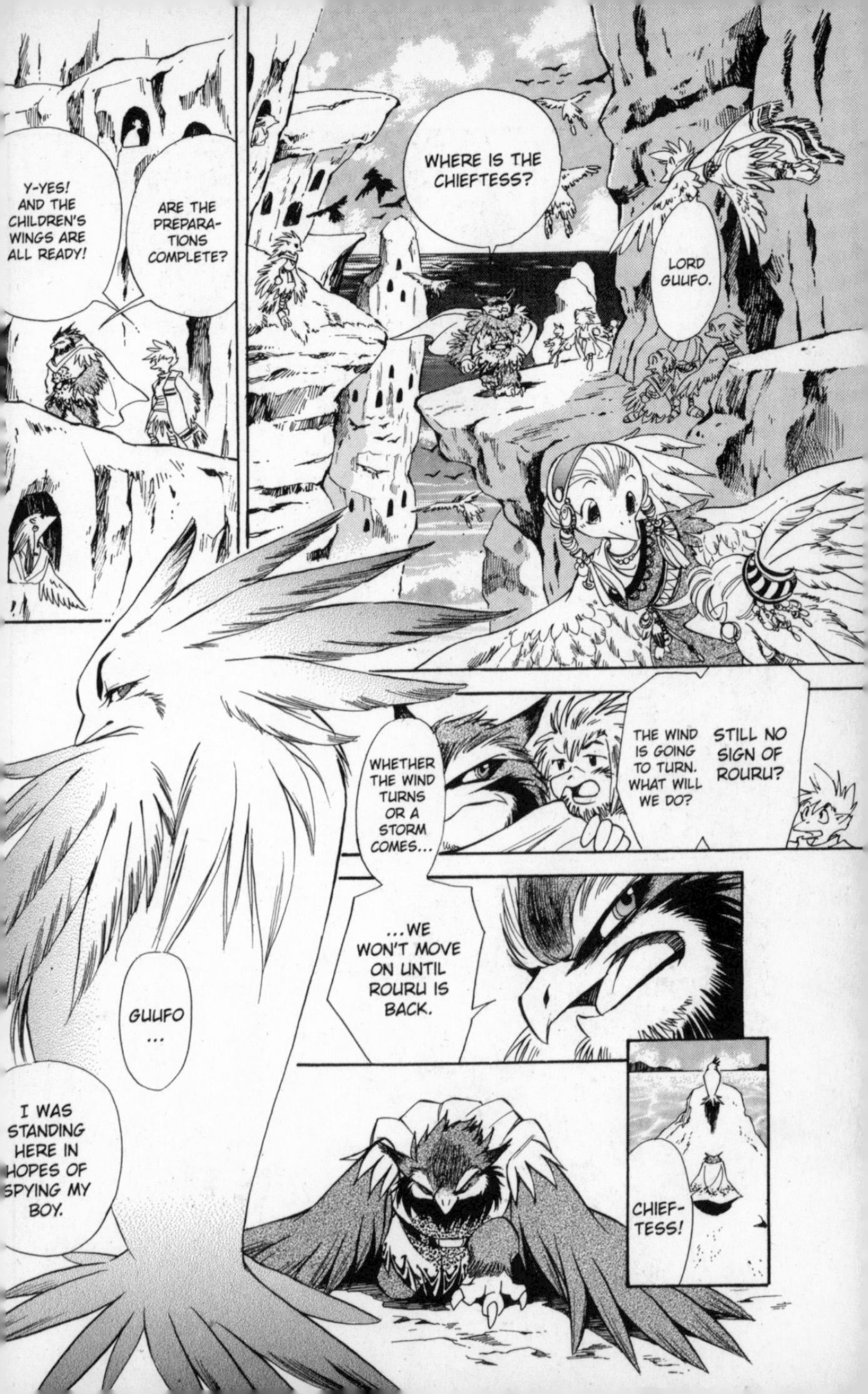

LORD GUUFO.
WHERE IS THE CHIEFTESS?
ARE THE PREPARATIONS COMPLETE?
Y-YES! AND THE CHILDREN'S WINGS ARE ALL READY!
STILL NO SIGN OF ROURU?
THE WIND IS GOING TO TURN. WHAT WILL WE DO?
WHETHER THE WIND TURNS OR A STORM COMES...
...WE WON'T MOVE ON UNTIL ROURU IS BACK.
CHIEF-TESS!
GUUFO...
I WAS STANDING HERE IN HOPES OF SPYING MY BOY.

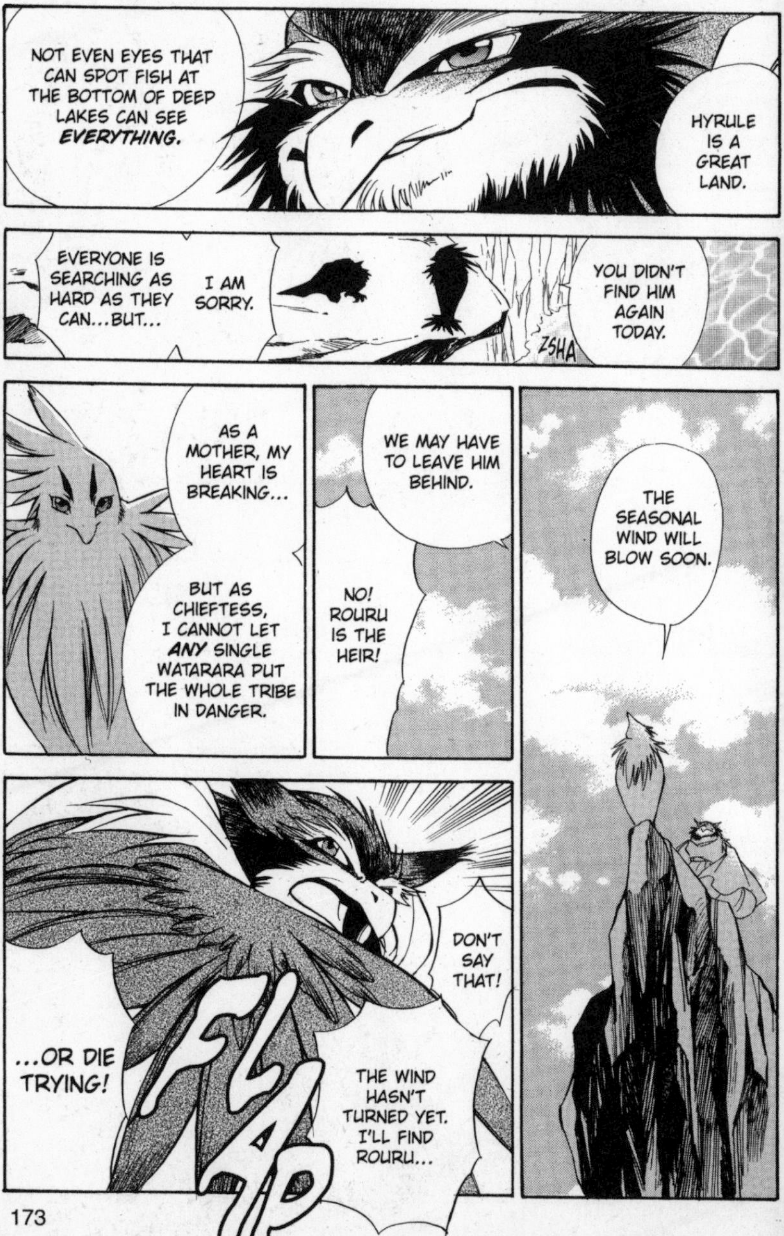
HYRULE IS A GREAT LAND.
NOT EVEN EYES THAT CAN SPOT FISH AT THE BOTTOM OF DEEP LAKES CAN SEE **EVERYTHING.**
YOU DIDN'T FIND HIM AGAIN TODAY.
ZSHA
I AM SORRY.
EVERYONE IS SEARCHING AS HARD AS THEY CAN...BUT...
THE SEASONAL WIND WILL BLOW SOON.
WE MAY HAVE TO LEAVE HIM BEHIND.
NO! ROURU IS THE HEIR!
AS A MOTHER, MY HEART IS BREAKING...
BUT AS CHIEFTESS, I CANNOT LET ***ANY*** SINGLE WATARARA PUT THE WHOLE TRIBE IN DANGER.
DON'T SAY THAT!
THE WIND HASN'T TURNED YET. I'LL FIND ROURU...
FLAP
...OR DIE TRYING!

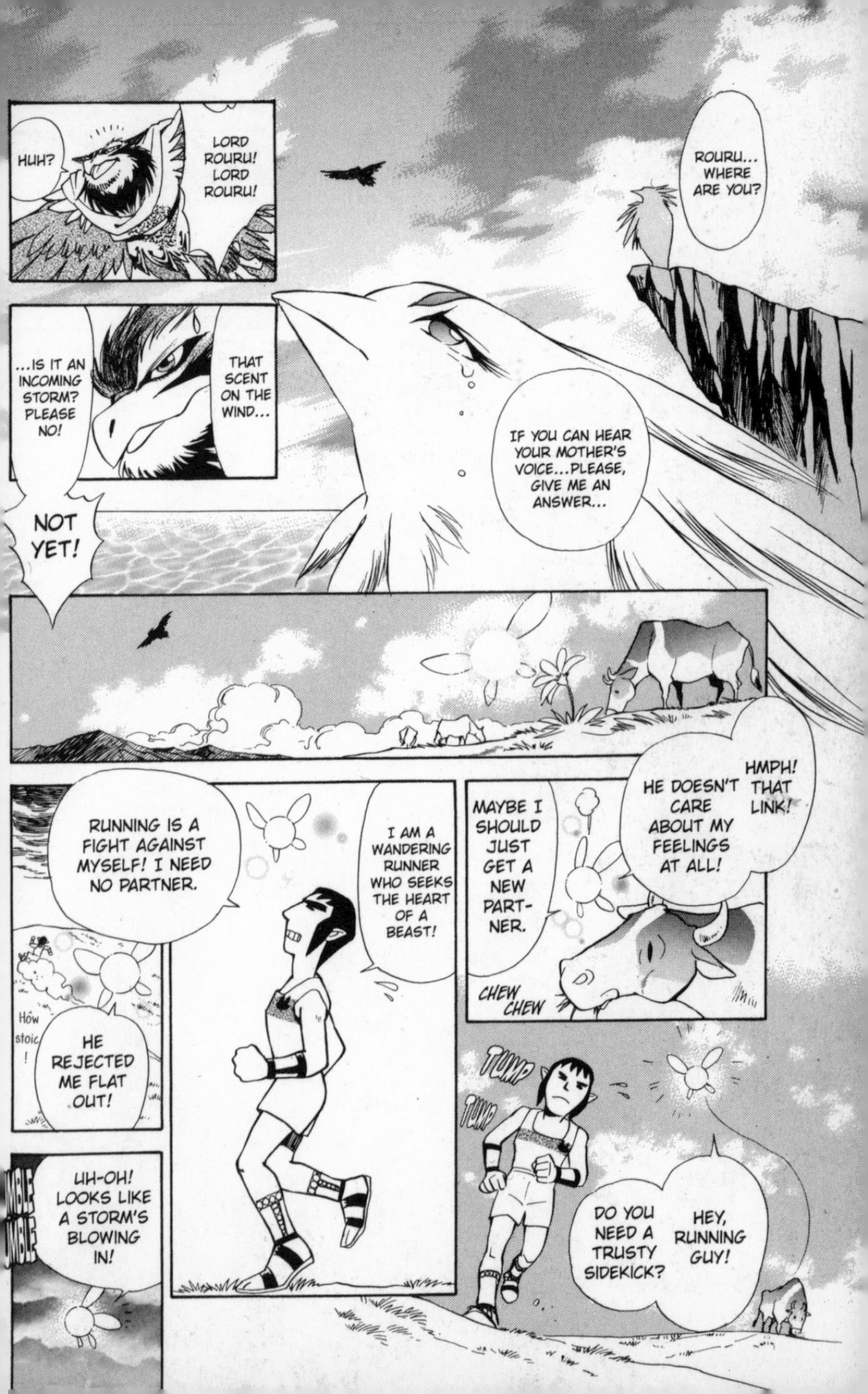
ROURU... WHERE ARE YOU?
IF YOU CAN HEAR YOUR MOTHER'S VOICE...PLEASE, GIVE ME AN ANSWER...
LORD ROURU! LORD ROURU!
HUH?
THAT SCENT ON THE WIND...
...IS IT AN INCOMING STORM? PLEASE NO!
NOT YET!
HMPH! THAT LINK!
HE DOESN'T CARE ABOUT MY FEELINGS AT ALL!
MAYBE I SHOULD JUST GET A NEW PART-NER.
CHEW CHEW
TUMP
TUMP
HEY, RUNNING GUY!
DO YOU NEED A TRUSTY SIDEKICK?
I AM A WANDERING RUNNER WHO SEEKS THE HEART OF A BEAST!
RUNNING IS A FIGHT AGAINST MYSELF! I NEED NO PARTNER.
HE REJECTED ME FLAT OUT!
How stoic!
UH-OH! LOOKS LIKE A STORM'S BLOWING IN!

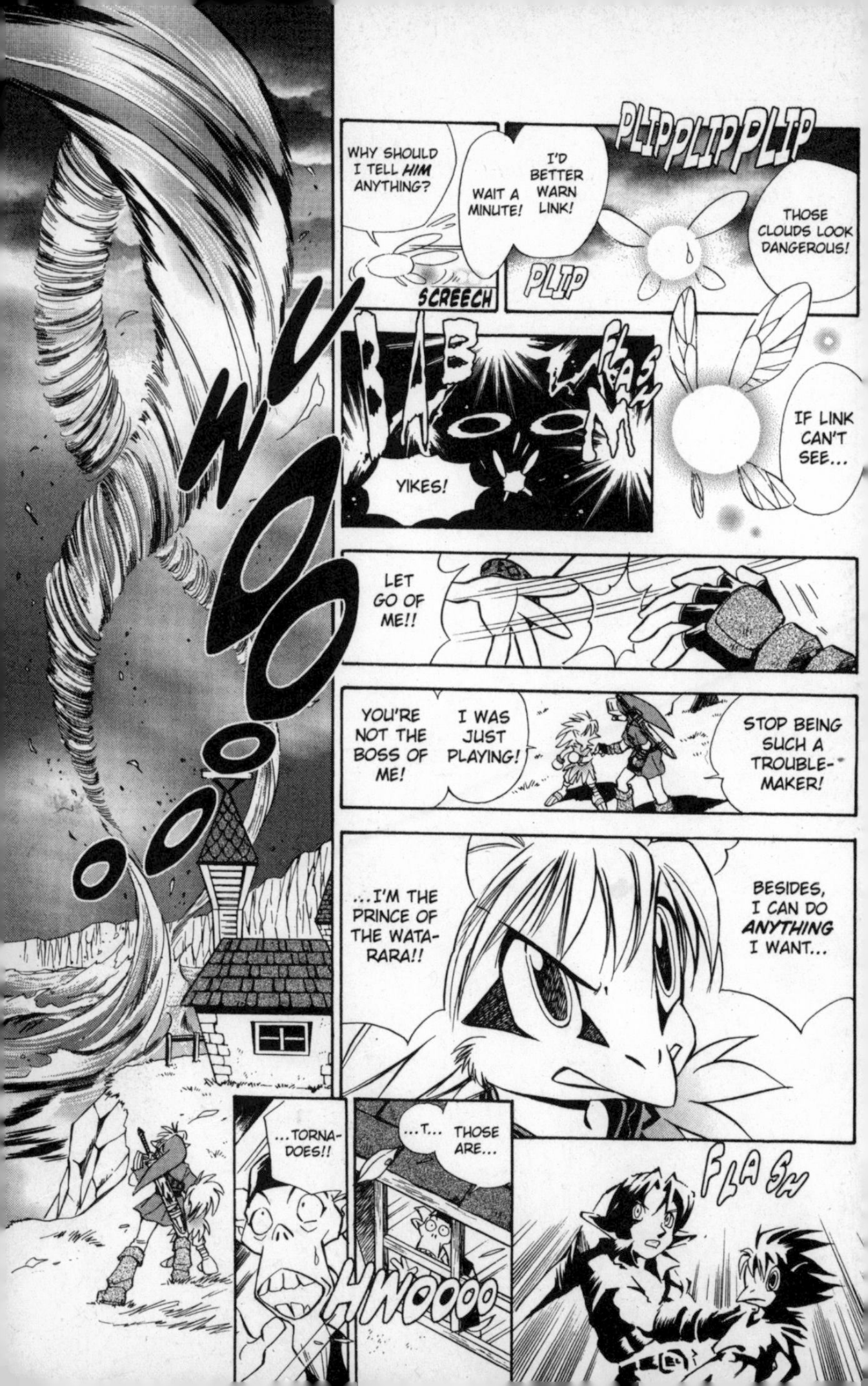

PLIP PLIP PLIP
THOSE CLOUDS LOOK DANGEROUS!
PLIP
I'D BETTER WARN LINK!
WAIT A MINUTE!
WHY SHOULD I TELL HIM ANYTHING?
SCREECH
IF LINK CAN'T SEE...
FLASH
BABOOM
YIKES!
LET GO OF ME!!
STOP BEING SUCH A TROUBLE-MAKER!
I WAS JUST PLAYING!
YOU'RE NOT THE BOSS OF ME!
BESIDES, I CAN DO ANYTHING I WANT...
...I'M THE PRINCE OF THE WATA-RARA!!
FLASH
...T... THOSE ARE...
...TORNA-DOES!!
HWOOOO
WHOOOOOO

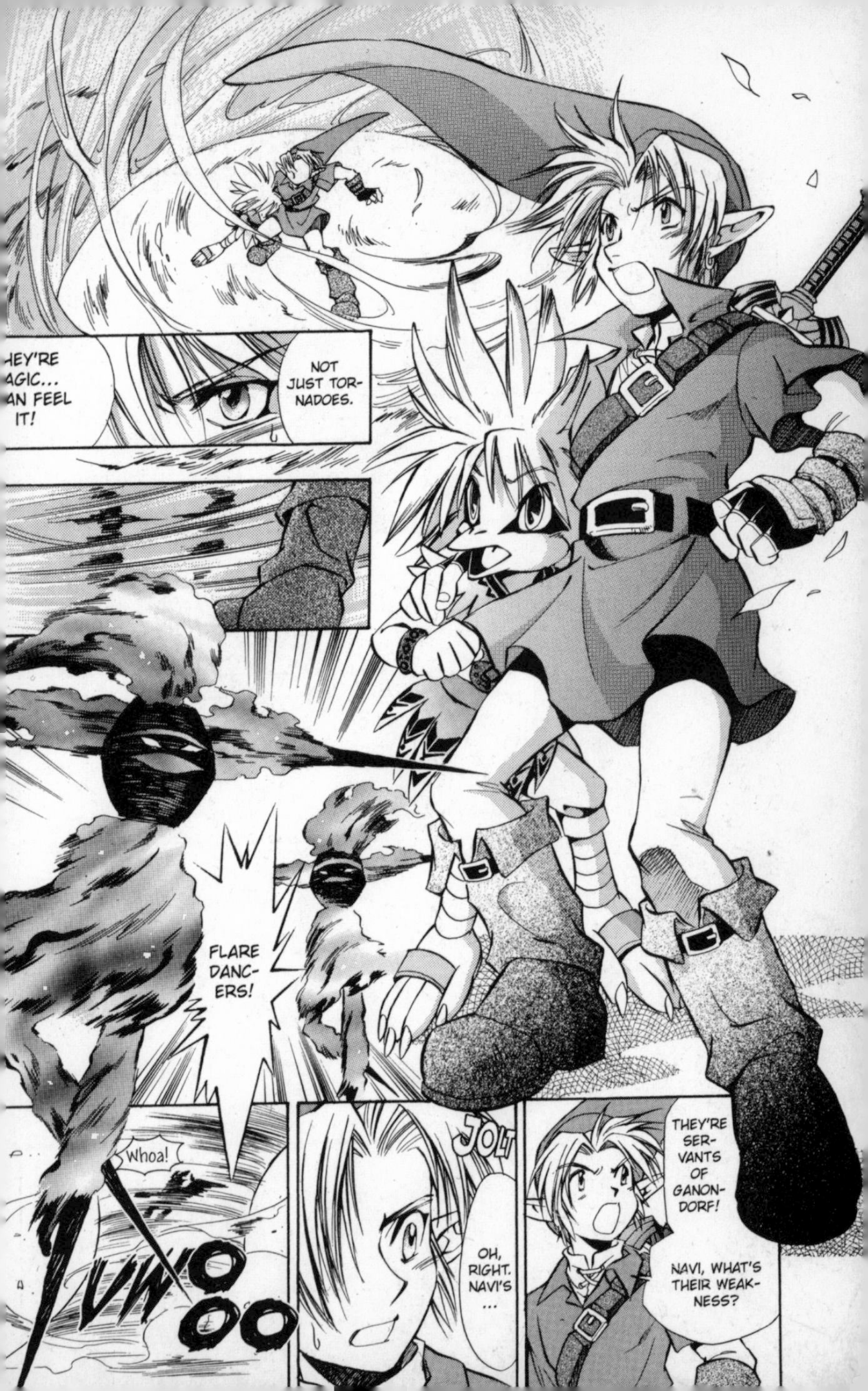
NOT JUST TOR-NADOES.
HEY'RE AGIC... AN FEEL IT!
FLARE DANCERS!
THEY'RE SER-VANTS OF GANON-DORF!
NAVI, WHAT'S THEIR WEAK-NESS?
JOLT
OH, RIGHT. NAVI'S ...
Whoa!
VWOOOO

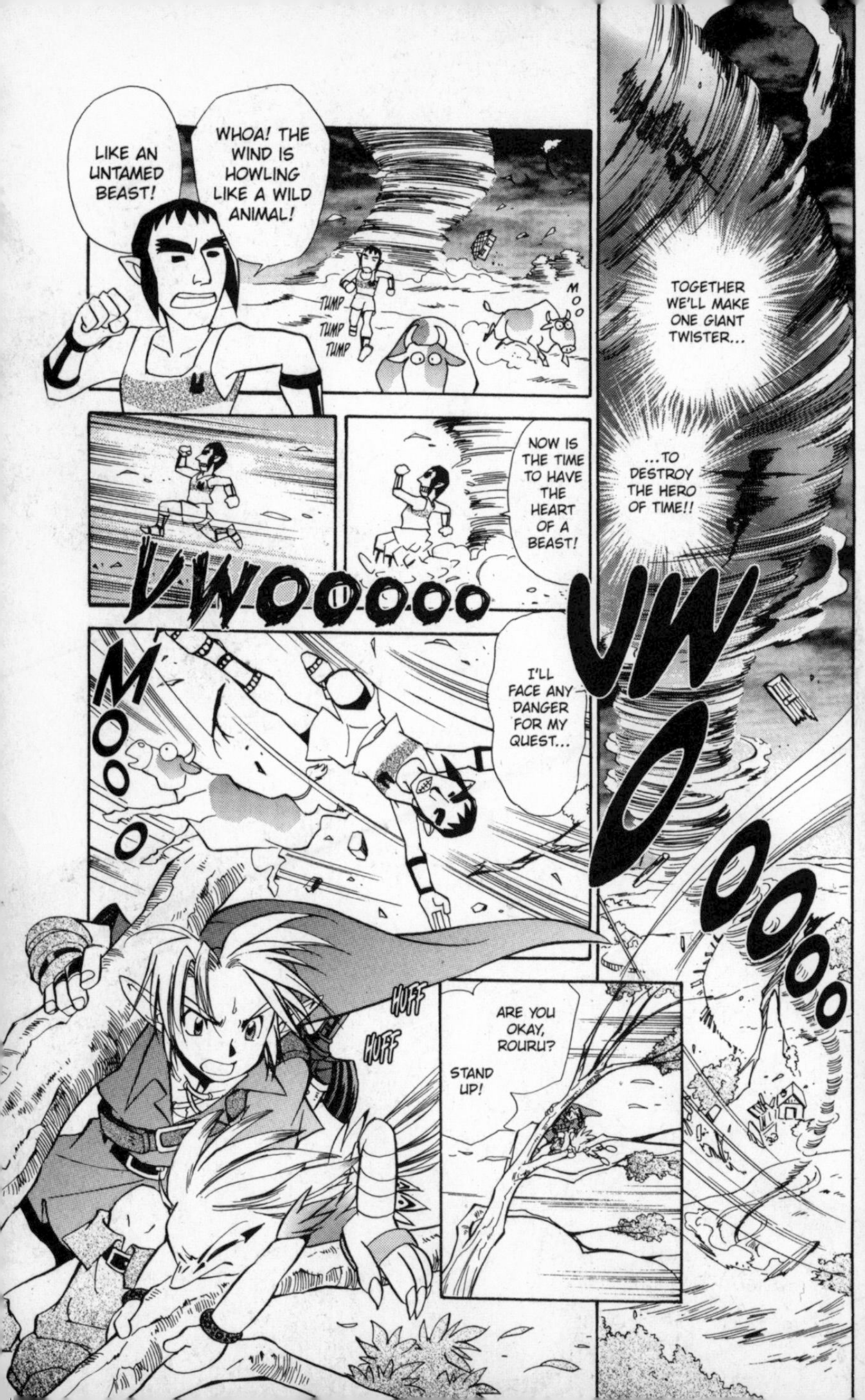
TOGETHER WE'LL MAKE ONE GIANT TWISTER...
...TO DESTROY THE HERO OF TIME!!
VWOOOOOO
WHOA! THE WIND IS HOWLING LIKE A WILD ANIMAL!
LIKE AN UNTAMED BEAST!
MOO
TUMP TUMP TUMP
NOW IS THE TIME TO HAVE THE HEART OF A BEAST!
VWOOOOOO
I'LL FACE ANY DANGER FOR MY QUEST...
MOOOO
ARE YOU OKAY, ROURU?
STAND UP!
HUFF
HUFF

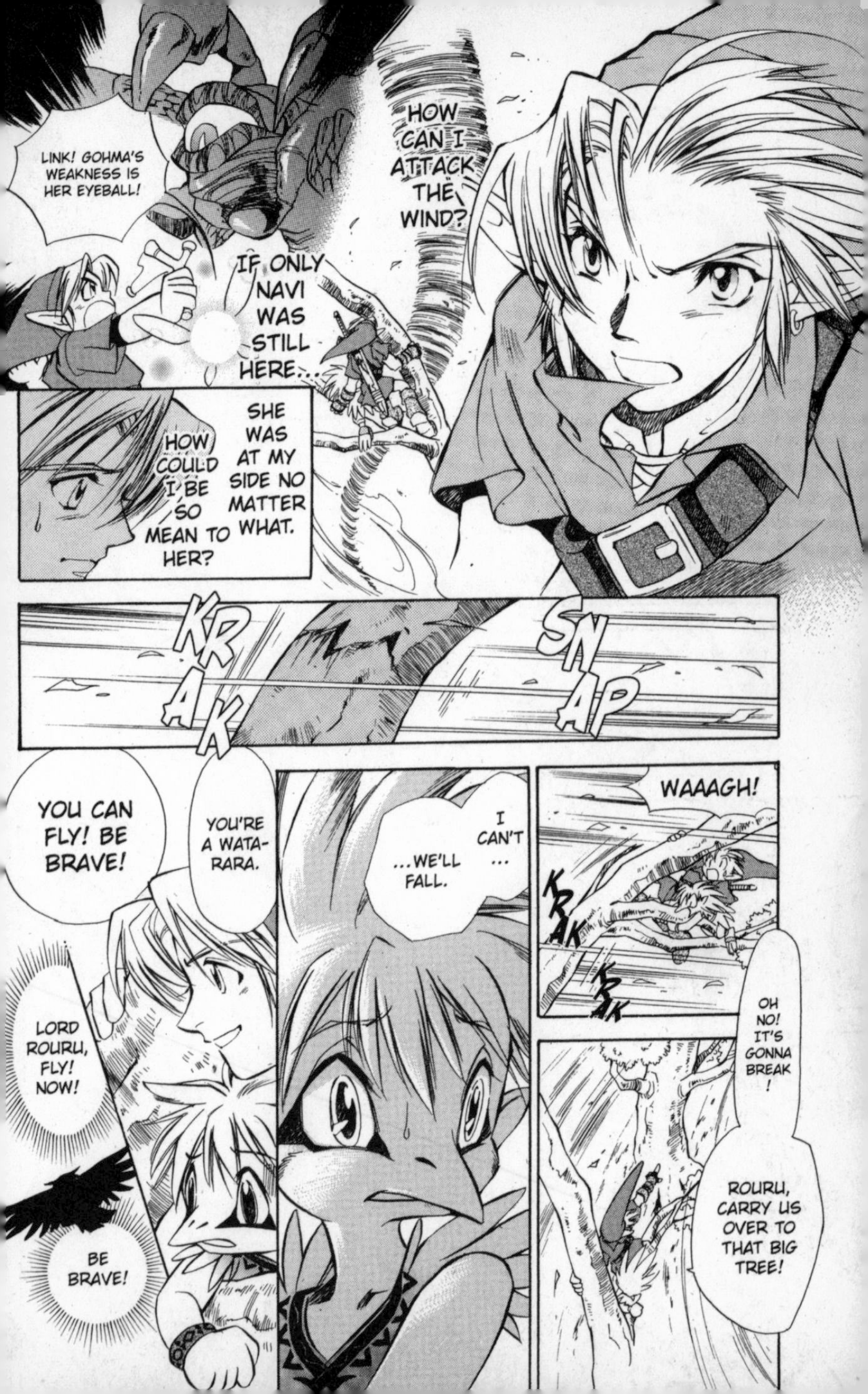
HOW CAN I ATTACK THE WIND?
IF ONLY NAVI WAS STILL HERE...
LINK! GOHMA'S WEAKNESS IS HER EYEBALL!
SHE WAS AT MY SIDE NO MATTER WHAT.
HOW COULD I BE SO MEAN TO HER?
SNAP
KRAK
WAAAGH!
KRAK
KRAK
OH NO! IT'S GONNA BREAK!
ROURU, CARRY US OVER TO THAT BIG TREE!
I CAN'T...
...WE'LL FALL.
YOU'RE A WATARARA.
YOU CAN FLY! BE BRAVE!
LORD ROURU, FLY! NOW!
BE BRAVE!

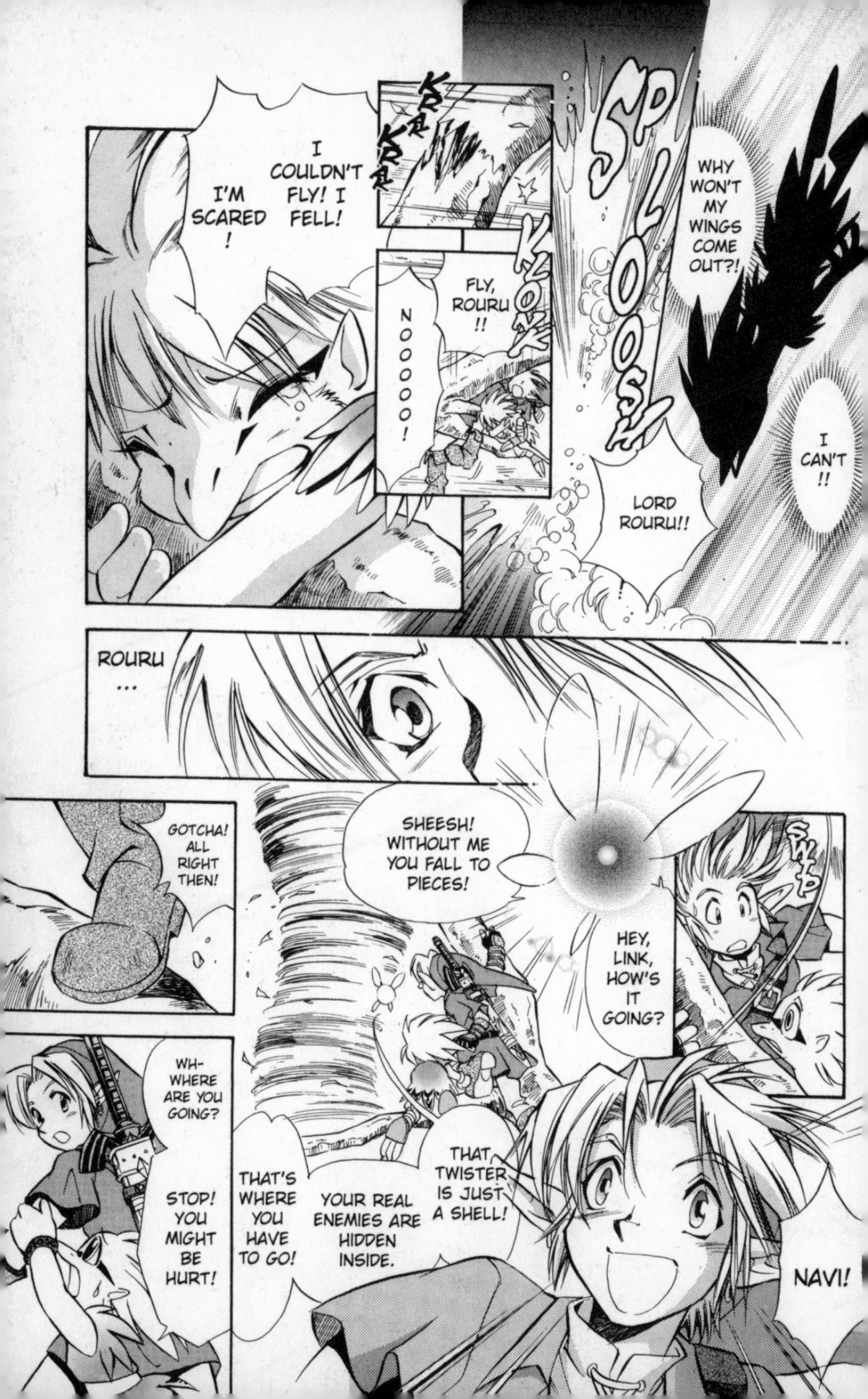
WHY WON'T MY WINGS COME OUT?!
I CAN'T !!
SPLOOOOSH
LORD ROURU!!
KRA KRA
FLY, ROURU !!
NOOOOOO!
I COULDN'T FLY! I FELL!
I'M SCARED !
ROURU ...
HEY, LINK, HOW'S IT GOING?
SHEESH! WITHOUT ME YOU FALL TO PIECES!
GOTCHA! ALL RIGHT THEN!
NAVI!
THAT TWISTER IS JUST A SHELL!
YOUR REAL ENEMIES ARE HIDDEN INSIDE.
THAT'S WHERE YOU HAVE TO GO!
WH-WHERE ARE YOU GOING?
STOP! YOU MIGHT BE HURT!

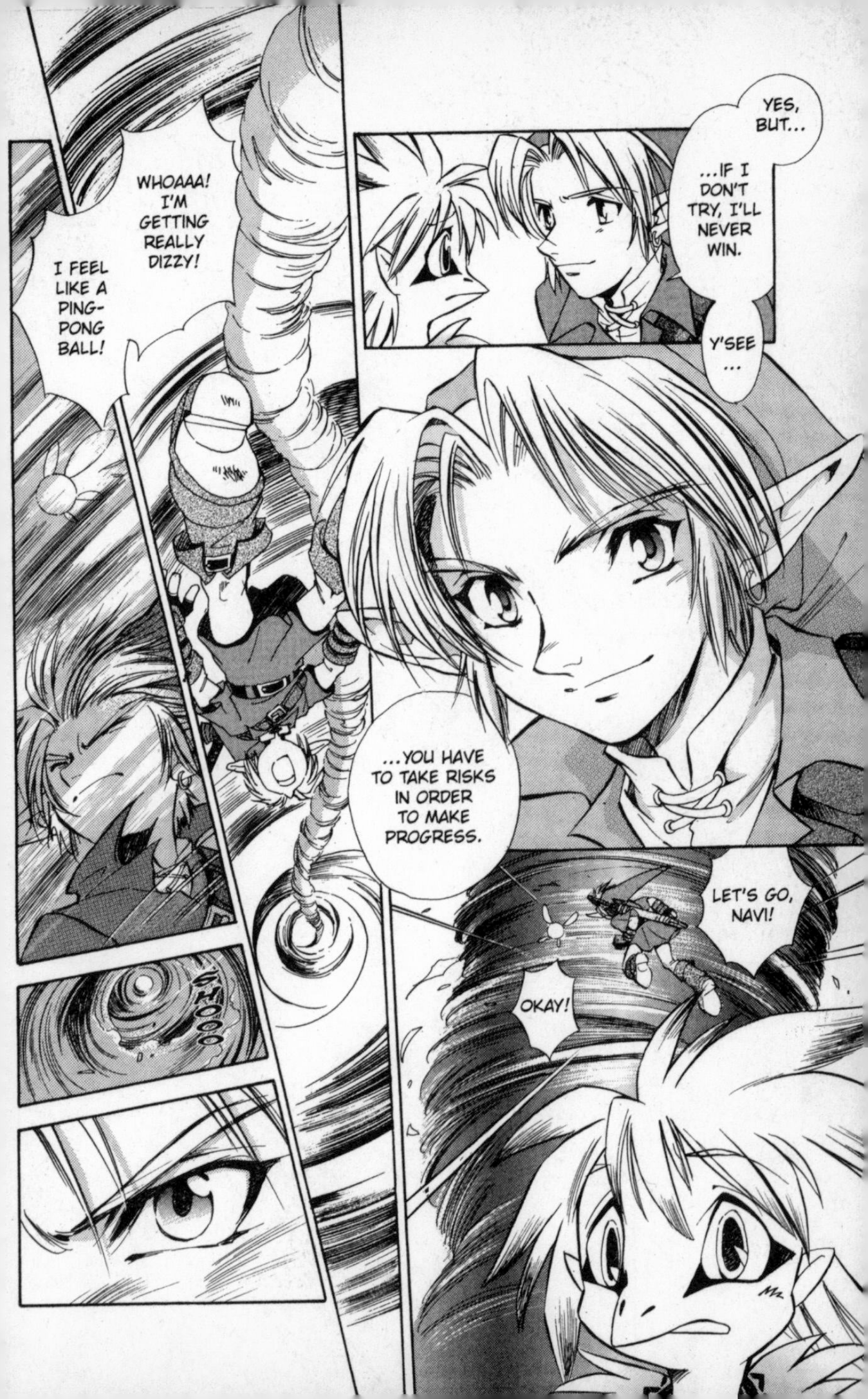
YES, BUT...
...IF I DON'T TRY, I'LL NEVER WIN.
Y'SEE ...
...YOU HAVE TO TAKE RISKS IN ORDER TO MAKE PROGRESS.
WHOAAA! I'M GETTING REALLY DIZZY!
I FEEL LIKE A PING-PONG BALL!
LET'S GO, NAVI!
OKAY!
SHOOOO

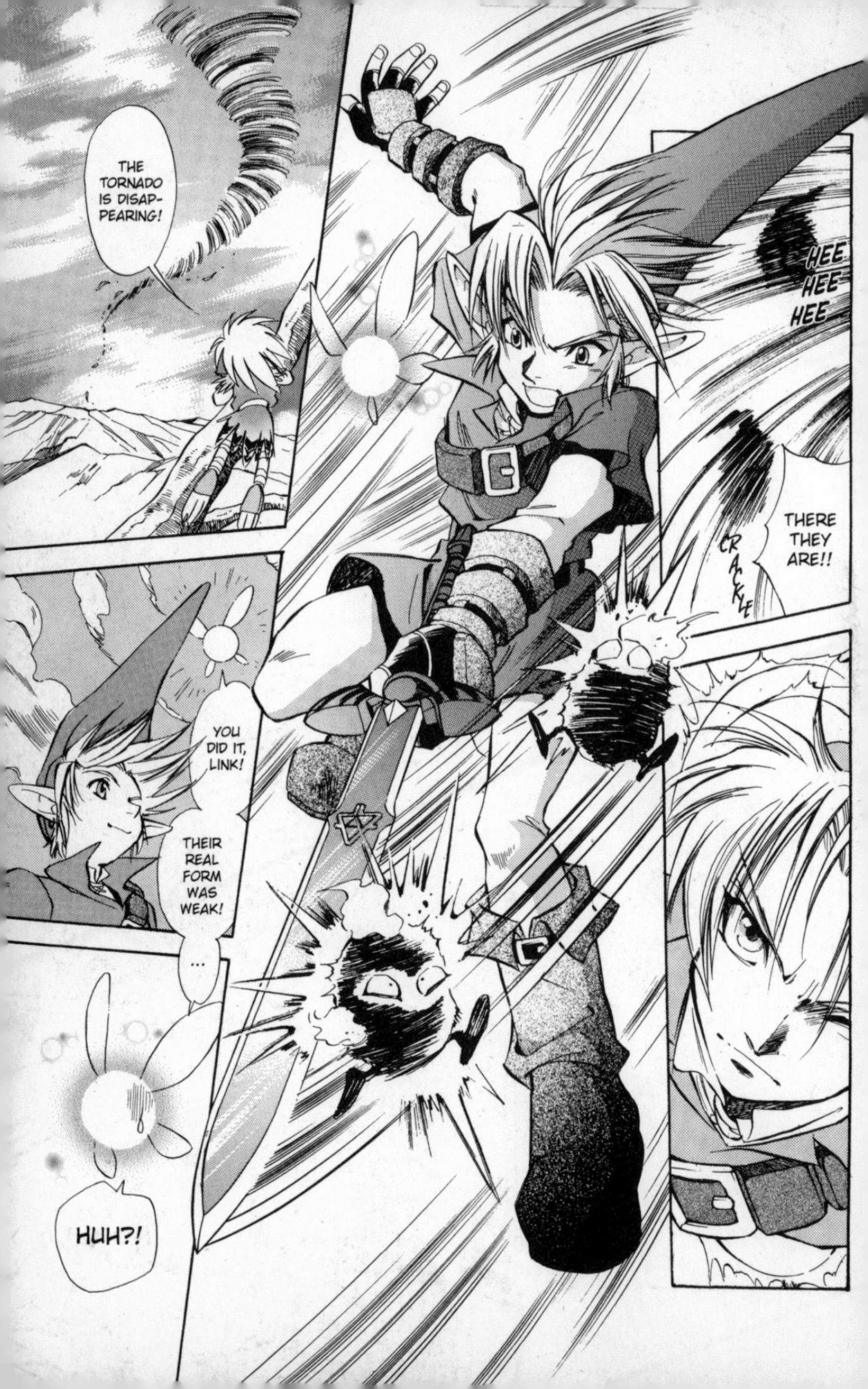
HEE HEE HEE
CRACKLE
THERE THEY ARE!!
THE TORNADO IS DISAPPEARING!
YOU DID IT, LINK!
THEIR REAL FORM WAS WEAK!
...
HUH?!

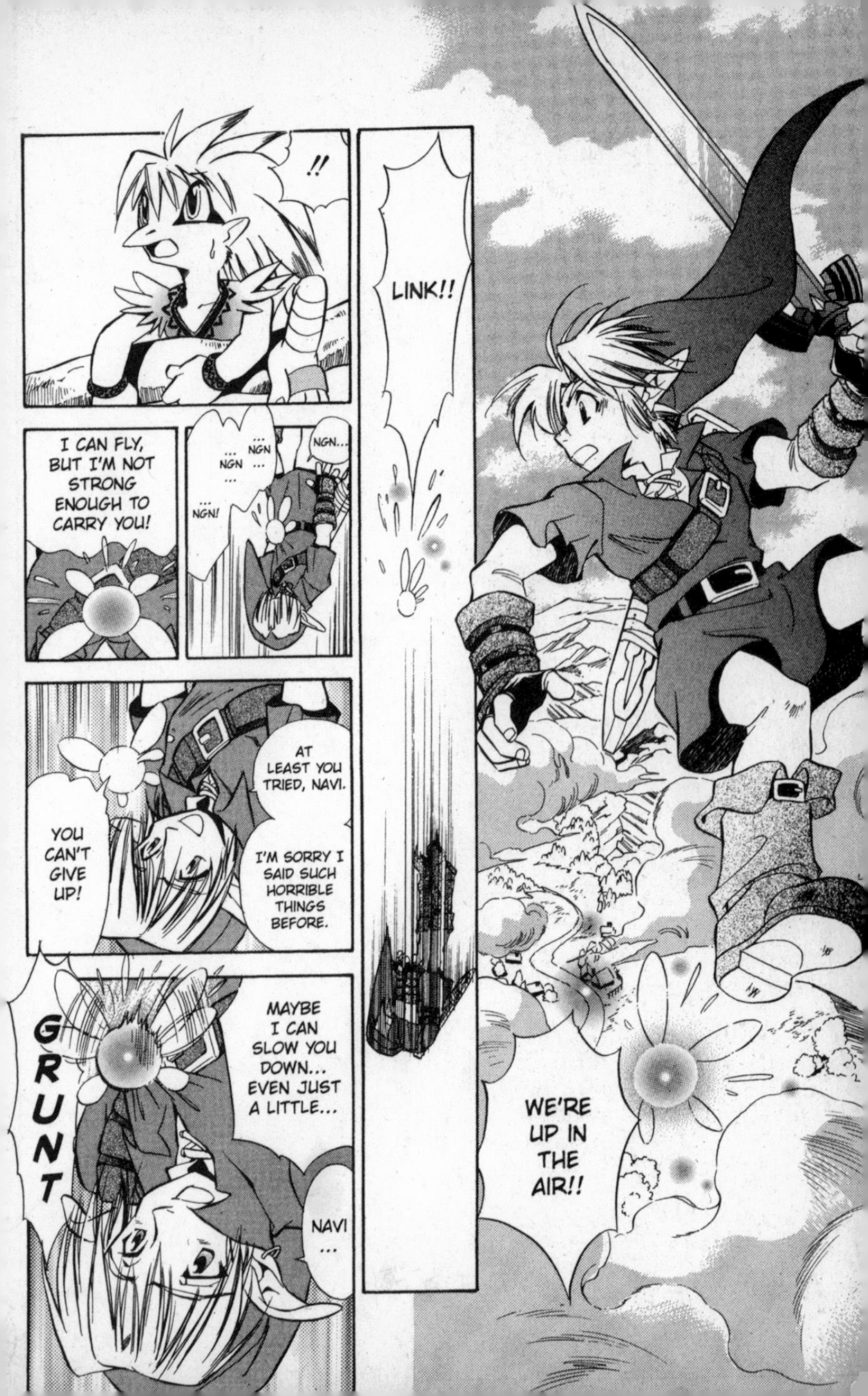
WE'RE UP IN THE AIR!!
LINK!!
!!
... NGN ... NGN ... ... NGN!
NGN...
I CAN FLY, BUT I'M NOT STRONG ENOUGH TO CARRY YOU!
AT LEAST YOU TRIED, NAVI.
I'M SORRY I SAID SUCH HORRIBLE THINGS BEFORE.
YOU CAN'T GIVE UP!
MAYBE I CAN SLOW YOU DOWN... EVEN JUST A LITTLE...
NAVI ...
GRUNT

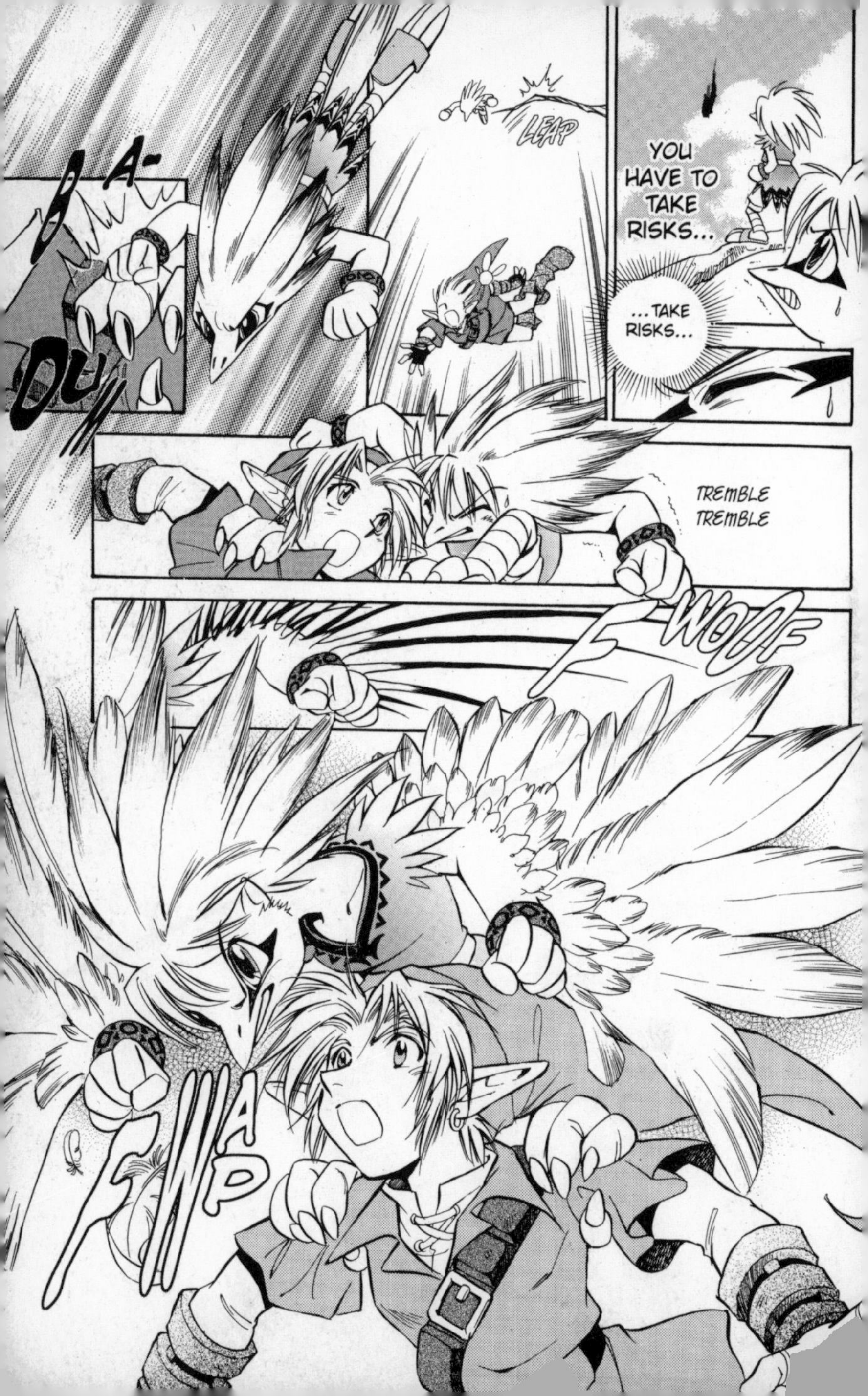

YOU HAVE TO TAKE RISKS...
...TAKE RISKS...
LEAP
BA-DUH
TREMBLE TREMBLE
FWOOF
FWAP

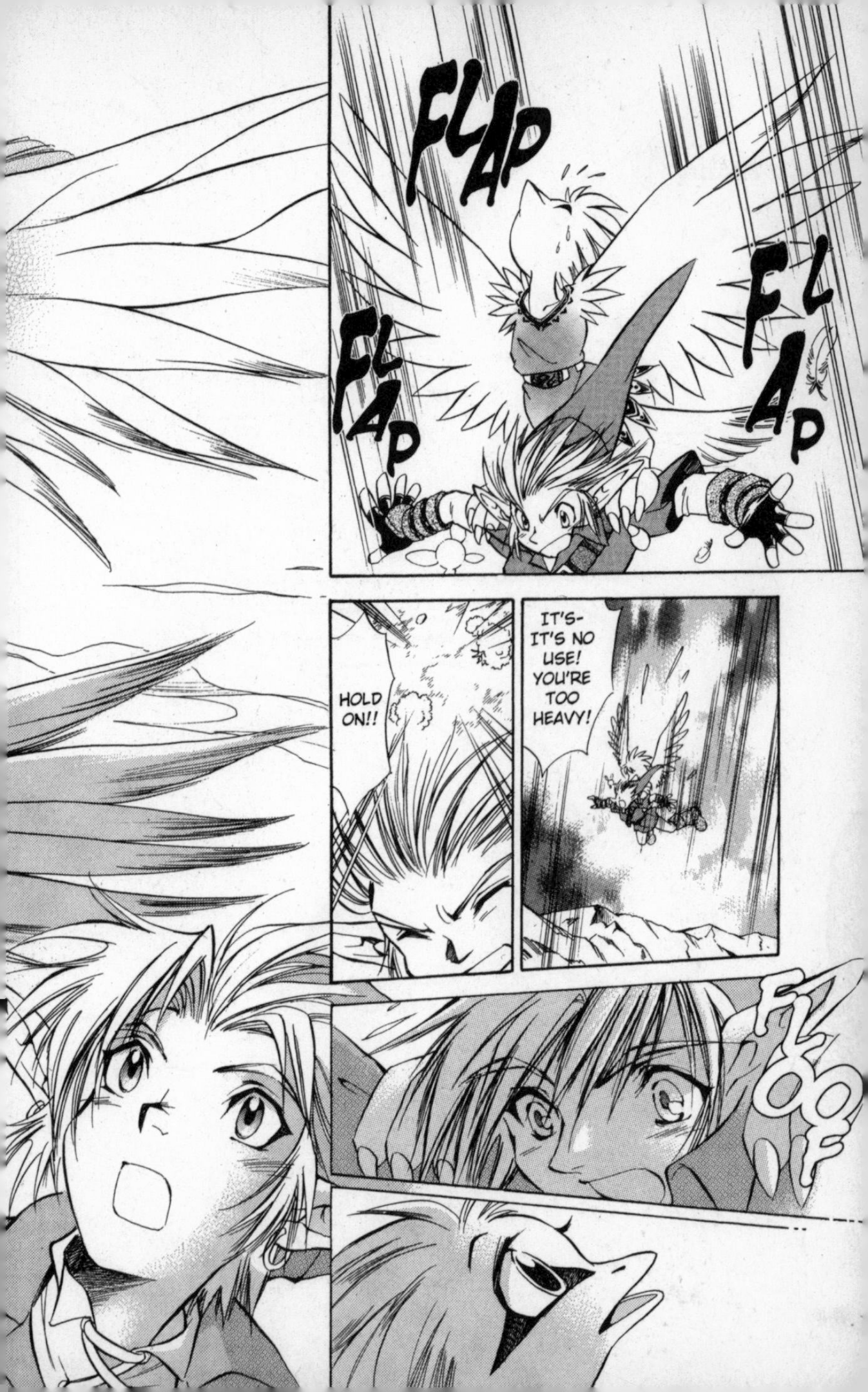
FLAP
FLAP
FLAP
IT'S- IT'S NO USE! YOU'RE TOO HEAVY!
HOLD ON!!
FLOOF

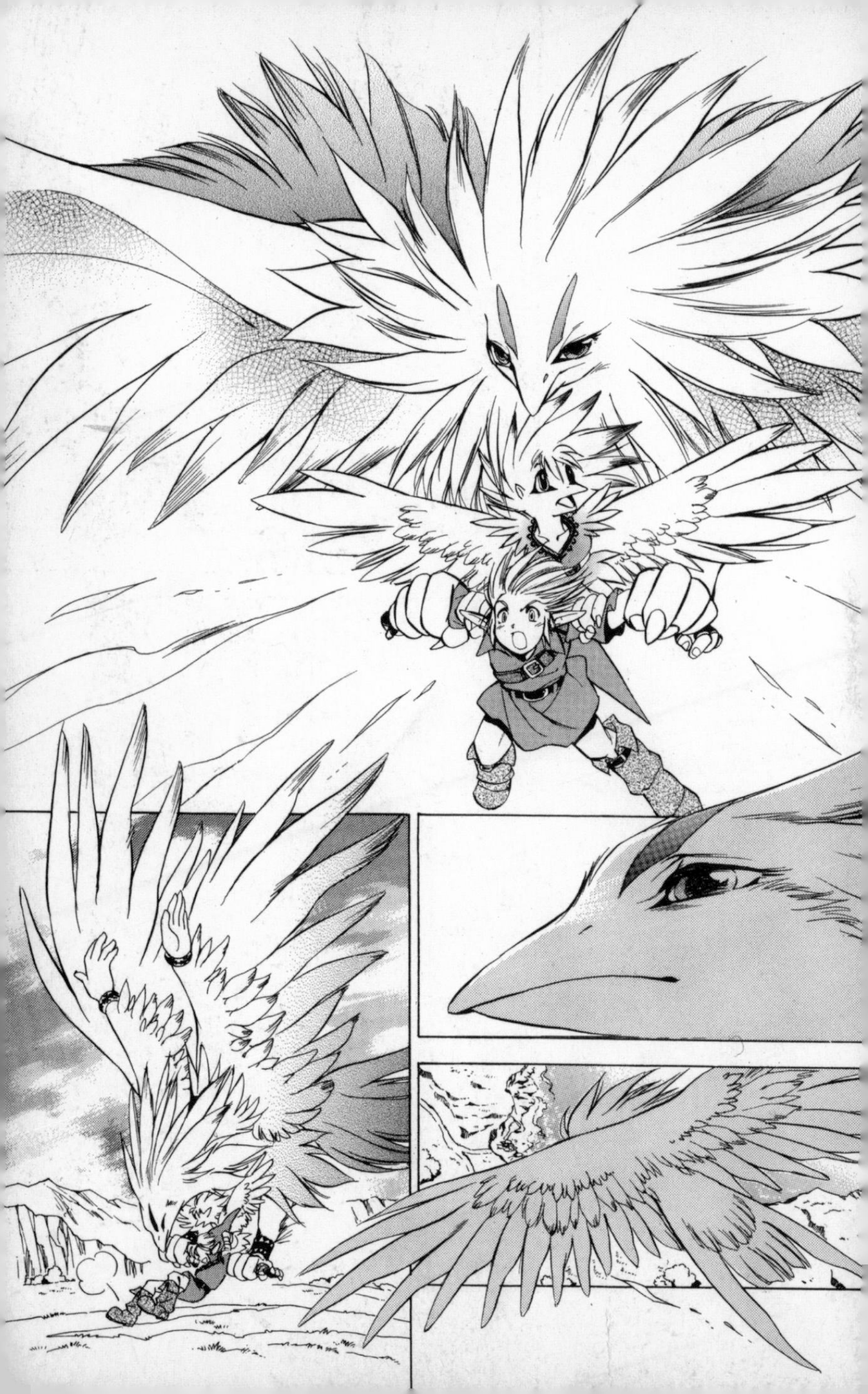

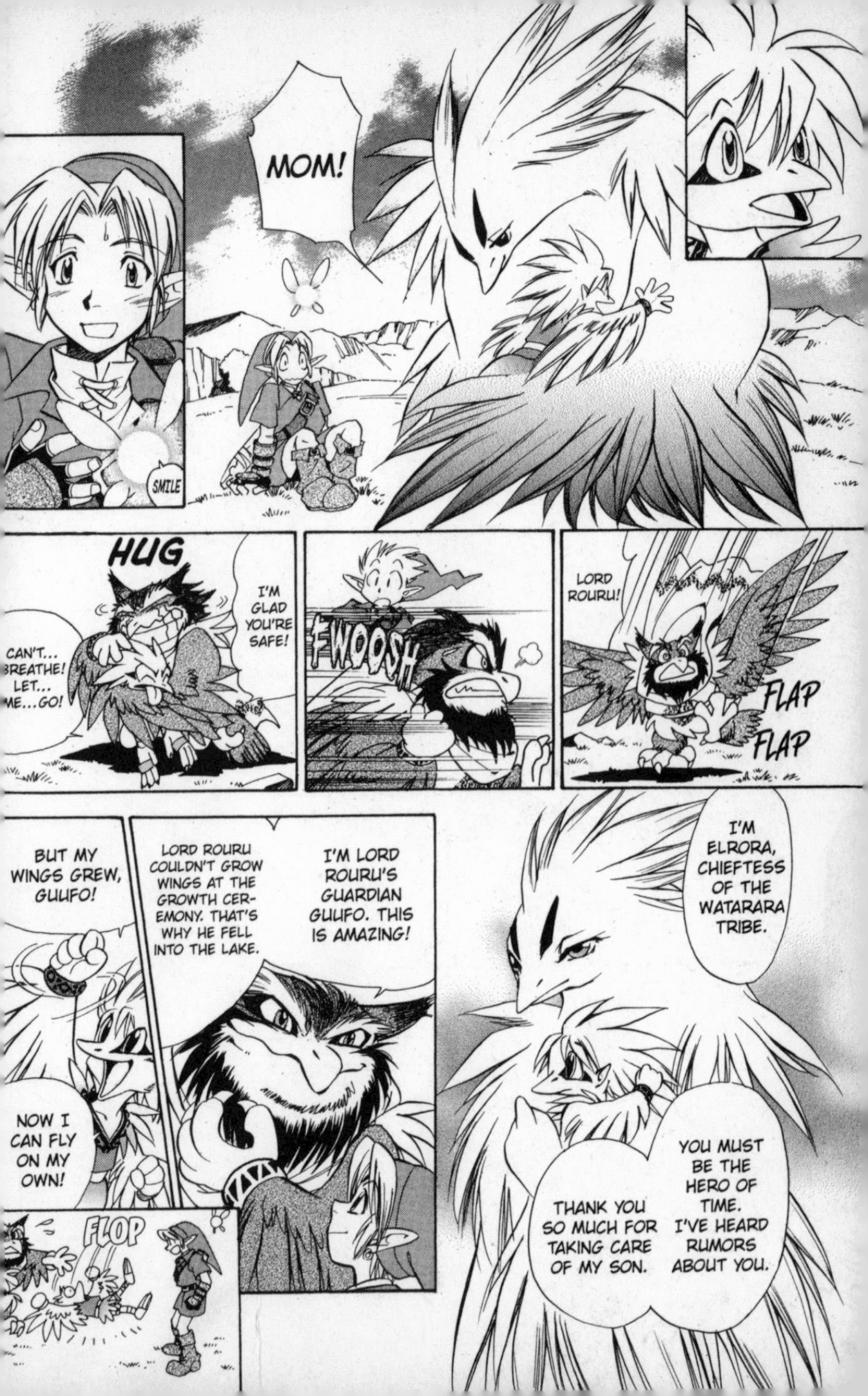
MOM!
SMILE
LORD ROURU!
FLAP
FLAP
FWOOSH
HUG
I'M GLAD YOU'RE SAFE!
CAN'T... BREATHE! LET... ME...GO!
I'M ELRORA, CHIEFTESS OF THE WATARARA TRIBE.
YOU MUST BE THE HERO OF TIME. I'VE HEARD RUMORS ABOUT YOU.
THANK YOU SO MUCH FOR TAKING CARE OF MY SON.
I'M LORD ROURU'S GUARDIAN GUUFO. THIS IS AMAZING!
LORD ROURU COULDN'T GROW WINGS AT THE GROWTH CER- EMONY. THAT'S WHY HE FELL INTO THE LAKE.
BUT MY WINGS GREW, GUUFO!
NOW I CAN FLY ON MY OWN!
FLOP

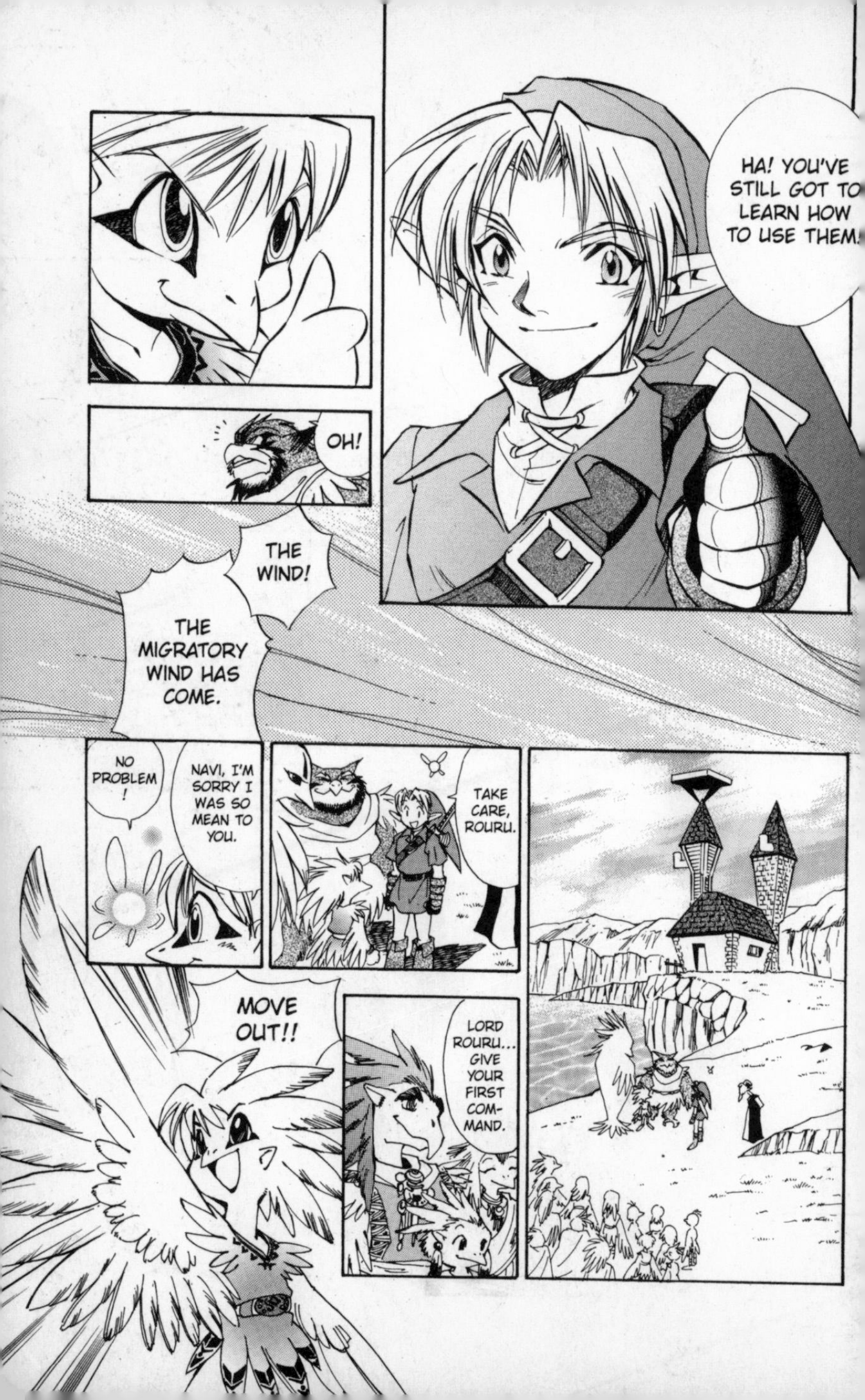
HA! YOU'VE STILL GOT TO LEARN HOW TO USE THEM!
OH!
THE WIND!
THE MIGRATORY WIND HAS COME.
TAKE CARE, ROURU.
NAVI, I'M SORRY I WAS SO MEAN TO YOU.
NO PROBLEM!
LORD ROURU... GIVE YOUR FIRST COMMAND.
MOVE OUT!!

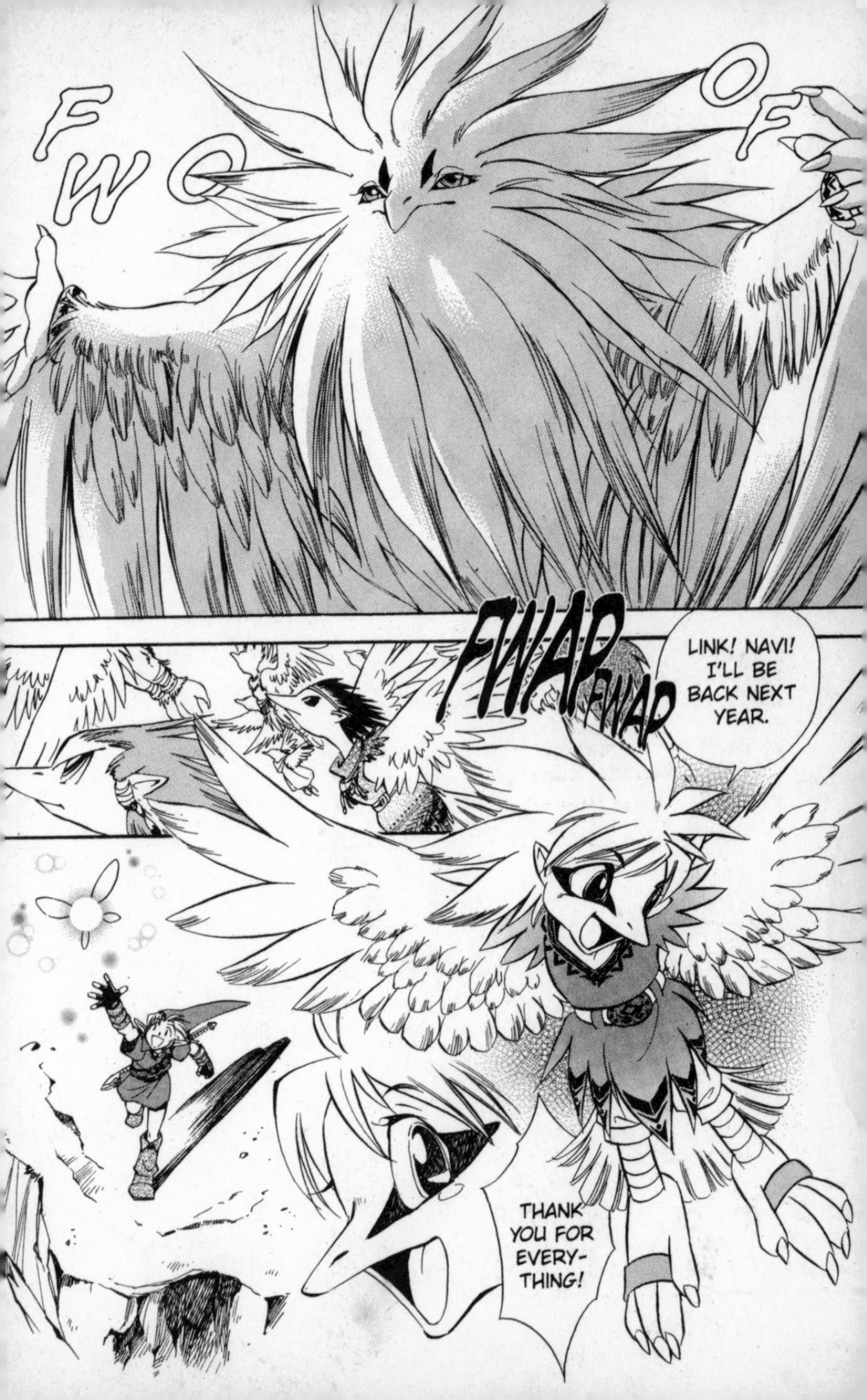
FWOOF
FWAP FWAP
LINK! NAVI! I'LL BE BACK NEXT YEAR.
THANK YOU FOR EVERY-THING!

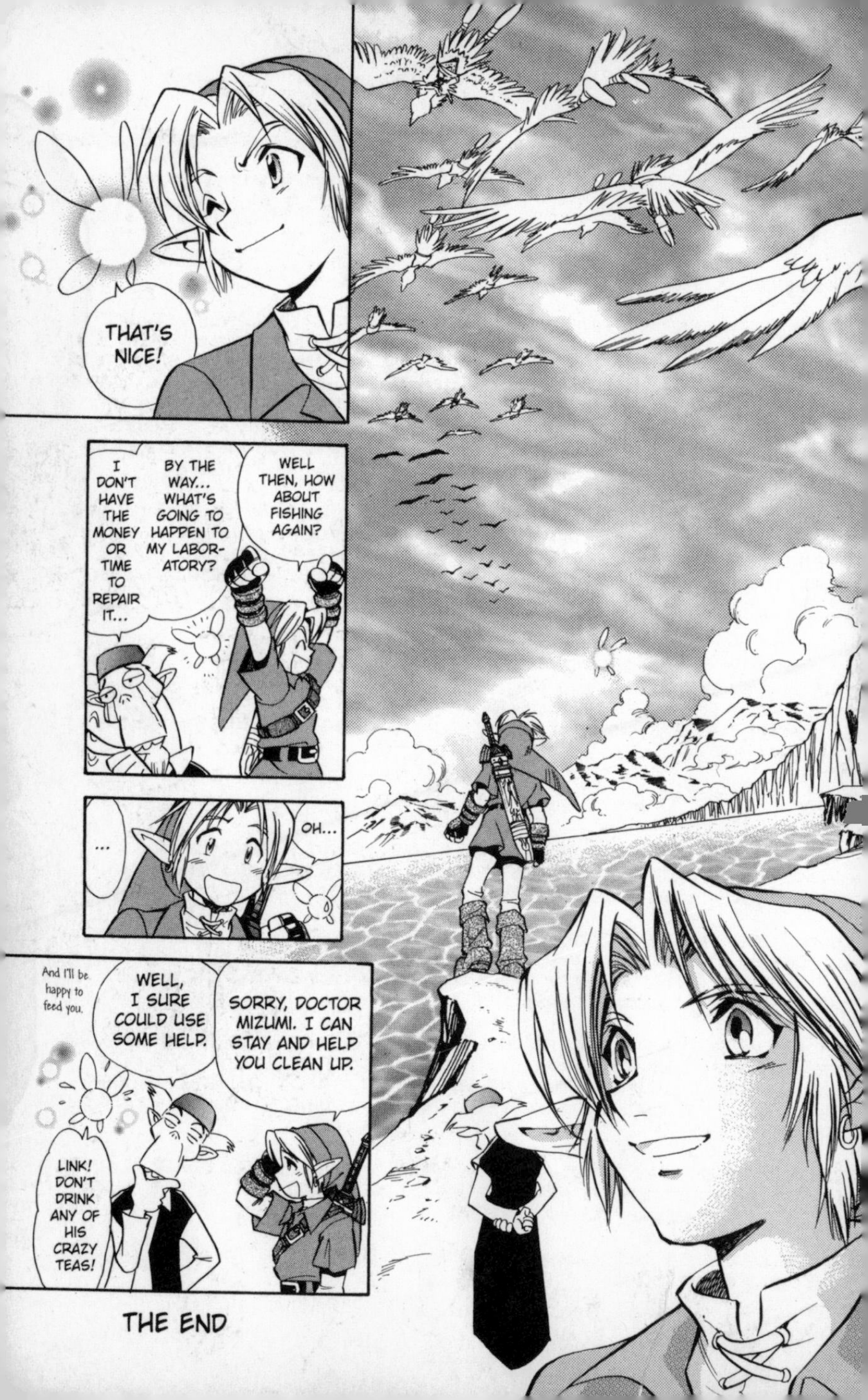
THAT'S NICE!
WELL THEN, HOW ABOUT FISHING AGAIN?
BY THE WAY... WHAT'S GOING TO HAPPEN TO MY LABORATORY?
I DON'T HAVE THE MONEY OR TIME TO REPAIR IT...
OH...
...
SORRY, DOCTOR MIZUMI. I CAN STAY AND HELP YOU CLEAN UP.
WELL, I SURE COULD USE SOME HELP.
And I'll be happy to feed you.
LINK! DON'T DRINK ANY OF HIS CRAZY TEAS!
THE END

AFTERWORD

THIS WAS LIKE PLAYING A VIDEO GAME FOR THE FIRST TIME.

IT'S NOT LIKE WE'D NEVER PLAYED VIDEO GAMES, BUT NEITHER OF US WAS VERY GOOD AT THEM. EVEN THOUGH WE BOTH PLAYED ONCE IN A WHILE, WE NEVER FELT ANY DRIVE TO PLAY MORE OFTEN. THEN ONE DAY IN 1998 A TV COMMERCIAL CHANGED OUR LIVES. IT WAS FOR LEGEND OF ZELDA: OCARINA OF TIME, AND IT SHOWED A YOUNG BOY BRANDISHING A SWORD FROM ATOP A HORSE THAT WAS REARING UP AGAINST A BACKGROUND OF FLAMES. AT THAT MOMENT, MY INTUITION (SO POOR AT VIDEO GAMES) SPOKE TO ME AND, AT THE SAME TIME, SO DID MY PARTNER'S. SOMEHOW WE KNEW THE CHARACTER IN THAT BRIEF TELEVISION COMMERCIAL HAD SOMETHING TO DO WITH US!!

BEFORE WE COULD GET OUT TO BUY A NINTENDO 64 FOR OUR STUDIO, WE RECEIVED A CALL FROM CHIEF EDITOR NAKAHARA (DEPUTY EDITOR AT THE TIME) OF SHOGAKU ROKUNENSEI MAGAZINE. HE WONDERED IF WE WOULD LIKE TO WORK ON A SERIALIZED MANGA FOR OCARINA OF TIME. WHAT INCREDIBLY GOOD TIMING! WE JUST LOOKED AT EACH OTHER AND BROKE OUT LAUGHING.

ACCEPTING THAT IT WAS FATE, WE STARTED WORK. AT FIRST WE THOUGHT THE MANGA MIGHT BE BEST SERVED BY SIMPLY BREAKING THE VIDEO GAME STORY INTO PANELS AND TURNING THOSE INTO EXCITING SCENES, BUT THAT DIDN'T GO WELL AT ALL. WE BEGAN TO REALIZE THAT THIS JOB WAS MORE COMPLICATED THAN JUST RE-TELLING THE SAME STORY. IT NEEDED MORE.

~ OCARINA OF TIME ~

FIRST, WE HAD TO PLAY THE GAME, THE WHOLE GAME, BEFORE WE COULD EVEN START. THAT WAS PRETTY HARD FOR US, BUT WHEN WE FINALLY FINISHED THE GAME WE LOOKED AT EACH OTHER AND SAID, "VIDEO GAMES ARE AWESOME!!"

FOR THE FIRST TIME WE UNDERSTOOD COMPLETELY HOW VIDEO GAMES CAN BE JUST AS FUN AND JUST AS INTERESTING AS MANGA. BOTH OF THEM TELL A STORY, BUT VIDEO GAMES TELL THAT STORY IN A COMPLETELY DIFFERENT WAY THAN MANGA DO. PLUS YOU GET COMPLETELY CAUGHT UP IN THE GAME!

THAT WAS IMPORTANT. PRECISELY BECAUSE WE WERE SO DEEPLY INVOLVED, WE WERE ABLE TO RELAX, STOP THINKING LIKE MANGA AUTHORS, AND JUST ENJOY THE STORY. MORE THAN ANYTHING ELSE, THE WORLD OF THE GAME WAS SO BEAUTIFUL. IT RADIATED LIFE AND WARMTH...A KIND OF HEAT...AND HUMAN EMOTION THAT WE'D NEVER FOUND IN A COLD DIGITAL WORLD BEFORE.

WE THOUGHT ABOUT THE FACT THAT SO MANY PEOPLE WORKED FOR LITERALLY YEARS TO MAKE THE GAME, BUT HERE WE WERE WORKING ON THE MANGA, JUST THE TWO OF US. SUDDENLY IT SEEMED LIKE TOO BIG A JOB. WE GOT A LITTLE FREAKED OUT.

BUT DISCOVERING THE TRUE CHARACTER OF LINK MADE US FEEL BETTER, LIKE A COOL BREEZE ON A SUMMER DAY.

LINK ISN'T STRIKINGLY GOOD-LOOKING. HE'S JUST MILDLY HANDSOME AND, FOR SOME REASON, THAT SEEMED APPEALING. AND IT'D BEEN A LONG TIME SINCE SUCH A NICE HERO APPEARED IN THE MANGA WORLD. (IT SEEMS LIKE THERE SHOULD BE MORE OF THEM, BUT THERE AREN'T). AT FIRST WE THOUGHT IT WOULD BE EASY TO CRAFT SUCH A HERO (SO WE HAD NO EXCUSE FOR FAILURE), BUT IT TURNED OUT TO BE QUITE DIFFICULT.

IN THE PAST, ALL THE HEROES WE CREATED WERE ANTI-HEROES (WHICH REFLECTED OUR VIEW OF THE WORLD). IF WE MADE HEROES TOO NICE OR TOO GOOD, WE THOUGHT THEY'D SEEM FALSE AND UNBELIEVABLE. BUT THE MORE TIME WE SPENT IN THE WORLD OF ZELDA, THE MORE WE REALIZED THAT IT HAD ITS OWN KIND OF REALITY.

I WAS USED TO WRITING MYSTERIOUS, CONFLICTED CHARACTERS LIKE SHEIK, BUT FOR THE FIRST TIME I UNDERSTOOD IN THE BOTTOM OF MY HEART THAT GOOD GUYS COULD BE COOL, TOO. LINK WAS COOL.

AND MY PARTNER ALWAYS THOUGHT THAT ATTRACTIVE VISUALS COULD ONLY COME FROM TOUGH, EDGY SETTINGS, BUT OCARINA OF TIME HAS A DIFFERENT KIND OF ATTRACTION. THE IMAGES FROM THE VIDEO GAME BREATHE WITH LIFE-INCREDIBLY SOFT, PURE, NOBLE AND WELL THOUGHT OUT. THE POLYGONS SOMEHOW REMINDED US OF THE STOP-MOTION ANIME WE USED TO LOVE (BUT WHICH NEVER FELT PARTICULARLY "REAL") AND PERFECTLY PORTRAYED A SENSE OF SPACE, GESTURES, AND TIMING. IN GENERAL WE PREFER GAMES THAT ARE NOT TOO INTENSELY CHEESY OR MELODRAMATIC.

WHEN WE HAD OUR FIRST MEETINGS WITH SHIGERU MIYAMOTO AND THE OTHERS DOING THE HARD WORK ON THE ZELDA GAMES, WE WERE EXCITED, NERVOUS, HAPPY, AND SCARED ALL AT THE SAME TIME. IT WAS AN INCREDIBLE HONOR THAT THEY WOULD ENTRUST ONE OF THEIR IMPORTANT WORLDS TO OUR HANDS.

THE LEGEND OF ZELDA

WE ALSO HAVE TO SEND UNENDING THANKS TO OUR CHIEF EDITOR, WHO INTRODUCED US TO THIS WORLD AND LET US BRING OUR OWN ARTISTIC VISION TO THE PROJECT, AND TO EVERYONE ELSE AT SHOGAKU ROKUNENSEI MAGAZINE! THANK YOU VERY MUCH!

IN ELEMENTARY SCHOOL WE BOTH READ A LOT OF MANGA MAGAZINES. AND WE AGREE THAT BACK THEN IT FELT LIKE ONE YEAR WAS A MUCH LONGER SPAN OF TIME THAN IT SEEMS NOW. THAT'S WHY WE REFUSED TO CUT ANY CORNERS, TREATED THIS WORK WITH LOVE, AND PUT ALL OUR CARE AND EFFORT INTO BRINGING IT TO LIFE. WE HOPE THAT YOU READERS, WHO ARE EVEN NOW ON THE CUSP OF ADOLESCENCE, WHEN THE DOORS OF SENSIBILITY ARE WIDE OPEN, WILL FEEL THE REALITY OF LEGEND OF ZELDA AND, IF EVEN JUST A LITTLE, FIND SOME OF LINK'S PURITY IN YOURSELVES.

AKIRA HIMEKAWA

Coming Next Volume

After sealing Ganondorf in the Sacred Realm, Link returns to the time when he was a boy. Peace has returned to Hyrule, but Navi is missing. Link decides to go on a quest to find his old friend. Along the way he runs into the mischievous Skull Kid who has Majora's Mask. When Skull Kid turns Link into a Deku Nut, Link's troubles are only just beginning!

Available Now!

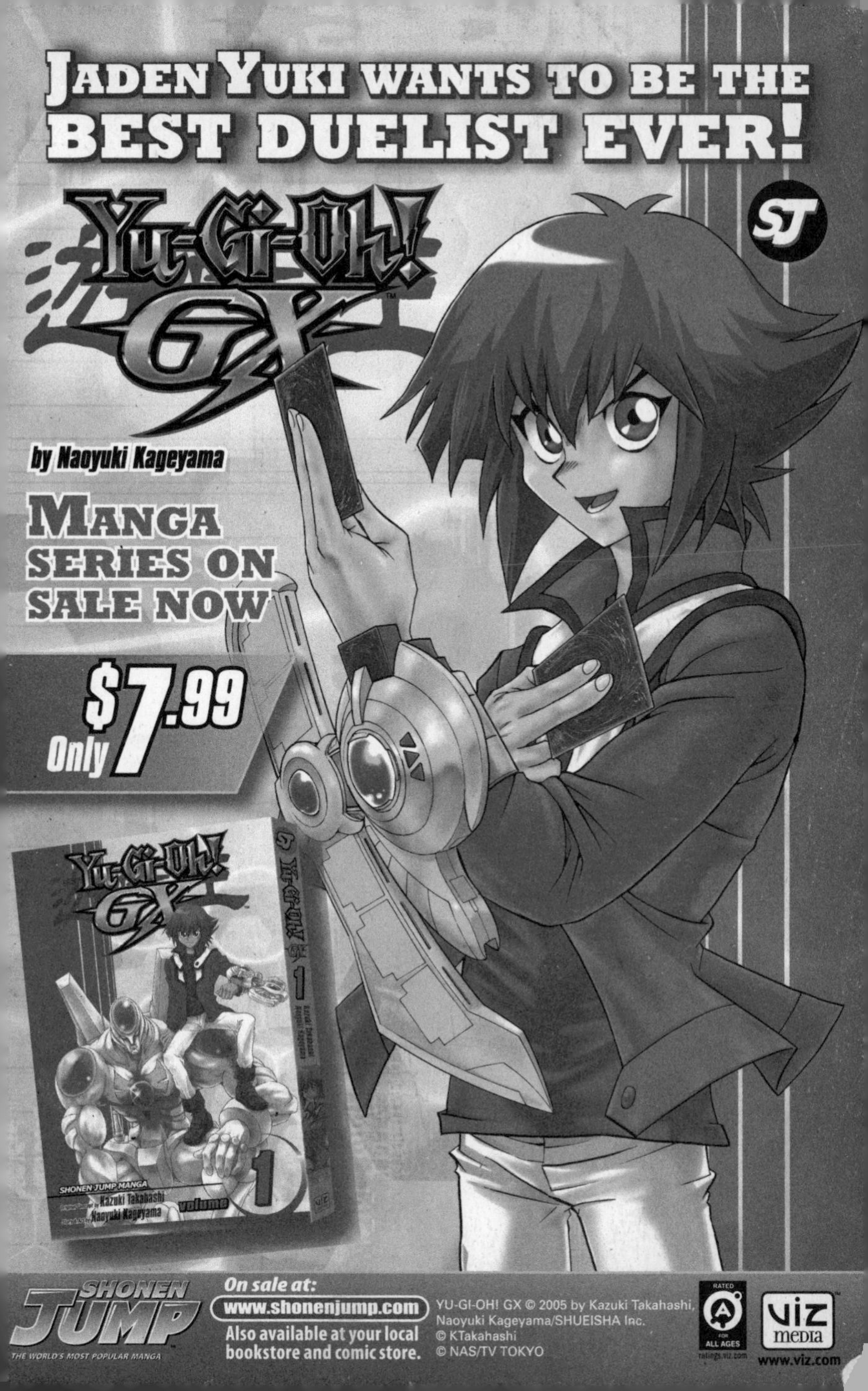

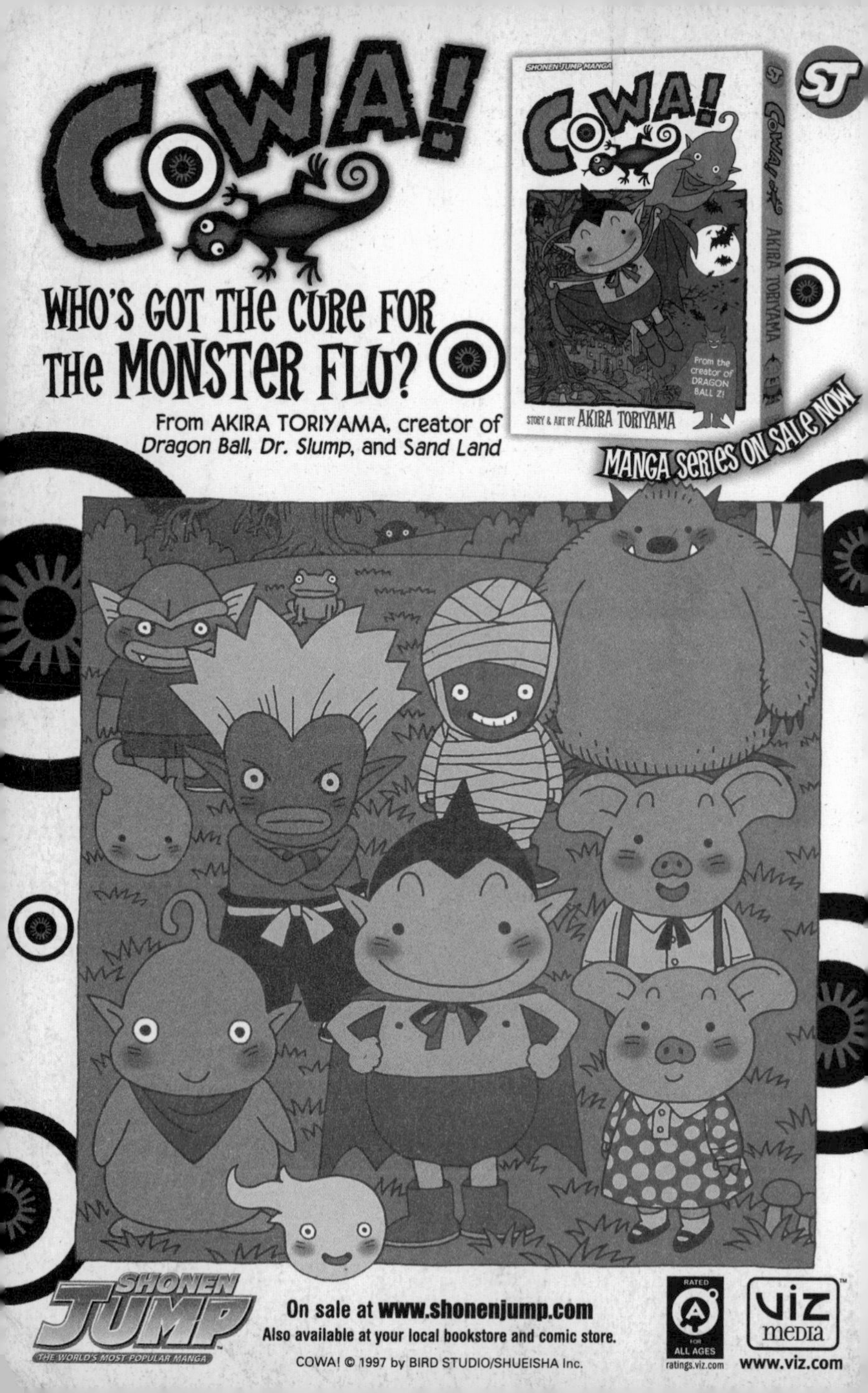
COWA!
WHO'S GOT THE CURE FOR THE MONSTER FLU?
From AKIRA TORIYAMA, creator of Dragon Ball, Dr. Slump, and Sand Land
SHONEN JUMP MANGA
COWA!
AKIRA TORIYAMA
From the creator of DRAGON BALL Z!
STORY & ART BY AKIRA TORIYAMA
SJ
MANGA SERIES ON SALE NOW
SHONEN JUMP
THE WORLD'S MOST POPULAR MANGA
On sale at www.shonenjump.com
Also available at your local bookstore and comic store.
COWA! © 1997 by BIRD STUDIO/SHUEISHA Inc.
RATED A FOR ALL AGES
ratings.viz.com
VIZ MEDIA
www.viz.com

THE LEGEND OF ZELDA™

– THE MINISH CAP –

VIZ Kids Edition

STORY & ART BY

AKIRA HIMEKAWA

Translation/John Werry, Honyaku Center Inc.
English Adaptation/Stan! Brown
Touch-up Art & Lettering/John Hunt
Cover & Interior Design/Sean Lee
Editor/Mike Montesa

VP, Production/Alvin Lu
VP, Sales & Product Marketing/Gonzalo Ferreyra
VP, Creative/Linda Espinosa
Publisher/Hyoe Narita

Printed in the U.S.A.

Published by VIZ Media, LLC
P.O. Box 77010
San Francisco, CA 94107

10 9 8 7 6 5 4 3 2 1
First printing, December 2009

viz media
www.viz.com

RATED A FOR ALL AGES
PARENTAL ADVISORY
LEGEND OF ZELDA is rated A and is suitable for readers of all ages.
ratings.viz.com

vizkids
www.vizkids.com

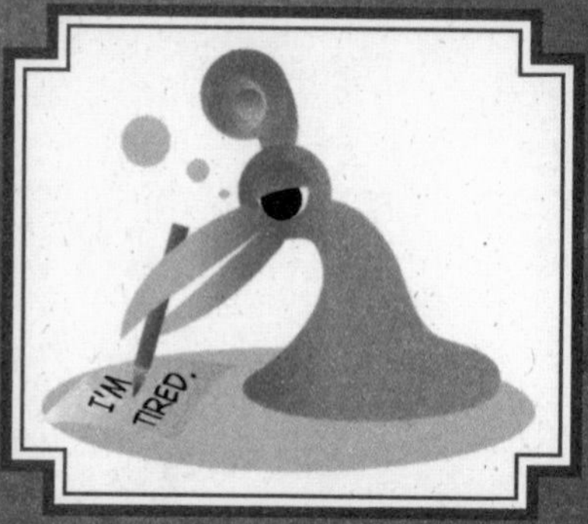
I'M TIRED.

Akira Himekawa

The world of *The Minish Cap* may be small, but the deeper you get into it, the more fun it becomes! I completed the figure! But no matter what I do, I can't find the last Kinstone. If Picori really existed, I'd wish for them to write my scripts while I sleep! LOL

Akira Himekawa is the collaboration of two women, A. Honda and S. Nagano. Together they have created nine manga adventures featuring Link and the popular video game world of *The Legend of Zelda*™, including *Ocarina of Time, Oracle of Seasons* and *Four Swords*. Their most recent work, *Legend of Zelda*™*: Phantom Hourglass*, is serialized in *Shogaku Rokunensei.*

Coming Next Volume

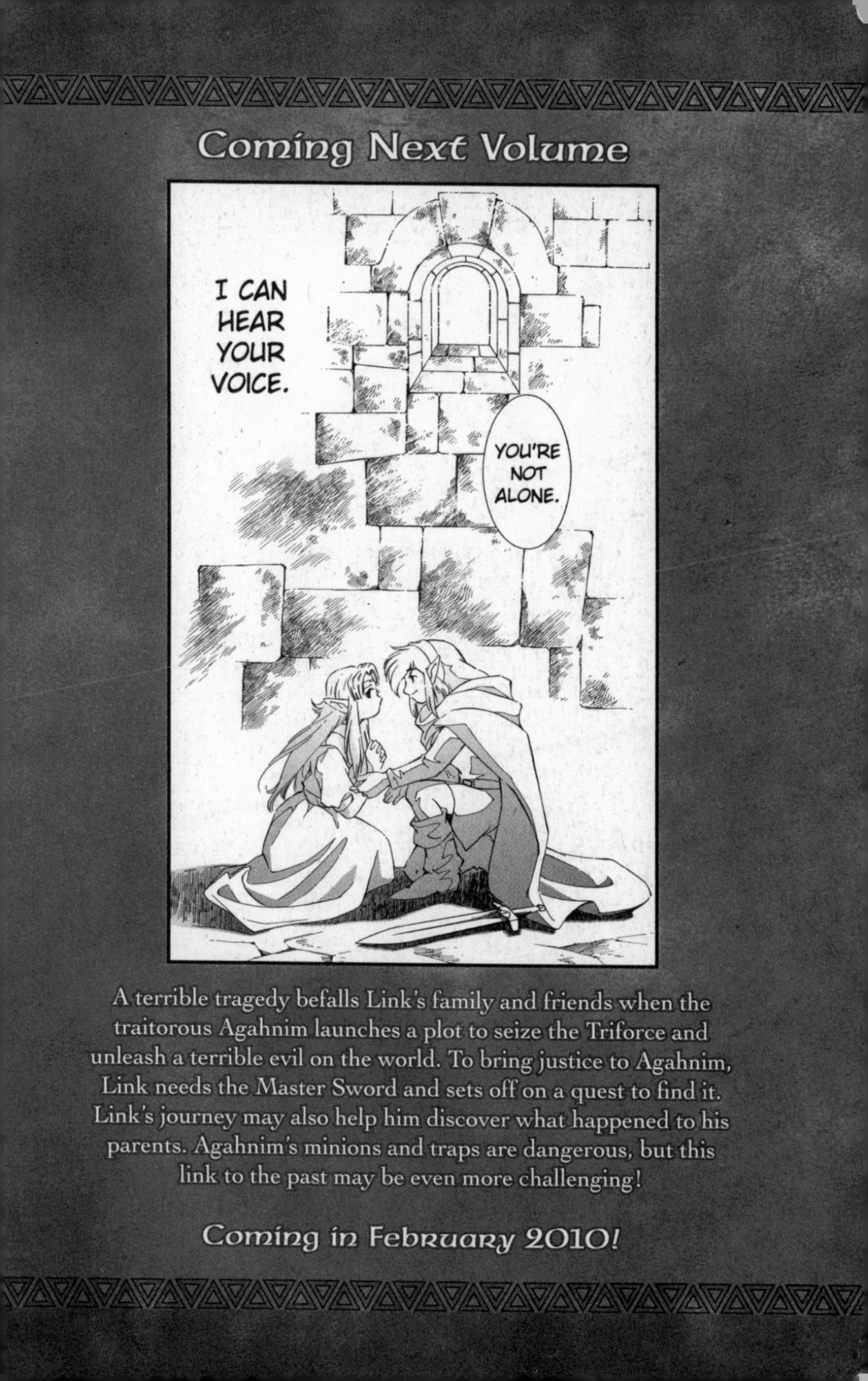

I CAN HEAR YOUR VOICE.
YOU'RE NOT ALONE.

A terrible tragedy befalls Link's family and friends when the traitorous Agahnim launches a plot to seize the Triforce and unleash a terrible evil on the world. To bring justice to Agahnim, Link needs the Master Sword and sets off on a quest to find it. Link's journey may also help him discover what happened to his parents. Agahnim's minions and traps are dangerous, but this link to the past may be even more challenging!

Coming in February 2010!

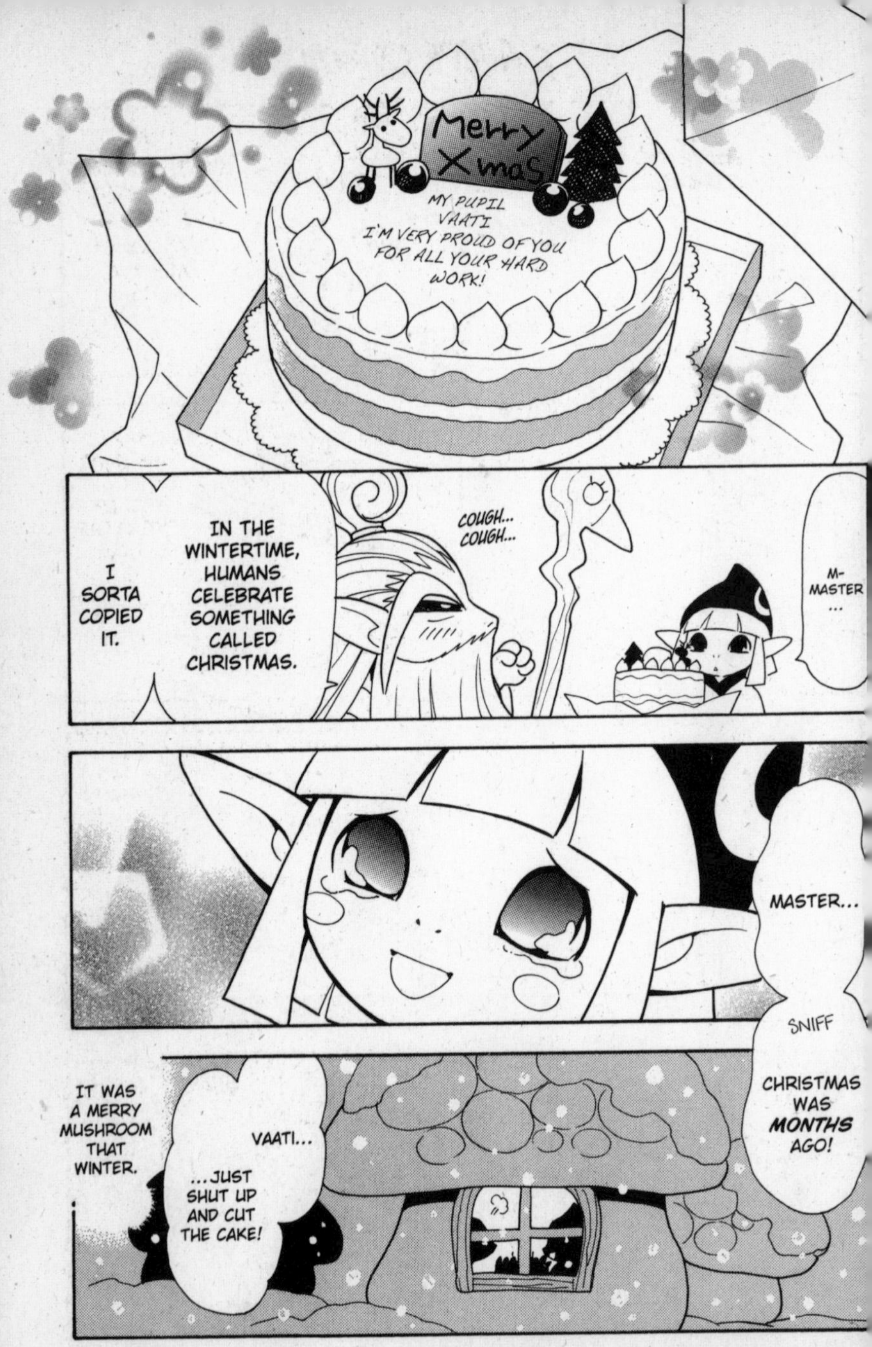
Merry Xmas
MY PUPIL VAATI I'M VERY PROUD OF YOU FOR ALL YOUR HARD WORK!
M-MASTER ...
COUGH... COUGH...
IN THE WINTERTIME, HUMANS CELEBRATE SOMETHING CALLED CHRISTMAS.
I SORTA COPIED IT.
MASTER...
SNIFF
CHRISTMAS WAS ***MONTHS*** AGO!
VAATI...
...JUST SHUT UP AND CUT THE CAKE!
IT WAS A MERRY MUSHROOM THAT WINTER.

THE END